W9-CLX-511

MANAGING BUSINESS COMPLEXITY

MANAGING BUSINESS COMPLEXITY
Discovering Strategic Solutions with Agent-Based Modeling and Simulation

Michael J. North *and* **Charles M. Macal**

2007

OXFORD

UNIVERSITY PRESS

Oxford University Press, Inc., publishes works that further
Oxford University's objective of excellence
in research, scholarship, and education.

Oxford   New York
Auckland   Cape Town   Dar es Salaam   Hong Kong   Karachi
Kuala Lumpur   Madrid   Melbourne   Mexico City   Nairobi
New Delhi   Shanghai   Taipei   Toronto

With offices in
Argentina   Austria   Brazil   Chile   Czech Republic   France   Greece
Guatemala   Hungary   Italy   Japan   Poland   Portugal   Singapore
South Korea   Switzerland   Thailand   Turkey   Ukraine   Vietnam

Published by Oxford University Press, Inc.
198 Madison Avenue, New York, New York 10016

www.oup.com

Oxford is a registered trademark of Oxford University Press

Library of Congress Cataloging-in-Publication Data
North, Michael J. (Michael John), 1969–
Managing business complexity : discovering strategic solutions with
agent-based modeling and simulation / Michael J. North and
Charles M. Macal.
p. cm.
Includes bibliographical references and index.

ISBN-13 978-0-19-517211-9

1. Management information systems.   2. Distributed artificial
intelligence.   I. Macal, Charles M.   II. Title.
T58.6.N67 2006
658.4′03—dc22   2005015235

9 8 7 6 5 4 3 2

Printed in the United States of America
on acid-free paper

To my sister Cindy, my father John, and my mother Shirley

Michael North

To my parents Dorothy and Charlie

Charles Macal

Preface

Why this book? The answer is because people need to know about one of the most exciting and practical developments in business simulation and modeling that has occurred since the invention of relational databases. The world is changing in terms of the *requirements* for solving business problems and the *capabilities* of information technology and computer modeling that the technical and analytical community is able to bring to bear on these problems. This change in requirements means that the problems confronting business are changing and becoming more complex. The change in capabilities means that problems that have been there all along can now be solved.

This book is designed to do two things: (1) to teach you how to think about agents, and (2) to teach you how to do something with agents by developing agent-based models and simulations. In doing so, this book provides you with a vocabulary for agent-based modeling and simulation that draws from a number of fields that people typically do not connect.

We believe that in the future virtually all computer simulations will be in the form of agent-based simulations. Why is this so? For simulations it makes sense because of the natural way that agent models can represent business issues and the close similarity of agent modeling to the predominant computational paradigm of object-oriented programming. In fact, we believe that in the future many optimization models will be agent-based as well, due to the flexibility of the algorithms applied in agent-based optimization and their applicability to solving real-time optimization problems.

This book is intended for managers, analysts, and software developers in business and government. Those interested in an overview of agent-based modeling should read chapters 1, 3, 4, 5, 7, and 15. Those interested in a more detailed discussion should read all the chapters. Those interested in practicing agent modeling for themselves should read all the chapters and duplicate the spreadsheet models described in chapter 8.

The book is the outgrowth of our agent-based modeling project work for the business and government communities. It has benefited from the agent-based modeling conferences that we have organized and the agent-based modeling courses that we have conducted.

The authors would like to thank the many people who made this book possible. We thank our respective families. In particular, Michael North thanks his sister Cindy, his father John, and his mother Shirley. Charles Macal thanks his wife Kathy. We owe much to our colleagues whom we have interacted with along the way to becoming proficient modelers. In particular, Charles Macal thanks his first simulation teacher, A. Alan B. Pritsker, a genuine modeler's modeler. We thank all of our friends at Argonne National Laboratory, with special gratitude to Tom Wolsko for his visionary insight, and to our fellow members of the

Argonne EMCAS development team: Gale Boyd, Dick Cirillo, Guenter Conzelmann, Vladimir Koritarov, Prakash Thimmapuram, and Tom Veselka. We thank our collaborators on the Repast development team, including Mark Altaweel, Nick Collier, Tom Howe, Miles Parker, David Sallach, Pam Sydelko, Eric Tatara, and Richie Vos. We thank the staff of the Santa Fe Institute, especially Susan Ballati, Shannon Larsen, and Chris Wood for their support in organizing business complexity modeling courses, and the SFI Business Network supply chain modeling team, including George Danner, Ed MacKerrow, and Owen Densmore. We thank Averill Law for recent discussions on the relationship between agent modeling and conventional simulation. We also thank the team at Oxford University Press, including editors Martha Cooley, Frank Fusco, and John Rauschenberg, managing editor Lisa Stallings, and copy-editor Alan Hunt of Keyword Group Ltd.

We thank the following individuals for many enjoyable and enlightening discussions about agent-based modeling over the years: Rob Axtell (George Mason University), Steve Bankes (Evolving Logic, Inc.), Roger Burkhart (Deere & Co.), Kathleen Carley (Carnegie Mellon University), John Casti (Technical University of Vienna), Lars-Erik Cederman (ETH Zürich), Ali Cinar (Illinois Institute of Technology), Claudio Cioffi-Revilla (George Mason University), Nosh Contractor (University of Illinois, Champaign Urbana), Harvey Drucker (Argonne National Laboratory), Thierry Emonet (University of Chicago), Josh Epstein (Brookings Institution), Nigel Gilbert (University of Surrey), Bryan Gross (MPSI Systems Inc.), Laszlo Gulyas (AITIA Inc.), Peter Hedström (Nuffield College), Cynthia Hood (Illinois Institute of Technology), Mark Kimura (MPSI Systems Inc.), Michael Macy (Cornell University), John Padgett (University of Chicago), Scott Page (University of Michigan), Randy Picker (University of Chicago), Bill Rand (Northwestern University), Bob Rosner (Argonne National Laboratory), Keith Sawyer (Washington University in St. Louis), John Sterman (Massachusetts Institute of Technology), Fouad Teymour (Illinois Institute of Technology), Seth Tisue (Northwestern University), Uri Wilensky (Northwestern University), and Peyton Young (Johns Hopkins University).

Michael J. North
Charles M. Macal

Contents

MANAGING BUSINESS COMPLEXITY

1

The Challenge

Why This Book?

This book was written because people need to know about one of the most exciting and practical developments in business modeling that has occurred since the invention of relational databases. Agent-based modeling and simulation (ABMS) promises to have far-reaching effects on the way that businesses in many areas use computers to support practical decision-making. ABMS represents a new way to understand data and generate information that has never been available before—a new way for businesses to view the future and to understand and anticipate the likely effects of their decisions on their markets and industries.

This book has two purposes. First, it teaches readers how to think about ABMS—how to think about agents and their interactions. This teaches readers how to explain the features and advantages of ABMS to other people—how to articulate the value of agent-based simulation. Second, it teaches readers how to do ABMS—how to go about building agent-based simulations.

This book is a complete ABMS resource, whether or not the readers have had any previous experience in building agent-based simulations or any other kinds of models for that matter. This book is also a collection of ABMS business applications resources, collected in one place for the first time.

The Who, What, Where, When, Why, and How of Agents

This book addresses the who, what, where, when, why, and how of agents.

- Who needs agents? Who should know about agent modeling? Who should do agent modeling? Who should use the information generated by agent-based models? Understanding the audience for agent-based modeling as a technique and as an information-creating enterprise is the key to its successful use.
- What are agents? What do agents allow us to do that cannot be done using standard modeling approaches? The agents modeling approach represents a natural view of how people think about and understand systems that before now has been barely tapped.
- Where agents? Where are the promising applications of ABMS in the everyday business problems that surround us? The growing preponderance of candidate areas for agent-based models means that there is no need to look far for promising applications.
- When agents? When it is appropriate to use agent-based modeling and simulation? The situations in which agent-based modeling can offer distinct advantages to more traditional modeling approaches, reveal new insights, and answer long-standing questions are becoming better understood every day.
- Why agents? Why do people use agent-based modeling? Agent-based modeling offers the agent focus and perspective as its central concepts and natural starting point. There is a natural evolution in the understanding of agent behaviors and the behaviors of a system as a whole. The authors believe that in the future virtually all computer simulations will be agent-based because of the naturalness of the agent representation and the close similarity of

agent models to the predominant computational paradigm of object-oriented programming.

- How agents? How should one think about agents? How should one go about building agent-based models? Experience is quickly accumulating on the steps that one goes through to be successful at building an agent-based model.

This book provides the answers to these critically important questions for anyone who has heard about agent-based modeling or for those who are considering undertaking an agent-based modeling enterprise.

Why Agent-Based Modeling and Simulation Is Needed Now

Why use ABMS now? There are many compelling reasons. The world is increasingly complex, and the systems that need to be analyzed are becoming more complex. Planning and management tools must capture this emerging complexity. Some systems have always been complex and traditional tools have not been adequate to analyze them. The full latent complexity must be captured as well. Data are now organized into databases at finer and finer levels of granularity. Competitive advantage must be wrung from this new data. Furthermore, many leaders in industrial and government organizations are finding that their planning and management tools lack robustness. These tools must be dependable. Properly applied agent modeling can answer these questions. This book will show how.

The world is becoming increasingly challenging because the systems that need to be managed are becoming more complex. Many organizations are facing shrinking resources and growing structural complications. For many, the following situation is all too familiar (Banham 2002):

> When the September 2001 quarter rolled around, computer chip maker Xilinx Inc. had missed its quarterly earnings forecast four times in a row. By then, of course, the company knew something was seriously wrong. Hard as it tried, it simply couldn't get its budget numbers in sync with customer demand . . . and that made planning and budgeting at the San Jose, Calif–based company a shot in the dark. "It was like flying a plane at night without instruments," says Xilinx CFO Kris Chellam.

Examples include increasingly fragmented consumer markets, more and more interwoven industrial supply chains, ever more connected transportation systems, as well as the fitful deregulation of the electric power, natural gas, and telecommunications industries and the growing interdependency of infrastructures such as electricity, natural gas, petroleum, water, and telecommunications (Anderson 2000). Many trends are contributing to this increase in complexity, including growing globalization, reductions in inventory, rising outsourcing, deepening information technology, expanding horizontal integration, ever more sophisticated products, and the escalating demands of customers. Each of these trends increases the range of possible outcomes that must be considered by decision-makers, while simultaneously reducing the time available for choices. This book presents a new solution to this widely recognized problem.

The growing complexity of the world is only part of the challenge being faced by modern organizations. Many systems are becoming much more complex, but complexity in systems is itself not new. Some systems have always been complex (Sterman 1989). Markets, especially those far from the standard forms analyzed in economic theory (perfect competition, monopoly, oligopoly, etc.), are an example. Social systems, particularly those within industrial and government organizations, are another example. Traditional tools have not been adequate to analyze these systems. To compensate, "heroic" assumptions are often used.

Heroic assumptions allow systems to be simplified enough to be modeled using traditional tools. These assumptions reduce the level of detail in systems and reduce the ranges of allowed interactions between components. Assuming that all products in an open market are identical is a classic heroic assumption in economics. Combining this assumption with the additional assumption that there are an essentially infinite number of competitors results in the idealization called a perfectly competitive market (McLean and Padgett 1997). This idealized model certainly can be used to understand some long-run market outcomes, but what about the details? In particular, what about the transient conditions along the way to the eventual outcome? Even worse, what if the market is perpetually perturbed by influences such as innovation and never is allowed to reach the assumed long-run state? Other examples abound. Assuming that employees in corporations behave according to strict organization charts or business processes is another heroic assumption that is sometimes used to produce simplified organizational models (Paul et al. 1999). What about the fact that people talk well outside of organization charts? Agent-based modeling and simulation can break the stranglehold of such assumptions.

In addition to model-driven simplification, heroic assumptions are also used to make up for missing data. In the past, this was often the only way to deal with a lack of adequate data detailing the behavior of systems and components within systems. Fortunately, data collection has been revolutionized in recent years. Data is now being collected at increasingly fine-grained levels of detail on a rapidly growing range of situations. The resulting data is commonly being stored into databases at the level of individual customers, employees, or items. This "micro-data" can be used to support increasingly finer-grained agent "micro-simulations."

Many leaders in industrial and government organizations are finding that their planning and management tools lack robustness in the sense that the tools fail to provide adequate warning about serious impending issues (Banham 2002). Who has not been surprised by the outcome of what seemed to be a well-understood situation? Who has not made sense of such surprises using the power of hindsight? What if there was no need to look back because there was no surprise at all? What if the effort put into hindsight analysis could have been used to recognize the situation before it happened? Agent-based modeling can be used to do this and this book will detail how.

Because of weaknesses in planning tools, many leaders are finding it increasingly difficult to convert their deep experience into strategic solutions for their enterprises. The increasing number of outcomes that must be considered for any decision makes it more and more difficult to consider all of the relevant possibilities. Furthermore, the growing novelty presented by restructured markets, reconfigured organizational structures, revised business processes, and innovative technology make it increasingly challenging to apply previous experiences. Properly applied agent-based modeling can convert deep experience with known situations into profound vision about novel circumstances. This book details how to apply agent modeling to real situations.

Why are leaders surprised so often? A simple analogy illustrates. Imagine a nighttime visit to a classic small American town on a long flat plain. Now imagine that the town is flooding and the water is rising fast.

Fleeing will take too long. The best approach is to find and stay at the highest point in the town. So, where to stay? The church steeple may seem attractive. The steeple is usually the highest point in most such towns. It is also usually extremely narrow. What if there is wind or more rain? Staying on the steeple could be hard and falling into the flood could be even harder. Maybe there is a better place.

How about staying on the broad, flat church roof? The roof is almost as high as the steeple and much higher than the rest of the town. It is also large so that wind and rain are unlikely to be a threat. It is a safe place to wait out the flood.

Similar to our imaginary situation, many organizations are perilously balanced on the points of church steeples that are highly optimized for one set of conditions, but which could result in disaster with a small shift to the left or right. Leaders in these organizations often make decisions using a combination of ad hoc informal methods, historical statistics, or inflexible optimization techniques. Unfortunately, these approaches all tend to find rigid rather than robust solutions. Ways to seek the stable success of high and broad roofs must be found.

Agent-based modeling and simulation is a new way to capture the behavior of complex business and government systems. Agent modeling captures a system's behavior from the ground-up. The behavioral rules of individual components are defined and then used to create an agent-based model. The model is then executed to reproduce the behavior of the complete system. The result is a ground-up approach to modeling that allows organizations to convert their knowledge of individual behaviors into an understanding of the overall system-level outcomes. The agent-based model thus provides connections that link the behavior of the individual components to the resulting system effects. Organizations with such a model can discover which combinations of individual-level actions and influences yield both positive results and negative consequences. They can also use such models as laboratories to explore the range of outcomes that can be expected from systems and to test the potential returns from possible future actions.

The Foundation of ABMS

ABMS builds on proven, highly successful techniques such as discrete event simulation and object-oriented programming. Agent-based modeling leverages these and other techniques as much as possible to produce returns more directly and quickly. Discrete-event simulation provides an established mechanism for coordinating the interactions of individual components or "agents" within a simulation. Object-oriented programming provides well-tested frameworks for organizing agents based on their behaviors. Both discrete-event simulation and object-oriented programming will be discussed in detail in chapter 5.

ABMS is sometimes confused with several other fields. In particular, agent modeling is occasionally confused with, but different from, typical mobile agent and artificial intelligence research.

Mobile agent research ultimately focuses on the creation of proxies that act as user representatives in selected situations such as online shopping (Thomsen and Thomsen 1997). In the best case, these proxies are expected to act as representatives or agents for their users. This is the source of the confusion in terminology. Some techniques used in mobile agent research can be applied with agent-based modeling, but there is a strong difference in emphasis. Mobile agent research produces individual agents that interact directly with users or other agents that in turn represent users. Their agents are intended to conduct transactions, monitor systems, or operate systems in place of a human user. Agent-based simulation produces agents that primarily interact with other agents, although user interactions can occur as well. ABMS agents are intended to represent the behavior of real system components to reproduce the behavior of a system.

Artificial intelligence research focuses on the creation of synthetic representations of individual human beings or major functions of individual human beings (Ginsberg 1993). Naturally, many artificial intelligence techniques can be used within agent-based models. Details on appropriate techniques are presented throughout the book. However, agent-based modeling is different from artificial intelligence research. While artificial intelligence research emphasizes the development of artifacts that in some sense appear to be human, agent-based modeling emphasizes the development of models that reproduce critical features of complex systems using component-level rules.

Why ABMS Is Useful, Usable, and Used

ABMS is a useful, usable, and used technique that can do many things for organizations. Agent-based simulation is useful for converting experience with detailed processes into knowledge about complete systems. Agent-based simulation is usable due to advances in computer technology and modeling techniques. Agent-based simulation is used by a growing number of organizations to solve real problems.

The usefulness of agent modeling arises from its ability to show the emergent connections between system components, tie experience with detailed processes to system-level knowledge, and to identify possible outcomes that are outside the range of typical thinking. Showing the connections between system components allows users to investigate possible interactions and test potential interventions. Discovering the ties between micro-level behavior and macro-level results increases the value of detailed expert experience by allowing this business experience to be leveraged in new ways. Expanding strategic managerial vision by revealing otherwise unanticipated potential outcomes allows business and government leaders to make better-informed decisions.

With agent modeling, decision-makers can even take advantage of conversational modeling. Conversation speed modeling, also called conversational modeling, is a way to use fast simulations to run live interactive tests of proposed options in real time during strategic planning meetings.[1] This book shows how to use agent modeling for conversational modeling.

Agent modeling is usable due to the iterative model construction process. This process starts with an initial description of the behavior of individual components or agent behaviors as well as supporting data. This description is then converted to a functioning model that can be executed with the given data. The resulting model is run and the initial results are examined. The behavior definitions in the model are then updated based on the initial results, and the model is rerun. This progressive refinement process is then continued until the model reproduces both the behaviors and results of the target system. Once this is complete, the resulting model can be used to answer business and government questions. This book shows how to do this for real problems.

A model that can be used to answer business or government questions is valuable in and of itself. However, the value of agent modeling in tying together micro- and macro-level behaviors is much greater. In particular, the process of building agent-based models has material benefits for business and government leaders as well. Building agent-based models can greatly increase an organization's understanding of the behaviors of system components. The requirement to specify the data access, adaptations, and actions of individual agents invariably compels the relevant experts to probe their areas of expertise with greatly increased attention to detail. This process drives experts to root out and document hidden and faulty assumptions that would escape other techniques. The improvement in the capabilities of business experts alone often justifies agent-based modeling projects. This book will illustrate how business and government leaders can win these results for their organizations.

Agent-based modeling and simulation is used for a variety of practical business and government purposes. Agent modeling is used to increase the capabilities of experts to grasp micro-level behavior and to relate this behavior to macro-level outcomes. Agent-based models are used to expand the scope of future possibilities considered in decision-making. This is particularly critical when business and government leaders face new and rapidly changing circumstances. As previously mentioned, what leader has not been surprised by unexpected events? Who has not said, "We should have known?" Who has not carefully developed a list of possible future scenarios only to face the real, unlisted outcome? Why does this happen? Even with the most thoughtful traditional projections, surprise can come from many directions, including unforeseen interactions and unexpected changes. In many cases, one of the biggest sources of difficulty is the human mind itself.

The human mind is in many ways a powerful simulator. People regularly consider future possibilities and their consequences alongside purely imaginary situations. However, most people find it difficult to consider more than about seven distinct items at once. This is exemplified by the classic "seven, plus or minus two" rule (Miller 1956). Basic aids such as notebooks and more sophisticated computer support tools such as spreadsheets do little to help. With these tools, the number of possible outcomes an individual can consider is still extremely small compared to the number of meaningfully distinct outcomes for most complex systems. Even with advanced organizational designs, people still have a hard time making truly informed decisions (Bendor and Kumar 2004). It is becoming recognized that adding more people to a problem can increase the chances of finding an effective solution because it increases the diversity and value of the available information (Surowiecki 2004). However, adding more people to a problem past a certain point often fails to improve the results because of the tendency of people to think alike, with groupthink being the ultimate extreme (Schwartz and Wald 2003). Thus, adding growing ranks of people to a problem will often generate increasing amounts of future projections that are similar to those already found. Merely generating more projects is not what is needed. What is needed are more possibilities that are genuinely new. Agent-based modeling can do this. This book will explain how.

Agent-based modeling focuses on incremental development to ensure stakeholder buy-in and progressively document return on investment. Incremental development means that agent-based models can be built over time in simple stages or steps. Each development stage adds new capabilities to the model and expands the range of business and government questions that it can answer.

As detailed in this book, agent-based model development steps are structured to ensure that the model is used at the end of each stage. Having stakeholders use the product at each step, rather than wait for a long-term final result, ensures that they will gain confidence in and develop ownership of the model over time. Furthermore, allowing stakeholders to work with the growing model encourages early and regular feedback. This informed feedback allows the development process to be simultaneously dynamic and focused. Regular user feedback allows the process to be dynamic since the model can be quickly adapted to changing business and government needs and because insights gained from model development can be immediately applied to future development. Adapting models to changing needs is critical since the pace of modern business and government virtually guarantees that modeling requirements, both for traditional modeling and agent modeling, will change before models are completed. Applying insights discovered during model development to future stages is equally critical since agent modeling intentionally involves learning about the system being modeled. Putting this new knowledge to work early and often will amplify the benefits of agent modeling. In addition, receiving regular user feedback allows managers to ensure that the model development process is always on track for success.

The recommended agent model development steps are purposely small, so that each stage requires only a limited investment and can be quickly completed. This allows model benefits to be progressively quantified without the need for major up-front costs. As the model grows and produces documented results, further model development stages can be completed. The ability to complete each step rapidly reduces the time required to begin reaping the benefits of agent modeling as well as minimizing the otherwise costly effects of changing requirements.

Good agent model development is not the only thing that proceeds incrementally. The examples in this book do too. Throughout the book, the examples grow from simple models that at best suggest the real world to complex models that match the world in detail. This style of exposition is intentional. The simple examples presented early in each chapter allow the reader to grasp the concepts of agent modeling without the distraction and confusion created by minutiae from the domain under study. The complex examples presented later in each chapter build on the earlier simple examples by adding the kind of details that make models useful for real applications. Along the way within each chapter, the reader is given the opportunity to see at first hand the incremental development processes that lead successfully from the simple to the complex.

An exposition that proceeds from the simple to the complex is always a point of tension for some readers since they often want to be immediately impressed with complex large-scale examples. Of course, some large and highly detailed models that have been carefully matched against the real world will be presented. However, the goal of this book is not to impress the reader with the raw overwhelming grandeur of the authors' example models. The goal is to arm readers with the knowledge and skills needed to use agent modeling in their own organizations. As with ABMS development, a willingness to work incrementally from the simple to the complex is the secret to success.

How ABMS Works: An Overview

So how does ABMS work? Imagine a trip to the sports stadium during a major event. The seats are filled with ten of thousands of fans. As part of the fun, the fans start to form "waves" in the crowd. To start a wave, a row of fans stands up quickly and then sits

back down a moment later. The next row of fans starts to stand up a moment later and then sits down. The fun continues as the following rows each stand up and sit down in turn. The individual people are each simply standing up and sitting down occasionally. The group as a whole forms a human wave that can sweep the entire stadium. Agent-based modeling works by applying the concept of a wave in a crowd. Each person or agent makes small, simple movements, but the group as a whole produces complex large-scale results.

Applying this analogy, senior managers' knowledge of consumers, employees, and business processes is their knowledge of the people forming the wave in the crowd. The resulting wave represents the large-scale system outcomes that every leader needs to know about ahead of time. Knowing about these outcomes and being able to relate them to their underlying causes can lead directly to the discovery of innovative answers to outstanding questions. Thus, with agent modeling, senior managers can use their knowledge of consumers, employees, and business processes to discover strategic solutions for their enterprises.

Incremental Discovery, Design, and Development

How does ABMS work in practice? As with most techniques, there are several approaches. The most powerful by far is incremental discovery, design, and development.

The ultimate goal of agent modeling is to create tools for evolutionary discovery. Agent-based modeling is best done incrementally. The discovery phase of agent modeling allows partial models to be built and then tested to yield insights. These insights can lead to both real-world innovations and improved model designs. These innovations and designs in turn can fuel further model development. This cycle can be repeated incrementally as desired. This book will show how to do this.

How This Book Is Organized

This book presents business and government agent modeling in great depth. Each of the main chapters presents and supports a key component of practical business and government ABMS. Throughout the book, each chapter builds upon a unified incremental discovery, design, and development approach.

The book starts out with a chapter that describes in detail the concepts underlying agent-based modeling and simulation. Chapter 2 introduces business and government leaders to the core concepts they need to know about agent-based modeling as well as comparing and contrasting the practical value of ABMS with traditional techniques.

Agent modeling is naturally about agents. Chapter 3 describes the crucial facts about agents and their environments that are necessary for useful applications.

Agent-based modeling and simulation has a rich history. Chapter 4 presents the facts that business and government decision-makers need to know about the origin and context of agent-based modeling and simulation.

Agent-based modeling is related to a variety of other techniques. Chapter 5 compares and contrasts agent modeling with the other major modeling techniques. Chapter 6 follows up with specific ways to address the central issue with agents, namely how agents behave.

The book then details the application of the crucial facts of ABMS using spreadsheets, mathematical scripting languages, participatory environments, and enterprise-scale computer systems. Chapter 7 provides a practical overview of agent modeling in an office setting. Chapter 8 describes the details of using spreadsheets and other desktop software to do basic agent modeling. Chapter 9 discusses how to engage people in interactive agent simulation. Chapter 10 discuss how to grow agent models along a continuum from small-scale prototypes to large-scale enterprise simulations.

Regardless of the tools used to do agent simulation, the resulting models must be properly checked. Following the chapters on agent-based modeling development, the book shows how to ensure that agent-based models are correctly developed, properly checked or "vetted," and are run using appropriate data. Chapter 11 shows how to ensure that agent models produce accurate results.

The book then visually illustrates effective techniques for finding good-quality data for agent-based models as chapter 12 details the key ABMS data topics. In particular, the data requirements of agent models are described, methods to find this data are discussed, and a visual approach to ensuring data quality is shown.

After discussing data collection and cleaning, the book then explains how to understand the results of agent-based models and how to communicate these results to nonmodeler business and government audiences. Chapter 13 discusses what to do with the results from agent models. The chapter details how to understand the type of results that are produced by agent simulation. Additionally, the chapter shows how to present these results to other decision-makers, including senior managers.

The book then provides practical approaches to managing agent modeling projects. Chapter 14 discusses the key issues of managing such projects, including project organization and individual project roles.

The book concludes with an integrative and forward-looking discussion of the concepts presented throughout the main chapters. Chapter 15 ties together the themes of the book and places agent modeling in the larger context of business and government management.

Case Studies

No book about agent modeling in business and government would be complete without a case study. This book includes many such examples. One major example is covered throughout the book, starting with chapter 3. This example is revisited from the perspective of the individual chapter in each of the chapters after this. This allows readers to the see how the concepts in the book progressively build to a complete understanding of agent modeling. The major example covers a market model. In addition, each chapter includes several specific examples in the main text.

Note

1. The term "conversational modeling," as used here, refers to processes for executing simulations interactively with decision-makers. The term can also refer to processes for developing models interactively with decision-makers (Sierhuis and Selvin 2002).

References

Anderson, J. A. (2000). What's Electrifying Natural Gas. *Business Week Online*, Sept. 19 (available at http://www.businessweek.com/).

Banham, R. (2002). Reality Budgeting. *CIO Insight Magazine*, Aug.

Bendor, J. and S. Kumar (2004). The Perfect Is the Enemy of the Good: Adaptive Versus Optimal

Organizational Reliability. *Journal of Theoretical Politics* **17**(1): 5–39.

Ginsberg, M. L. (1993). *Essentials of Artificial Intelligence*. San Francisco: Morgan Kaufmann.

McLean, P. A. and J. F. Padgett (1997). Was Florence a Perfectly Competitive Market? Transactional Evidence from the Renaissance. *Theory and Society* **26**: 209–244.

Miller, G. A. (1956). The Magical Number Seven, Plus or Minus Two: Some Limits on Our Capacity for Processing Information. *Psychological Review* **63**: 81–97.

Paul, R. J., G. Giaglis, and V. Hlupic (1999). Simulation of Business Processes: A Review. *American Behavioral Scientist* **10**(42): 1551–1576.

Schwartz, K. and M. L. Wald (2003). Smart People Working Collectively Can be Dumber Than the Sum of Their Brains: "Groupthink" Is 30 Years Old, and Still Going Strong. *New York Times*, Mar. 9.

Sierhuis, M. and A. Selvin (2002). Towards a Framework for Collaborative Modeling and Simulation. *ACM 2002 Conference on Computer Supported Cooperative Work*. New Orleans, La.: ACM, 16–20 Nov.

Sterman, J. D. (1989). Modeling Managerial Behavior: Misperceptions of Feedback in a Dynamic Decision Making Experiment. *Management Science* **35**(3): 321–339.

Surowiecki, J. (2004). *The Wisdom of Crowds*. New York: Doubleday.

Thomsen, L. L. and B. Thomsen (1997). Mobile Agents—The New Paradigm in Computing. *ICL Systems Journal* **12**(1): 14–27.

2

The ABMS Paradigm

Parts Make the Whole

Agent-based modeling and simulation (ABMS) is founded on the notion that the whole of many systems or organizations is greater than the simple sum of its constituent parts. To manage such systems, the systems or organizations must be understood as collections of interacting components. Each of these components has its own rules and responsibilities. Some components may be more influential than others, but none completely controls the behavior of a complete system. All of the components contribute to the results in large or small ways. Such a collection of components is said to be a complex adaptive system (CAS).[1] System reactions where the complete results are more than the sum of the individual components' outcomes are called emergent behavior. CAS regularly exhibit emergent behavior. Managing a CAS requires a good grasp of emergent behavior. ABMS combines this fundamental insight with proven, highly successful techniques such as discrete-event simulation and object-oriented programming to produce a new way to discover strategic, tactical, and operational business solutions.

How does ABMS compare to traditional system-modeling techniques? Specifically, how does ABMS compare to statistical modeling, risk analysis, optimization, systems dynamics, standard participatory simulation, or traditional event simulation? Each of these approaches is useful in its own right and each has proven its value over the years. However, these

system-modeling techniques alone are often not adequate to address many of today's business questions. In particular, they tend to have difficultly capturing the highly nonlinear interactions that are common in the problems addressed by industry and government. These nonlinear interactions regularly combine to produce emergent behavior. Ultimately, each of these approaches has strengths and weaknesses that are considered in chapter 5.

The Two Fundamental Types of Models

There are two fundamental types of models. These two types are deterministic models and stochastic models. Deterministic models tend to be simpler to use but much less expressive than stochastic models.

Deterministic models always produce the same outputs when they are repeatedly run with identical inputs. An example is a simple reactive market model with bidding agents that raise prices by a fixed amount when their last bid was accepted and lower prices by another fixed amount when their last bid was rejected. This model will always produce the same outputs given the same inputs, since each of the agents always acts the same way given identical inputs. In principle, deterministic models can be run once to produce a final answer for any given situation. Even with uncertain inputs, a limited range of runs is often all that is required to produce a complete answer. Furthermore, the input information required to represent a situation is often simpler when working with a deterministic model rather than a stochastic model. These factors mean that deterministic models are usually simpler to work with than stochastic models. Unfortunately, this simplicity comes at a price. Deterministic models are more limited in the kinds of behaviors that they can represent than stochastic models. In particular, requiring that agents always produce the same output for the same input restricts agents from performing unexpected actions or from producing "creative" responses. It also means that behaviors must often be modeled in detail at every stage of development, rather than relying on probability distributions to limit the required specificity.

Stochastic models can produce different outputs when they are repeatedly run with identical inputs. Stochastic models can produce different outputs because they include agent behaviors or environmental responses based on random or probabilistic elements. The assumption is that agent behaviors or environmental responses are not known with complete certainty, so these factors are characterized by ranges of possible values, means, variances, and other statistical measures. An example is a market model with bidding agents that raise prices by a randomly chosen amount when their last bid is accepted and lower prices by a randomly chosen amount when their last bid is rejected. In this example, new values for random price changes are selected during each step of the simulation. The responses of the agents to market activity will change from run to run since the random numbers will vary each time they are generated. The variation in agent behavior will cause the simulation results to vary as well.

Stochastic simulations are models that can produce different outputs given the same inputs. By definition, such models need to be executed many times to produce valid general results. Any one run of such a model produces at best one narrative or one possible sequence of events. Even though these models must be run many times to produce general conclusions, individual runs can have great value in their own right. With a properly constructed model, each run can represent a different possible historical trace or future path given a particular set of assumptions. A path or trace can be used to understand how individual agent interactions can contribute to system behavior. Furthermore, paths or traces can be used to illustrate the operation of the model, to explain conclusions reached by using the model, and to support

training exercises based on the model. These topics are discussed in detail in chapter 13. Still questions remain. What does all of this variability really mean? Alternatively, is it just plain wrong? The answer to these questions requires a clear definition of these terms.

Variability

Variability is the natural variation that is exhibited by a system or an organization (Berleant et al. 2003). Variability is often called stochastic uncertainty, or irreducible uncertainty (Berleant et al. 2003). This type of variation is stochastic because the outcomes change in unpredictable ways. This type of variation is irreducible because there is no way to anticipate the changes in outcomes ahead of time. In academic circles, the term "aleatory uncertainty" is also used since the word aleatory refers to a "depending . . . on chance" (Berleant et al. 2003; Oxford 2004). Variability is the result of system behavior that prevents models from giving exact answers. Virtually all real-world systems and organizations have substantial variability. An example is the variation in electricity demand driven by uncertainties in the weather. This leads to the question, what is the point of modeling in the face of all this variability? Why even bother?

Modeling systems with substantial variability can be beneficial for two reasons. First, variation itself cannot be predicted but ranges, bounds, and sets of potential paths often can be. Thus, extremely useful information about systems outcomes can be provided despite the variability built into real systems. Techniques for doing this are discussed in detail in chapter 13. Second, not all system variation is variability. Many types of variations in system outcomes can be represented with models. These variations are called uncertainties.

Uncertainty

Fundamentally, uncertainty is a "potential deficiency in any phase or activity of the modeling process that is due to lack of knowledge" (AIAA 1998). Uncertainty is caused by modeling oversights driven by incomplete information (Copas and Eguchi 2003). Uncertainties are not strictly mistakes. They are possible mistakes driven by guesses to fill in missing facts. Uncertainties can be reduced by finding and using the facts. In academia, uncertainty is also called "epistemic uncertainty" since epistemology is the philosophical study of knowledge itself (Stirling 2002).

This emphasizes that uncertainties are not mistakes but rather are ambiguities caused by incomplete information.

An example of uncertainty is supply chain performance variation caused by undocumented ordering policies at warehouses. Documenting the ordering policies and disseminating the results could reduce delivery surprises. Thus, uncertainties can be resolved with suitable investments in research. Fortunately, agent-based models are ideally suited to support this research since they can be used to test hypotheses about the operation of systems. Ultimately, variation is unavoidable but uncertainty can to some extent be controlled.

Uncertainty is often categorized as model uncertainty or reducible uncertainty (Finkel 1990). Model uncertainty is the difficulty in deciding between competing model structures that all may at least partially match the known facts. In this case, more facts need to be collected to resolve the ambiguity. Reducible uncertainty occurs when the model structure is clear but there are still open questions about the details. So, how do actual mistakes fit in?

Error

An error is a "recognizable deficiency in any phase or activity of modeling and simulation that is not due to lack of knowledge" (AIAA 1998). Errors are not necessarily recognized. The key point is that enough is known about the system that errors could be recognized with suitable attention to detail. Errors come in two flavors, namely unacknowledged errors and acknowledged errors.

Unacknowledged errors are hidden problems that no one is aware of at the current time (AIAA 1998). An example is a typographical error in an agent behavioral specification that leads to incorrect responses during simulation runs. There is no ambiguity here. This issue could be easily corrected if it is recognized. Techniques for finding these types of errors are presented in chapter 11. Once unacknowledged errors are found, they become acknowledged errors.

Acknowledged errors are known problems (AIAA 1998). An example is assuming that supply chain customers only visit retail stores once a day to simplify agent model design and development. Of course, allowing customers to have a variable number of store visits each day is relatively easy, but the incremental development approach might suggest that one visit a day is a good intermediate stepping-stone.

Can models be made entirely error free? In general, the answer is no. The only prefect model of a system is the system itself. Everything else is an approximation. The entire purpose of modeling is to produce simpler representations of the system under study. The hope is that these simpler representations will be correspondingly easier and cost less to work with than the real thing. Thus, no real model can or should contain every possible detail from the real system. Normally, not even all of the known facts can be accommodated. Modeling is therefore the art of approximation. Acknowledged error is more than just unavoidable. Acknowledged error can be desirable. Skillful modelers find good answers to the question of what kind of error is acceptable.

Nondeterminism

Addressing the question raised by nondeterminism in agent models leads in two different directions. Which direction an individual takes depends on their outlook on life. From one perspective, the world as we know it today is at least in some ways an accident of history. From this viewpoint, nondeterminism is a natural feature of the world that is entirely appropriate in agent models. From another perspective, the world is deterministic or at least highly structured and failure of many agent models to reflect this predictability may appear to be a problem. However, as we will see, appearances can be deceiving.

Assume for a moment that the world itself is nondeterministic. This means that if the clock of history could be turned back and then allowed to progress forward to the current time, then the path of events could be very different. From this perspective, the history that we know represents only one possible chronology of events. Other chronologies are also possible. By chance, the other paths did not happen and the one that we know did. In fact, an interpretation of quantum mechanics proposed by physicist Hugh Everett III states that all of the possible things that could happen actually do happen in disjoint universes (Everett 1957). This results in a tree-like branching of historical paths. The path that we are on is just one branch in a complete tree of all possible universes. Either way, from one point of view the universe we know is just an accident of history. What can be said about the other paths?

Continuing the nondeterministic point of view, the other possible historical paths that did not happen but could have represent an interesting opportunity.

Historians and history aficionados have long recognized this with their studies of what might have happened in a variety of historical situations, particularly those involving war (Cowley and Ambrose 2000; Cowley 2001). Some historians are now beginning to use agent-based modeling to add quantitative rigor to what otherwise would be qualitative debates about the causes and implications of historical events (Brantingham 2003). Biologists investigating the origins of life and the definition of life itself have long fought with this problem since they have essentially only one example to consider for each of these topics (Langton 1997, 2000). According to Christopher Langton (2000):

> Biology is the scientific study of life—in principle, anyway. In practice, biology is the scientific study of life on Earth based on carbon-chain chemistry. There is nothing in its charter that restricts biology to carbon-based life; it is simply that this is the only kind of life that has been available to study. Thus, theoretical biology has long faced the fundamental obstacle that it is impossible to derive general principles from single examples.
>
> Without other examples, it is difficult to distinguish essential properties of life—properties that would be shared by any living system—from properties that may be incidental to life in principle, but which happen to be universal to life on Earth due solely to a combination of local historical accident and common genetic descent. In order to derive general theories about life, we need an ensemble of instances to generalize over. Since it is quite unlikely that alien life-forms will present themselves to us for study in the near future, our only option is to try to create alternative life-forms ourselves—artificial life—literally "life made by Man rather than by Nature."

As with history, some researchers have developed agent-based modeling systems to answer hard questions about life and self-organization (Minar et al. 1996). Business people can do the same for their questions. Previous historical events can be analyzed to determine not only what did happen but also what might have happened. This is particularly valuable to speed up organizational learning, avoid problems before they happen, and recognize opportunities before they are obvious to everyone.

Given a historical event, it is often, but of course not always, possible to develop an understanding of why the event happened. Once the event is in some sense understood, plans can be developed to either cause or avoid the outcome in the future. This "relentless error correction" process can be and usually is repeated, ad infinitum (Bendor and Kumar 2004). This basic approach has been one of the drivers of business innovation, engineering progress, and medical advances for several centuries. In many ways, this is a proven approach that works. Clearly, this process should be continued in order to wring as much progress from each event as possible. This has been done for centuries. There is only one question. How many businesses have centuries during which to experiment?

The Cycle of Innovation

According to Bendor and Kumar (2004), "relentless error correction—the agency first putting out one fire . . . and then putting out another . . . is suboptimal: it prevents the organization from finding, even in the long-run, the optimal combination of . . . reliability." Thinking more broadly about the standard cycle of innovation leads to another way to view the issue. The cycle begins with the simple process of business as usual. Organizations proceed forward following the trail of business as usual until a problem or something unexpected occurs. In due course, the problem is investigated and in some sense resolved. The resolution becomes the new approach to business as usual. What does this "trial and error" process suggest? Does it suggest a growing tree? No, it more likely suggests a mouse lost in a maze. What would happen if the mouse could look over the walls? What would be possible if the mouse had a map?

Agent-based models can be used to investigate not only what happened in a given business situation but also what might have happened. Uncovering unexpected issues through "trial and error" in the real world can be quite costly. Instead, agent models can be used to quickly explore a wide range of circumstances and eventualities. An example illustrates.

As many know, the United States armed forces are undergoing a long-term transition from platform-centric warfare to network-centric warfare (Gartska 2000). According to Admiral Vern Clark, "future naval operations will use revolutionary information superiority and dispersed, networked force capabilities to deliver unprecedented offensive power, defensive assurance, and operational independence to Joint Force

Commanders" (Clark 2002). Many signs of this transition can already be seen in the growing interconnection of U.S. military communications systems (Book 2002).

Platform-centric warfare focuses on the use of many separate weapons systems or platforms, each with its own unique communications systems (Gartska 2000). Transmitting data from one platform to another requires custom translation programs or complicated gateways. In principle, one custom translator or gateway is needed for each possible pair of platforms. In practice this requirement can be reduced somewhat, but the number of translation systems is still large. Worse, translators can add substantial processing delays, can create data flow bottlenecks, and can be vulnerable to attack. Properly tracking targets often requires the use of multiple platforms that must exchange information rapidly. The use of layers of translators can greatly complicate an already difficult environment.

Network-centric warfare focuses on common standards to achieve seamless interconnection or interoperability between communications components (Gartska 2000; Clark 2002). In a network-centric world, two platforms located near one another can directly exchange data without needing intermediary translators. According to Admiral Clark, the U.S. military has "been talking about network-centric warfare for a decade" and has already achieved some parts of this vision (Clark 2002). However, much more remains to be done (Gartska 2000; Book 2002; Clark 2002). In particular, battlefield computer communications standards that are more comprehensive may be required to ensure that different types of equipment are fully interoperable. This conclusion led to experiments.

For some time, parts of the U.S. military have recognized the need for common battlefield computer network standards (Office of the Secretary of Defense 1997; Book 2002). Some standards have already been successfully defined for some applications (Hamilton et al. 1999). Despite these successes, it was felt that there was an unmet need for extremely general standards with wide applicability (Office of the Secretary of Defense 1997). An existing, widely used standard was a natural choice. A large experiment involving a substantial number of real military units was commissioned. The battlefield computer communications experiment applied a widely used standard in a highly dynamic environment. The communicating military units were constantly moving around the battlefield relative to one another. The chosen standard was designed to support variable communications on a fixed network. The battlefield network changed constantly. As a result, the standard performed quite poorly. To be clear, the chosen standard was exceptionally well designed for its purpose. Its purpose was simply different from its new application.

The most obvious standard for battlefield computer communications had performed quite poorly in a realistic experiment. It seemed clear that quite a few other choices might need to be tried before a good fit was found. Then someone asked a question: Could agent-based modeling reduce the potential cost? Could an agent-based model be used to screen potential military communications standards? One of the authors reviewed the situation with military officials and identified several key issues:

1. The military needed a cost-effective way to test potential battlefield communications standards. In this case, a model would be considered cost-effective if it was at least an order of magnitude less expensive than "live" testing performed with actual units.
2. The military needed a rapid method to test communications standards. A model would be considered rapid if it took at least an order of magnitude less time to test a given protocol.
3. The military needed a flexible system that could be easily configured to test a wide range of protocols under a diverse set of operating conditions.
4. As a secondary benefit, the military hoped to be able to make long-term use of the model for detailed network and staff deployment planning.

The communications situation to be modeled posed a variety of challenges:

1. Battlefields normally include large numbers of organized but nonetheless independent decision-makers. These decision-makers included everything from tanks, trucks, boats, and airplanes all the way down to individual soldiers. Friendly forces, hostile forces, and even civilians needed to be considered. Basic interactions between these components also needed to be modeled. These independent decision-makers would be the agents in the system.
2. Communications needs that vary with the circumstances had to be considered. For example, a group of soldiers near enemy forces might need to communicate either more or less than an isolated group in open country.

Simply put, the U.S. military's defined goal for the project was to develop a model that could be used to prescreen candidate computer communications standards. Given these basic requirements, agent-based modeling was a natural choice. In particular, the need to capture the behavior of a large number of complex interacting components directly called for agent simulation. The model could be used to eliminate large numbers of possible communications protocols at low cost. Of course, no military communications protocol should be used in real situations without appropriate live testing. However, the agent-based model could be used to reduce the cost of screening out candidate protocols with hidden problems. The best candidates to survive the model-driven screening process could be tested using live exercises. Furthermore, the model could be used to subject the surviving contenders to extremes of operation that would be difficult if not impossible to achieve with live testing. This was a natural situation for agent-based modeling.

Other Angles on Nondeterminism

For those who reject the notion of nondeterminism being directly inherent in the world, there are several other philosophical views of randomness that still lead naturally to nondeterministic modeling. One is founded on our limited ability to know or measure the physical or business world. The other is based on the inevitability of approximation, both in theory and practice.

One of the core discoveries of modern physics is the Heisenberg uncertainty principle. Briefly, it states that there are definite bounds on how well anyone can measure and record events (Eisberg and Resnick 1985). Furthermore, it says that these bounds really matter. Even if the world secretly is completely deterministic, many facts we really wish to know are forever shrouded in uncertainty. Things are even tougher within real-world businesses. Collecting good information costs serious money. Maintaining deep databases takes real investment. The quality of information is never perfect and never will be. Measuring and knowing in the business world requires business leaders to handle more uncertainty than physicists ever will.

Recall that a deterministic process always produces precisely identical outputs given identical inputs. Does this sound like any substantial business process anyone has ever heard of? This is not likely.

No matter how clearly business processes are defined, no matter how automated a task is, variations seem to abound. If the results of a process are always completely predictable, then that process could essentially run on its own. For everything else, there are managers.

Even if every process in a given business was entirely deterministic, there is still the question of measurement. The growing use of logging databases was noted in the opening chapter of this book. The huge volume of data meticulously stored in commercial and government databases is a testament to the enormous faith that modern organizations place in the value of information. As was also noted, agent-based modeling is a powerful way to help convert this accumulating data into useful facts. However, no data collection system is perfect. In the best of circumstances, a perfectly deterministic business process will still seem partially nondeterministic due to data collection error. Of course, the best of circumstances are rarely achieved in real-world businesses. From this perspective, nondeterministic agent models are a way to both deal with and represent the inherent imperfection of data collection.

If there are not yet enough ways to think about randomness in models, here is one more. Suppose the world is completely deterministic. Suppose that data can be recorded with absolute accuracy. Imagine building a model that captures every possible interaction that can produce meaningful data. Think big. Even for a simple process, the amount of detail required to capture everything everywhere that might possibly influence the outcome is overwhelming. The great mathematician John von Neumann once posited that the "simplest description of the human brain may be the human brain itself" (quoted in Batchelor 2004). If this were even partially true, how hard would it be to model a business process, let alone a complete business or even a market? Is agent-based modeling of business doomed? Fortunately, the answer is no. There is a simple answer that leads to an important conclusion.

The fact is that modeling is by definition an act of artful approximation. This is true for all types of modeling, not just agent-based simulation. The principle that is now known as Occam's Razor suggests that simpler explanations should be preferred to more complicated ones (Thorburn 1915, 1918). Following this rule, good modelers design and implement parsimonious models. Such modelers carefully balance the expressive power of more details with the cost of additional complications. Successful modelers achieve this balance through a combination of prior experience and iterative experimentation. Naturally, experience helps to keep modelers on paths that have led to success in the past. On the other hand, the iterative model development approach described throughout this book helps even experienced modelers be successful in complex evolving domains. Iterative model development and use is the ABMS paradigm.

It has been said that engineering is the art of tradeoffs. In some ways, each engineering specialty faces a different set of more or less well-understood tradeoffs. Electrical engineers specializing in digital systems trade off heat dissipation, speed, size, and cost among other things. Mechanical engineers trade off such factors as strength, size, weight, and cost. Good modelers are engineers in the sense that they intimately understand that they are weighing tradeoffs to achieve a goal. Modelers trade off detail, complication, and cost. So how are all of these approximations used?

At the most basic level, good models contain all of the details that impinge on the processes of interest, and everything else is approximated. When considering each candidate behavior or property that might be added to a model, good modelers ask themselves a question. What are the chances that this behavior or property will have a significant effect on the model's results? Of course, the meaning of the word "significant" depends on the problem being addressed. If the answer is high, then the behavior is a good candidate for incorporation into the model. If the answer is low, then do not include it. If the answer is moderate or unclear, then the behavior is a marginal initial candidate. Ideally, such candidates would be evaluated or tested without going through the investment of a full implementation.

Deciding whether to model agent behaviors that marginally contribute to system-level results is one of the most challenging parts of simulation design. It is also one of the most critical areas for project success. Most reasonably analytical people can identify behaviors that obviously contribute to outcomes. They can also eliminate behaviors that clearly do not influence results. Deciding about marginal behaviors is difficult because the need to have enough detail to have a usable model directly competes with the need to limit model development time and cost. Fortunately, there is an effective solution.

Choosing Behaviors to Model

Not long ago, the authors helped to lead a large-scale agent-based market simulation project focused on developing a detailed electricity market simulation. The model was being designed to show the interrelated effects of physical system structure, market rules, and corporate behavior on deregulated electricity markets. The market rules ranged from system-level pricing and operating policies all the way down to individual-level options and obligations. The structural issues ranged from the basic rules of electrical current flow all the way to the need to account for the details on thousands of power distribution points in each state being modeled. The corporate behaviors ranged from those typical of risk-prone startup companies to those characteristic of risk-averse incumbent monopolies. Furthermore, the corporate behaviors included not only previously observed activities but also potential activities that might be undertaken in the near future. This substantial scope sprang from the variety of constituencies directly involved with the modeling effort.

The need to model physical system structure in detail derived from the fundamental problem of electricity markets. On the scale of power systems, electricity is a commodity that cannot be stored and that is distributed according to complicated rules imposed by nature. Stating that electricity cannot for practical purposes be stored means that the supply of electricity and the demand for electricity must precisely balance on a continuous basis. This balance depends sensitively on the results of the distribution rules. In turn, the results of these rules are a function of a huge number of localized details. For example, accurately determining the flows of power in a state such as Illinois requires the calculation of a variety of factors on nearly two thousand points distributed throughout the state. This number does not even include the simultaneous calculations that are required for supporting points in neighboring states. To make matters even more complicated, prices and payments need to be derived for these power flows. As might be expected, prices and payments depend in part on the market regulations, which themselves can vary significantly.

The ability to simultaneously model a broad assortment of market regulations at a number of levels was the answer to questions posed by federal and state regulators as well as other organizations that might face shifting regulatory sands. The regulators were interested in learning which regulatory choices tended to lead to stable and efficient markets and gauging the consequences of current rules in existing markets. This information could be used to set regulations as well as investigate possible violations and abuses. The other organizations were interested in discovering better responses to existing regulations and in assessing their prospects under possible future rules.

The requirement to model an expansive array of corporate behavior was derived from the need to test the interactions of companies and the environment in which they function. As previously stated, prices and payments depend in part on the rules of the market in which they occur. Of course, these quantities also depend on the choices of corporations in the market.

The Spectrum of Model Uses

For business purposes, model applications can be characterized along a spectrum running from the most specific uses to the most general. Specific uses can be categorized as operational. General uses can be categorized as strategic. In the middle are tactical uses. Some models can span multiple uses and are thus multipurpose. Each of these has its own unique characteristics, including differing output accuracies, output precisions, input requirements, execution time requirements, and execution capacity requirements.

Model Accuracy and Precision

The output accuracy of a model refers to the closeness of the match between the results produced by a model and the corresponding real-world values. Output accuracy measures a model's ability to reproduce real-world behavior. Output accuracies can be expressed in several ways. They can be expressed as a qualitative measure of the fit between a model result and real-world value. For example, if a market model price tends to move in the same direction under a given situation as a corresponding real-world price, then this might be considered a qualitative match. Alternatively, output accuracies can be expressed as a percentage of a real-world value. For example, a commodity market model might produce prices that are within 8% of the real-world value for the same conditions. As we have discussed, agent-based models are often stochastic. Thus, multiple runs are needed to derive general conclusions. The references to specific model outputs raise the question of how the values are defined in the first place. The answer depends on the model's output precision.

The output precision of a model refers to the closeness of the match between the various results produced by a model. Unlike output accuracy, no comparison is made to corresponding real-world values. Output precision is expressed either qualitatively or as a percentage, similarly to output accuracies. Instead of referencing the real world, qualitative output precision compares model results from independent runs to one another. For example, a market model that produces rising price values for a series of stochastic runs could be said to generate precise market price directions. Models with this kind of narrow result range or high output precision are said to be stable. Precision only compares the model to itself. The real-world price direction may have nothing to do with the model's results. In this case, the model price directions would be precise but inaccurate. Normally, fewer stochastic runs are required for highly precise models than for less precise ones.

Guidance Horizons

A simulation guidance horizon is the time span accurately simulated by a given model. Of course, accuracy is relative to the model's intended use. Despite initial appearances, the tradeoff between simulation guidance horizons and agent behavioral variability is not really a modeling limitation for properly constructed simulations. This tradeoff is actually inherent in the nature of real systems.

The relationship between guidance horizons and agent behaviors is actually a tradeoff between what is known and what is possible. In simple terms, the more that is known about a situation, the less that is possible. For example, what if someone asked what was likely to happen next week in a market? People ask questions such as this all the time. The speaker simply assumes that the listener knows the context of the question. Often the listener does not. However, what if these few words were all that the speaker said? What if they did not indicate which market or even what type of market they where referring to? Replying to the main question with a specific answer is impossible. Why is this so?

From one perspective, there are too many possible answers to a general question about an unnamed market. Any market might be involved. Any events might be of interest. What if the speaker now stated that they were asking about a commodity market? This is not much help, but at least it is a little more specific. There are still too many possible answers. What if the speaker now stated that they wanted to know about a corn market? Still, little can be said, but now there is at least a small enough set of possible answers to provide some general thoughts. Continuing along this line, the speaker might say that they are interested in the corn futures market in Chicago. Knowing these details limits the scope of possible answers enough that there is at least the hope of answering the question. Knowing more about a situation means that there is less to be determined. This in turn means that statements about the remaining details can become more specific. The same can be said for models.

Knowing a little about a situation to be modeled leaves open a huge range of possible outcomes to be simulated. As details are filled in, the list of potential outcomes shrinks. These details include facts about what has happened as well as information on the types of actions that are likely in the future. Both of these factors constrain the behavioral choices of agents. Thus, as more is known about a situation, the range of agent behaviors tends to be reduced.

Normally more is known about the near term than is known about the distant future. As such, modelers running simulations with shorter and nearer time horizons tend to have more information available to them then those that are investigating possible events further in the future. These modelers are able to eliminate unlikely or impossible agent behaviors by specifying the appropriate initialization data. Others with less data need to simulate the extra outcomes since they cannot be strictly eliminated.

Operational Models

Operational models start with well-known information on the long-term commitments of organizations and use this background to study shorter-term decision-making. Since they are working on short time intervals, major changes such as strategic realignments tend to happen quite rarely. Forecast accuracy of 3% to 10% is usually appropriate. With a few notable exceptions, nearly all strategic decisions and the majority of tactical choices can be input rather than calculated. This can simplify the task of operational modeling

and can free up effort to gain the high levels of required accuracy. Accuracy requires details, but these can be suitably dealt with as discussed throughout this book.

What are the exceptions to the notion that operational modelers can hold strategic and tactical choices constant? Two primary situations raise red flags. These situations are boundary conditions and feedback loops.

Boundary conditions occur when strategic and tactical changes are implemented during the time horizon of an operational model run. An example is an operational market model that simulates a day during which market rules change. In this example, the daily market has margin requirements that are changed at noon for participants, if the requirements are changed at all. Say that the margin requirements are strategically set by regulators to ensure market stability. As such, these requirements are rarely changed to avoid adding to the uncertainty already present in the market. Further stabilizing the situation, the mandated changes that do occur in this example are announced well in advance of their implementation. These market rule changes could be reasonably modeled using simulation input parameters. These parameters can be time indexed or scripted, as described in chapter 12. In many ways, the example seems contrived. Many assumptions were made about when, how often, and why the model parameters needed to change. Furthermore, the example did not include a situation where varying input parameters may not be enough. Can things really be this simple? Fortunately, the answer is yes.

Strategic models have to deal with all of the cited complications and variations. However, operational models do not. Changes such as market rule modifications are usually in the domain of tactical or strategic modeling. The important point is the tradeoff between accuracy and flexibility. Large changes that can reduce accuracy move a model into the tactical or strategic realm. The example is realistic for an operational model.

Until now, the discussion of guidance horizons and agent behaviors assumed an extremely high-quality model. This does not automatically apply to all models. Obviously, it is also possible to have an incomplete model that necessitates a less than ideal tradeoff between these two factors. No model is perfect, so it is expected that at least some of the uncertainty in agent behaviors will come from shortcomings in the model itself. It is easy for poorly constructed or incompletely validated models to themselves introduce uncertainty beyond that inherent in the world. In fact, models do not even have to be bad to have this problem. All models add some of their own uncertainly to output results. However, some models do add more uncertainly than other models. How much uncertainty is introduced by simulation inaccuracies is discussed in detail in chapter 11.

Tactical Models

Tactical models are typically used to answer monthly and quarterly questions. These questions usually involve moderate levels of decision-making within the bounds created by higher-level strategic plans. For most business applications, tactical models need to produce quantitative forecasts that are within 10% to 15% of the corresponding real-world values. This accuracy level is generally high enough to provide clear guidance for medium-term decision-making. As with operational models, some tradeoffs in flexibility normally must be made to achieve this accuracy. However, far fewer tradeoffs are needed than with operational models. As before, the main factors are the model guidance horizon and the allowable range of agent behaviors. Tactical models are commonly used for both periodic planning sessions and for training.

Tactical models are regularly used to support intensive monthly and quarterly planning sessions. These sessions bring together a group of decision-makers for a day in the case of monthly planning and for a few days in the case of quarterly planning. The sessions are best held away from the decision-maker's offices to allow the decision-makers to avoid daily distractions and concentrate on planning. To prepare for these meetings, all of the data required to run the model should be collected and formatted as described in chapter 12. It is important that all of the key decision-makers who are affected by the planning be present. This avoids delays and ensures that choices can be made within the allocated meeting time. Normally the main purpose of these intensive meetings is to assess the current state of the organization relative to its stated monthly and quarterly goals. The model helps to project the current situation forward far enough to make this assessment feasible. If the organization is found to be performing differently than desired, then the model can be used to help determine why this is happening and to determine what can be done to improve things.

Strategic Models

Strategic models are generally used to answer questions covering annual or longer durations. These questions assume quite little about the possibilities for the future. Forecast accuracy of 15% to 30% is usually appropriate. To be effective, finding answers to these questions requires "outside the box" thinking and fundamental reconsiderations of the way the world might be rather than what it currently is. The answers are ultimately long-term visions for change rather than detailed daily plans. Of course, such long-term visions cannot be generated by models alone.

The creation of practical long-term strategies using agent-based models is an iterative process just like model development. The process is designed to be reliable, reviewable, and repeatable. The process is reliable since it includes intensive evaluations during each stage of model development and each stage involves a small step. The process is reviewable since it requires traceable intermediate products and documented feedback during each development stage. The process is repeatable since the iterative pattern allows organizations and individuals to accumulate experience that can be applied going forward.

The iterative ABMS development process normally involves a feedback between managers and modelers. The managers use their deep experience to create candidate strategies and form situational insights. In return, the modelers use agent simulations to provide unbiased evaluations of the strategies and generate unexpected outcomes to fuel new insights. These contributions build on one another during repeated feedback cycles.

The feedback cycles between management and modelers during strategic planning tend to follow a common pattern. Initially the generality and range of the scenarios being considered tend to grow. This is driven by both the managers and the model. Many situations have obvious projections into the future. These projections are not necessarily the only outcomes or even the most probable ones. They are just the ones people are most likely to think of. Once managers document these projections within the strategic ABMS process, they are freed to think of possibilities that are more complex. On the other hand, most strategic agent models will generate new possible future outcomes that would otherwise be difficult to discover. Many of these scenarios are found during the early model runs. This also contributes to the early expansion of thinking characteristic of strategic ABMS.

As time progresses, strategic ABMS tends to focus more on detailed refinement. The feedback cycles following the initial period usually converge on a number of different paths. These paths of convergence may be, and usually are, extremely different from one another! Regardless of their differences, convergent paths can be a natural result of the strategic ABMS process itself. During the process, a large number of combinations of corporate choices, competitor choices, and environmental factors are considered. This leads to the elimination of poor corporate choices and the selection of corporate choices that tend to be robust to the capriciousness of competitor choice and environmental factors. Furthermore, over time the feedback between management and modeling tends to reveal and remove repetitious scenarios even if at first the paths seemed superficially different.

As has been previously discussed, agent models are typically stochastic. Therefore, a potentially large number of alternatives can be easily generated from a given set of starting assumptions. This allows multiple future paths to be considered and dramatically reduces the possibility of unwanted surprises.

It should be noted that the typical strategic modeling cycle of expansion followed by focus is usually repeated in both the small and the large during a strategic modeling project. In the large, such cycles often occur when whole ranges of possibilities are eliminated and new ranges are brought under consideration. Thanks to agent-based modeling, it is realistic and practical to analyze complex long-term plans. This is one of the strengths of strategic ABMS. In the small, the ABMS feedback cycles often occur within individual convergent paths. Much like the large-scale feedback loops, this occurs when possible interactions along similar paths are considered, eliminated, and then replaced with new candidates. An additional ABMS strength is that these new candidate interactions are often highly unexpected.

In ideal situations, the feedback loops between high-level decision-makers and modelers can occur quickly enough for real-time interactions. When this happens, conversational modeling approaches can be used. More details on this are presented in chapter 11. Conversational modeling is most commonly used with strategic modeling but, in principle, it can be used for any type of agent simulation that executes fast enough for interactive execution.

There are two fundamental strategic modeling approaches. The direct approach focuses on future potential scenarios without considering how those situations might have come about. The transitional approach focuses on the possible transition paths between the current situation and possible future scenarios. These approaches are in many ways complementary.

The direct approach simply begins with a scenario set sometime in the future. The initial simulation scenarios are normally based on either probable conditions or ones of special interest. Likely conditions are often used since there is a high expectation that they will be faced in the future. Several kinds of special scenarios are also commonly employed. These special scenarios include those that represent unusually bad, unusually good, or radically changed future environments. Unusually bad environments are normally investigated to assess risk. Unusually good environments are investigated to determine upside potential and to ensure that a given organization is ready to take advantage of opportunities. Radically changed environments are investigated to see if there is any value in attempting to make the requisite changes.

The direct approach is relatively easy in the sense that only data for one or more future scenarios is required. Furthermore, the direct approach encourages open-ended exploration and the discovery of genuinely new future possibilities. This is so because there is no need to find a path from the present world to the future possibilities. Of course, this is also the direct approach's greatest weakness.

The transitional approach begins with the current situation and builds toward the future. The initial simulation scenarios are based on the present environment. This starting point is used to simulate possible future paths.

Developing initial simulation scenarios starts with the collection of basic descriptive information about the current situation as well as background information on the agents. This information is used to set up the baseline scenarios and to define the initial agent behavioral selections. The agent's choice of behaviors typically becomes more variable as the simulations move forward in time. For stochastic models, the increasing variability ultimately leads to a branching of possible future paths as this baseline scenario is projected forward into the future.

So, how do the direct and transitional approaches compare? The direct approach normally requires less data that the transitional approach since only possible future scenarios are needed rather than the exact current data. However, the direct approach only shows what would happen in the projected future state. It does not tell how to reach the hoped-for or feared starting state. It does not even say whether the starting state can be reached at all. On the other hand, properly executed transitional studies only deal with future states that can actually occur. Such studies also precisely detail how to reach the states under investigation. In fact, accurately logged transitional simulation runs produce what amount to scripts for the paths being examined. As might be expected, all of this precision and detail comes at a price. The transitional approach depends on the ranges of allowed agent behaviors. If the agents are substantially limited in their choice of actions, then certain outcomes may not be found. This seems to be at odds with the notion of agent-based models as open-ended discovery tools. How could this be?

Simply put, agent models can be used to uncover a wide range of possible future scenarios, but only if users allow this to happen. It is common for model users or input data collectors to limit agent behaviors based on preconceived notions of what is possible. For example, in a large industrial market model, several model users declared that their organization would never offer certain types of contracts to other groups. Nevertheless, what if the organization changed its mind and decided to offer these contracts anyway? Many other groups offered the contracts. It turned out that making such offers could greatly increase the flexibility of the original organization. Transitional modeling tied solely to the current situation would have precluded this option. Obviously, this is not the fault of the transitional modeling approach per se. A properly constructed baseline transitional modeling scenario would have allowed such agent behaviors. To reflect the current policies, the baseline transitional scenario would probably have limits on how often such offers were made. These limits would then have been allowed to fall as the simulations proceeded forward in time. However, most people have a hard time thinking this way. The direct modeling approach has the distinct advantage of encouraging people to think in this more open-minded way right from the start.

Multipurpose Models

It is possible for a single agent-based model to span the operational, tactical, and strategic level. In fact, many agent models are used this way. The ability to use models in this flexible way is one of the great strengths of ABMS. An operational run requires data

that is more detailed and normally has fewer options set for adaptation than a strategic model run. In return, operational runs tend to produce much more accurate results.

Multipurpose models should not be confused with multiscale models even though the terms sound similar. The word "multipurpose" refers to running a model with different input and output expectations. An example is a market model the authors developed that can be run for operational purposes with realistic but fixed descriptions of each market participant or run for strategic purposes with adaptive but general participant descriptions. The word "multiscale" refers to simulating several different levels of behavior or time scales at once in an integrated fashion. An example is a market model that simulates the detailed decision processes of individual companies on a level that is nested within a complex market on a second, higher level. While there is no necessary relationship between these two classifications, it is common for agent models to be both multipurpose and multiscale. The example market models cited above are in fact the same model described from two different perspectives.

Discovering That the Whole Is Greater Than the Parts

ABMS represents the unique rules and responsibilities of system components in the form of individual agents. Since agents have varying influence, none of them solely determines the ultimate system outcome. Every agent factors into the results one way or another.

ABMS can provide decision-makers with useful tools to allow systems or organizations to be understood as collections of interacting agents. These tools allow decision-makers to act on the fact that the totality of many systems or organizations is greater than the simple sum of the fundamental parts. The ABMS paradigm is to iteratively develop and use models of complex systems. The result is an ability to leverage the emergent behavior exhibited by complex adaptive systems.

Summary

Agent-based modeling and simulation is founded on the notion that the whole of many systems or organizations is greater than the simple sum of their constituent parts. The models that result from this view can be deterministic or stochastic. Stochastic models are generally more difficult to work with than deterministic models, but the extra effort is often handsomely rewarded with greater realism. Either type of model can be used in an operational, tactical, or strategic mode depending on the required guidance horizon and the fundamental capabilities of the model.

Note

1. The modeling approach presented here is a pragmatic combination of concepts from complexity science, as defined by those such as Phelan (1998, 2001), and systems theory, as defined by those such as Sterman (1994, 2000). This approach focuses on producing practical results that are of value to business and government and thus embraces a systems view of complex phenomena. The approach's goal is to produce simple models that can replicate the behavior of systems. The approach's method is highly iterated model development and testing.

References

AIAA (1998). *AIAA Guide for the Verification and Validation of Computational Fluid Dynamics Simulations*. Reston, Va.: American Institute of Aeronautics and Astronautics.

Batchelor, B. G. (2004). *Natural and Artificial Vision*. Cardiff, U.K.: Cardiff University.

Bendor, J. and S. Kumar (2004). The Perfect is the Enemy of the Good: Adaptive Versus Optimal Organizational Reliability. *Journal of Theoretical Politics* 17(1): 5–39.

Berleant, D., M.-P. Cheong, C. Chu, Y. Guan, A. Kamal, S. Ferson, and J. F. Peters (2003). Dependable Handling of Uncertainty. *Reliable Computing* 9: 1–12.

Book, E. (2002). Information Warfare Pioneers Take Top Pentagon Positions. *National Defense Magazine*, Jan. (online at http://www.nationaldefensemagazine.com/).

Brantingham, P. (2003). A Neutral Model of Stone Raw Material Procurement. *American Antiquity* 487–509.

Clark, V. (2002). Sea Power 21: Projecting Decisive Joint Capabilities. *Proceedings of the Naval Institute*. 128: 32–53. Annapolis, Md.: U.S. Naval Institute.

Copas, J. and S. Eguchi (2003). Model Uncertainty and Incomplete Data. *ISM Research Memorandum* (Institute of Statistical Mathematics, Japan) 884: 45.

Cowley, R. (2001). *What If? 2: Eminent Historians Imagine What Might Have Been*. Emeryville, Cal.: Putnam Publishing Group.

Cowley, R. and S. E. Ambrose (2000). *What If? The World's Foremost Military Historians Imagine What Might Have Been*. Berkeley, Cal.: Berkeley Publishing Group.

Eisberg, R. and R. Resnick (1985). *Quantum Physics of Atoms, Molecules, Solids, Nuclei, and Particles*. Chichester, U.K: Wiley.

Everett, H. (1957). Relative State Formulation of Quantum Mechanics. *Review of Modern Physics* 29: 454–462.

Finkel, A. M. (1990). *Confronting Uncertainty in Risk Management: A Guide for Decision-Makers*. Washington, D.C.: Center for Risk Management Resources for the Future.

Gartska, J. (2000). Network Centric Warfare: An Overview of Emerging Theory. *Phalanx* 33(4): 1–33.

Hamilton, J. A., J. L. Murtagh, and J. C. Deal (1999). A Basis for Joint Interoperability. *Command and Control Research and Technology Symposium*. Newport, R.I.: Naval War College, U.S. Department of Defense Command and Control Research Program.

Langton, C. G., Ed. (1997). *Artificial Life: An Overview?* Cambridge, Mass.: MIT Press.

Langton, C. (2000). What is Artificial Life? Biota Publications website (available at www.biota.org/papers/cglalife.html).

Minar, N., R. Burkhart, C. Langton, and M. Askenazi (1996). The Swarm Simulation System: A Toolkit for Building Multi-Agent Simulations. Working Paper 96-06-042. Santa Fe, N.M.: Santa Fe Institute.

Office of the Secretary of Defense (1997). *Defense Technology Area Plan*. Washington, D.C.: U.S. Department of Defense.

Oxford (2004). *Compact Oxford English Dictionary Online*. Oxford: Oxford University Press.

Phelan, S. E. (1998). A Note on the Correspondence Between Complexity and Systems Theory. *Systemic Practice and Action Research* 12: 237–246.

Phelan, S. E. (2001). What Is Complexity Science, Really? *Emergence*, Special Issue on "What Is Complexity Science?," pp. 120–136

Sterman, J. D. (1994). Learning In and About Complex Systems. *System Dynamics Review* 10(2–3): 291–330.

Sterman, J. D. (2000). *Business Dynamics: Systems Thinking and Modeling for a Complex World*. Boston: Irwin McGraw-Hill.

Stirling, W. C. (2002). *Satisficing Games and Decision Making with Applications to Engineering and Computer Science*. Cambridge, U.K.: Cambridge University Press.

Thorburn, W. M. (1915). Occam's Razor. *Mind* 24: 287–288.

Thorburn, W. M. (1918). The Myth of Occam's Razor. *Mind* 27: 345–353.

3

Agents Up Close

Agents: An Overview

This chapter details the main approaches to implementing computational agents. This chapter builds toward chapter 6. Chapter 6 in turn shows how to decide which agents should be used to model a given situation, how to determine which of the agent implementation approaches to apply for modeling, and how to document the choices that are made. Chapters 3 and 6 are presented separately because of the way chapter 6 depends on the background provided by chapters 4 and 5.

Agents are the decision-making components in complex adaptive systems. Agents have sets of rules or behavior patterns that allow them to take in information, process the inputs, and then effect changes in the outside environment. The information processing within agents typically includes some form of adaptation or learning. As will be discussed in chapter 4, this is one of the two main sources of adaptation in complex adaptive systems. The other main source is structural change in the system itself in the form of the relationships between agents.

As shown in figure 3.1, anything that makes choices in a business can be viewed as an agent. Executives, managers, and other decision-makers can be modeled as agents. Organizations can be modeled as agents. Computer systems can be modeled as agents. Naturally, agents form the core of ABMS.

In ABMS, an agent is an individual with a set of attributes and behavioral characteristics as shown in figure 3.2. The attributes define what a given agent is.

The behavioral characteristics define what a given agent does. Typically, there is variation among many of the agents in the model.

Agent Attributes

There are many kinds of agent attributes. Some common attributes used to represent people include age, income, sex, history, and various preferences. As shown in figure 3.3, some common attributes used to represent corporations competing within markets include resources, size, decision time, and various strategic preferences such as risk tolerance. Common behaviors include operations and planning. Of course, these attributes and behaviors need to be specialized and fleshed out for specific applications. Typical attributes used to represent organizational management within a corporation include a network of employees each with their own status, the work pending for the organization, the work outputs of the organization, and any other resources the organization may have available. In this case, the employees within the organization are often agents. In the most detailed situations, the result is a multiscale model of organizational behavior with the smaller-scale employee interactions combining to produce the larger-scale activities of the organization as a whole. An example is outlined in figure 3.4.

Some agents' attributes such as age can be represented in a simple form. However, many agent attributes, such as preferences, are multifactorial and

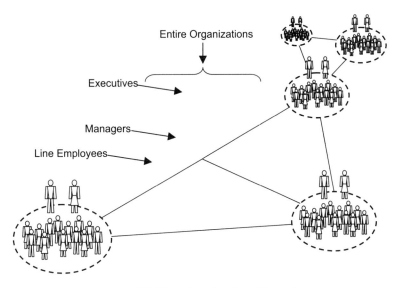

FIGURE 3.1 Examples of real-world agents.

thus are defined at multiple, nested levels. In an agent-based simulation, these attributes are carried by each agent and can often evolve or change over time as a function of each agent's experiences. An example is corporate strategic preferences.

Corporate strategic preferences within complex markets can be decomposed in many ways. One common approach is to factor out several critical components such as risk tolerance and planning time horizon. These components can then be used to build an initial agent model that can be iteratively elaborated upon as required by the context of the application area.

Risk tolerance can be seen as a measure of how much an individual will put at stake to gain a specified

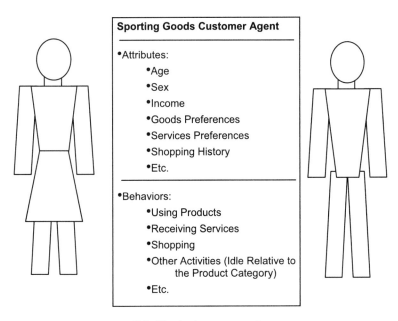

FIGURE 3.2 The basic structure of an agent.

Corporation

•Attributes:
    •Resources
    •Decision Response Time
    •Profit Targets
    •Volume Targets
    •Market Share Targets
    •Risk Tolerance
    •Etc.

•Behaviors:
    •Unexpected Event Response
    •Daily Operations
    •Weekly Operations
    •Monthly Operations
    •Annual Planning
    •Etc.

FIGURE 3.3 Common corporate attributes and behaviors.

return (Raiffa 1970). More simply, risk tolerance represents how much value differing possible returns have to an individual (Raiffa 1970). The relative value of a specified return is called utility (Raiffa 1970). Figure 3.5 shows a chart that relates corporate profit

to corporate utility for two hypothetical firms. The firm represented by the upper curve will tend to avoid risk and the firm represented by the lower curve will tend to take risks.

The firm characterized by the upper curve places great value or receives much utility from moderate returns, but gains little by increasing returns above a modest level. For this corporation, increasing returns from zero to a small value below the bend or "knee" in the curve greatly increases utility. However, increasing the returns beyond the knee in the curve provides very little additional or marginal benefits. Thus, this corporation will take actions to reach the knee in the curve but it will not knowingly take action beyond this point. Given that smaller returns typically involve less risk than larger returns, this corporation will tend to take fewer risks than firms that derive more utility from large returns. This firm is said to be risk-averse.

The firm represented by the lower curve places limited value or receives little utility from moderate returns. However, much greater returns substantially increase the firm's perceived utility. Critically, the improvements in utility far outpace the improvements in the actual returns. For this corporation, increasing returns from zero to a small value below the knee in the curve have almost no utility. Increasing the returns beyond the knee in the curve provides substantial

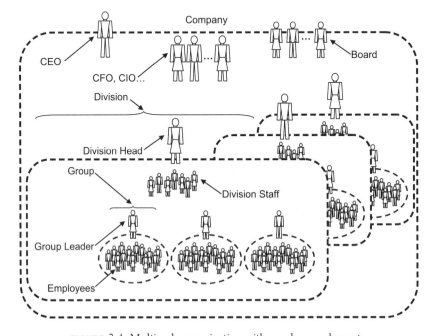

FIGURE 3.4 Multiscale organization with employee subagents.

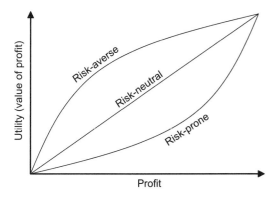

FIGURE 3.5 Utility curve with risk-averse, risk-neutral, and risk-prone agents.

additional or marginal benefits. This corporation will do whatever is required to get returns well beyond the knee in the curve. Given that larger returns usually involve more risk than smaller returns, this corporation will tend to take more risks than firms that derive less utility from large returns. This firm is said to be risk-prone.

Agent Behaviors

Agents have several behavioral features. These features include decision rules to select actions, adaptation capabilities to learn from experiences, perceptual capabilities to sense its surroundings, and optional internal models to project the possible consequences of decisions. These features are indicated in figure 3.6. These behavioral features often vary from agent to agent to reflect the diversity commonly found in real situations. As shown in the figure, there are essentially two levels of agent rules (Casti 1998). The first are base-level rules. These rules specify how the agent responds to routine events. The second level contains "rules to change the [base-level] rules" (Casti 1998). These second-level rules provide adaptation by allowing the routine responses to change over time. Thus, according to Casti, agents have "rules and rules to change the rules" (Casti 1998). Of course, this simple hierarchy can be greatly elaborated depending on the application. The diverse range of approaches for specifying agent "rules and the rules to change rules" are reviewed in detail in the sections that follow (Casti 1998).

Agents have sets of decision rules that govern their behaviors. These rules allow agents to interact with and communicate with other agents as well as to respond to their environments. These rules can provide agents with responsive capabilities on a variety of levels from simple reactions to complex decision-making.

Agent behaviors follow three overall steps. First, agents evaluate their current state and then determine what they need to do at the current moment. Second, agents execute the actions that they have chosen. Third, agents evaluate the results of their actions and adjust their rules based on the results. These steps can be performed in many ways, including the use of simple rules, complex rules, advanced techniques, external programs, or even nested subagents. Each of these approaches will be discussed in detail.

Simple Agents or Proto-Agents

Many agent models are composed of agents that do not have all the characteristics that have been used to describe an agent, even though the simulations are described as or structured as agent simulations. Characteristics that have come to be associated with agents are that they are:

- adaptive;
- have the capability to learn and modify their behaviors;
- autonomous; and
- heterogeneous, resulting in a population of agents having diverse characteristics.

Does the fact that a model may consist of agents lacking one or more of these properties imply that the model is not an agent model? If not having all agent characteristics in all the agents of the model disqualifies the model from being an agent model, then the results can be quite undesirable. For example, such a nonagent model may suddenly be transformed into an agent model if the missing characteristic is added. This situation can happen for a number of reasons. For example, the model may be developed incrementally, with the essential agent characteristics to be added at a later stage of development. This is a common development approach for agent models. How can this situation be described and articulated to others? The answer is to define proto-agents, which are agents that lack one or more of the defining characteristics of agency.

Not all agents in all agent models are fully developed agents in the sense that they have all of the agent characteristics. But, depending on the model, the important

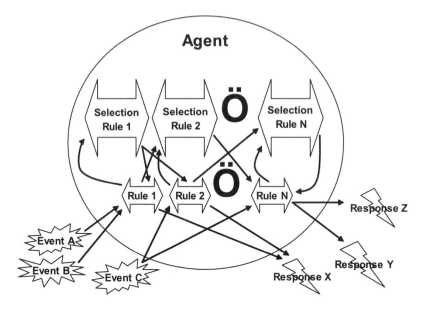

FIGURE 3.6 Basic agent behavioral features.

question is whether the model is structured in such a way that these missing features could be added within the established modeling framework. They could have these characteristics if there was a reason to add them to the model, and maybe there even is an intention to add some of the characteristics to the model in the future.

A good example is a traffic simulation in which individual drivers are modeled by a set of simple rules that govern their driving behavior. The rules may cover when drivers change lanes, when they speed up, even when and how they brake for stopped traffic. These rules are not adaptive in the sense that they change in any way over time as drivers learn how to drive or negotiate traffic. Nor is the population of drivers adapting to the driving conditions over time. Yet this represents a useful model of traffic systems based on individual driver behavior, and it could readily be expanded to include adaptive driver strategies for dealing with traffic or novel situations that are not specified in the core set of rules governing driver behavior. In the case that a simulation is structured as an agent model, but the agents do not exhibit the requisite characteristics of agents as noted above, then it is not an agent-based model. Instead, the agents in question are prototype agents, or "proto-agents," and the simulation is a proto-agent model.

Simple reactive decision rules allow proto-agents to perform essential interactions with their neighbors and to respond to basic environmental changes. Simple reactive rules normally associate or map each external stimulus with specific responses. An example is shown in figure 3.7.

Figure 3.7 shows a proto-agent that is offering a commodity for sale in an open outcry market over a series of days. When the market opens each day, each agent is allowed to declare an asking price for its products. This price is fixed throughout the day. At the end of the day, agents total their sales and check the market price boards to find the day's average market-wide price. The agent in the figure simply bases its asking price on the previous day's average or a threshold value. If the previous day's average price was above the agent's marginal production cost, then the agent simply asks the average market price the next day. If the previous day's average price was less than or equal to the agent's marginal production cost, then the agent simply asks their marginal production cost. The result is a basic trend-following agent. ABMS agents are normally more complex than this. This example is presented only to illustrate the simplest of rules.

A second example is shown in figure 3.8. This example shows another proto-agent that is offering a commodity for sale in the same open outcry market. As before, the agent needs to set an asking price for its products at each step in the simulation. The agent begins with an initial price and then adjusts this price

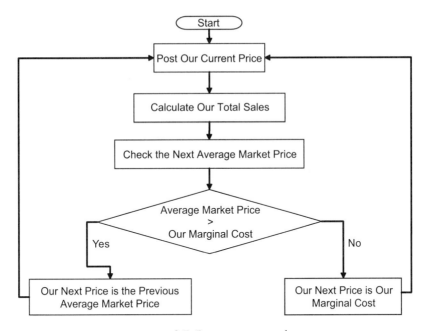

FIGURE 3.7 Proto-agent example.

based on its sales volume. If the volume is below the desired level, it lowers its price, limited only by its marginal production costs. If the volume is above the threshold level, it raises its price in the hopes of increasing unit profits. As a result, the agent performs a simple price discovery process. A group of these agents acting together can perform market-level price discovery. In this case, the agent has an extremely simple learning mechanism, the last price, which it adjusts over time to improve its performance.

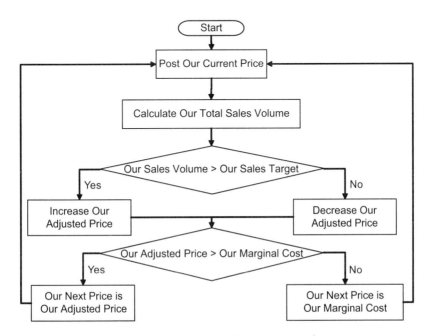

FIGURE 3.8 A simple market agent example.

With proto-agents, the external stimuli or trigger conditions for the rules are normally either mutually exclusive or prioritized. Normally only a single simple rule is selected for activation during each decision-making cycle for proto-agents. Complex agents relax this constraint and allow many behaviors to be potentially activated during each decision-making cycle. Complex agents are discussed in detail in the next section. The agent shown in the next example is a moderate elaboration of the agent shown in figure 3.8. The new agent now has a set of price-setting rules. The first rule is used to set prices during time steps with a normal balance between supply and demand. The second rule is used when there is a sudden shortage of products. Both rules work the same way as the single rule shown in figure 3.8. The differences in the activation conditions for each of the two rules allow the agent to choose between them appropriately. Each of the rules has a simple but independent adaptation mechanism that allows the agent to learn different price points for typical markets and markets with shortages. Agents with short lists or small sets of such rules can react to the world around them. However, since the rules are extremely simple, they usually involve little or no adaptation. So how is the adaptation normally found in complex systems modeled using agents with simple decision rules?

Adaptation is represented using simple reactive agents through the configuration of the agents themselves. The agents change little, if at all. The interaction structure of the agents can change over time in response to the changes in the system state. This change in the interaction patterns reflects "learning" or adaptation on the system level. As an example, consider a group of simple production agents trying to coordinate their production activities to satisfy a set of customers. In the example, the results from any one stage of production are used as the raw material for the next step in the chain. The situation is made more complicated by the fact that production levels cannot be instantly changed. Say that production level changes take two days. As a result, changes in downstream demand propagate slowly up through the production group. Imagine further that each agent can only use extremely simple rules. Can rules be written that allow the agents to coordinate their production levels to match the requirements of the downstream customer?

One possible rule set has each agent performing daily checks of their own current production level and their requested demand downstream. Agents then attempt to adjust their current production level to match their expected future downstream demand. Even though each agent has no learning capabilities, these simple rules allow the production group as a whole to adapt over time to a range of customer demand patterns.

Simple rules have several advantages. Representing agents using simple reactive decision rules allows focus on core mechanisms, permits models to be quickly developed, shortens verification and validation times, and enables rapid model use.

Simple rules can help ABMS users to focus on core mechanisms. Core mechanisms are the key behaviors and interactions that give models their essential structure. One of the principal advantages of models that use simple rules is that these key behaviors and interactions can be given center stage. In some cases, the presence of complicated mechanisms can obscure the fundamental rules that drive overall system outcomes. In general, the fewer mechanisms there are in a model, the easier it is to see the contribution each mechanism makes to the overall results. The simpler each mechanism in a model is, the clearer the operation of each rule becomes. One counter is that excessive abstraction can sometimes make it difficult to relate the agents in a model to the real-world components they are intended to represent. Developing useful, usable, and used models requires a careful balance between clarifying generalization and excessive simplification. This balance is usually best achieved by starting simple and then applying the iterative development approach described throughout this book.

Simple rules can provide more than just clarity. Model designs that use simple rules can often be implemented in less time than models that depend on complicated rules. The benefits are straightforward on the surface. Building less takes less time and less effort. However, the actual advantages run much deeper. As described later in the book, building in small iterative stages yields a much more efficient overall development process. A model built starting with simple rules can provide a firm foundation for later work and avoids the inefficiency of building unnecessarily complicated models. Designing models using simple rules is a fast and wise way to begin most ABMS projects.

Verification is the process of making sure that an implemented model matches its design. Validation is the process of making sure that an implemented model matches the real world. Practical approaches to verification and validation are described in detail in chapter 11. For now, it is enough to note that for a variety of reasons, models with simple rules are easier to verify and validate than models with more complex rules. The reasons include the fact that less complicated mechanisms have narrower ranges of distinct inputs and outputs; that simple rules are conceptually easier to work with than more complicated mechanisms; and that simple rules result in smaller designs and implementations with less to check than designs that are more sophisticated. The major disadvantage of simple rules concerning verification and validation is that, in some circumstances, it can be more difficult to match such models to real-world events due to the number of simplifying assumptions required.

It is usually easier for people to learn how to use models built using agents with simple rules than it is for them to learn to use models that are more complicated. Furthermore, it is often much easier to operate and apply the results from simpler models. Simpler models can be learned more quickly since there are fewer details to learn and less complexity to master. Operating such models is usually both faster and easier since there is less cognitive overhead and fewer inputs to prepare. Furthermore, models with simpler rules generally execute in less time than models with more complicated rules. This can provide more rapid feedback to users and allow more iterative cycles during a given investigation with the model. Even though simple rules can allow models to be learned, configured, and executed rapidly, there are some advantages to more complex rules. Occasionally, models with more complex rules can be easier to learn, operate, and explain than models that are more abstract. This is because of the potential for a more direct relationship between the model agents and the corresponding real-world components, due to the potential for a direct use of common domain terminology and readily available data and to a reduction in overall abstraction. It is important to note that building a more complex model with such advantages over simpler models requires a careful balancing of necessary detail and optional minutiae. The iterative development approach presented throughout this book provides an accessible path to achieving this balance.

Simple rules are usually a good starting point for prototyping, design, and implementation.

Furthermore, models that rely on simple reactive decision rules can still produce adaptation at the system level. Even when modeling systems with highly adaptive individual agents, it is strongly recommended that the iterative model development process begin with simple reactive agents. It is true that simple rules may not always have enough expressive power to implement the desired model. Even in this case, beginning with a simple simulation permits basic premises to be tested, lets the overall model structure be verified, allows immediate feedback to users, provides a strong foundation for future development, and prevents unnecessary investments by trying simpler possibilities first. The proto-agents can always be made more complex later.

Complex Agents

What about agents that are complex enough to be individually adaptive? These agents have the ability to change or adapt decision rules over time. These types of agents are required when simple rules are not enough to represent the level of adaptation found in the system being modeled. Such agents normally have measures of performance applied to their decisions—by themselves and by their environments. They may even have internal models of their environments and of other agents' decision-making processes. There are many ways to create such agents within agent-based models. Complex rules, advanced techniques, external programs, and nested subagents can all be used. Each of these approaches has unique strengths and requirements that will be discussed in detail.

The overall difference between the strengths and requirements of simple and complex agent-based modeling is large enough to have produced two major camps in the agent-based modeling community. Following Einstein, one camp holds that models should be "as simple as possible." This group strongly resists making models complex and focuses on clarity as the ultimate ideal. In principle, this group tends to value broadly applicable but general conclusions over detailed domain-specific deductions. The other camp insists that complex models are required to completely represent complex situations. This group tends to be more interested in producing detailed domain-specific results than discovering universal patterns. This group focuses on realism or verisimilitude as the ideal.

Verisimilitude is the appearance of truth. This book takes a pragmatic view that the importance of clarity or verisimilitude depends on the system or systems being modeled. Thus, from the perspective of the authors, either goal is equally valid.

Complex Rule Agents

Complex rules can be used to increase the detail, fidelity, and expressiveness of models compared to that achievable with simple rules. Complex rules as described here are structurally similar to simple rules but have more sophisticated activation conditions. As with simple rules, the external stimuli or trigger conditions for complex rules are normally either mutually exclusive or prioritized. Unlike simple rules, it is common to have multiple complex rules activated during a single agent decision-making cycle and it is common to have nested rules.

Multiple complex rules can be activated during a single decision-making cycle when the activation conditions for more than one rule are triggered. The activation sequence for the selected rules is normally prioritized so that the chosen rules are executed in an intelligible sequence. Nested rules are rules within rules. These rules specify behaviors that depend on other behaviors within the agent. As discussed in detail later, particularly complex prioritized or nested rule sets can be implemented using predicate databases, logic programming systems such as Prolog (Bratko 1990), or embedded rules engines for languages such as Java.

An example of a moderately complex agent with nested rules that can activate more than one rule during a decision-making cycle is shown in figure 3.9. This agent extends the market example from the proto-agents section. The enhanced agent uses a wider range of behaviors to determine its offer price. The resulting overall behavior is complex enough to be somewhat realistic. The agent now considers not only the success of its previous offer, and the current balance between supply and demand, but also takes into account basic offer price trends over time. In the example, the agent adjusts its offer price based on whether it has achieved its target sales level for the previous two days. If its sales targets are missed consistently for two or more days in a row, then the agent will attempt to get ahead of the trend with a larger than usual price change. This decision rule is executed every day so that looking two days back allows the agent to begin to recognize simple trends.

Next, the agent considers whether it has recently changed its price in offsetting directions. If so, the agent recognizes that it is cycling its price up and down and takes steps to stabilize its offer. It achieves this by checking the direction of the previous day's price change, if any, against the next price change it is planning. If there is a change in direction, then the price is left alone for the next day. Finally, the agent checks to see if a sudden shortage has occurred. If so, the agent will modify its previous decision and adjust its price upward on a temporary basis. The parameters used in the model should be based on known market information. It is expected that the parameters will typically vary from agent to agent. As will be discussed shortly, this agent has nested rules, several of which can be activated at the same time.

Figures 3.10 and 3.11 show traces through the agent decision-making process presented in figure 3.9. The trace in figure 3.10 shows a simple trip through the process. The trace in figure 3.11 shows a more complex trip that activated several nested rules.

During the figure 3.10 trace, the agent checked the results of its offers for the last two days and found that it was successful both times. Because of this, the sales target trend is good so that it will attempt to increase its offer price by an amount greater than what it would have if it had not been as successful. Next, the agent checks the change it made yesterday in its offer price against the new change it is planning for its next offer price and finds that both prices changed upward. The cycle prevention mechanism is ignored since both price changes were increases. Finally, the agent checks for a temporary shortage and finds that no disruption is expected for the next day. This simple trace through the decision-making rules of figure 3.9 results in an offer price that is somewhat higher than the previous value.

The rule trace shown in figure 3.11 is much more complex that that shown in figure 3.10. In figure 3.11, the agent had mixed sales results over the last two days. Two days ago, the agent missed its sales target. Therefore, yesterday it reduced its price. The result was a sufficient increase in sales for it to achieve its sales target today. Because of this success, it will initially choose to increase its price. However, it will next check to make sure that it is not simply cycling its price up and down. Yesterday the agent reduced its price. Today it initially plans to increase its price. When it compares these two pricing directions, it finds that it is cycling. To prevent this, the agent

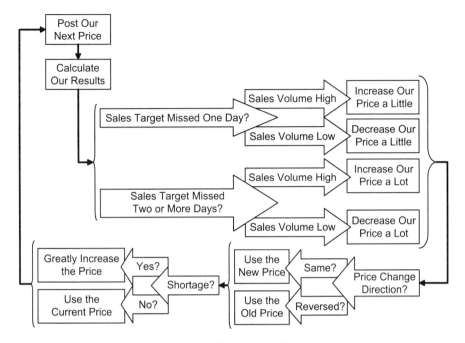

FIGURE 3.9 Moderately complex agent.

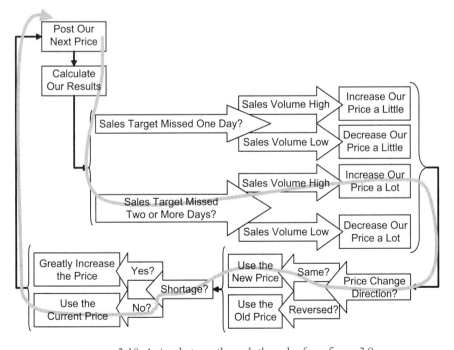

FIGURE 3.10 A simple trace through the rules from figure 3.9.

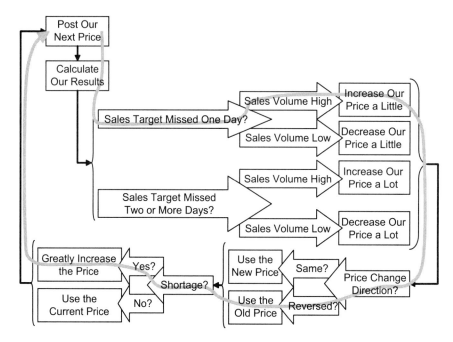

FIGURE 3.11 A complex trace through the rules from figure 3.9.

decides to keep its price the same. Finally, the agent checks the trends in the market supply level and finds that a temporary shortage is expected for the next day. This causes the agent to increase its price above the constant level selected to avoid cycling. This example trace shows multiple pricing rules being triggered in a priority order as well as the activation of nested price adjustment rules.

As previously discussed, the use of complex rules has several advantages. However, the use of complex rules also has some disadvantages. In comparison to models built with simple rules, complex rule models can make it harder to focus on underlying patterns, can raise development costs, and can increase the required verification and validation efforts. Furthermore, sometimes even complex rules may not have enough expressive power to implement the desired model.

One of the primary goals of agent-based modeling is to improve the modeler's understanding of the system under study. Parsimonious models built with the simplest possible agents naturally have fewer distracting details than more complicated models. The improved ability of richer models to represent the systems under study and their greater verisimilitude for domain experts can come at the price of reduced generality.

The complexity of the rules within these models can obscure the underlying patterns.

Obviously, the more complicated a model is, the more effort is required for design, implementation, and operation. As a result, complicated models generally have higher design, development, and operation costs. There are a few caveats though. First, highly abstracted models can sometimes require more design effort due to the need for detailed refinement. Second, the extra expense of more detailed models is often more than paid for by the greater fidelity of the answers that they provide.

The classic statement that anything that can go wrong will go wrong is as applicable to modeling as to most other things. In principle, there is simply more that can go wrong with complex rules than with simpler variations. Thus, complicated rules are often harder to verify and validate than simple rules. This manifests itself in terms of increased verification and validation time, greater costs, and higher data requirements.

Complex rules have several disadvantages. Despite these disadvantages, complex rules are usually a good intermediate point for prototyping, design, and implementation. Furthermore, simple rules often lack the richness required to represent complex systems at the necessary level of detail. In these situations in particular, complex rules are required for accurate modeling.

Advanced Technique Agents

Sometimes, even complex rules are insufficient to represent the agents within some systems due to the sophisticated nature of some agent behaviors. In this case, advanced techniques can be used to represent agent behaviors. Advanced techniques include the use of statistical methods such as multinomial logit modeling, the use of artificial intelligence methods such as neural networks, and the use of optimization methods such as genetic algorithms.

Statistical Methods

Statistical methods are commonly used within agents to do forecasting. Statistical methods are useful for rigorously finding numerical correlations in quantitative data. An example of the use of one of these methods, namely linear regression, is shown in figure 3.12 (Mendenhall et al. 1990; McClave and Benson 1994). In this example, the previously discussed market agent uses linear regression to attempt to forecast the market price based on the ratio of demand to supply predicted by the market clearing house. The agent develops its forecast by finding the line that best relates the historical market prices to the historical demand-to-supply ratios. The line is found by calculating the parameters that minimize the difference or error (formally the mean average of the square of the error) between the predicted and actual values. This line is then used with the next day's predicted demand to supply ratio to estimate the next day's market price. Of course, this regression example is intentionally

quite simple. Both a larger number of inputs and more sophisticated statistical methods can be used to improve the example agent's market price forecasts. A large number of inputs can be included in the agent's forecasting procedure, including absolute supply, absolute demand, supply volatility measures, demand volatility measures, and timing information. Many statistical methods may also be applicable, including general nonlinear regression, various types of statistical hypothesis testing, and multinomial logit modeling.

Multinomial logit modeling is one example among a range of sophisticated statistical methods that can be used within an agent to represent more realistic behaviors (de Rooij and Kroonenberg 2003). As with most of these other statistical methods, it is commonly used as a forecasting method. Similar to linear regression, multinomial logit modeling is used to find a predictive between inputs and outputs. Unlike linear regression, which focuses on continuous variables, multinomial logit modeling is designed to predict the likelihood of discrete events such as bid acceptance or rejection. This approach can allow agents to estimate the chances that a given action will succeed or fail. Multinomial logit modeling assumes that the overall likelihood of success is given by a particular curve, namely the logit function. The method uses historical data to set the function's parameters to match the shape to the situation being considered. The resulting function is then used to estimate the likelihood of future events. Once these events occur, the resulting data points can be used on an ongoing basis to refine the shape of the prediction curve.

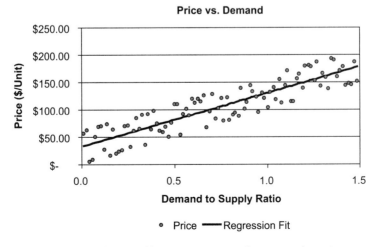

FIGURE 3.12 The use of linear regression to forecast market prices.

Consider an example market agent that uses multinomial logit modeling to determine the chances that a bid at a given price will be accepted. In the example, the logit model would map an input bid price to an output probability of acceptance. The logit model's parameters and resulting curve represent the observed relationship between historical bid prices and bid acceptance rates. This curve can be used to determine the probability of future bid acceptances given selected bid prices.

Multinomial logit modeling is one example of a set of methods that can be used to find predictive mappings for discrete events (de Rooij and Kroonenberg 2003). Another example is multinomial probit modeling. This method works similarly to multinomial logit modeling but replaces the predictive logit curve with an exponential prediction function. A large number of other statistical techniques are also available.

Artificial Intelligence Methods

A variety of artificial intelligence methods can be used within agents. The methods include the previously mentioned logic programming, neural networks, advanced search techniques, distributed problem solving, and nonmonotonic reasoning.

Logic Programming As was discussed previously, logic programming or predicate databases can be used to store and execute complex rules. These rules are stated in the form of asserted truths or facts that are then matched to queries in a recursive fashion. In other words, queries are matched to facts. Any outstanding parts of the query that could not be resolved become new queries that are then matched against the stored facts. This process is repeated until all of the queries are matched or some of the queries are shown to be unmatchable given the current facts.

Predicate databases can be easily updated as a model evolves. Predicate rule engines that operate on these databases can be easily embedded into agents. Using these tools to implement complex rules can save substantial amounts of time and significantly reduce development cost by leveraging existing off-the-shelf components.

Neural Networks Neural networks are particularly well suited for prediction and pattern recognition tasks (Rich and Knight 1991). In principle, neural networks do essentially the same thing as statistical regression.

In practice, some problems seem to be more naturally addressed using neural networks than statistical methods. These problems include learning in complicated environments with large numbers of potential inputs of unknown quality, learning in situations with high ongoing rates of change, and recognizing patterns in data amidst substantial amounts of noise.

Neural networks often operate using variations of a technique called back propagation (Rich and Knight 1991). This technique starts out with an initial set of parameters and then adjusts these parameters through a series of steps. Each step involves using the network to make a prediction and then observing the actual results. The difference between the neural network's prediction and the actual results is called the error. This error is traced backward or back-propagated from the network's outputs to its inputs. During the trace, the parameters of the network are adjusted to reduce the error in the previous prediction. These steps can occur over data points at one time, over data points at different times, or both.

As an example, consider the previously discussed linear regression model that was used to forecast market prices. In place of linear regression, the market agent could use a neural network to recognize when its special shortage price increase action should be triggered. In this case, the neural network would accept the market clearing house's predicted supply and the demand levels as inputs. The network would output a price increase signal. The success or failure of the price increase decision would be back-propagated on an ongoing basis over time. Errors are considered to have occurred if the network signaled the opportunity for a bid price increase that subsequently failed to be accepted, or if the network did not signal the opportunity for a bid price increase immediately before the market price rose to a level that would have supported an increase.

Swarm or Mob Intelligence Swarm intelligence is the ability of a group of agents to collectively find a solution that is better than any one of them could have found alone (Bonabeau et al. 1999). Swarm intelligence is sometimes also referred to as mob intelligence. Swarm intelligence uses large groups of agents to solve complicated problems. Swarm intelligence uses a combination of accumulation, teamwork, and voting to produce solutions. Accumulation occurs when agents contribute parts of a solution to a group. Teamwork occurs when different agents or subgroups of agents accidentally or purposefully work on different parts of a large problem. Voting occurs when agents propose solutions or components of solutions and the other agents vote explicitly by rating the proposal's quality or vote implicitly by choosing whether to follow the proposal.

Swarm intelligence can be effective when applied to highly complicated problems with many nonlinear factors, although it is often less effective than the genetic algorithm approach discussed later in this chapter. Swarm intelligence is related to swarm optimization covered in the "Optimization Methods" section. As with swarm intelligence, there is some evidence that at least some of the time swarm optimization can produce solutions that are more robust than genetic algorithms. Robustness here is defined as a solution's resistance to performance degradation when the underlying variables are changed.

Swarm intelligence fits well with the nested sub-agent approach detailed later in this chapter. When these approaches are used together, swarm intelligence is normally used to solve a problem for a parent agent that contains a swarm of smaller agents. The parent agent defines the problem that the smaller agents solve. The smaller agents actually perform a swarm optimization procedure to locate possible solutions for their parent agent.

Other Artificial Intelligence Techniques Many other areas of artificial intelligence are particularly fruitful for agent rule implementation. These areas include the use of advanced search techniques, nonmonotonic reasoning, and paraconsistent reasoning (Rich and Knight 1991; Ginsberg 1993; Arieli and Avron 2000).

Optimization Methods

Optimization methods seek to find the "best" value among large sets of possible values. The best value is usually defined to be either the highest or the lowest value possible. For example, a search for the highest value can be used to find the most profitable portfolio amidst a range of options. Another example is the use of a search for the smallest value within a list of costly choices. In principle, searches for highest or lowest values are interchangeable. A method that can find one type of extreme value or "extremum" can be easily refocused to find the other type of value as well. There are a huge number of methods and variations

for finding extrema and more continue to be developed. These methods can be categorized into two major groups.

The first group of search methods is called algorithms (Baase 1988). These search methods are guaranteed to work if they are properly applied (Baase 1988). Thus, at first glance, they can seem quite attractive. However, the success guarantees often come with strings attached. For example, the simplest of these algorithms is exhaustive search. To use this method, an agent just checks all possible options. An agent looking for the most valuable portfolio would calculate the net present value of each portfolio and then select the most profitable one. Clearly, this guarantees that the portfolio with the highest net present value will be selected. However, if there are huge numbers of possible portfolios to check, then this method will likely be impractical. This is a common occurrence with search algorithms. Examples of search algorithms are linear programming and quadratic programming. Even though search algorithms are guaranteed to work for appropriate problems, they often can be too slow to use for many agent-based applications and are typically limited to solving selected categories of problems. These difficulties led to the development of the second group of search methods.

The second group of search methods is called heuristics. Heuristics have been described by Edward Feigenbaum as "rules of thumb" (Ginsberg 1993). These rules are more formally known as heuristics (Rich and Knight 1991; Ginsberg 1993). Heuristic search methods are not guaranteed to work, even if they are properly applied. In general they will often, but not always, find extrema or values close to extrema. However, unlike many algorithms, heuristic search methods commonly consider only a limited number of possible options and thus can be quite fast. They typically limit their searching to the most promising or likely values and ignore less promising or unlikely values. These limits are the source of both the strength and weakness of heuristics. The reduction in searching can save time and improve performance. The reduction in searching can also cause extrema to be missed. Examples of search heuristics include simulated annealing, genetic algorithms (GAs), and swarm optimization.

Search heuristics can be organized into general-purpose frameworks that allow many different heuristics to be both easily substituted and efficiently used together. Constraint programming is an example of a search heuristic framework.

Linear and Quadratic Programming   Linear programming finds the best value for a mathematical objective function subject to a set of limiting constraints (Vanderbei 1997). The limiting constraints define the range of possible solutions to the problem being solved. The objective function defines the criteria by which the competing solutions are ranked. Linear programming requires that both the constraints and the objective function be linear equations, that the constraints produce a convex, bowl-shaped range of possibilities, and that the objective function gives the best result in the middle of the bowl. Linear programming can be extremely effective for problems that have this structure. Linear programming uses rigorous algorithms to test a series of candidate solutions to find the best alternative. Several linear programming algorithms are currently known. All of these algorithms will find the best solution for every linear programming problem. However, for the most part each of these algorithms has a different set of problems for which it is the fastest. The difference in performance can be substantial, so picking the best algorithm is usually worthwhile. Many modern linear programming packages include automatic checks to either select or recommend the best approach for a given problem. Linear programming is discussed in detail in chapter 5.

Quadratic programming generalizes linear programming and relaxes the restrictive assumptions of linear relations by allowing constraints with squared terms. This allows the boundaries of the bowl shape discussed previously to include simple curves. Naturally, the solution methods are more complicated and take more time than with linear programming. Quadratic programming is otherwise much like linear programming.

Constraint Programming   Constraint programming is in some ways similar to linear and quadratic programming. In particular, constraint programming searches for the best value for a mathematical objective function subject to a set of limiting constraints (Schulte 2002). As before, the limiting constraints define the range of possible solutions to the problem being solved while the objective function defines the criteria by which the competing solutions are ranked. The difference is that constraint programming associates one or more solution heuristics or algorithms called

propagators with each constraint. The solution process begins by setting each variable to be solved to the maximum range of allowed values. The propagators then work together to narrow the range of each variable in the solution. This allows constraint programming systems to be applied to problems that are much more general than those solvable by linear or quadratic programming. In fact, linear or quadratic programming can be viewed as specialized types of constraint programming. Some constraint programming systems even include propagators that do linear programming (ILOG Inc. 2004; Mozart Consortium 2004).

Consider an example of a production optimization model for a frozen dinner factory. Say that the daily factory output range starts with a minimum of zero and a maximum of 1 million dinners. There might be a break-even minimum of 10,000 dinners and a raw material limit of 100,000 dinners. This will allow the propagators to determine that the factory output must be between 10,000 and 100,000 dinners. Going further, say that 5,000 dinners can be made per hour. The propagators can then find that the current range of 10,000 to 100,000 dinners implies that the number of working hours must be between 2 and 20. However, it might be that workers must be given full shifts, so that there can be either zero, 8, 16, or 24 hours worked in one day. Thus, the propagators can determine that the factory must be running for either 8 or 16 hours, but not zero or 24, since the number of hours must be between 2 and 20. Thus, production can be either 40,000 or 80,000 dinners. Adding nonlinear profitability constraints, and the corresponding propagators, might show that the optimal output is 80,000 dinners.

With appropriate tuning, constraint programming can be very effective for complicated nonlinear problems that have reasonably smooth objective functions. Highly irregular objective functions usually lead to extremely long searches. Both GAs and simulated annealing are better choices for these types of spaces.

Simulated Annealing   Simulated annealing is well suited to finding the best option among a large and irregular set of similar, but not identical, competitors (Rich and Knight 1991; Ginsberg 1993). Simulated annealing can be used within agents for complex search and optimization. Annealing or tempering is the controlled cooling of metals to increase their strength. Annealing works by slowly cooling a hot metal to allow the crystals that form within the metal to align. Simulated annealing uses this concept to try ranges of neighboring choices with limited excursions to more distant possibilities. Thus, simulated annealing starts with a given choice and then tries nearly identical choices or immediate "neighbors" to see if they are better. If they are, then the search process is repeated with this new option. The result is that the process usually quickly finds the best solution in a local neighborhood. In fact, if properly used, the process is guaranteed to do this. Unfortunately, this best local value or local extremum is not guaranteed to be the best value everywhere in the search space or global extrema. To break out of this tendency to be trapped in local solutions, the simulated annealing heuristic randomly jumps to a new place occasionally. If this new place turns out to be better than the current location, then choices from this area are used instead of starting from the previous values. If this process is repeated, then the global solution can be found. However, making this process efficient requires that the random jumps be activated carefully. Jumping too infrequently wastes time with fruitless local searches. Jumping too often wastes time through lack of focus. Adjusting the jump rate or "cooling schedule" is something of an art. The need to adjust the "cooling schedule" makes simulated annealing a heuristic.

Genetic Algorithms   GAs are well suited to simulate "outside the box" searches of complicated nonlinear spaces (Goldberg 1989; Mitchell 1996). GAs are inspired by the mechanics of biological genomes. Like simulated annealing, GAs can also be used within agents for general complex search and optimization. Unlike simulated annealing, GAs can also be conveniently used to create new combinations of fundamental building blocks and thus simulate evolutionary or innovative processes.

GAs work by maintaining and adapting populations of competing solutions. Each solution is composed of a set of fundamental building blocks (Goldberg 1989; Mitchell 1996). The value or fitness of each solution is calculated using a fitness function. GAs operate over a series of steps or generations. Each step begins by calculating the individual fitness of each current member of the population. The best solution found thus far is noted. The least fit members are killed or deleted while the fittest members are either copied or mated. Copying is a simple process of introducing more than one instance of the solution into the population. Mating is a somewhat more complex process that involves "crossing over" or mixing

the building blocks from two different solutions to produce two new solutions. The resulting population is then often subject to "mutation" or random interchanges of a limited number of building blocks within individuals in the population. These steps are then repeated for a fixed number of generations or until the improvement in the results drops below a selected threshold.

Clearly, it can be seen from the large amount of randomness in the process that it is not guaranteed to work. What is somewhat amazing is that it often works quite well (Goldberg 1989; Mitchell 1996). In fact, the combination of crossover and mutation often produces new solutions that are significantly different than previously calculated solutions. These new solutions are often in areas of the search space that are far from previously calculated values. Thus, GAs can be considered for use in agent simulations any time creativity or innovation needs to be simulated. An example is a corporate management agent that uses a GA to develop new business strategies or an entrepreneurial agent that uses a GA to invent new business models. GAs are also excellent choices for solving highly complicated nonlinear problems that cannot be addressed using standard techniques such as linear programming.

Swarm Optimization   Swarm optimization uses the idea of swarms or groups of solution-tracing components to find answers to difficult problems (Bonabeau et al. 1999). Each tracing component starts with an initial solution and then picks a sequence of follow-up solutions. The sequences are usually chosen so that successive solutions are quite similar and thus in some sense are "near" one another. The candidate solutions can change dramatically over time from an accumulation of these smaller changes. Many separate tracing components are normally used so that a wide range of options is being explored at any one time. Different tracing components often exchange information on the quality of the solutions they are finding and then use this information to select more promising future steps. This information exchange often results in a flocking behavior over time, particularly when good solutions are found.

Swarm optimization is one use of swarm or mob intelligence. In principle, swarm optimization is suited for the same complicated problems addressable with GAs. In fact, swam optimization is often combined with GAs (Bonabeau et al. 1999).

Special-Purpose Techniques

Special-purpose techniques above and beyond those already discussed are sometimes required to model complex agents. These techniques are often highly customized heuristics focused on solving one particular problem. However, these techniques have disadvantages similar to complex rules. As before, the complexity of the rules can obscure underlying patterns. In addition, the results are harder to verify and validate than those from simple rules. However, any verification and validation completed for the special techniques can be leveraged for the agent model.

External Program Agents

Agents do not always have to be built from scratch. External agents can be implemented using external programs. These external programs may already exist or may be adapted for use in an agent framework. Furthermore, external programs may be used to provide supporting software libraries or external functions. An example of the use of external programs is shown in figure 3.13.

A wide variety of external programs can be accessed by agents to guide their behavior. Existing programs, such as standard deterministic models, can be used. Mathematics packages such as MathWorks MATLAB (The MathWorks Inc. 2004),[1] Wolfram Research Mathematica (Wolfram Research Inc. 2004),[2] and others can be used. Complex commercial or open-source optimizers, such as linear programs, can also be used if they include interfacing mechanisms or protocols.

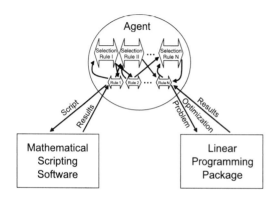

FIGURE 3.13 Example of use of external programs to implement agents.

The use of external programs has several advantages, including leveraging of existing knowledge and programs and the simplification of verification and validation. The selection of external programs currently in use in an organization eliminates the need to train staff on a new tool. This choice also allows programs that have been custom written for other projects to be potentially applied to the agent-based modeling efforts. Verification and validation efforts can be reduced since the work invested in checking the external programs and custom scripts is already done.

Despite the potential advantages, external programs must be used with a cautious eye toward possible compatibilities and incompatibilities. Not all programs are compatible with one another. Furthermore, even if programs can operate together they may not have consistent views of the world. Testing the individual components together before committing to use them is critical.

Nested Subagents

Agent-based models can be used to represent complex adaptive systems. If an agent is itself a complex adaptive system, then why not represent it with an agent model? This leads to the use of nested subagents to represent agents.

Quite simply, nested subagents are agent-based models within agent-based models. One object is identified as the agent. This object then contains or maintains references to the other objects that make up the agent. Some of these objects may themselves be agents. This approach allows recursive nesting where high-level agents are themselves composed of many subagents. The behavior of the containing agent can then be an emergent result of the simpler behavioral rules of the subagents. In principle, this process can be repeated, allowing complex recursive hierarchies to be formed. In practice, this recursive nesting must be used with caution to keep ABMS projects manageable.

An example of the use of nested subagents is shown in figure 3.14. In this example, each major agent represents a corporation within a competitive market. Each subagent represents a division or department within its containing corporation. The decisions and ultimate performance of each corporation depend in large measure on the choices and results of its constituent divisions.

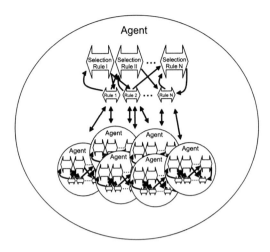

FIGURE 3.14 Example of nested subagents.

A Market Example

This section introduces a case study example that will be followed throughout the book. The Electricity Market Complex Adaptive Systems Model (EMCAS) electric power market simulation is an agent simulation that represents the behavior of an electric power system and the producers and consumers that work within it (North et al. 2003).

The EMCAS model contains a variety of major agents and other supporting environmental elements. These major agents and supporting environmental elements are shown in figure 3.15. The agents include generation companies, transmission companies, distribution companies, and demand companies. The supporting elements include an underlying electric power grid and negotiation forums.

The electric power grid in the EMCAS model transfers electric power between the various agents and passive components within the system. The grid provides a high-power backbone for bulk energy transfers. For many simulation applications, the grid configuration closely matches the real physical grid being studied. The data are normally derived from published national and state sources. There are often several thousand physical components such as major power lines and significant transformers in an EMCAS scenario. These components are grouped into tap points or electrical buses. There are often several hundred taps in a scenario. In many jurisdictions, each tap point has its own hourly unique electricity price. The prices

often vary by tap due to the arbitrage opportunities created by physical power line transmission limits between taps. The electricity grid is not considered an agent since it is a purely passive component with no individual adaptability or memory. Instead, this component and its constituent power lines and simple transformers are represented as part of the environment.

The model has generators and several other active physical components. The components produce, route, and consume power. As with grids, many simulation applications have generators that closely match the real generators being studied using data from published or private sources.

The EMCAS model includes electric power production companies that own and operate individual portfolios of generators. For most model usages, these companies are created based on the actual firms present in a given market. As before, the generation unit portfolios and corporate behaviors are configured to match the actual organizations being modeled. Naturally, these highly active decision-making entities are modeled as adaptive agents. The generation companies' adaptive features include the use of complex statistics to project potential future market prices and the use of heuristics to develop bidding portfolios. The statistics are used to estimate future prices at each of the electricity tap points where a company can buy or sell power. Prices are estimated for each of the markets into which generation companies sell power. There are six power generation markets, including a privately negotiated bilateral power market, a publicly cleared spot market, and four publicly cleared backup services markets. These markets differ by both time availability and whether they trade options or futures. The five publicly cleared markets are also called pool markets. As discussed previously in this chapter, heuristics are "rules of thumb" used to discover approximate solutions to complicated problems (Feigenbaum, quoted in Ginsberg 1993). EMCAS generation companies use heuristics to determine the prices for their individual generation bids as well as to determine the sizes of the bid blocks to use. The details of these behaviors are discussed in the chapter 6. Like most producers, EMCAS generation companies make profits on the difference between their final accepted bid prices and their individual costs of production.

The EMCAS generation companies produce power that is sold to distribution companies. These distribution companies are often electric power retailers

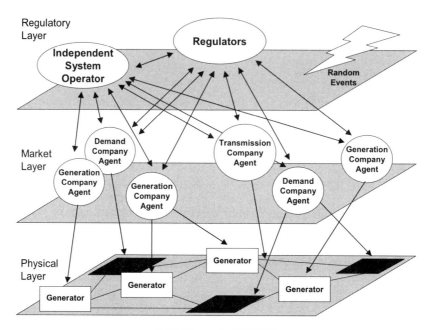

FIGURE 3.15 The main EMCAS agents.

in that they buy from producers as well as some brokers and then resell the resulting power to the final consumers. The delivery of power from suppliers to the retailers is handled by transmission companies.

Transmission company agents act as bulk long-distance power transporters. They are paid through one of three common mechanisms. In some markets, they are paid a fixed fee per unit of shipped power. The fees are normally set by government regulatory bodies. In other markets, the transmission companies are paid using open or sealed transmission services bidding. Finally, some markets use payment formulas that set the hourly value of each transmission line based on the price arbitrage differences between power grid taps. Many markets use a combination of these mechanisms for different classes or locations of lines. Smaller lines and less heavily used lines tend to be assigned simpler mechanisms. EMCAS transmission company agents can work with many different payment systems. In each of the cases, the transmission company agents must determine their operational responses given the payment mechanisms they face. Transmission companies make money based on the difference between their line usage fees and their power line construction and maintenance costs. Transmission companies sell into a variety of markets

including the privately negotiated bilateral power market, the publicly cleared spot market, and the four publicly cleared backup services markets. It is important to note that transmission companies normally do not take ownership of electric power. They only ship power. As with generation companies, these activities are discussed in chapter 6.

Distribution companies are often electric power retailers. They buy wholesale power from generation companies and from intermediate brokers. Distribution companies are responsible for delivering power across the "last mile" of wire that runs between the high-voltage transmission backbone operated by transmission companies and the meter on each customer's premises. Distribution companies receive payments either directly from customers or from other distribution companies that are leasing lines. Distribution company profits come from two sources. First, they can make money on the difference between the retailer power payments they receive from consumers and the sum of power purchase costs and local-line maintenance costs. Second, they can make money on the difference between local-line lease fees and line maintenance costs. Line lease fees are paid by distribution companies that are selling to customers in another distribution company's service area. In this case, the host distribution company manages local power delivery but not retail sales. These types of hosting arrangements are becoming increasingly common in deregulated markets since they allow retail customers a choice of power suppliers.

Distribution companies normally buy in the same power markets as generation companies except for the reserve options markets. The reserve options markets are managed by the independent system operator. The independent system operator is normally either a highly regulated private firm or a government agency that acts as a clearing house for pooled bidding, is charged with maintaining the overall stability of the power grid, and handles pool market payment clearing. The independent system operator charges distribution companies for the options fees needed to buy reserve power as well as any costs necessary to exercise the options in times of crisis.

Distribution companies face a problem similar to generation companies. They both must determine how much to charge for scarce resources in the face of substantial uncertainties. EMCAS distribution company agents need to determine the asking prices that they will offer for electric power as well as the retail prices that they will offer to consumers. Of course, these various offer prices need to be correlated to increase the chances for profits.

In EMCAS, as previously mentioned and shown in figure 3.15, independent system operator (ISO) agents operate the five pool markets. The ISO works to match bids and asks, handle final payments, check bilateral contracts for physical limits, and update the system status bulletin board. This bulletin board lists historical generation levels, previous outages, historical weather, past loads, historical location-based prices, projected outages, forecast weather, and forecast loads.

Discover, Design, and Develop

As was discussed throughout this chapter, agents are decision-makers in complex adaptive systems. Managers, organizations, computer systems, and anything else that makes business choices can be modeled as agents. There are two main types of agents, namely proto-agents and full agents. Proto-agents have rules. Following Casti, full agents have "rules and rules to change the rules" (Casti 1998). Full agents use complex rules or advanced techniques such as statistical methods, artificial intelligence methods, optimization methods, special-purpose techniques, external

programs, or even nested subagents. These techniques allow agents to absorb, process, and produce information as well as make changes to their environment. Agent learning and the related structural changes in the environment are the two main sources of adaptation in complex adaptive systems. The remaining chapters will consider many ways to incrementally discover, design, and develop models of agent behavior.

Notes

1. MATLAB is a registered trademark of The MathWorks, Inc.
2. Mathematica is a registered trademark of Wolfram Research, Inc.

References

Arieli, O. and A. Avron (2000). General Patterns for Nonmonotonic Reasoning: From Basic Entailments to Plausible Relations. *Logic Journal of the Interest Group in Pure and Applied Logics* 8(2): 119–148.

Baase, S. (1988). *Computer Algorithms: Introduction to Design and Analysis*. Redwood City, Cal.: Addison-Wesley.

Bonabeau, E., M. Dorigo, and G. Theraulaz (1999). *Swarm Intelligence: From Natural to Artificial Systems*. Oxford: Oxford University Press.

Bratko, I. (1990). *Prolog Programming for Artificial Intelligence*. Wokingham, U.K.: Addison-Wesley.

Casti, J. L (1998). *Would-Be Worlds: How Simulation Is Changing the World of Science*. New York: Wiley.

de Rooij, M. and P. M. Kroonenberg (2003). Multivariate Multinomial Logit Models for Dyadic Sequential Interaction Data. *Multivariate Behavioral Research* 38(4): 463–504.

Ginsberg, M. L. (1993). *Essentials of Artificial Intelligence*. San Francisco: Morgan Kaufmann.

Goldberg, D. E. (1989). *Genetic Algorithms in Search, Optimization, and Machine Learning*. Redwood City, Cal.: Addison-Wesley.

ILOG Inc. (2004). ILOG Home Page. Gentilly, France: ILOG, Inc.

McClave, J. T. and P. G. Benson (1994). *Statistics for Business and Economics*. Englewood Cliffs, N.J.: Prentice-Hall.

Mendenhall, W., D. D. Wackerly, and R. L. Scheaffer (1990). *Mathematical Statistics with Applications*. Boston: PWS-Kent.

Mitchell, M. (1996). *An Introduction to Genetic Algorithms (Complex Adaptive Systems)*. Cambridge, Mass.: MIT Press.

Mozart Consortium (2004). Mozart Programming System. Brussels, Belgium: Mozart Consortium.

North, M., P. Thimmapuram, R. Cirillo, C. Macal, G. Conzelmann, V. Koritarov, and T. Veselka (2003). EMCAS: An Agent-Based Tool for Modeling Electricity Markets. *Proceedings of Agent 2003: Challenges in Social Simulation.* Chicago: University of Chicago, Argonne National Laboratory.

Raiffa, H. (1970). *Decision Analysis: Introductory Lectures on Choices under Uncertainty.* Reading, Mass.: Addison-Wesley.

Rich, E. and K. Knight (1991). *Artificial Intelligence.* New York: McGraw-Hill.

Schulte, C. (2002). *Programming Constraint Services: High-Level Programming of Standard and New Constraint Services.* Berlin: Springer.

The MathWorks Inc. (2004). The MathWorks Home Page. Natick, Mass.: The MathWorks Inc.

Vanderbei, R. J. (1997). *Linear Programming: Foundations and Extensions.* New York: Springer.

Wolfram Research Inc. (2004). Wolfram Research Home Page. Champaign, Ill.: Wolfram Research, Inc.

4

The Roots of ABMS

ABMS in Context

ABMS has connections to many other fields, such as complex adaptive systems, complexity science, and systems science, and draws on them for techniques and applications. An understanding of where ABMS came from is helpful for establishing the context in which ABMS is being applied to solve business problems today and promising areas for its application in the future.

Historical Roots

Agent-based modeling and simulation has its historical roots in the study of complex adaptive systems (CAS). CAS was originally motivated by investigations into the adaptation and emergence of biological systems. The field of CAS concerns itself with systems composed of individual, interacting components and the adaptive mechanisms that such systems exhibit. The defining characteristic of CAS is the ability to adapt to a changing environment. Complex adaptive systems learn over time to effectively respond to novel situations. CAS also have the ability to self-organize and reorganize their components in ways better suited to surviving and excelling in their environments. Furthermore, CAS exhibit organization and adaptation at multiple scales as suggested by figure 4.1. The ability to adapt is one of the key capabilities of a complex adaptive system. Murray Gell-Mann (1994)

describes this adaptive capability in terms of the application of schemata or building blocks:

> . . . a complex adaptive system acquires information about its environment and its own interaction with that environment, identifying regularities in that information, condensing those regularities into a kind of "schema" or model, and acting in the real world on the basis of that schema. In each case there are various competing schemata, and the results of the action in the real world feed back to influence the competition among those schemata.

Gell-Mann (1995) has gone on to state the following:

> What is most exciting about our work is that it illuminates the chain of connections between, on the one hand, the simple underlying laws that govern the behavior of all matter in the universe and, on the other hand, the complex fabric that we see around us, exhibiting diversity, individuality, and evolution. The interplay between simplicity and complexity is the heart of our subject. . . .
>
> The name that I propose for our subject is "plectics," derived, like mathematics, ethics, politics, economics, and so on, from the Greek. . . . It is appropriate that plectics refers to entanglement or the lack thereof, since entanglement is a key feature of the way complexity arises out of simplicity, making our subject worth studying . . . I hope that it is not too late for the name "plectics" to catch on. We seem to need it.

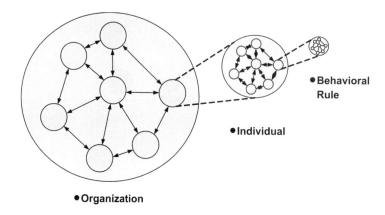

FIGURE 4.1 A complex adaptive system.

The scope of ABMS continues to expand well beyond its origins in biological systems, drawing on a number of other fields for its motivations, techniques, and applications. ABMS also draws upon the techniques and approaches of a number of other traditional fields. Systems science, complexity science, computer science, management science, and the social sciences are a few of the fields that have made significant contributions to the techniques and applications of ABMS. Agent-based modeling and simulation as currently practiced also owes much to the fields of traditional modeling, simulation, and computation.

ABMS has found applications to solving practical business problems, and agent-based modeling has quickly gone from the laboratory to the boardroom. A number of companies and organizations have been formed to facilitate and promote the practical applications of ABMS to solving problems in business. This chapter reviews some of the major developments of ABMS and their implications for business applications.

Many have heard some of the terminology of complexity, complex adaptive systems, and agent-based modeling and simulation. The terms autonomous agents, swarm intelligence, artificial life, self-organization, evolutionary programming, and artificial societies are just a few of the commonly applied terms in the field. Figure 4.2 provides a list of commonly used CAS and ABMS terminology. Complexity science is an umbrella term that includes CAS.

Complexity Science

Complexity science is a field that focuses on the universal principles common to all systems. Physical systems, emphasizing universal principles, as well as biological systems, emphasizing adaptation and emergence, are the focus. Issues such as information, entropy, emergence, and how these arise from "bottom up" principles are questions central to complexity science. One of the fundamental physical laws of nature is that disorder, that is, entropy, in the universe is constantly increasing. If disorder is increasing, how is it that systems can self-organize, effectively increasing order (i.e., decreasing disorder) in the universe? Such questions among others are the province of complexity science.

The discussion on the roots of ABMS begins with a simple game, the "Game of Life," or GOL as it is called. The GOL is based on what are called cellular automata.

Cellular Automata

Perhaps the simplest way to illustrate the basic ideas of agent-based modeling and simulation is through cellular automata (CA). The original notion of cellular automata was developed by the physicist Stanislaw Ulam in response to a question posed by the famous twentieth-century mathematician John von Neumann. The question was, "Could a machine be programmed to make a copy of itself?" (Casti 1994). In effect, the question had to do with whether it was possible to develop a structure that was complex enough to completely contain all of the instructions for replicating itself. The answer was yes, and it was eventually found in the abstract mathematical representation of a machine in the form of a cellular automaton.

Complex Behavior from Simple Rules

A typical cellular automaton (CA) is a two-dimensional grid divided into "cells." Each cell assumes one

- Individual-based/actor-based/particle simulation
- Autonomous agents, and multi-agent systems (MAS)
- Rational agents, and bounded rationality
- Adaptation, and learning algorithms
- Emergence, and self-organization
- Artificial life
- Swarm intelligence, and swarm optimization
- Endogeneity, hypercycles, and autocatalytic networks
- Rugged landscapes
- Downward causation
- Increasing returns, and positive feedback
- Dynamic small-world networks, and six degrees of separation
- Coevolution

FIGURE 4.2 Some CAS-related terms.

of a finite number of states at any point in time. A set of very simple rules determines the value of each cell. Every cell is updated each time period according to the rules. The next value of a cell depends on the cell's current value and the values of its immediate neighbors in the eight surrounding cells. Each cell is the same as the next and the update rules are the same for all the cells. A CA is deterministic in the sense that the same state for a cell and its neighbors always results in the same updated state.

John Conway's "Game of Life," developed in the 1970s, is a good example of a CA (Gardner 1970; Poundstone 1985). The GOL has three rules that determine the next state of each cell:

- The cell will be on in the next generation if exactly three (out of eight) of its neighboring cells are currently on.
- The cell will retain its current state if exactly two of its neighbors are on.
- The cell will be off otherwise.

Figure 4.3 shows some snapshots from a simulation of the Game of Life. Initially, cells that are on are randomly distributed over the grid (on cells are shaded in the figure). After several updates of all the cells on the grid, distinctive patterns emerge, and in some cases these patterns can sustain themselves indefinitely throughout the simulation. Note how the neighborhoods shown in figure 4.4 determine the scope of agent interaction and locally available information. Also, note that the idea of local availability is not limited to a small spatial neighborhood.

Rather, it can refer to any moderate-sized set of items of interest. In terms of people, one might say that "I have neighbors, I just don't happen to live near them!"

Two observations are important pertaining to the rules in the GOL:

- The rules are simple.
- The rules use only local information. The state of each cell is based only on the current state of the cell and the cells touching it in its immediate neighborhood.

Although the rules are extremely simple, Conway proved that the GOL rules are actually complicated enough to admit patterns of cells that are capable of self-reproduction. But the pattern would be extremely large, 10^{14} cells—much too large to be represented on a real game board!

Although these are interesting findings, and observing the patterns created within repeated simulations of the GOL reveals a world of endless creations, other observations are even more interesting, counterintuitive, and have implications for practical ABMS. The GOL demonstrates that sustainable patterns can emerge in systems that are completely described by simple rules that are based on only local information. And the patterns that may develop can be extremely sensitive to the initial conditions of the system. These findings have direct implications and applications for more practical and realistically complex agent-based models.

Exploring All the Rules

Since the 1970s, Steven Wolfram has been exploring the broadest implications of cellular automata. Wolfram is investigating the range of all possible rules that can be used in the most basic of CA models and is developing what he terms a new kind of exploratory, computational science. He has demonstrated that varying the rules in cellular automata produces a surprising range of resulting patterns, and these patterns correspond directly to a wide range of algorithms and logic systems (Wolfram 2002). In effect, this means that simple rules such as those in CAs can be used as the building blocks of much more complex systems. This suggests that simple rules can be used to understand much of the complexity observed in real systems. For example, he has used CAs to explain how randomness arises

(a) Generation 0

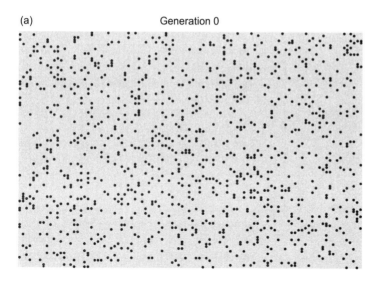

(b) Generation 1

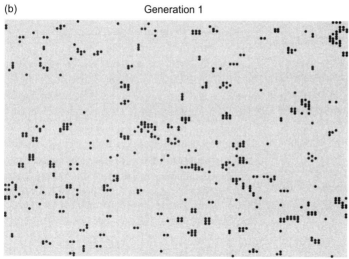

(c) Generation 100

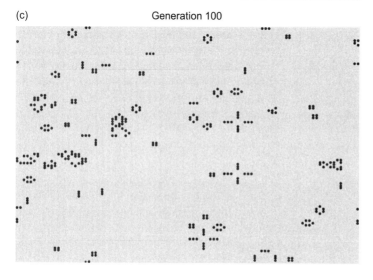

FIGURE 4.3 Snapshots from the Game of Life simulation: (a) initial random distribution of cells in the on state; (b) after the first generation of applying the rules; (c) after 100 generations, showing sustainable patterns of organization.

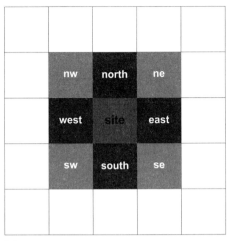

(a)

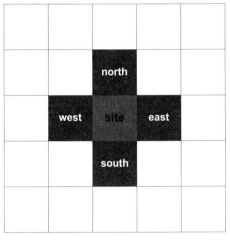

(b)

FIGURE 4.4 Neighborhoods in cellular automata: (a) a Moore neighborhood; (b) a von Neumann neighborhood.

in financial markets and traffic systems based on deterministic rules.

Onward to Complex Adaptive Systems

The field of complex adaptive systems concerns itself with adaptive mechanisms in nature. How do complex behaviors arise in nature among myopic, autonomous agents?

Adaptation and Emergence

John Holland, a pioneer in the field of complex adaptive systems, identifies the properties and mechanisms common to CAS (Holland 1995). The properties of CAS include:

1. *Aggregation*: allows groups to form.
2. *Nonlinearity*: invalidates simple extrapolation.
3. *Flows*: allow the transfer and transformation of resources and information.
4. *Diversity*: allows agents to behave differently from one another and often leads to robustness.

The mechanisms common to all CAS are as follows:

1. *Tagging*: allows agents to be named for later identification.
2. *Internal models*: allow agents to reason about their worlds.
3. *Building blocks*: allow components and even whole systems to be composed of many simpler components.

The properties and mechanisms of CAS provide a useful framework for designing agent-based models.

John Holland also developed genetic algorithms (GAs) in the 1960s and 1970s as a general mechanism for modeling adaptation. Genetic algorithms are search procedures based on the mechanics of genetics and natural selection, specifically the operations exhibited by chromosomes, such as genetic crossover and mutation. The GA concept was instrumental in understanding the mechanisms of change and adaptation, linking behaviors across small and large scales alike. GAs are one of the most commonly used adaptive mechanisms in ABMS. Genetic programming, evolutionary programming, and evolutionary computation are generalizations of genetic algorithms that have been used extensively as mechanisms for modeling adaptive processes in agent rules (Fogel 1995).

Swarm Intelligence

How is it that an ant colony can organize itself to carry out the complex tasks of food gathering and nest building and at the same time exhibit an enormous degree of resilience if disrupted and forced to adapt to changing situations? Natural systems are able not only to survive, but also to adapt and become better suited to their environment, in effect optimizing their behavior over time. They seemingly exhibit collective intelligence, or swarm intelligence as it is called, even without the existence of or the direction provided by a central authority. Swarm intelligence has inspired a practical optimization technique, often called "ant colony" optimization, that has been used to solve practical scheduling and routing problems in business (Bonabeau et al. 1999).

Swarm optimization, as well as genetic algorithms and evolutionary programming, are techniques that have also been applied in ABMS for doing whole-system optimization.

Network Science

Recently, much attention has been paid to the importance of networks in society, due in part to the rise of the Internet and the World Wide Web. Much progress has been made in understanding networks (Barabási 2002). Understanding how networks are structured and grow, how quickly information is communicated through networks, and the kinds of relationships that networks embody are important to businesses. Figure 4.5 shows three types of common graphs, including a regular graph in which every node is connected to its nearest neighbors, a random graph in which nodes are randomly connected, and a small-world or scale-free network in which most nodes have few links and a small number of nodes have many links. Regular networks occur in many planned or hierarchically structured situations. Random graphs approximate many unordered situations. Small-world networks, which are common structures for real-world networks, are structured in such a way that many nodes have very few links and a small number of nodes have many links. These networks are extremely robust, shrugging off most disturbances, but are vulnerable to a well-planned assault.

Networks are central to businesses' understanding of their customers, operations, and even their own organizations. There are many important examples of networks in business, including:

- Supply chains and supply networks.
- Electric power grids, natural gas customer delivery systems.
- Personal relationships, such as business relationships, friendship, and kinship.
- Page linking in the World Wide Web.
- Membership on corporate boards and organizations.

"Network thinking" in terms of connectivity, tipping points, and cascading effects of the information propagated through networks has important implications for businesses applications of ABMS (Gladwell 2000).

Some of the more fundamental discoveries of network science are important to keep in mind when developing ABMS. Stuart Kaufman has discovered how networks of chemical reactions can emerge and become self-sustaining (Kaufman 1993, 1995, 2000). These so-called autocatalytic chemical networks are the chemical basis of life. Kaufman's discoveries suggest how aggregations of chemical and gene networks working together can take on higher-order, emergent properties and behaviors. They also have implications for how human organizations become established and sustain themselves (Padgett 2000). Duncan Watts has investigated the properties and implications of various types of network structures and applied this knowledge to modeling social relationships (Watts 1999, 2003). Steven Strogatz has investigated how autonomous agents resonate their behaviors with each other and become synchronized across loosely connected networks (Strogatz 2003).

How the networks of agent relationships are structured can have significant effects on the behaviors observed in the agent-based simulations. When developing an ABMS, several aspects of networks are relevant, such as the following:

- What is the appropriate type of connectivity for the network of agent relationships?
- Are network links and relationships externally specified or generated by processes within the model?
- How does network connectivity affect agent and system behaviors?

Network science provides knowledge and techniques for understanding the representations of agent connectedness and interaction in agent-based models.

Social Simulation

In applications of ABMS to simulating social processes, agents represent people or groups, and agent relationships represent social interaction. Social simulation and its applications are progressing rapidly (Gilbert and Troitzsch 1999). The fundamental assumption is that people and their interactions can be credibly modeled at some reasonable level of abstraction for some specific purpose. The modeling of social systems is the basis for business applications of ABMS.

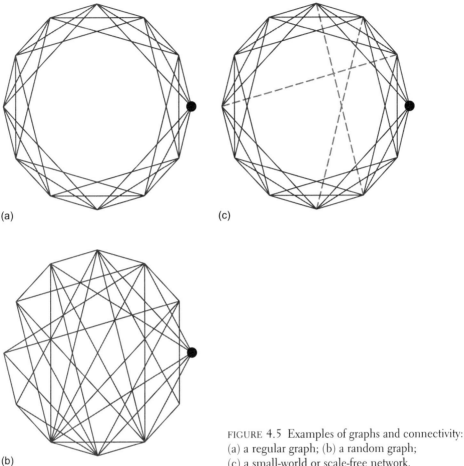

FIGURE 4.5 Examples of graphs and connectivity:
(a) a regular graph; (b) a random graph;
(c) a small-world or scale-free network.

Social Processes

Thomas Schelling is credited with developing the first agent-based simulation in which agents represented people and agent interactions represent a socially relevant process (Schelling 1971, 1978). Schelling applied notions of cellular automata to study housing segregation patterns. He posed the question, "Is it possible to get highly segregated settlement patterns even if most individuals are, in fact, color-blind?" In Schelling's model, there are two kinds of agents. An individual who is not satisfied with the number of neighbors who are like themselves is motivated to move to the nearest empty site that has a sufficient number of neighbors of the same type. The unexpected finding from Schelling's model is that an agent only has to require a relatively small number of neighbors who are similar to themselves, 25% or 2 out of 8 neighbors, to result in large-scale segregation patterns.

The Schelling model demonstrated that ghettos can develop spontaneously. In other words, Schelling showed that patterns can emerge that are not necessarily implied or even consistent with the objectives of the individual agents. It is not hard to see that this effect could at least partially explain the clustering of people by gender or age at a social gathering, or even by ethnicity or race in society at large.

The Schelling model is an extremely simple and abstract social agent-based simulation. There are three agent movement rules:

1. An agent calculates the percentage of neighbors with same color.
2. If the number is greater than the preference factor, the agent is satisfied and does not move.
3. Otherwise, an agent looks for the nearest unoccupied site that satisfies its preference and moves there, if one can be found.

Schelling's results showed that a preference factor set as low as 25% resulted in extensive segregation patterns. Similar results are shown in figure 4.6.

Schelling's initial work was done in the days before desktop computers. He used coins to represent agents laid out on a checkerboard on his kitchen table. The simulation was done by executing the agent rules for each coin and manually moving the coins to their new locations on the grid. Since then, this basic cellular automata approach has been used to model many types of social systems from settlement patterns to international conflict, from financial markets to environmental impacts, and from status symbols and fads to the adoption of social norms and conformity.

Economic Processes

Some of the fundamental assumptions of standard microeconomic theory include:

- Economic agents are rational, which implies that agents have well-defined objectives and are able to optimize their behavior.
- Economic agents are homogeneous, that is, agents have identical characteristics and rules of behavior.
- There are decreasing returns to scale in terms of economic processes, decreasing the marginal utility, decreasing the marginal productivity, and so on.
- The long-run equilibrium state of the system is the key information of interest.

Each of these assumptions is relaxed in ABMS applications to economic systems. The field of agent-based computational economics (ACE) has grown up around the application of ABMS to economic systems (Tesfatsion 2002, 2005). So, how true are these assumptions?

First, do organizations and individuals really optimize? Herbert Simon, a famous Nobel Laureate who pioneered the field of artificial intelligence, developed the notion of "satisficing" to describe what he observed people and organizations doing in the real world (Simon 2001). Satisficing means that a decision-maker selects a satisfactory alternative when it presents itself, rather than selecting an "optimal" alternative from an exhaustive investigation into all possibilities. This decision "heuristic" is due to the decision-maker's inability to encompass all the complexities

(a)   Generation 0

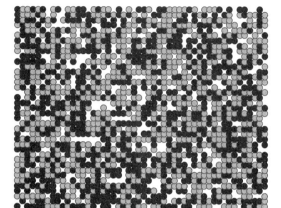

(b)   Generation 5

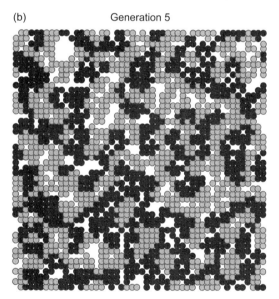

FIGURE 4.6 Emergent patterns in Schelling's housing segregation model: (a) initial random distribution of agents; (b) distribution of agents after several iterations for preference factor of 50%.

of the situation (such as the inability to formulate the optimization problem) or to the lack of a method that can find the optimal solution (for example, the inability to solve the complex optimization problem). This view of decision-making has come to be known as "bounded rationality."

Second, Brian Arthur has researched "positive feedback loops" and "increasing returns" as the underlying dynamic processes of rapid exponential growth in economics (Arthur 1996, 1999; Arthur et al. 1997). Positive feedback loops can create self-generative processes that take a system to a stable point that is far from its starting point. For example, traditional economics has difficulty explaining how a product rapidly attains a dominant market share, often eclipsing competing products that are lower in quality and price. Increasing returns leads to lock-in, a stable, irreversible state.

Third, what does agent diversity contribute to the emergent structure and complexity of complex systems? Agent-based simulations in which agents have diverse characteristics and rules of behavior often exhibit stable populations for the various agent types. Exploring the important effects of diversity among social agents and what diversity means for system behavior is an ongoing area of research in CAS.

Fourth, are long-run equilibrium states the only results of interest? Generally, the answer is no. Knowing about long-run equilibrium states certainly has value, but so does being aware of what might happen along the way to the final results. Furthermore, not all systems come to equilibrium. Knowing what might happen to these systems has value too. In the words of the noted economist John Maynard Keynes, "in the long run we are all dead." Clearly, it would be nice to know what lies along the road.

Growing Artificial Societies

Can an entire society, at least a computational one, be built from the ground up by modeling the society's agents and their interactions? Extending the notion of modeling people to modeling entire societies through agent simulation was taken up by Joshua Epstein and Robert Axtell's groundbreaking Sugarscape model (Epstein and Axtell 1996). Sugarscape was the first comprehensive computational study of entire artificial societies. A version of the Sugarscape model is shown in figure 4.7. In numerous computational experiments, Sugarscape agents emerged with a variety of characteristics and behaviors, highly suggestive of a realistic, albeit rudimentary society, such as:

- life, death, and disease
- trade
- wealth
- sex and reproduction
- culture
- conflict and war
- externalities such as pollution.

Epstein has gone on to apply agent simulation to a diverse number of social system applications that are not amenable to standard modeling or analysis approaches. He has used ABMS to investigate how and why adaptive organizations emerge (Epstein 2003) as well as the processes that lead to civil disobedience and violence (Epstein et al. 2001). Axtell has applied agent simulation to a diverse number of social topics such as the growth of firms and the number of firms in a mature industry, issues of importance to strategic business planning (Axtell 1999).

Some of the important modeling techniques of ABMS have their origins in models of physical systems. For example, the Ising system is a model of imitative behavior in which individuals modify their behaviors to conform to the behavior of other individuals in their vicinity (Callen and Shapero 1974). Originally developed by Ernest Ising in 1925, the Ising model was used to study phase transitions in solids, for example, how individual atoms become aligned in a material causing it to become magnetized. In the Ising model, atoms are arranged in a rectangular lattice and are either in a positive or a negative state. Atoms exert forces on neighboring atoms only, and there is an exogenous force that affects all atoms equally. In the 1990s, social scientists adapted the Ising model to study social processes. For example, opinion formation can be modeled by an Ising approach if the lattice assumption is relaxed so that individuals are free to interact with neighbors defined by a social network. The basic idea is that in each time period, an agent's probability of changing its mind is proportional to the number of adjacent agents who disagree. The key behaviors of such a model are the sudden phase transitions that can occur without warning, signifying rapid opinion change. The Ising model is a powerful way to think about modeling social influence. It has been used to model:

- opinion change
- diffusion of new ideas
- fads
- friendship formation
- social communication
- the spread of disease and epidemics.

Anthropologists are developing large-scale agent-based simulations to model ancient civilizations. ABMS has been applied to help understand the social and cultural factors responsible for the disappearance

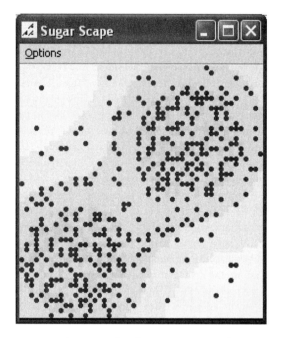

FIGURE 4.7 Example of a Sugarscape simulation.

of the Anasazi in the southwestern United States (Dean et al. 1998) and the fall of the ancient Mesopotamian civilization (Christiansen and Altaweel 2004). Large-scale ABMS applications to contemporary society and culture are the next logical step.

Cooperation in Organizations

How did cooperation among individuals originate? What are the essential requirements for cooperative behavior, whether in human or animal societies, to emerge and be sustained? Identifying the social interaction mechanisms for how cooperative behavior emerges among individuals and groups is an interesting question with practical implications. These questions are actively being pursued using ABMS. Evolutionary game theory is a field related to traditional game theory in economics that takes into account the repeated interactions of the players and their effect on strategies. Robert Axelrod has discovered that a simple tit-for-tat strategy of reciprocal behavior toward individuals is enough to establish cooperative behavior (Axelrod 1984, 1997a, 1997b). H. Peyton Young has investigated how larger social structures, social norms and institutions, arise from micro-level interactions between individuals (Young 1998). This type of work has important implications

for modeling how people behave in organizations and business.

Multi-Agent Systems

ABMS is related to the field of multi-agent systems (MAS) which is concerned with social interaction among machines such as robots (Jennings 2000). MAS has addressed and solved several of the computational problems inherent in modeling the behaviors of large number of agents. The MAS approach tends to be a normative rather than a descriptive one, that is, it focuses on design questions of what machines should do rather than what people actually do. Nonetheless, MAS has made important contributions to how agent systems can be effectively modeled and implemented computationally.

Systems Science

Systems science consists of systems analysis, a way of thinking about problems; systems dynamics, a set of modeling methods and computational techniques for modeling systems; and management science, a set of practical quantitative techniques for supporting management decisions.

Systems Analysis

Systems analysis (SA) is a way of "systematically thinking" about a system. SA views a system as composed of component parts and focuses on how the relationships among the components affect the system as a whole. Feedback, amplification, and cascading effects are exhibited by systems, which are not observable by viewing the components in isolation. SA was pioneered in the 1950s as a way of thinking about systems composed of people and technologies by Churchman, Ackoff, and others (Miser 1996). SA consists of a worldview, a set of principles, and a process for analysis. SA principles are applicable to analyzing complex systems and building ABMS. Systems dynamics extends SA with a modeling framework and computational techniques.

Systems Dynamics

Systems dynamics (SD) is a simulation technique designed specifically for modeling business and social systems. Developed by Jay Forrester in the 1950s (Forrester 1958), SD is a "whole system" modeling approach applied to dynamic processes that change continuously over time. In line with its modeling philosophy, SD models tend to be highly aggregate representations of component processes and their relationships. In this regard, SD is a "top down" approach to systems modeling, in contract to the bottom-up approach of ABMS. Yet if done successfully, an ABMS model of a system should yield the same results at comparable levels of aggregation as does an SD model. SD has been used to model everything from industrial supply chains (Forrester 1961), to the growth and decay of cities (Forrester 1969), to the entire world (Forrester 1971).

Systems Dynamics is much more than a modeling technique; it is a comprehensive approach to modeling systems (Roberts 1978) as well as a way of thinking about the world. John Sterman has used systems dynamics thinking to understand the limitations and pitfalls of normal human decision-making, which tends to be based on linear thinking (Sterman 1994, 2000). SD offers a set of computational tools and a well-defined end-to-end process for building a model (Ventana Systems Inc. 2000; isee systems inc. 2005; Powersim Software AS 2005). Causal loop diagrams are graphical depictions of key system variables and their qualitative causal relationships. Peter Senge has used the systems dynamics philosophy to develop the notion of the "learning organization" (Senge 1990). Figure 4.8 shows a causal loop diagram for a learning organization.

Management Science

Management science (MS), and the related field of operations research (OR), is concerned with the quantitative analysis and solution of problems in business and management (Gass and Harris 2000; Gass and Assad 2005; Hillier and Lieberman 2005). Operations research developed as a discipline from analytical work conducted in World War II on the identification of efficient search patterns for enemy submarines. Management science is primarily a normative science, prescribing solutions that should be implemented, rather than a predictive or descriptive science.

MS has developed an enormous number of standard models and simulations covering a wide range of idealized cases of business and management problems. The basic techniques of MS include linear programming, probability theory and stochastic processes, statistics, and traditional discrete-event simulation. The use of models in supporting business decisions and the field known as decision analysis are also the province of management science. The basic problems of defining, developing, applying, validating, and having the results from any kind of computational model impact a decision are valuable lessons from the field of management science for ABMS applications.

Several of the techniques discussed in subsequent chapters have antecedents in management science. What is new is the inclusion of agents within the models and the agent perspective. MS, and systems science as a whole, has traditionally focused on the process view of the world—the processes are the central focus of analysis and modeling. The agent view of the world is not the traditional approach taken by MS to modeling business problems.

The Diffusion of ABMS

Business Applications

Many of the ideas of complexity science have implications for business and the management of organizations. Several recent books translate the findings of complexity science into business philosophy and practice and explain how companies have incorporated these techniques into their business processes (Stacey 1996, 2001; Kelly and Allison 1998; Axelrod and Cohen 1999; Clippinger 1999).

The development of computational agent-based models and simulations is actively being pursued by businesses and government to cover a number of applications in many areas, including:

- Designing optimized systems for businesses and organizations.
- Improving manufacturing and operations.
- Managing supply chains and supply networks.
- Understanding the interdependencies within industries such as insurance and reinsurance.
- Predicting consumer response to marketing programs and other activities in consumer markets.
- Developing insights into market trends, designing efficient markets.
- Improving the efficiency of financial markets.
- Increasing trading profits.
- Better managing energy markets.
- Restructuring electric power markets.
- Improving control of crowd behavior.
- Understanding pedestrian and vehicular traffic patterns and growth.
- Designing buildings for accessibility and evacuations.

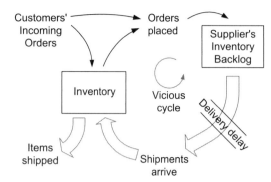

FIGURE 4.8 Systems dynamics causal diagram for an inventory system (adapted from Senge 1990).

- Designing new communication protocols and information fusion approaches for military command and control systems.

The nature of these applications covers everything from the design and analysis of complex systems to their operational development and deployment.

Tools for ABMS

The Santa Fe Institute (SFI) had an active role in developing the first widely used ABMS tools. SFI was founded in 1984 as an independent research institution for the dedicated study of complex adaptive systems and the emerging science of complexity. Although SFI is dedicated to advancing research into CAS, it was quickly realized that the same CAS thinking and techniques motivated by biological systems had analogous applications in the business world. The concepts of adaptation and emergence were central to the business/biology metaphor. The Santa Fe Institute Business Network was established in 1992 to make accessible and promote the use of complexity science in the business world. In addition, several firms specializing in consulting on applications of complexity science and ABMS to business have been formed as spinoffs of the Santa Fe Institute.

Under the auspices of SFI and to complement its research program in artificial life, the agent-based simulation software toolkit Swarm was developed by Chris Langton and others. Swarm was the first widely available software toolkit for modeling the mechanisms of artificial life. Swarm quickly became a tool of choice for modeling agent-based systems in general. Agent-based simulation became an established discipline for practical applications (Casti 1998) and became an educational vehicle to teach computing and systems principles from the bottom up (Resnick 1994). Swarm is the predecessor of current ABMS toolkits. ABMS toolkits, including Swarm, are discussed extensively in chapter 10.

Popular Culture

How widespread is interest in agent-based systems and complexity? Autonomous agents have penetrated popular culture and become the stuff of recent science fiction movies. In the *Terminator* movie series, autonomous machines are deployed to form a protective satellite network called SkyNet. The complexity of the networked machines suddenly attains a level at which SkyNet reaches consciousness and turns against its human creators as an act of self-preservation. The *Matrix* movie series is another example. Autonomous machines attain collective consciousness and again turn against their creators, relegating all humanity to a life deep underground. Swarms of autonomous agents are even starring in Michael Crichton's recent book, *Prey*. In that book, autonomous agents based on nanotechnology learn to self-organize and progressively adapt to the series of measures thrown at them by their human creators.

Although these examples portray what amounts to agent-based technology that is out of control, it is far beyond what is currently known or even thought to be possible. The prognosis for agent technology to benefit humanity is very bright.

Plectics Redux

This chapter has discussed the relationships of ABMS to several fields of knowledge and technology, with a particular emphasis on complexity or plectics. Each field contributes a little knowledge, a beneficial modeling technique, or a useful way of thinking about how to model agents, behaviors, and interactions. ABMS as a modeling approach is at the confluence of these fields. Integration of this diverse knowledge, these techniques, and these ways of thinking about problems is a sizable task of synthesis. This is the challenge of ABMS. The remainder of the book incorporates this knowledge into a unified, practical approach to ABMS.

References

Arthur, W. B. (1996). Increasing Returns and the New World of Business. *Harvard Business Review* **74**: 100–109.

Arthur, W. B. (1999). Complexity and the Economy. *Science* **284**(2): 107–109.

Arthur, W. B., S. N. Durlauf, and D. A. Lane, Eds. (1997). *The Economy as an Evolving Complex System II.* SFI Studies in the Sciences of Complexity. Reading, Mass.: Addison-Wesley.

Axelrod, R. (1984). *The Evolution of Cooperation*. New York: Basic Books.

Axelrod, R. (1997a). Advancing the Art of Simulation in the Social Sciences. In R. Conte, R. Hegselmann, and P. Terna (Eds.), *Simulating Social Phenomena*. Berlin: Springer Verlag, pp. 21–40.

Axelrod, R. (1997b). *The Complexity of Cooperation: Agent-Based Models of Competition and Collaboration*. Princeton, N.J.: Princeton University Press.

Axelrod, R. and M. D. Cohen (1999). *Harnessing Complexity: Organizational Implications of a Scientific Frontier*. New York: The Free Press.

Axtell, R. L. (1999). The Emergence of Firms in a Population of Agents: Local Increasing Returns, Unstable Nash Equilibria, and Power Law Size Distributions. Working Paper 03-019-99. Santa Fe, N.M.: Santa Fe Institute.

Bonabeau, E., M. Dorigo, and G. Theraulaz (1999). *Swarm Intelligence: From Natural to Artificial Systems*. Oxford: Oxford University Press.

Barabási, A.-L. (2002). *Linked: The New Science of Networks*. Cambridge, Mass.: Perseus Books.

Callen, E. and D. Shapero (1974). A Theory of Social Imitation. *Physics Today* **27**: 23–28.

Casti, J. L. (1994). *Complexification*. New York: HarperCollins.

Casti, J. L. (1998). *Would-Be Worlds: How Simulation Is Changing the World of Science*. New York: Wiley.

Christiansen, J. H. and M. Altaweel (2004). Simulation of Natural and Social Process Interactions in Bronze Age Mesopotamian Settlement Systems. *Proceedings of Society for American Anthropology 69th Annual Meeting*, Montreal, Canada.

Clippinger, J. H., Ed. (1999). *The Biology of Business: Decoding the Natural Laws of Enterprise*. San Francisco: Jossey-Bass.

Dean, J. S., G. J. Gumerman, J. M. Epstein, R. Axtell, and A. C. Swedlund (1998). Understanding Anasazi Culture Change Through Agent-Based Modeling. Working Paper 98-10-094. Santa Fe, N.M.: Santa Fe Institute.

Epstein, J. M. (2003). Growing Adaptive Organizations: An Agent-Based Computational Approach. Santa Fe, N.M.: Santa Fe Institute.

Epstein, J. M. and R. Axtell (1996). *Growing Artificial Societies: Social Science from the Bottom Up*. Cambridge, Mass.: MIT Press.

Epstein, J. M., J. D. Steinbruner, and M. T. Parker (2001). Modeling Civil Violence: An Agent-Based Computational Approach. Working Paper No. 20. Washington, D.C.: Brookings Institution.

Fogel, L. J. (1995). *Evolutionary Computation: Toward a New Philosophy of Machine Intelligence*. Piscataway, N.J.: IEEE Press.

Forrester, J. W. (1958). Industrial Dynamics: A Major Breakthrough for Decision Makers. *Harvard Business Review* **36**(4): 37–66.

Forrester, J. W. (1961). *Industrial Dynamics*. Cambridge, Mass.: MIT Press (currently available from Pegasus Communications, Waltham, Mass.).

Forrester, J. W. (1969). *Urban Dynamics*. Cambridge, Mass.: MIT Press (currently available from Pegasus Communications, Waltham, Mass.).

Forrester, J. W. (1971). *World Dynamics*. Cambridge, Mass.: Wright-Allen Press (currently available from Pegasus Communications, Waltham, Mass.).

Gardner, M. (1970). The Fantastic Combinations of John Conway's New Solitaire Game "Life." *Scientific American* **223**: 120–123.

Gass, S. I. and A. A. Assad (2005). *An Annotated Timeline of Operations Research: An Informal History*. New York: Kluwer.

Gass, S. I. and C. M. Harris (2000). *Encyclopedia of Operations Research and Management Science*. New York: Kluwer.

Gell-Mann, M. (1994). *The Quark and the Jaguar: Adventures in the Simple and the Complex*. New York: W.H. Freeman.

Gell-Mann, M. (1995). Let's Call It Plectics. *Complexity* **1**(5) (online).

Gilbert, N. and K. G. Troitzsch (1999). *Simulation for the Social Scientist*. Buckingham, U.K.: Open University Press.

Gladwell, M. (2000). *The Tipping Point: How Little Things Make Can Make a Big Difference*. New York: Little Brown.

Hillier, F. S. and G. J. Lieberman (2005). *Introduction to Operations Research*. New York: McGraw-Hill.

Holland, J. H. (1995). *Hidden Order: How Adaptation Builds Complexity*. Reading, Mass.: Addison-Wesley.

isee systems inc. (2005). STELLA. Lebanon, NH.: isee systems.

Jennings, N. R. (2000). On Agent-Based Software Engineering. *Artificial Intelligence* **117**: 277–296.

Kaufman, S. A. (1993). *The Origins of Order: Self-Organization and Selection in Evolution*. Oxford: Oxford University Press.

Kaufman, S. A. (1995). *At Home in the Universe: The Search for the Laws of Self-Organization and Complexity*. Oxford: Oxford University Press.

Kaufman, S. A. (2000). *Investigations*. Oxford: Oxford University Press.

Kelly, S. and M. A. Allison (1998). *The Complexity Advantage: How the Science of Complexity Can*

Help Your Business Achieve Peak Performance. New York: McGraw-Hill.

Miser, H. J., Ed. (1996). *Handbook of Systems Analysis*. New York: Wiley.

Padgett, J. F. (2000). Modeling Florentine Republicanism. Working Paper 01-02-008. Santa Fe, N.M.: Santa Fe Institute.

Poundstone, W. (1985). *The Recursive Universe: Cosmic Complexity and the Limits of Scientific Knowledge*. Chicago: Contemporary Books.

Powersim Software AS (2005). Powersim Studio. Bergen, Norway: Powersim Software, AS.

Resnick, M. (1994). *Turtles, Termites, and Traffic Jams: Explorations in Massively Parallel Microworlds*. Cambridge, Mass.: MIT Press.

Roberts, E. B., Ed. (1978). *Managerial Applications of System Dynamics*. Cambridge, Mass.: Productivity Press.

Schelling, T. C. (1971). Dynamic Models of Segregation. *Journal of Mathematical Sociology* 1: 143–186.

Schelling, T. C. (1978). *Micromotives and Macrobehavior*. New York: Norton.

Senge, P. M. (1990). *The Fifth Discipline: The Art and Practice of the Learning Organization*. New York: Doubleday/Currency.

Simon, H. (2001). *The Sciences of the Artificial*. Cambridge, Mass.: MIT Press.

Stacey, R. D. (1996). *Complexity and Creativity in Organizations*. San Francisco: Berrett-Koehler.

Stacey, R. D. (2001). *Complex Responsive Processes in Organizations: Learning and Knowledge Creation*. London and New York: Routledge.

Sterman, J. D. (1994). Learning In and About Complex Systems. *System Dynamics Review* 10(2–3): 291–330.

Sterman, J. D. (2000). *Business Dynamics: Systems Thinking and Modeling for a Complex World*. Boston: Irwin McGraw-Hill.

Strogatz, S. H. (2003). *Sync: The Emerging Science of Spontaneous Order*. New York: Hyperion.

Tesfatsion, L. (2002). Agent-Based Computational Economics: Growing Economies from the Bottom Up. *Artificial Life* 8(1): 55–82.

Tesfatsion, L. (2005). Agent-Based Computational Economics (ACE) web site, www.econ.iastate.edu/tesfatsi/ace.htm.

Ventana Systems Inc. (2000). VENSIM. Harvard, Mass.: Ventana Systems Inc.

Watts, D. J. (1999). *Small Worlds*. Princeton, N.J.: Princeton University Press.

Watts, D. J. (2003). *Six Degrees: The Science of a Connected Age*. New York: W.W. Norton.

Wolfram, S. (2002). *A New Kind of Science*. Champaign, Ill.: Wolfram Media, Inc.

Young, H. P. (1998). *Individual Strategy and Social Structure: An Evolutionary Theory of Institutions*. Princeton, N.J.: Princeton University Press.

5

The Role of ABMS

This chapter sets the stage for the practical application of agent-based modeling and simulation and creates the context for agent-based modeling by answering the question, "Why does business engage in modeling and simulation?" This question is considered in the specific context of using modeling and simulation to support decision-making. This chapter describes the broader context for modeling beginning with systems analysis, then the need for modeling and simulation in general, and finally by taking a close look at the traditional types of modeling approaches that have been widely used in practical business applications. The focus is on the most widespread modeling techniques in use today in terms of their intended purposes, their capabilities, the kinds of applications for they are most appropriate, and the limitations or drawbacks in their application.

This discussion creates a context for agent-based simulation, emphasizing its unique capabilities and the "value added" from its application and use. The traditional modeling approaches that this chapter discusses are as follows:

- *Systems dynamics*: A computer simulation approach that models the inner workings of a dynamic, high-level, strategic process, usually at an aggregate level of detail, and simulates how processes unfold over time.
- *Discrete-event simulation*: Another simulation approach that models the inner workings of an operational process, usually at a highly detailed level, and simulates the occurrence of events that move the process forward from time period to time period.
- *Participatory simulation*: A noncomputerized simulation approach that uses people as the primary components of the model to "simulate" the dynamic decision-making processes and the participants' interactions as they are reflected in the real system.
- *Optimization*: A modeling approach that seeks to find the best, better, or even "optimal" solution to a well-defined problem that can be expressed in mathematical notation. Not all problems are so amenable to being expressed mathematically.
- *Statistical modeling*: A modeling approach that treats a system, or a system's components, as a "black box," and focuses on how a system's outputs depend on its inputs, without regard to the system's internal structure or causal processes.
- *Risk analysis*: A common use of modeling in the business world that focuses on one aspect of an organization—the factors that threaten the organization and put its survival at risk.

Several of these traditional modeling approaches take what could be called a strategic perspective, by taking a view of the whole system. Others are capable of taking either a strategic or a more tactical view, and are applicable at the operational level as well. For each modeling approach, this chapter briefly discusses the background of the modeling approach, where it came from, and how it is being used. Taking a look at the background of a modeling approach can provide insights into understanding the original intended use for the approach, which in turn sheds light on the technique's appropriateness and limitations. Usually there are many applications for a modeling approach that are well beyond the purposes for which it was originally intended, some of which may be inappropriate. This chapter addresses the appropriateness of each modeling approach as a systems modeling tool and identifies the situations in which it would be most useful. The drawbacks and limitations of the modeling approaches for specific modeling situations are also discussed.

As a prelude to describing the modeling approaches in detail and to make the discussion more concrete, this chapter introduces a simple example of a supply chain model. The supply chain model will be used throughout the chapter to illustrate how the various modeling approaches could be applied, comparing and contrasting the kinds of information that could be provided to decision-makers in their practical application. The supply chain example will be carried through subsequent chapters of the book to illustrate various principles of agent-based modeling and simulation as well.

Finally, this chapter concludes by describing agent-based modeling within the same framework as the other modeling approaches, comparing and contrasting the capabilities of ABMS. This chapter also proposes a new approach to modeling systems, called "blended modeling," which provides a framework for ABMS to most effectively be applied and used together with the traditional modeling approaches. First, this chapter will discuss one issue of fundamental importance, namely, why do businesses do modeling and simulation?

The Big Picture of Modeling and Simulation for Business Applications

Modeling and simulation is part of a much larger analytical framework undertaken to understand and ultimately control business processes and organizations. Systems analysis is the name given to the general task of systematically identifying and understanding the goals, objective, processes, activities, tasks, resources, and constraints of the organization (Miser and Quade 1985). Sometimes systems analysis goes by other names or is part of a larger framework, such as business process re-engineering, which includes normative goals of transforming the organization and making it better. Systems analysis is motivated by various goals and can be approached from various perspectives. For example, as shown in figure 5.1, systems analysis can be approached from the perspective of information in an organization: What information is required, and where in the organization it is required? By whom? What information is generated by the organization? Is the information used? How is the information used? How much does it cost to generate the information? The questions go on.

Systems analysis creates much useful information, insights, and understanding about the organization. The information is usually qualitative, in the form of ideas, diagrams, documents, and so on. Systems analysis may be a useful end in itself and does not necessarily have to lead to a modeling and simulation activity to be beneficial. But systems analysis also lays the groundwork for a comprehensive modeling and simulation effort, and most modeling and simulation development begins with systems analysis as a necessary prelude to developing a model. No matter what type of model is developed or what modeling approach is used, systems analysis is an essential part of developing any kind of model, including an agent-based model. Systems analysis is an important activity of any business organization, but who are the analysts?

The Analytical Perspective

By definition, the analyst is concerned with analyzing the details, identifying the root causes, searching for more basic explanations, and finding a deeper understanding of a situation or phenomenon. Modeling and simulation are the tools of the analyst or model user. Modeling and simulation, if done properly, offer a way for the analyst to investigate the world and create new knowledge, much of which may be of great practical importance to the efficient functioning and survival of a business.

Anecdotal life experience reveals an obvious fact—not everyone is an analyst. Not everyone is inclined to delve into the details, know what to do with them, and live in what is often a confusing and self-contradictory world for extended periods of time. Not everyone derives satisfaction from separating the wheat from the chaff when it comes to information and sorting out the relevant details. Not everyone enjoys

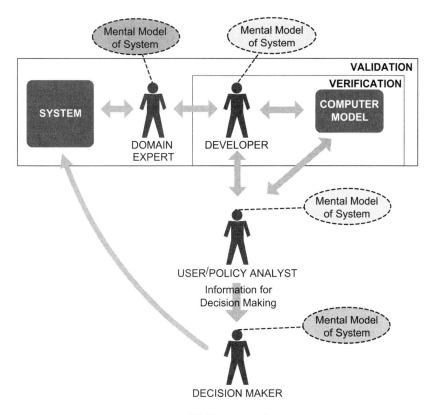

FIGURE 5.1 Systems analysis.

finding yet another possible connection to new information—yet more details that must be woven into the big picture.

The downside of being an analyst is the propensity to become lost in the details. Getting lost in the details means losing perspective—losing sight of the big picture and the practical significance of the information being compiled, analyzing the information as an end in itself, rather than as a means to an end, that end being to provide information for an informed decision.

Of course, not all analysts get lost in the details, nor do all managers eschew the details. Yet there is a constant tension in any modeling project emanating from the conflict between the level of detail necessary for a credible and valid model, and the amount of time and effort required to collect and compile the needed information. Some people prefer to spend the majority of their time looking at the big picture, and making decisions based on instinct, or intuition, or simply recognizing patterns. In a sense, they intuitively search for larger patterns and identify key indicators or variables to use as the basis for their decisions and actions. Nonetheless, these types of people are "agents" in the organization, each with their own goals, perspective, and approaches to decision-making.

Why Does Business Do Modeling and Simulation?

Modeling and simulation is the quantitative part of systems analysis. Some of the reasons why modeling and simulation is used to support business decisions are:

- No one can understand how all the various parts of the system interact and add up to the whole. The system is simply too complex given all of the complexities of its components and their interactions. Business managers need to simulate a system on the computer first, rather than build an untested new system only to have it fail or fall into gross inefficiencies.
- No one can imagine all the possibilities that the real system could exhibit. This may be true even if managers have a good handle on operating the

real system through a limited range of experience. To be confident that they are minimizing costs and optimizing operations, managers need to consider possibilities beyond their experience, perhaps thousands of possibilities, far beyond the capabilities of their mental models to conceive and anticipate.

- No one can foresee the full effects of events with limited mental models. Human mental models are often based on "linear" thinking, and this greatly limits the ability to extrapolate to new situations. The human mind is limited in its ability to trace a causal chain of events as they cascade throughout a system and have consequences in parts of the system far from their original source.
- No one can foresee novel events outside of their mental models. The complex, nonlinear interactions that occur in models may create new and unforeseen events and behaviors.
- Managers want to model as an exercise in "thought space" to gain insights into key variables and their causes and effects. Secondary and tertiary effects of decisions and actions can be modeled much more effectively on the computer.
- Managers want to model to make predictions of the future. No model can predict the future. But how close can modeling come to predicting the future? Modeling can provide educated guesses about what can happen in the future, given necessary assumptions used to construct the models. Modeling can show the range of possible futures and the situations in which these futures could come about. This can be extremely useful and important information, but not always.

Agent-based modeling in particular can be used to address each of these motivations for modeling and simulation, often in ways that are novel and provide new insights not achievable with traditional modeling and simulation approaches.

How can maximum modeling and simulation effectiveness be achieved, avoiding the pitfalls in modeling that, in some cases, have been painfully gained through the experiences of the past fifty years?

How Does Business Do Modeling and Simulation?

There are two common approaches to modeling:

- *Modeling the problem*: This approach focuses on developing concrete tools to answer specific questions.

- *Modeling the system*: This approach focuses on developing concrete tools to reproduce behavior.

The "modeling the problem" approach tends to be successful for businesses since it concentrates development effort on the areas of greatest benefit and it helps modelers to avoid adding unnecessary simulation features. In contrast, the "modeling the system" approach, although effective in many other fields of application, is risky for businesses since it is rarely based on a clear definition of the behavior to be reproduced and can often lead to investments in vague lines of model development and unneeded model features.

How can one proceed down the right path of "modeling the problem?" The "End Products Presentation Method" (EPPM) is a practical approach to defining business modeling questions. This method focuses directly on "modeling the problem." Using EPPM, the project manager writes the final presentation that they would like to show about the modeling effort, before the project even begins in earnest. This presentation is then used to define the appropriate questions to be asked. The approach is flexible in that the questions being asked can evolve over time, as previous questions become successfully answered with a given model, and new directions or even the real purpose of the activity becomes better defined.

Common Aspects of All Modeling Approaches

All modeling requires going through the steps of a modeling process and facing the same issues, no matter what modeling technique is employed. As a practical matter, the two main things that people other than the modelers are most concerned about when it comes to working with the information from any type of model are as follows:

1. *Data*: Where does, can, will, or could the data come from?
2. *Model validation*: How can users know that they can trust the model results? How can users be shown that the model meets their needs?

Whatever modeling approach is employed, these two issues need to be addressed first and foremost, and the approach to addressing them is largely the same across the modeling techniques, with some important variations. For example, a statistical model cannot begin to be built without the data, whereas a simulation model can often be constructed first and the data collected, possibly in parallel as part of a multistep process.

Another common modeling challenge is the need to stay focused on constructing the model so that it produces the information that the model is supposed to provide. Loss of focus is one of the greatest dangers in any modeling effort. Sometimes the intended focus of the model is vague to begin with; this situation presents special challenges. Ensuring that the modeling effort does not become an end in itself is a challenge that must be addressed continually in the modeling process.

In reality, many of the modeling approaches bring with them a whole process or procedures for how to go about each step of the modeling process, from requirements definition to model implementation on the computer. Many elements of various modeling approaches can be combined, by taking the best parts of each, into an effective model development strategy.

This chapter next turns to an important system in business and one that is often modeled to gain insights for decision-making—that of supply chains. This supply chain model will be used throughout the remainder of the chapter to illustrate important modeling concepts and approaches.

A Supply Chain Example

Supply chains are everywhere in today's modern society involving every aspect of the production and provision of goods and services. A supply chain consists of several stages, from suppliers and manufacturing to distribution, wholesaling, and retailing, providing final goods and services to customers as shown in figure 5.2. Supply chains have flows between stages in the form of goods and information. Goods flow down the chain or flow downstream in response to orders that flow up from the customers or flow upstream. The flow of payments in the upstream direction completes the picture. In reality, a supply chain is a complicated and dynamic structure in the form of a complex network of interrelationships among firms, with relationships and linkages that are constantly in flux. Even the simplest supply chains can exhibit complex system behaviors that are difficult to understand and manage, as customer demand and inventories fluctuate in unanticipated ways.

This chapter will describe a relatively simple model of a supply chain to illustrate how various modeling approaches can be applied to the supply chain to provide important information for decision-making. The supply chain model, inspired by Sterman's Beer Game, also establishes a basis for comparison of traditional modeling approaches with agent-based modeling and simulation (Sterman 1992). Although simplified, the supply chain model is well grounded in thinking about and modeling supply chains. The supply chain consists of four stages: factories, distributors, wholesalers, and retailers, responding to customers' demand. There are multiple participants, or agents, at each stage, and they are interrelated through a network. Suppliers and assembly operations are ignored for the purposes of the simplified model, but without losing the most important aspects of realistic supply chain behavior. Note that suppliers could easily be incorporated into the model if so desired. There is only one commodity. No transformation of goods is made and no assembly of materials into products is required. The flow of goods and information, in the form of orders, between participants is included in the model, but the flows of payments and the additional complexities of pricing, negotiation, and financial accounting that this could entail are not included in the example model.

At each time period, the following steps occur in the supply chain:

- Customers place orders with retailers.
- Retailers fill the orders immediately from their respective inventories, if they have enough inventory in stock. If a retailer runs out of stock, the customer's order is placed on backorder, to be filled when stock is replenished.
- Retailers receive shipments from wholesalers in response to orders they placed previously. Retailers then decide on how much to order from wholesalers, based on an "ordering rule." The decision on how much to order is based in part on how much the retailer expects customer demand to be in the future. Retailers estimate future customer demand using a "demand forecasting" rule. The retailers order items from the wholesaler.
- Similarly, each wholesaler receives shipments from the distributors, forecasts future demand by the retailers, and places an order with the distributors. This process continues up the chain to the factories, who instead of placing orders upstream, decide on how much to put into production.

It is assumed in this model that there is a one-period delay in the order being received at a stage

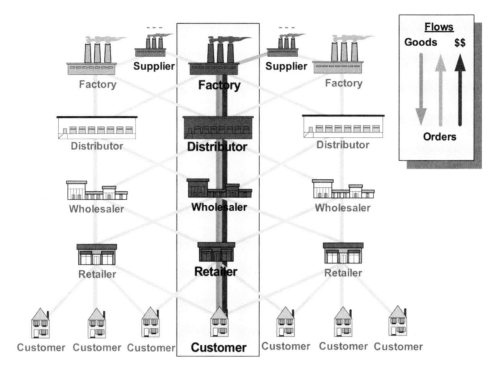

FIGURE 5.2 A supply chain.

from the time is sent from the downstream agent. There is a two-period delay in items being shipped and reaching the next downstream stage. There is a three-period production delay at the factory level.

This supply chain model is "simulated" by processing the above steps over several time periods. This supply chain model can be thought of as a flow model. Goods flow down the supply chain from stage to stage in response to orders that flow up the chain, beginning with the customer. What the model does is to track the flows of information or orders and goods through time from the customer upstream through the supply network through the factory. For the purposes of this discussion, each of the stages in the supply chain is populated by a number of "agents," although it has been traditional to refer to the various stages as sectors or players.

The goal of the agents in the model is to manage their inventory in such a way as to minimize their costs through judicious decisions based on how much to order each period. When inventories are too low and there is a danger of running out of stock, agents order more; when inventories are too large and agents incur high inventory holding costs, agents order less. Each agent incurs a cost when holding stock in

inventory. This is called the inventory holding charge in standard inventory planning. In the supply chain model, it is assumed that an inventory holding charge of $0.50 per unit of stock in inventory per period. Agents also incur a cost when they receive an order and cannot immediately meet that order because they have no inventory stock. This is called the backorder charge in inventory planning. In the supply chain model, the backorder charge is $2.00 per unit of unmet demand per period. The notion is that it is more costly to the company, in terms of losing customers and customer goodwill by not being able to fill an order at the time it is demanded, than it is to hold an extra unit of stock in inventory. This assumption naturally leads to the desire on the part of a supply chain agent to hold a positive inventory, to always have some level of the costly inventory on hand rather than to possibly incur the even more costly "stockout" situation.

The overall objective of each supply chain agent is to minimize costs, which are composed of inventory stock and backorder costs. This entails the agent striking a delicate balance between having too much inventory, which runs up inventory holding costs, and too little inventory, which puts the agent at a greater risk of running out of stock and incurring extensive backorder charges. As will be shown in the section on systems dynamics, the desire to have a positive inventory leads to the need for agents to have decision rules for determining orders and effectively managing inventory.

One of the features of the supply chain example is the fact that players only have access to and make use of local information in making their decisions. No agent has a global view of the system or notion of optimizing the system as a whole, that is, of minimizing the total cost of operating the supply chain, other than through the collective decisions made by the individual agents. Agents adopt decision rules that use this key local information in making decisions.

The supply chain model can be an excellent foundation for more complex and realistic models of real supply chains. Numerous additions and enhancements easily come to mind to make the model more realistic and potentially relevant, but this chapter will press on in describing how one could apply various modeling techniques to this highly simplified version. In fact, several agent-based models of supply chains have been developed that examine various enhancements to this basic supply chain example (Brugali et al. 1998; Fu et al. 2000; Garcia-Flores et al. 2000; Garcia-Flores and Wang 2002; Ahn et al. 2003; Macal 2003a, 2003b; Macal et al. 2003).

Effective modeling is driven by focused questions. What kinds of questions about the supply chain example can be answered using the various modeling approaches? Even this simple supply chain model can be used to answer a host of important questions about the supply chain:

- The effects of various ordering policies or the rules supply chain agents use to determine orders on inventory levels and costs can be studied. Does inventory fluctuate over time, or can it be brought to a stable desired level? This is the "system behavior" of the supply chain. System behavior comes in two types: the short-run, in which the system transitions from an initial state through a series of fluctuations before possibly finally settling down, and the long-run, in which the system falls into a steady pattern of behavior. These types of questions can be answered using systems dynamics modeling.
- The effects of demand fluctuations and variations in delivery times on overall supply chain performance can be studied. These types of questions can be answered using discrete-event simulation modeling.

- What kind of rules would it be reasonable to expect that people would come up with and use in the course of managing the supply chain, given limited time and the need for making fast decisions? What factors would they consider in making ordering decisions, and what strategic or even irrational behaviors might occur? These types of questions can be answered using participatory simulation.
- What is the cost-minimizing solution for the entire supply chain solution? What results in the most stable positive inventories, enough to meet the desired inventory and pipeline goals, minimizing backorder costs at reasonable costs? These types of questions can be answered using optimization modeling.
- What is the relationship between profits and orders, inventory, the pipeline, and recent demand for each agent in the supply chain? These types of questions can be answered using statistical modeling.
- What is the risk for all the supply chain agents of having too much investment tied up in inventory? These types of questions can be answered using risk analysis modeling.
- What are the effects of the rules used by the supply chain agents on the overall behavior and profitability of the supply chain? Do smarter and better-informed supply chain agents make greater profits? What strategic behaviors might agents find effective in increasing profits? These types of questions can be answered using agent-based modeling and simulation.

The modeling sections that follow will explain how the various modeling techniques could be used to address these and other questions. These kinds of questions provide the mechanism to achieve several important organizational goals of the modeling project:

- They help to determine the appropriate level of detail for the models.
- These questions define the end state of the modeling effort, so that the model can be developed using progressive refinement toward a focused goal.
- Based on how well the questions are answered, they can be the criteria for determining the overall success and effectiveness of the modeling project.

Answering these questions is the essence of "modeling the problem."

A Survey of Modeling Approaches

A wide range of modeling approaches are surveyed in this section. These approaches include systems dynamics, the discrete-event simulation approach, the participatory simulation approach, the optimization approach, the statistical modeling approach, the risk analysis approach, and finally the agent-based modeling and simulation approach. This survey provides both a foundation for later discussions and a comparative analysis of each approach.

Systems Dynamics

Systems dynamics (SD) is a "whole system" modeling approach that is used to model dynamic processes, which change continuously over time. SD models tend to be highly aggregated, or higher-level, representations of systems and processes. Systems dynamics models consist of two main elements: stocks that represent the state variables of the system, and flows that describe how the stocks change over time. This is much like a system of rivers and lakes, with water continually flowing.

Background

Systems dynamics originated as a modeling approach designed specifically for modeling business and social systems, by Jay Forrester in the late 1950s (Forrester 1959). It has been used to model everything from industrial supply chains (Forrester 1958), to the growth of cities (Forrester 1969), to the entire world (Forrester 1971). Systems dynamics is much more than a simulation technique, it is a comprehensive structured approach to modeling a complex system (Roberts 1978; Checkland 1981). It offers a world-view, a set of tools, and a well-defined end-to-end process for building a model, from defining the components of the model through its implementation. More recently, John Sterman of the Sloan School of Business at MIT has extensively used systems dynamics concepts in exploring specific areas of human decision-making in business processes. SD even has its own professional society, the Systems Dynamics Society, to communicate advances in and promote SD applications.

Systems dynamics, as with the general field of simulation, began as a modeling tool with the widespread use of computers. It owes its roots to the field of systems engineering, which is primarily concerned with physical systems such as electronics—not systems that contain human decision-makers and social processes. The first computers were analog in nature, as opposed to today's widespread digital computers, and analog computer simulations were common. It was natural for analog simulations to operate in continuous time, as opposed to today's digital, discrete-event simulations. In continuous simulation, one represents a system by its most important variables and describes how each of these variables changes over time. An engineer might describe the situation as one in which "the system is represented by a set of state variables and a set of differential equations that indicate the rate of change of each of the state variables as a function of the state." A common approach in analog simulation was to define the state variables of the simulation to correspond to the voltages and currents in an electrical circuit and to model how these varied over time in response to external factors. The continuous-time analog simulations were directly applicable to modeling systems that could be represented in the form of differential equations, owing to the fact that differential equations are a natural representation for Kirchhoff's laws of electricity on how voltages and currents in electrical circuits are conserved and change over time. The promise of modeling dynamic business systems as systems of differential equations motivated the development of the systems dynamics modeling technique, and elements inherent in the original approach are carried over in the application of the technique to this day.

Systems dynamics takes the approach of modeling the dynamic behavior of a system as it changes over time at discrete time points, through the use of difference equations that relate the state of the system from one time point to the next. Usually the time increment for updating the system is kept constant at one time unit, whether it be one hour, one day, one year, and so on. This contrasts with the differential equation approach in which systems are modeled in continuous time. For some systems it is clear that the precise time trajectory of variables needs to be accurately modeled. For example, weather modeling is a case in point in which accuracy demands that the dynamics of the atmosphere be modeled at the highest levels of resolution in time and space. But for social and business processes, the simplification of representing the system only at discrete time steps produces results that are the same as or very similar to what would be obtained from a differential equation approach. Most importantly, using discrete time points greatly simplifies the computations of the model.

Another aspect of systems dynamics modeling is its treatment of uncertainty. SD models are generally deterministic in nature—the variability or randomness in key variables is not considered in the model. This is largely due to the fact that the focus of systems dynamics models is not to explore the effects of uncertainty, but rather to understand the nature of whole-system behavior. The notion is that the system still exhibits the same kind of systems-wide behavior whether or not the variability of key parameters is considered, and ignoring the uncertainty in the model's parameters allows one to focus on the more fundamental determinants of system behavior. The consideration of this small set of variables is the essence of using the information from models and simulations in business decision-making.

Several systems dynamics modeling tools are available and widely used. Among them are Vensim, STELLA, and Powersim (Ventana Systems Inc. 2000; isee systems inc. 2005; Powersim Software AS 2005).

A Systems Dynamics Model: Sterman's Beer Game Simulation

The systems dynamics approach to modeling the supply chain is illustrated by the well-known "Beer Game" simulation, originated by John Sterman (Sterman 1989a, 1989b; Mosekilde et al. 1991). The Beer Game originated as a noncomputerized, participatory simulation game, but has since been computerized as a business simulation and studied extensively. The game is widely played and used in business schools and executive education programs to illustrate key points of human decision-making behavior and fundamental aspects of the behaviors of systems. This model, although simple, captures the essence of supply chain behavior and illustrates pitfalls inherent in dynamic decision-making behavior (Sterman 2000). Many business programs have since picked up the Beer Game and use it in their classes as well.

More recently, a computational version of the Beer Game was developed as a systems dynamics model and studied extensively to explore the effects of individual decision-making on systemic properties of the supply chain, the results of which are reproduced in figures 5.3–5.7, 13.1–13.17, and 13.19–13.20 (Sterman 1989a, 1989b, 2000, 2003; Mosekilde et al. 1991).

The computational Beer Game simulation, although a highly simplified model of real-world supply chains, is well studied and well published—an example of a classic supply chain simulation. Even though it is simple, the Beer Game still exhibits an important characteristic observed in real-world supply chains—the "bull-whip effect." In the Beer Game simulation, each agent has the goals of achieving both a desired inventory level to buffer against unexpected fluctuations in demand and a desired level of orders in the pipeline (i.e., orders made but not received) to buffer against the delays between placing an order and receiving shipments. Agents keep track of two key parameters in determining the amount to order each period. These are the amount of inventory the agent has on hand and the number of outstanding orders. The inventory is composed of two parts, the physical stock that the agent has on hand, or if there is no stock, the number of backorders. If an order comes in but it cannot be met immediately because there are no inventory stocks, the order is placed on backorder.

Similar to the supply chain example introduced earlier in this chapter, the Beer Game supply chain consists of four stages: retailer, wholesaler, distributor, and factory. Each stage of the supply chain makes ordering decisions based only on locally available information. For example, the order placed by a supply chain agent at a stage is based on the information that the agent has access to, which consists of:

- Current inventory level.
- Desired inventory level.
- Number of items in the pipeline (i.e., shipments in transit from upstream agent and outstanding orders placed to agent upstream).
- Desired level of items in the pipeline.
- Current demand.
- Expected demand for the next period based on a forecast.

Each agent has two goals to be met: achieve both the desired inventory level to buffer against unexpected fluctuations in demand and the desired pipeline level to buffer against the delays in placing an order and receiving supplies.

How can the influence between these factors be represented? In systems dynamics there is a standard approach to visually depicting the key variables in a system, called a "causal loop diagram." A causal loop diagram for the retailer agent in the Beer Game is shown in figure 5.3. The other agents have similar

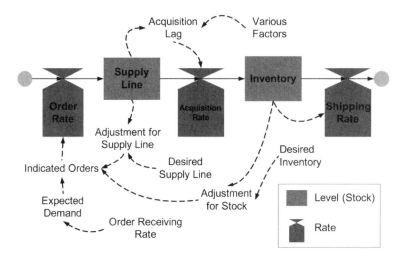

FIGURE 5.3 Systems dynamics causal loop diagram. (Adapted from Mosekilde et al. 1991, fig. 3.)

causal diagrams with appropriate modifications for the fact that wholesalers and distributors do not interface directly with customers, and the factory does not interface with an upstream agent. The causal loop diagram shows which state variables are related to each other. Some causal loop diagrams also show whether the relationship is positive, with larger values of one variable causing another variable to increase (denoted by a "+" sign), or negative, with larger values of a variable causing another variable to decrease (denoted by a "–" sign). If two or more variables taken together form a chain that closes back onto itself, it is called a causal loop. If all of the relationships in the chain are positive, the loop is called a positive feedback loop. Positive feedback loops are very important parts of SD models because they result in a process that is self-reinforcing. That is, increasing one variable results in an increase in another variable, which in turn leads to an even larger increase in the first variable. The process often leads to exponential growth, with the variables involved increasing to the point at which they cannot be sustained, resulting in a large "crash" of the system. If the relationships in the loop are negative, the loop is called a negative feedback loop. Negative feedback loops tend to stabilize the entire system. The mix of positive and negative feedback loops comprising the relationships among the variables in an SD model leads to realistic system behaviors that are often counterintuitive. The causal diagram can be used to construct a set of equations

that constitutes a complete systems dynamics model. These equations are solved repeatedly, once each time period during the simulation.

Causal diagrams have value in their own right in representing and articulating the system's important components and variables and how these variables are interrelated. For example, Peter Senge has shown how to use causal diagrams to represent and communicate important processes in learning organizations (Senge 1990).

The precise form of the supply chain agent ordering rule that is commonly used in the computational Beer Game begins with each agent placing an order based on their estimate of the demand in the next period and adjustments to be made to inventory and the orders they have in the pipeline. (Many other plausible rules could also be considered.) For example, if inventory is especially low, the agent may order extra items in an effort to raise the inventory to desired levels. Agents seek to close the gap between the desired and the actual levels of inventory stock and what they have in the pipeline compared to their desired levels. One strategy is for agents to include an extra amount in their order to "split the difference" between their current inventory and their desired inventory, and do the same for the pipeline. Another strategy could be for agents to try to close the gap completely with one order. Either of these strategies can be represented by specifying ordering parameters that represent the fraction of the gap to be closed between desired and actual levels of inventory and orders in the pipeline. The values of these two weighting parameters, one for the inventory shortfall and the other for the pipeline shortfall, are typically set between zero and one. Alternative ordering policies are represented by varying these values in this range.

Agents also base their orders in part on forecasts of future demand coming from the downstream. A simple demand forecasting rule is used for this purpose. The demand forecasting rule commonly used in the computational Beer Game begins with agents weighing the current period's actual demand and the projection of demand made in the previous period to estimate the demand for the next period. The relative weight given to actual demand and the projection of demand made in the previous period is specified by a forecasting parameter set by the agent. This weight is held constant for the entire period of the game or simulation. The value of this parameter is typically set between zero and one. At the extremes, a value for the forecasting parameter close to one indicates that more weight should be placed on the actual demand as an indicator of the next period's demand than the forecasted amount; a value closer to zero indicates that more weight should be placed on the forecasted demand, regardless of the actual demand incurred. Different values correspond to different assumptions regarding demand "smoothing," a common approach to demand forecasting in standard texts on operations management. Sterman has shown that this is a good behavioral decision model for this Beer Game and describes how people really behave (Sterman 1987a, 1987b, 1989a, 1989b; Mosekilde et al. 1991).

The Beer Game example begins with 12 items in the inventory and in the pipeline for each agent. The system begins in complete equilibrium—the orders received equal the orders sent at every stage, and customer demand is always satisfied. The supply chain model is completely deterministic, that is, there are no random elements in this model, demand is constant and never fluctuates, and so on. If demand does not change, the system continues forever in complete equilibrium as shown in figure 5.4.

Continuing with this simple model, a single change in the system is made at time 5. At time 5, customer demand ramps up from the initial value of 4 to 8, and it stays there for the remainder of the simulation as shown in figure 5.5. That is all that changes in this simple supply chain model. In response to the change in customer demand at time 5, each agent begins to use the ordering rule to determine how much to order given the new situation. The ordering rule uses information that is only locally available to the agent. For example, the distributor agent knows only how much is in its inventory and in its pipeline, not the inventories and pipelines of the other agents. Then the system is simulated forward from that point in time. Agents try to cope with this simple change in the system.

One might expect that, after an initial period of adjustment, the agents are able to adjust to this seemingly minor change quickly and bring the system back to a point of stability and equilibrium. This turns out to be far from what happens. The ramp-up in demand has the effect of rippling through the various stages of the supply chain, causing alternating behaviors of overordering and underordering on the part of each of the agents. The system never stabilizes or adjusts to the ramp-up in demand as shown in figures 5.6 and 5.7. This effect has been observed in real-world supply chains and is known as the "bull-whip effect" (Chen et al. 2000).

Using Systems Dynamics Models

Systems dynamics simulations are straightforward to build, consisting of three kinds of variables: levels,

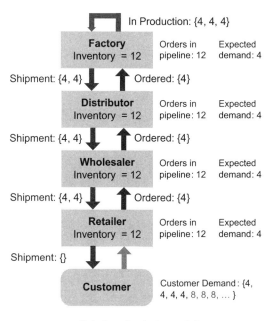

FIGURE 5.4 Supply chain model setup.

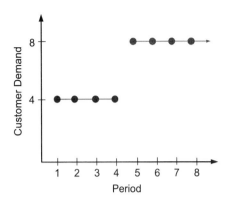

FIGURE 5.5 Ramp-up in customer demand.

- A need to define processes that may not be fully or completely known and difficult to model at a high level of aggregation.
- Difficulty of modeling learning or adaptation of the system components.
- Difficulty of modeling discrete events or fixed duration activities.

Since SD models tend to be aggregate representations, it is often not clear what the right amount of aggregation or detail is in developing a model. The right balance between too little and too much detail must be struck. With too much detail, the modeling effort bogs down. With too little detail, the model lacks credibility and is open to criticism.

rates, and auxiliary variables. Their aggregate, high-level approach means that there are fewer variables and data requirements. Use systems dynamics to find out:

- How a system changes over time.
- The system's transition patterns and long-run behavior.
- Whether the system contains inherent instabilities.

There are also drawbacks of systems dynamics models. These include:

- An emphasis on the fixed processes that do not change in structure and interrelatedness.

Systems Dynamics and Agent-Based Modeling

Systems dynamics and agent-based simulation share many similarities. It is possible to develop an agent-based version of a systems dynamics model and obtain exactly the same results from the simulation. This is done by rearranging the information within the model. In an agent model, the information in the model is grouped by agent, but one can infer the agent behaviors from the system state variables and how the state variables change. It is also possible, at least theoretically, to develop a systems dynamics version of an agent-based simulation for many systems. In an SD model, the information in the model is

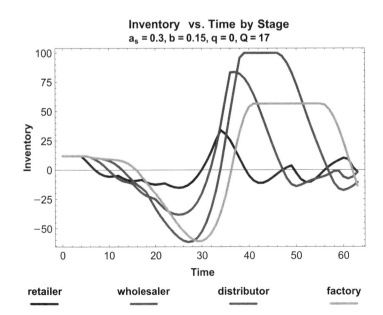

FIGURE 5.6 Unstable system behavior for 60 periods. (Reproduced from Mosekilde et al. 1991, fig. 5a.)

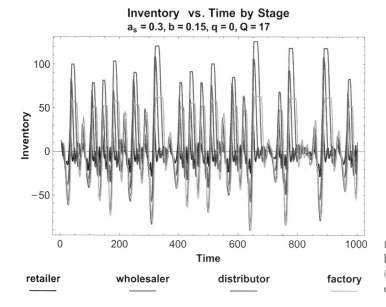

Inventory vs. Time by Stage
$a_s = 0.3, b = 0.15, q = 0, Q = 17$

FIGURE 5.7 Unstable system behavior for 1,000 periods. (Reproduced from Mosekilde et al. 1991, fig. 6a.)

grouped by state variables and how they change, but one can determine or infer how these variables describe agents and agent behaviors. Systems dynamics takes the process perspective, and using it to explicitly model agents and their interactions is outside the realm of its original intended purpose as a modeling methodology. Systems dynamics has great difficulty in modeling certain types of problems, which are generally outside the original scope for which the methodology was intended. Do not use systems dynamics modeling:

- When the problem has a strong spatial or geographical component, as when agents need to interact over a spatial landscape, for example in modeling the locations of consumers and retail markets.
- When the problem involves networks of agents that interact over time, especially if these networks are dynamic in the sense that they are created and transform themselves as a result of the agent interactions that go on within the model.
- When the problem has discrete decision variables, as when a state variable is required to be a whole number at all times and fractional levels do not make sense, such as when items being ordered and shipped can only come in whole units.
- When the problem has constraints on decision variables, for example when a state variable is required to be within a range, such as when there is a need to maintain inventory within capacity limits.

In contrast, ABMS readily addresses these aspects of modeling a system because it was in part developed to do so. This chapter next considers a more general approach to simulation than systems dynamics, namely discrete-event simulation.

The Discrete-Event Simulation Approach

Discrete-event simulation (DES) is a technique that models a process as it unfolds over time. The emphasis is on the process. The approach has discrete in its name because time is represented only at discrete points. DES is event-oriented in that events are scheduled to occur only at these discrete time points. An event in turn causes a chain of future events to be scheduled and processed as the simulation progresses through time.

Background

Discrete-event simulation gradually became a well-established modeling tool with the widespread use of digital computers (Law 2007). DES owes its emphasis on modeling uncertainty of key variables to what is called Monte Carlo simulation.[1] Monte Carlo simulation, named for the Monte Carlo casinos, was originally developed to understand the nature of combinations of probabilities of events that were too numerous and complicated to be worked out by hand (Metropolis and Ulam 1949). Stanislaw Ulam invented the Monte Carlo method while trying to determine the mathematical likelihood of winning at solitaire. The main idea of Monte Carlo simulation is to lay out a problem, test or sample values for its random elements from their respective probability distributions, tally up the outcomes of various types, and repeat this process, many, many times. The result is a set of probability distributions for the main outcome variables of interest. Ulam went on to apply the same technique to understanding neutron diffusion, which proved very useful for his work in designing the hydrogen bomb (Eckhardt 1987). Monte Carlo simulation went from a theoretical construct to a useful modeling technique when Ulam realized that computers can easily perform this otherwise daunting and repetitive task.

One of the most widespread uses for discrete-event simulation is modeling waiting lines, or queuing systems. Waiting lines are ubiquitous for people in everyday life, encountered in their daily routine of shopping, driving, banking, and so on, as well as for business and industry, encountered in the interconnected aspects of production, transport, and distribution. Discrete-event simulation goes beyond static Monte Carlo simulation to the level of modeling a dynamic process that has random elements and decision points. Because of its roots in Monte Carlo simulation, a typical discrete-event simulation includes elements of uncertainty and randomness, in contrast to systems dynamics models which are deterministic for the most part. The key questions typically addressed by discrete-event simulations concern how the variability of important system variables results from the variability of the system components. The simulation is used in effect to derive the probability distributions for these key variables. Many discrete-event simulations take the form of models of complex queuing networks, in which the durations of activities and events that occur are probabilistic in nature.

Discrete-event simulation became widely used as an accepted business tool beginning in the early 1960s with the development of dedicated simulation languages, which began as collections of software subroutines and prescribed methods for how one should go about modeling dynamic systems. Systems such as GASP, SIMSCRIPT, and GPSS made simulation modeling accessible to a wide audience of modelers in business and government (Nance 1995). The initial simulation systems and languages were very successful and led to a continuous stream of new developments in languages and commercial products that continues to this day. Simulation systems and languages vary in

terms of their generality and applicability across problem domains. Some simulation systems are designed for specific problem domains, such as manufacturing. Others are generally applicable, but require users to develop more of the model for the specific domain of application. Simulation systems include Arena, SLAM, and many others (Pritsker 1986; Swain 2003a, 2003b).

There are also common variations on the discrete-event simulation theme. For example, in time-stepped simulation, every discrete time point is visited in the simulation to check for and execute the events that may be scheduled for that time. Usually in discrete-event simulation, only time points are visited for which events are scheduled. There are also fully developed simulation systems that combine both continuous simulation, as in systems dynamics, and discrete-event simulation in a logically consistent framework (Pritsker 1986). Using combined simulation, one could model a system as it smoothly evolves over time but is suddenly interrupted by events that are the result of crossing thresholds for some of the variables. These threshold events change the state of the system at that point in time and significantly alter the evolution of the system from that point forward, effectively sending the system off in new directions.

A DES Supply Chain Example

This section shows a typical use for discrete-event simulation as applied to the supply chain example. Consider the following daily routine for a supply chain agent, for example, the distributor. The distributor experiences this ordered sequence of events and activities:

1. An order arrives from the wholesaler downstream.
2. A shipment arrives from the factory upstream.
3. The distributor processes the shipment and adds it to the inventory.
4. The distributor processes the order and adds it to the list of backorders.
5. The distributor makes a new shipment, if there is stock in the inventory and there are backorders to be filled.
6. The distributor forecasts demand for the following day.
7. The distributor determines how much to order and sends the order to the factory upstream.

If the distributor knows precisely how much the incoming orders from the wholesaler and the shipments from the factory will be, the distributor's problem can be easily solved: simply order and ship at the rates of the incoming orders and shipments, respectively. But suppose the distributor does not know exactly when the next order will be received or what the quantity ordered will be, or how much will be received in the next incoming shipment.

Suppose the distributor has carefully recorded data on how the incoming orders and the incoming shipments have varied over time. This data can be used to describe orders and shipments in probabilistic terms, by applying probability distributions characterized by means and variances and possibly other parameters depending on the particular distributions employed. This data can then be used to drive a simple discrete-event simulation model. The model in turn can be used to experimentally determine

a good ordering policy. Figure 5.8 shows an approach to modeling this process as a discrete-event simulation model, using notation based on the SLAM modeling system. A structured simulation language, such as in SLAM, and its accompanying notation is an unambiguous visual representation of the problem, and can be used to generate and run the underlying computer code for the simulation without the need for the model developer to write computer code.

The simulation process begins by making assumptions about the key input variables, such as the probability distributions of duration times for all activities. Solving the discrete-event simulation model consists of (1) beginning the simulation by sampling the orders and shipments from their respective probability distributions to initialize the arrival events in the simulation; (2) moving the simulated time forward to

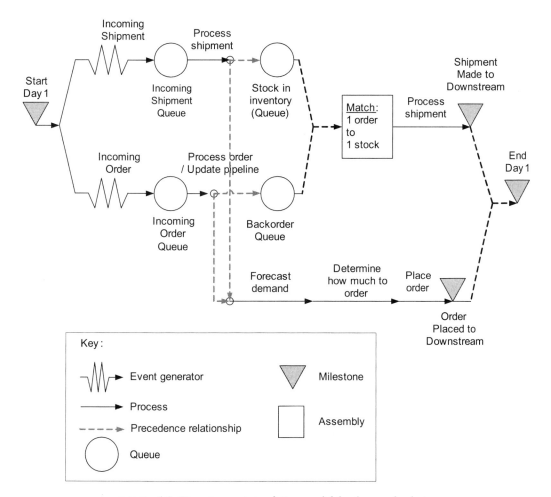

FIGURE 5.8 Discrete-event simulation model for the supply chain.

the first event and initiating an activity; (3) scheduling more events that result from the completion of activities initiated by previous events; and (4) stepping forward through time repeatedly for the series of events and activities that constitute the duration of the simulation.

The main results of running the model are shown in figures 5.9 and 5.10 for the first two days of the simulation. Normally, the simulation would be extended out over many days until a statistically significant sample of observations is collected. Sophisticated procedures exist for making this determination. Figure 5.9 shows the timeline of events and activities that are computed in the simulation. One important piece of new information that the simulation adds is how long incoming orders and incoming shipments have to wait before being processed. Note that the distributions for the waiting times were not input into the model; they are completely a result of the simulated activities within the model. These statistics can be used to answer the basic questions of "How long do backorders have to wait before they are met?" and "How long does stock have to wait in inventory before it is ordered?" These statistics are important to determine, as they affect the bottom line.

Figure 5.10 shows the variability in the inventory for the entire simulation period, in the form of stock, if positive, and backorders, if negative. These statistics can be used to determine inventory costs, the likelihood of having stock outages, and other undesirable situations. This information would be essential in setting meaningful levels of desired inventory. The simulation can also provide information on resource utilization. Finally, good simulation modeling practice would suggest the need to conduct sensitivity analyses around the most important parameters in the model, and to be able to answer such questions as "What would be the effect of decreasing processing times on inventory levels?"

It is easy to imagine extending the supply chain simulation example to cover all the stages and processes in the entire supply chain. The results would then be a systems model of the supply chain very similar in scope and content to the systems dynamics version described earlier. The important difference would be that by using the DES approach the model could capture the uncertainties in the underlying data, such as the customer demand and transit times, to the extent this was salient information for the decisions that the model was being used to support.

Using Discrete-Event Simulation

Simulation of any kind is basically a "what if" type of model. Each simulation run conditionally answers a question based on the assumptions that were made in formulating the simulation and the data used in the model. Change an assumption, and it changes the result. Simulation does not identify the "optimal" solution, as an optimization model does. Optimization is discussed in the following section. But simulation can be used to effectively explore a broad range of decision-makers' questions and the likely situations the organization can face.

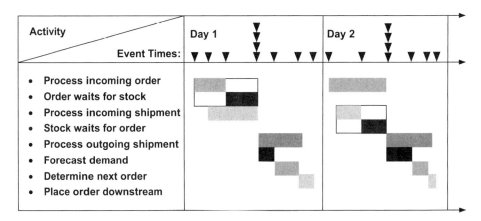

FIGURE 5.9 Supply chain discrete-event simulation results: event schedule.

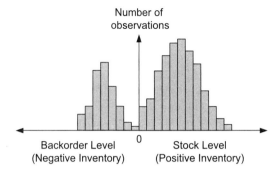

Number of observations

Backorder Level 0 Stock Level
(Negative Inventory) (Positive Inventory)

FIGURE 5.10 Supply chain discrete-event simulation results: inventory for distributor.

There are drawbacks to using discrete-event simulation, depending on the application:

- There is an emphasis on fixed sets of processes and relationships that are typically defined at the start of the simulation, rather than being generated within the simulation.
- Changes in system structure over time are not captured. Where do these processes and their interrelationships come from to begin with? A typical discrete-event simulation cannot be asked to identify the best set of processes for managing a supply chain.
- Complex processes with multiple levels of decision-making can be increasingly difficult to model with standard discrete-event approaches.

In summary, discrete-event simulation is most useful:

- When there is a need to simulate a complex process as it progresses through time.
- When the processes and the relationships between processes do not change over time, and are well understood and well defined.
- When important factors have a strong element of variability or uncertainty, and this variability can be represented by well-defined probability distributions.

Discrete-Event Simulation and Agent-Based Modeling

Agent-based simulation with its emphasis on modeling adaptive behavior and emergent systems properties is designed to address many of the drawbacks of traditional simulation. An important aspect of discrete-event simulation has to do with how events are generated within the simulation as it moves through time, and how these events are ordered or sequenced to occur in the future. This is called "event scheduling" and is usually handled by the "event scheduler" within a simulation. Scheduling is a complicated topic and similar problems arise in a variety of contexts in addition to simulation modeling, including scheduling computer jobs across a set of distributed processors and multi-agent systems in which robots must negotiate and schedule their activities. Agent-based simulation borrows from all of these fields to address the problem of modeling agent interactions, and in this regard is most similar to discrete-event simulation of all the traditional modeling approaches. Discrete-event simulation has an important role to play in agent-based simulation, as will be seen in the concluding section of this chapter.

The Participatory Simulation Approach

Participatory simulation is a noncomputerized approach to simulating the interactions between the components of a system and understanding the dynamics of system behavior. In participatory simulation, system components are usually composed of people or groups of people. Systems composed of a mixture of people and nonhuman physical or simulated components, such as those used in military planning simulations and virtual exercises, are common as well. By design, participatory simulations focus on the behaviors and interactions of the participants. Some have said that participatory simulation is a form of simulation that does not allow computers to get in the way!

Background

Participatory simulation has been around a long time, well before the days of computers, but it has not always been called this. In fact, some have made the point that Aristotle was the first simulation scientist, and an agent-simulation modeler, no less (Gable 2003)! Consider the following (Gable 2003):

> Aristotle devoted a treatise to simulations: what they are, how they differ from other products of the mind, and what the standards are for evaluating them. The treatise is the Poetics, Aristotle's analysis of how the human propensity to imitate what we observe can eventuate in complex symbolic

simulations (Aristotle 1973). The simulations Aristotle had in mind were ancient Greek dramas.

Plato, Aristotle's teacher, was a philosophical idealist, and tended to see simulations as merely imperfect images of reality and of no intrinsic interest. This attitude is one that I would guess some of you have encountered in one guise or another.

But Aristotle understood that simulations—properly performed—offer a unique way of gaining knowledge about the world. Or, as Aristotle put it: "The poet's function is to describe, not the thing that has happened [that is, empirical or historical data], but a kind of thing that might happen, i.e., to describe what is possible as being probable or necessary (Aristotle 1973)." That is why, he goes on to argue, a simulation such as a drama "is something more philosophical and of graver import than history, since its statements are of the nature of universals . . . . By a universal statement I mean one as to what such and such a kind of man [or agent!] will probably or necessarily say or do (Aristotle 1973)."

I could continue with this exercise of discussing Aristotle's reflections on drama (which are very much in a scientific spirit) and argue further that his reflections reveal that he understood drama as essentially a simulation, and that he believed simulations can yield a kind of knowledge that is available to us in no other way. But if you did not already accept the proposition, you probably would not be here.

The modern era of what has now become know as standard participatory simulations began in the mid-1960s. Since that time, participatory simulations have been developed in many fields, ranging from international relations to political science to business and government (Guetzkow et al. 1972). A good example of a recent participatory simulation is the automotive steel supply chain simulation (Holweg and Bicheno 2002).

Nearly everyone has been involved in a participatory simulation at some level of sophistication. Schools commonly use participatory simulation for classroom exercises. Commercial airlines and the military often use computer-assisted participatory simulations for tasks such as pilot training. Participatory simulation has come to be much more than role-playing or game-playing.

Participatory simulations must be carefully constructed to achieve their full potential as a realistic learning vehicle for the participants. Careful attention must be paid to what information the participants are allowed to have, how and when they are able to have it, and most importantly when and how the participants are able to interact. Participatory simulations can be highly structured to isolate a few key decision variables and situations to serve as an experimental laboratory for deriving explicit knowledge, or they can be more free form, depending on their intended purpose. One of the advantages of participatory simulation over computer simulation is the ability to transcend the need for mathematical, verbal, or symbolic representations of behavior. Participatory simulations include all the variables present, whether they are physical, environmental, cognitive, emotional, or social in nature. The non-programmed aspect of participatory simulation allows novel events and unanticipated situations to develop, often leading participants to respond in unexpected and creative ways.

A Participatory Simulation Example for the Supply Chain

The supply chain example for a participatory simulation is the original manual version of the Beer Game. Sterman developed the Beer Game and used it for pedagogical purposes to drive home the need for systems thinking when it comes to understanding the behavior of modern complex systems (Sterman 1992). Many other groups have also adopted the Beer Game as an in-class teaching tool. Here are the key aspects of the manual Beer Game. The participants are in teams of two for each stage in the supply chain, and sit across from each other to facilitate communication as shown in figure 5.11. The Beer Game is highly structured in terms of how the game is played, and who does what when, but not how they go about doing it. One of the challenges each team faces is to divide up the tasks they have to perform. The "rules of the game" enforce this structure. The main decision each team has to make is how much to order on a daily basis from the downstream stage or the downstream team. The information that the players have available to them for making this decision is highly constrained, and consists only of locally available information. Direct communication across levels in the supply chain is not allowed. In effect, teams communicate only by passing or receiving orders and shipments. This information is communicated in the form of

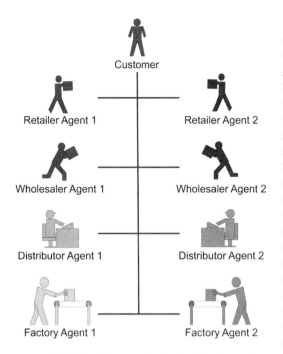

FIGURE 5.11 Participatory simulation for the supply chain.

sheets of paper that are passed between adjacent stages. Each team has as its goal minimizing its own long-run inventory costs, consisting of inventory holding charges if inventory is positive, and backorder charges if inventory is negative, as discussed in the previous examples in this chapter. The only variable that players have under their control to achieve this goal is how much to order each period from the next, upstream stage or team. At the factory level, the control variable is how much to place into production. As a general observation on the Beer Game, each stage's long-run inventory cost is minimized if the system as a whole exhibits steady and stable behavior in terms of inventory fluctuations over the long run. As a point of fact, it is a peculiarity of the Beer Game that costs are minimized for the system as a whole when each stage minimizes its own cost, but this is generally not the case for most systems. That is, minimizing the costs for each stage does not minimize the total cost for the system as a whole. This is one aspect of the Beer Game that is overly simplified to the point that it can lead to negative learning—learning about a side effect of the oversimplification process.

For each period the game is played, each team is free to determine its order in any way it can, based on its situation and the available information. Available information consists of the stage's inventory, how much it has ordered but not yet received (i.e., orders in the pipeline), and the incoming orders (i.e., demand) previously received from the downstream agent as shown in figure 5.12. Participants go through an initial rehearsal period for the game, in which they learn to go through the motions, to learn the rules of the game, establish the basic mechanics of the game (e.g., receiving orders, making shipments, etc.), and form relationships with their team partner, all without experiencing the added challenges of the game that follow in the next phase. A single event occurs to initiate the second phase of the Beer Game. Customer demand increases from the constant level of four items per period to a new level of eight items per period, and remains at that level for the remainder of the game. No other changes are imposed on the system after the time of the ramp-up in customer demand. From that point forward, the participants have to manage the supply chain and try to minimize the costs they incur over time. More often than not, they find this to be a daunting task, as inventories throughout the system fluctuate wildly and seemingly uncontrollably. Inventory fluctuations are amplified up the supply chain, with the factory receiving the largest impacts. This is the bull-whip effect, observed even in this simple game. In this regard, the Beer Game is a success in demonstrating realistic supply chain behavior.

The main result, and the most surprising finding of playing the Beer Game, is the observation that people have a great deal of difficulty meeting their inventory goals and managing the supply chain, even

- **Ordering rules**
- **Information used in the ordering rules**
- **Identification of situations for which the ordering rules apply**
- **Strategies for applying the ordering rule**
- **Additional information that one would like to have for basing the ordering decision**

FIGURE 5.12 Information from the participatory supply chain simulation.

in highly simplified situations in which the number of variables to consider is greatly reduced from what they would face in the real world. Sterman attributes this to the difficulty that people have in managing systems composed of many interacting parts. Most people are not good systems thinkers, and they cannot account for the second- and third-order effects of their decisions, as these decisions play themselves out up and down the supply chain.

Another important observation about the Beer Game, and one that is most germane for agent-based simulation, is that as participants play the game over time, they observe the successes and failures of their decisions and begin to develop structured ordering rules, which are rules of thumb for decision-making. The rules that are developed vary across the teams, with some rules being much better than others, but nonetheless the rules serve the same purpose. The rules provide a shorthand for the decisions that have to be made within an environment constrained by limited information and limited time and effort that can go into making decisions. These rules work well in an ever-increasing number of identifiable situations, as players gain experience, as they learn and adapt over time.

Using Participatory Simulation

Participatory simulation is very beneficial but also has several obvious limitations. Participatory simulations tend be limited to a small number of participants. The simulations are not scalable in the number of participants and in the number of time periods simulated. This is due in part to the increased difficulties of coordinating the participants' interactions as more individuals participate (e.g., the number of interactions grows according to n^2, where n is the number of participants). The practical limitations of having many people available to participate in the simulation for extended periods of time is another drawback. For these reasons, participatory simulations tend to be limited to shorter time horizons than the corresponding computerized versions. For example, the Beer Game is typically played for a period of several weeks, with one real-time day corresponding to a few simulated days. But as a computer simulation, a supply chain can be simulated for years on end in a virtual instant. Participatory simulation tends to set up an environment in which a small number of simpler behavioral rules are employed by the participants. And participatory simulation does not address the deeper question of "Where do observed behaviors come from?"

In summary, participatory simulation is most useful:

- As a teaching tool or for training to impart knowledge to the participants.
- To understand what behaviors people might exhibit and what strategies they might develop in response to specific situations.
- To understand how participants interact and posture in dealing with each other.
- When higher-level behavior rules that deal with a relatively small amount of information and situations are appropriate.

Participatory Simulation and Agent-Based Modeling

Agent-based simulation makes good use of the principles of standard participatory simulation but does it with a different emphasis, as a means to an end, not an end in itself. Agent-based simulation uses participatory simulation with the goal of identifying agent behaviors. Standard participatory simulation commonly focuses on macro-level behaviors rather than on micro-level interactions and is rarely used to derive micro-level rules. And agent-based simulation does this with an eye toward using this information to build agent models that include a rich set of agent behaviors, or at an even more fundamental level, as a basis for generating agent behaviors from more basic determinants.

The Optimization Approach

Optimization is a modeling technique that is applied in situations where the goal is to select the best solution from a set of well-defined alternatives. An optimization model consists of an objective that is to be maximized, such as profit, or minimized, such as cost, and a set of constraining factors that limit the objective from being achieved, such as limits on capacity, labor, and so on. The solution to such an optimization problem is usually far from obvious, even for a problem with a relatively small number of variables and constraints. Identifying a solution that is truly optimal, as opposed to a solution that is just "good enough," can significantly increase profits and reduce costs in many cases. This is the motivation for the optimization approach to modeling.

Background

Optimization is widely used as a modeling approach for business applications. Optimization has been around since the days of Isaac Newton, who invented the calculus and discovered that the minimum value taken on by a mathematical function could be found by setting the function's first-order derivative to zero and solving for the result. Given these humble beginnings, how did optimization come to be a very useful and widespread business modeling technique, critical to modeling people, processes, and organizations? Optimization came into its own as a useful business technique in the last sixty years because of two factors: the invention of digital computers, as with most of the other modeling and simulation techniques discussed in this chapter, and the development of specialized algorithms for solving optimization problems that have inequality constraints. As a practical matter, most useful optimization models include limits on resources, upper and lower bounds, and these limits are represented as inequality constraints. For example, if the amount of labor is limited in terms of total hours available, then one of the constraints in the optimization model should be an upper limit on available labor hours. To ensure that the optimization model gives plausible solutions, the modeler would also need to include the obvious fact that the use of labor cannot have a negative value by including another constraint specifying a lower bound of zero on the use of labor.

Although applications of inequality-constrained optimization problems to important practical problems had been formulated many years earlier, it remained to find an efficient method for solving such problems. In 1947, George Dantzig developed a practical way to solve such problems by developing the simplex method for solving linear programs. Linear programs are the most common type of constrained optimization problem in which the objective function and the constraints are linear in all of the variables. As the story goes, Dantzig was a young graduate student at Berkeley when, arriving late to class one day, he mistakenly assumed that the problem written on the blackboard was the day's homework assignment. Dantzig solved the problem that night and in the process invented the simplex method, only to find out later that the problem he had copied from the blackboard that day was in reality one of the "unsolvable" problems in all of applied mathematics (Dantzig 1982). Linear programming quickly found wide-scale application to a number of problems faced by industry, government, and the military with the growing needs of these sectors to operate and manage systems of ever-increasing complexity. Early applications of linear programming include blending materials in

the proper proportions, scheduling conflicting activities, and allocating scarce resources. More recently, just as computers have continued to become more powerful, major advances in methods of solving constrained optimization models have continued. Larger and larger problems are now possible to solve, and more complex problems are solvable in terms of their degree of nonlinearity. "Interior point methods" have made it practical to solve larger models, including millions of variables, and require much less in the way of computational resources to do so (Karmarkar 1984). In effect, with continuing advances in computers and algorithms, the optimization problem that is too large to solve today may be readily solved tomorrow.

Optimization modeling finds extensive application in specific industries, especially at the operational level. These include the airline industry, for solving aircraft and aircrew scheduling problems, the petroleum refining industry, for optimizing the product mix slate, and the commercial transportation industry for optimally routing and scheduling vehicle fleets. Several commercial firms specialize in developing optimization models for business (Nash 1998a, 1998b; Fourer 1999a, 1999b).

The notion of individuals and organizations as optimizers and the ability to represent the optimization problem as a rigorous mathematical statement is central to optimization modeling. The notion is one of the basic tenets of economics: all economic agents are rational agents who seek to make choices and decisions based on the criteria of optimizing their welfare, whether it be individuals maximizing utility or firms maximizing profits. This is a descriptive view of decision-making. It describes the goals that people have, but it also has implications for how they behave. It is a theory of what people actually do. The motivation for optimization also has another origin, that being that individuals and organizations should optimize, whether or not they already do. This is the normative view taken by the fields of operations research and management science. It is a prescription for what people and organizations should do.

The distinction between the normative and descriptive views of optimization is quite an important one, and is often confused and sometimes lost in the practical development and application of optimization models. This distinction also has great bearing on the development and application of agent-based models to business problems because it harks back to step one of the modeling process—answering the fundamental modeling question, "Why is the model being built?" The normative and descriptive views of modeling are continually interleaved in discussions of agent modeling, as will be seen.

An Optimization Model Example

This section considers an optimization model as applied to the supply chain. What would an optimization model applied to the supply chain look like? An optimization model must be well defined in the mathematical sense in terms of the objective or objectives to be maximized or minimized, the constraints that limit the choices, and the complex relationships among the various system components. An optimization model requires a rigorous mathematical representation of the problem. The following example eschews a rigorous mathematical definition for the optimization model, choosing instead to concentrate on its graphical representation and the information that the "optimal" solution provides.

Consider the following typical product mix problem in the supply chain for which an optimization model is the logical approach to obtaining the much-needed information. A factory produces two versions of a product, a standard version and a deluxe version. The deluxe version can command a higher price than the standard version (e.g., $50 for the standard version and $75 for the deluxe version), but the deluxe version costs more to produce. Each version requires a different mix of resources to produce it in terms of labor, measured in person-hours, and materials, measured in pounds. The standard version requires 2 pounds of material, compared to 1 pound for the deluxe version, and 0.5 hours of labor, compared to 2 hours for the labor-intensive deluxe version. Assume that labor is $10 per hour and materials are $10 per pound. The question is, how many standard versus deluxe items should be produced so as to maximize profits? This problem can be formulated as an optimization model, specifically a linear program, since all of the variables are continuous (i.e., each variable can take on any values in a range) and the relationships are linear (e.g., doubling production will use double the amount of labor and materials as well as doubling the cost of production). The problem can be represented graphically as shown in figure 5.13.

What does it mean to solve this optimization model? Optimization models are solved by applying a solution procedure, called an algorithm, which finds the optimal solution, if such a solution exists. The solution to the supply chain optimization example

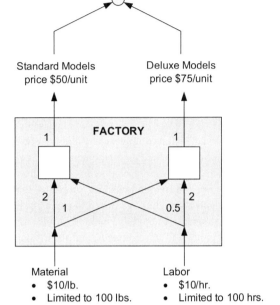

FIGURE 5.13 Optimization problem setup.

is illustrated graphically in figure 5.14. The optimal solution is to produce 28 units of the standard version and 42 units of the deluxe version. This combination of products maximizes profits at $1,642. No other combination of standard and deluxe versions that can be produced results in as much net profit. The shaded region in the figure is the feasible region that indicates all the combinations of labor and materials that are possible, although not necessarily optimal, within the set of constraints selected for the problem. Figure 5.14 also shows that only one of the feasible solutions is the best combination of labor and materials in terms of maximizing profit.

Solving optimization problems is not always so clear-cut as this example suggests. In some optimization problems, it is possible that more than one solution exists, each solution resulting in the same level of maximum profit. In this case, there is a choice of solutions that can be implemented in practice. If the optimization problem does not have linear relationships or if some of the problem variables can only take on discrete values, it is also possible that several solutions may exist and/or the solution algorithm may not be able to find a solution. In this case, each solution may be the best solution in a small area of the feasible region but at the same time may not be the best solution for the entire problem.

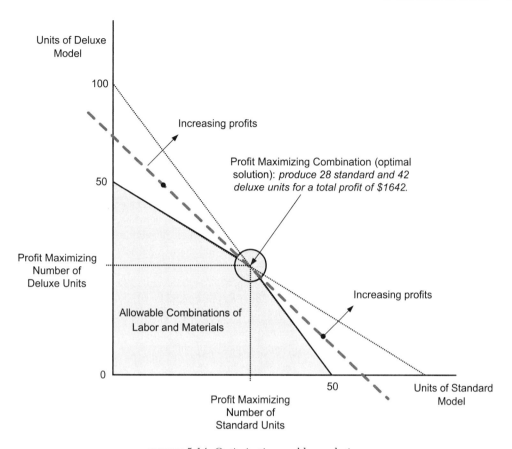

FIGURE 5.14 Optimization problem solution.

Using Optimization Models

Optimization models can be, and have been, applied at every level of a business, from the strategic to the operational (Carson and Maria 1997; Helbing 2003; Lee 2003). They could be used to find maximum profits for the supply chain as a whole, in terms of optimizing production schedules and product mix, or just as easily to find minimum cost schedules that balance a single assembly line for an agent in the supply chain. The supply chain optimization example suggests a broad range of possibilities for applications of optimization models to the supply chain. However, there may be additional questions about the optimization example, such as "How much would these parameter values have to change to appreciably affect the optimal production combination of standard and deluxe versions?" or "How much should be produced if maximizing profits was not the sole objective?" Optimization models can be used repeatedly with different assumptions on the parameter values to answer these kinds of questions.

Optimization models and solution methods go far beyond the linear programming model used in the supply chain example. Nonlinear programming goes beyond the requirements of linearity in the problem's objective function and constraints. Integer programming considers variables that are restricted to take on discrete values only, and 0–1 programming considers variables that are restricted to two values, zero or one, a useful technique for modeling problems in which variables are either true or false, such as in capital budgeting (e.g., do the project or not) and location planning (e.g., build the plant here or not). There is also a rich set of methods for including uncertainty regarding the values for the variables in optimization models, and there are specialized algorithms for solving problems with uncertainty. Optimization models that include uncertainty go by the name of programming under uncertainty, stochastic programming, and chance-constrained programming. Multiple-objective programming considers situations in which there are several competing objectives and provides optimal solutions considering the tradeoffs among the various objectives. Finally, goal programming considers the relative ranking of goals without the need to explicitly specify numerical values for the weights on the individual goals.

Optimization models provide valuable information when there is a need to find the best solution from a set of alternatives that are well defined in the rigorous mathematical sense. There can also be drawbacks to the application of optimization models as well. Drawbacks with traditional optimization modeling include the fact that it is often difficult to identify and quantify the objective to optimize. Do organizations and individuals really optimize? Herbert Simon, a famous Nobel Laureate who pioneered the field of artificial intelligence, developed the concept of "satisficing" to describe what he observed people and organizations doing in the real world (Simon 1955, 1969, 1979, 1982). Satisficing means that a decision-maker selects a satisfactory alternative when it presents itself, rather than selecting an "optimal" alternative from an exhaustive investigation into all possibilities. The decision-maker has aspiration levels that they try to attain and chooses the first alternative that satisfies acceptable levels. In effect, the decision-maker chooses the first alternative that meets the decision-maker's constraints. This compromise is due to the decision-maker's inability to encompass all the complexities of the situation, such as the inability to formulate the optimization problem or the lack of a method that can find the optimal solution such as the inability to solve the complex optimization problem. This view of decision-making has come to be known as "bounded rationality." The optimization approach of goal programming addresses the notion of satisficing by attempting to prioritize a decision-maker's goals based on their personal preferences and finding the solution that best meets the goals.

Quantifying the objective to be optimized can be difficult, especially for systems that extend beyond a single organization. Can everyone agree on what it means for the company to maximize profits? There are many examples of such systems in which a clearly defined objective is not obvious. Consider a complex manufacturing supply chain containing many firms. Each firm seeks to optimize its individual profits, potentially at the expense of the larger organization. Despite standard economic theory, neither maximizing combined total profits nor minimizing combined total costs for all of the firms may actually be reasonable objectives for such a system. In fact, there may be no system-level metric that is uniquely optimized for the organization as a whole.

Another drawback of standard optimization models is the brittleness of the model formulation. A change in one aspect of the model formulation, such as requiring that a variable take on integer values, can completely change the applicable solution algorithms. It is important to note that if the structure of an optimization model changes in terms of going from linear to nonlinear relationships, or going from continuous variables to discrete variables, then an entirely different solution algorithm is called for to find the optimal solution. In this regard, standard optimization algorithms are not "robust" in their application to the range of business problems that are often encountered.

Aside from the formulation, the optimal solution may also suffer from "brittleness." Optimization models commonly produce "church steeple" solution points that are highly optimized for one set of conditions, but are highly unstable when slight changes are made in the problem data. Perturbing the data or slightly changing the data can result in a new optimal solution that is very different from the original solution.

There can also be practical difficulties in implementing the model's optimal solution, that is, in doing what the model says to do. Necessary simplifications and assumptions that were made in constructing the model can result in a solution that is feasible in the modeled world, but infeasible in the real world! The overall approach may not be realistic, since few organizations or individuals really optimize. Some of these difficulties can be avoided with agent-based modeling.

In summary, optimization modeling is most useful when:

- There is a need to find the best solution from a set of mathematically well-defined alternatives.
- There is agreement on the objective function, and the objective function can be quantified.
- Brittleness of the model formulation and solution is not an important consideration.
- The data in the optimization problem and the structure of the problem is fairly static and not changing rapidly, at least not changing within the time that it takes to solve the optimization problem.

- There is a clear path within the organization for implementing the optimal solution.

Agent-Based Optimization Approaches

Recently, there have been some new developments in how optimization models are formulated, solved, and applied, coming from outside of the traditional optimization field. Examples include genetic algorithms, swarm optimization, and constraint programming. These techniques are motivated by an agent perspective—essentially optimization is done through the use of autonomous agents that operate on locally available information. Genetic algorithms (GAs) and swarm optimization (SO), which is also known as ant colony optimization, are motivated by biology—how living systems manage to survive, adapt, and thrive in an ever-changing environment. Constraint programming (CP) is motivated by developments in the field of artificial intelligence; it addresses the question of "How do autonomous entities search through a number of alternative courses of action to achieve a goal?"

GAs, invented by John Holland (Holland 1992), is a field that has motivated approaches to solving optimization problems. However, GAs as a field extend far beyond their use in solving optimization problems of the type discussed in this section. Genetic algorithms are motivated by the observation that living organisms can somehow adapt and optimize their situation, even if their environment is undergoing a process of radical disruption and change. How is this possible? The notion, adopted from genetics, is that living systems encode information in modular building blocks, and through a process of selective and chance assembly, substitution, alteration, and recombination, piece together new combinations of these building blocks. The result is a new organism having new characteristics and capabilities that allow it to better cope with its environment. The building blocks and how they are encoded is very general in algorithmic terms, so genetic algorithms can be as easily applied to solving a numerical optimization problem as they are to evolving an organism. In terms of numerical optimization, the building blocks can consist of the discrete parts of the feasible space as in traditional optimization.

Genetic algorithms are widely used in business and engineering applications for solving a host of problems including scheduling, engineering design, and virtually every type of optimization problem to which traditional optimization methods have been applied. GAs are an attractive alternative to standard optimization techniques, as they put few restrictions on the forms of the objective function and constraints for their application. The same basic solution algorithm can be applied to a wide range of problems and a good starting solution can be found very rapidly. It is a characteristic of GAs that an optimal solution is seldom obtained, only near-optimal solutions are typically found. This approach resonates with the notion of satisficing in which the search for an optimal solution is tempered by practical limits on time and effort. The notion of a genetic algorithm is a general one, and GAs can be used to solve not only numerical problems but also problems consisting of symbols.

There is another field known as genetic programming (GP), which generalizes the GA notion (Koza 1993). GP is a powerful technique with the potential to solve problems in qualitative reasoning, the kinds of problems that come up all the time in daily life. For this reason, GP is often used in artificial intelligence applications.

Swarm optimization (SO) is another recent optimization technique inspired by observation of living systems (Bonabeau et al. 1999). How is it that some living organisms with no recognizable capacity for intelligence can organize themselves, coordinate their actions, and perform complex tasks? How can they exhibit seemingly intelligent behavior? As a group, they are able to adapt and improve their behavior over time, even when their environment is undergoing rapid change. An ant colony with its ability to organize and perform complex tasks, such as nest building and food gathering, is the archetypal example of swarm intelligence. Swarm optimization is based on the idea that a system can be optimized, or at least attain performance levels that are "good enough," based entirely on successive refinement of the local interactions between the system's components. Communication among components is achieved through use of the environment as an intermediary in a process called "stigmergy." Stigmergy reduces the amount of information that needs to be exchanged between system components to manageable levels, and, in effect, makes the system "scalable"—able to increase in size with a concomitant increase in complexity of the component interactions. Swarm optimization techniques have been successfully applied to solving business optimization problems, such as vehicle routing and factory scheduling, as well as engineering design. The fact that the swarm optimization process relies on local interactions, rather than being directed by a central authority, means that SO algorithms are particularly well suited to real-time optimization of systems in dynamic, rapidly changing environments. This is similar to the observation that an ant nest can still continue functioning quite effectively even after losing a large portion of the ants in the nest. In abstract terms, the problem-solving strategy is distributed over the entire system; if part of the system is lost, the portion of the system that remains can recreate the problem-solving strategy of the original whole.

Constraint programming (CP) is another technique that allows a complex problem to be formulated with few restrictions on the form of the relationships or the variables in the problem (Schulte 2002; Apt 2003). Variables can be continuous, discrete, or even symbolic. Relationships can be nonlinear. In CP, an algorithm is applied repeatedly to find a solution that meets all of the problem constraints. Solutions are feasible but not necessarily optimal at each step. The algorithm continues finding more feasible solutions or feasible solutions that are better than those previously found. The algorithm continues until an optimal solution is found, or time and resources run out for continuing the search, similar to the situation with satisficing.

Optimization and Agents

Agent-based simulation can make good use of the principles of optimization in the representation of agents behaviors. Optimization is useful when the theory for agent behavior is that of optimization, for example, because it is reasonable to assume that the agents could come reasonably close to solving their actual optimization problem rather than merely satisficing. If the agent's problem is simple enough, the use of optimization problems for representing agent behavior is a reasonable approach.

Another application of optimization applied to agent behavior is for comparison purposes—comparison to an ideal agent that optimizes behavior. If the theory of agent behavior is that an agent optimizes, for example, maximizes profits, then there is a single model of agent behavior. If the theory of agent behavior is one of satisficing, however, there are many plausible models of behavior. Which model of satisficing behavior is the closest to describing what the agent actually does? That is, there may be several competing theories of agent behavior and there may be a need to compare each of them to the ideal case in which the agents behave as if they were behaving optimally.

The Statistical Modeling Approach

Statistical modeling is an approach that focuses on how the outputs of a system depend on its inputs. The system is modeled as a "black box," with no visibility on its internal structure, the processes responsible for its observed behavior, or any other details. As defined here, statistical modeling refers to using a statistical representation as the complete model, rather than using statistics as a tool to support larger models in which it is embedded or directly for decision-making without an intervening model.

Background

The use of statistical methods in decision analysis has become an important technique in the solution of business problems since the late 1950s. Statistical modeling has its business roots in applications ranging from quality control to process engineering, statistical decision-making, and economic forecasting (McClave and Benson 1994). Regression analysis, response surface methodology, and other types of statistical modeling are widely used in business, often in conjunction with some form of simulation.

A Statistical Model Example

A statistical model consists of a set of independent variables, a set of dependent variables, and an explicit relationship that states how the dependent variables depend on the independent variables. What might a useful statistical model look like in the context of the supply chain example? Suppose there is an interest in how profits vary as a result of ordering decisions made by an agent. This information could be used to develop better ordering rules that make the best use of the information available at any point in time, rules of the type that the players in the participatory simulation of the last section arrived at by trial and error and through experience. The dependent variable in the supply chain example is profit. To keep the example simple, the independent variables are orders placed by the distributor and the recent orders received from downstream. The independent variables may be appropriately lagged over time to allow for the time delays involved in ordering and receiving shipments.

To make the example more interesting, consider the perspective of a new distributor entering the market for the first time. Having no experience working as a distributor in the industry, there is a need to develop an effective ordering rule. Further, suppose there are several distributors already in the industry, all with fairly similar characteristics, varying only by how they go about making their ordering decisions. Suppose data are available for all the distributors on the variables of interest over an extended period of time, and the data cover a wide range of cases and situations, that is, a wide range of values for the independent variables. The formulation of the statistical model consists of first selecting the form of the model relationship (e.g., linear, nonlinear) expected to best relate the independent variables to the dependent variables. The formulation also includes the model parameters, the values of which need to be estimated from the data in a way that provides the best fit of the modeled relationship to the data. "Solving" the statistical model means applying an algorithm that finds the parameters for the specified functional relationship that results in the "best fit" to the data. The end result is the relationship between profits and the key independent variables. Continuing with the example, using standard statistical methods, a statistical relationship can be derived between recent observations for the points consisting of orders, recent demand, and profits. The solution to the supply chain statistical model is a surface as illustrated in figure 5.15. The figure shows the orders that maximize profits given any level of recent demand that may be encountered.

Using Statistical Models

It is easy to imagine expanding the simple statistical model to make it more elaborate. The resulting model could be used to determine how profits depend on orders, which in turn depend on other variables such as inventories. In fact, this is exactly what economic forecasting models of specific industries do in estimating the future growth of the industry based on a few key parameters.

Statistical modeling has some drawbacks. The data for the statistical model is the complete basis for the model. Whether the data are historical or empirical, deriving valid relationships between outputs and inputs depends critically on the availability and credibility of that data. The solution to the statistical model is a fixed relationship that reflects a process

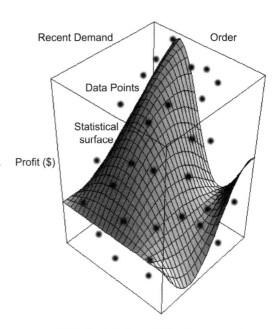

FIGURE 5.15 Statistical model for the supply chain.

frozen in time. If, in the future, some of the processes or the relationships among the components of the system change, the relationships between inputs and outputs also change, but the statistical model does not capture this. The model must then be re-estimated from new data that properly reflects the new situation. It would be wise to ask additional questions about the statistical model, such as "How long will the derived relationships be valid?" and "Has something that is likely to occur in the future not been captured in the underlying data set?"

Statistical models indicate correlations between or among variables without providing any indication as to why the derived relationships exist or where they came from. Statistical models rarely identify causal relationships, and can only indicate that one variable appears to change in relation to one or more other variables. These models can also require substantial simplifications or simplifying assumptions to coerce the data into a form amenable to analysis and estimation of the parameters for the hypothesized form of the relationship.

The most important drawbacks to statistical modeling when it comes to their use in supporting decision-making are the following:

- The derived statistical relationships are brittle. Changes in system structure over time are not captured.

- The models are not sensitive to many assumptions or amenable to "what if" scenarios.
- Statistical models rarely provide insight into why things happen.
- Statistical models lack the capability for spatial representation. Statistical models are specified over a set of key important factors, and this may include time, but including a spatial representation is not a standard part of the statistical modeling.

These observations imply that statistical modeling should not be used when the following occurs:

- The process being modeled is new or has novel elements that could not possibly be reflected in the data. In other words, even if all the data on the system were readily available, the data would simply not reveal information about the underlying processes that will govern the behavior of the system in the future.
- The process being modeled is rapidly changing.
- The data are not available to support the estimation of a statistically valid model using the standard tests for such models.

By the reverse logic, use statistical modeling when:

- Little is known or can be known about the internal workings of the process.
- Data are readily available relating system outputs to inputs.
- The relationships of a small number of outputs are to be related to the system inputs.
- There is reason to believe the historical process indicates something about how the process will behave in the future.
- The process does not change very quickly, at least not relative to the time frame for which the information from the model will be used.

Statistical modeling, by virtue of its view of the system as a black box, is a top-down approach. In many ways, ABMS, with its philosophy of building a model from the bottom up, is the antithesis of statistical modeling. Not only are details of the processes and the agent interactions of the system the central focus, how these processes change and how agents adapt are the main motivations for ABMS. Nonetheless, statistical modeling can have an important role to play in agent-based modeling, as will be seen in the last section of this chapter.

The Risk Analysis Approach

Risk analysis is a commonly used modeling technique in business applications to assess the exposure of firms to events that adversely affect the value of the firm. Fundamentally, risk analysis consists of identifying the drivers of risk that are specific to the organization. Risk analysis, as traditionally done, is a two-step process: identify the likelihoods of detrimental events, and translate the events into quantifiable impacts. Similarly to other modeling approaches, risk analysis can be applied to a specific aspect of a firm's operation or to the system as a whole. Risk analysis is often the only modeling technique that a business uses, as risk directly affects the bottom line and the very survival of the business.

Background

Risk analysis, as traditionally conducted, relies largely on the practical application of probability and statistics. Often there is limited information on the likelihood of the events under consideration, and various decision analysis techniques, such as decision-making under uncertainty, are employed to quantify the situation when data are scarce. Related techniques include value at risk (VaR), operational risk (OpRisk), and extreme value theory (EVT).

Value at risk tries to answer the question of how much value a firm can lose due to normal market movements for a particular time horizon and for a given confidence level. VaR concentrates on financial price risk, often of a financial portfolio, and ignores credit, operational, legal, and other risks to the firm. There are several quantitative techniques for calculating VaR, including variance/covariance, Monte Carlo simulation, and historical simulation, but they all rely on the availability of a good deal of historical market data and applicable statistical techniques. Operational risk, applied widely in the financial industry, has many definitions, but a good working definition is the "risk of direct or indirect loss resulting from inadequate or failed internal processes, people and systems, or from external events" (Harmantzis 2003). OpRisk is the risk associated with everything other than market risk and credit risk, which by comparison are well understood and routinely quantified components of risk. EVT concerns itself with statistical techniques for fitting the tails of probability distributions characterizing extremely rare events. The use of EVT can be a supplement to estimating VaR or OpRisk.

A Risk Analysis Example for the Supply Chain

How can risk analysis be applied to the supply chain example? It was shown earlier that the inventory levels in the supply chain could be subject to wide variations depending on customer demand, whether various agents in the chain are able to meet orders, and other factors. The uncertainty stemming from inventory levels creates risk for the supply chain agents. A natural application of risk analysis to the supply chain example is to quantify the risk arising from inventory volatility. Consider the problem from the viewpoint of one of the retailers.

Solving the Risk Analysis Model

How would the retailer quantify the risk of having capital tied up in inventory? First, the retailer identifies the likelihood of various levels of customer demand, possibly based on historical data and judgmental factors. For each demand scenario, the retailer calculates the long-run inventory taking into account the ability of the wholesalers to meet the retailer's orders in each case. The result is a probability distribution of inventory for the retailer, taking into account all of these factors as shown in figure 5.16a. Next, the retailer estimates the cost of the inventory for various inventory levels as shown in figure 5.16b. If the inventory consists of perishable goods, the retailer includes the inventory holding charge, which increases on a per unit basis as more inventory space is required, and considers the probability that the goods will lose value the longer they sit in inventory. Combining this information in a quantifiable risk analysis framework results in an estimate of risk for the retailer—the likelihood that various levels of capital will be tied up in inventory given the uncertainty in all of the market and operational factors. Figure 5.16c illustrates the result that there is a 10% chance that more than $1 million of the retailer's total assets will be tied up in inventory.

Using the Risk Analysis Model

Risk analysis, as illustrated by the supply chain example, has the advantage of simplicity. It is a transparent framework, in which the main assumptions are made explicit. Risk analysis can apply to the business as a whole, or can be built up from separate risk analyses of business units. When applied broadly across the business enterprise, it can provide a quick idea of where risk

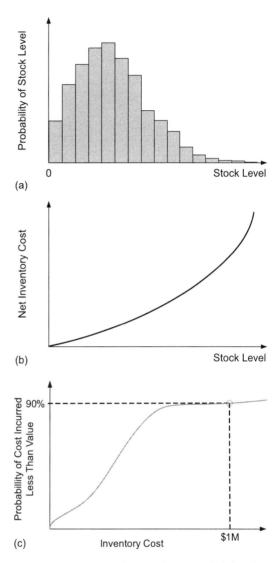

FIGURE 5.16 Risk analysis results: (a) probability distribution of inventory for the retailer; (b) inventory cost estimates; (c) probability that less than $1 million will be tied up in inventory.

is inherent in the firm's operations and the degree to which the firm's assets are at risk.

As with all modeling techniques, there are drawbacks to risk analysis. The main drawback is the difficulty of obtaining credible data. Risk models require the estimation of probabilities and likelihoods for events that may never have occurred or may never actually occur, which makes them difficult to validate. Risk models are necessarily focused on exposing the worst possible outcomes, rather than on discovering the future actions the firm can take. Risk models do not account for complex, nonlinear behavior outside the model user's typical thinking.

Risk Analysis and Agents

Recently, risk analysis has been extended beyond its traditional focus on the individual firm to consider entire industries. Recent disasters, such as the devastation brought by Hurricane Andrew and the September 11 attack and its effect on capital markets throughout the world, have highlighted the interdependencies of the global economy and the need to consider the ripple effects of events as they cascade throughout an industry. Unlike the statistical approach to quantifying and describing risk used by the risk analysis techniques mentioned above, newer risk analysis modeling approaches have sought to identify the underlying causal factors that are the determinants of risk and to explicitly model how risk is propagated through the system as a whole. Both the direct as well as the indirect consequences of risk are considered. The modeling approach taken has been to consider the entire industry as a closely interconnected system and to model the companies within the industry as individual agents (Melymuka 2002).

The risk analysis example applied to the supply chain illustrates the traditional approach to risk analysis, which is based on estimating probability distributions for key factors, such as inventory levels. Another approach to modeling the constituent factors of risk is to model them as part of a system-wide model. In the supply chain model, an alternative way to compute the risk due to inventory would be to use the entire supply chain model to directly calculate the inventory levels. Specifically, one could run the model for various demand scenarios and assumptions about order policies adopted by the agents throughout the supply chain. This would be another way to estimate the distributions of retailer inventory that were only statistically or judgmentally estimated in the example.

Insurance World is another example of a system-wide approach to modeling risk (Jones and Casti 2000). Insurance World is a model of the reinsurance industry or the organizations that provide insurance to insurance companies. All of the companies involved in insurance and reinsurance are included in the model as separate entities with distinct behaviors. The relationships among the agents as companies are also modeled. Simple but sophisticated models are included for each of the agents. The agent models focus on the most important information relative to risk as generated by the agents within the firm. The agent approach allows the model to incorporate different aspects of individual companies, including customer loyalty, pricing strategy, and the degree to which such risks as litigation, product liability, changing regulatory policies, and changing demographics differ among individual firms. The ability to model the diverse behaviors of the agents allows for a rich set of future possible scenarios to be created by the model, many of which are beyond what is possible to predict otherwise.

The Agent-Based Modeling and Simulation Approach

Unlike the other modeling approaches discussed in this chapter, the primary focus of agent-based modeling and simulation is the agent—a discrete entity, having its own individual characteristics and behaviors. The primary characteristic of an agent is that of autonomous behavior. An agent has goals and is able to take independent actions that allow it to strive toward the attainment of those goals. ABMS has strong roots in the fields of multi-agent systems (MAS), artificial intelligence (AI), and robotics. But ABMS is not only tied to designing and understanding "artificial" agents. It also has roots in modeling actual human behavior and individual decision-making. With this comes the need to represent social interaction, collaboration, and group behavior (Gilbert and Troitzsch 1999). The agent perspective allows one to come at the modeling problem from the standpoint of the individuals who comprise the system, considering their individual decision-making behaviors and rules. This will be illustrated in the application of ABMS to the supply chain model.

An Agent-Based Supply Chain Model

Supply chains readily lend themselves to being modeled as agent-based models. In the agent approach, agents are the "decision-making members" of the supply chain. Whether that means the agents are the individuals, the organizations, or the decision-making processes themselves, depends on the precise perspective one wants to take in modeling the actual system.

The world of a supply chain agent consists of interacting with other supply chain agents (e.g., receiving shipments from upstream agents and receiving orders from downstream agents) and then making decisions (e.g., deciding how much to order from the upstream and how much to ship to the downstream) as shown in figure 5.17. As a basis for these decisions, each agent has a notion of what tomorrow's demand will be and has to decide on how to forecast this demand. Agents have decision rules that they use to answer these questions. Where these decision rules come from, whether they are generated by the agents themselves over time, perhaps by trial and error, or whether they are taken as given, perhaps inherited from previous occupants of the supply chain agent role, is an important concern of the field of ABMS as a whole, but somewhat outside the scope of the current discussion. In the broader perspective of the agent, the agent needs to decide how to organize these rules into a workable "business process."

To illustrate the nature of agent simulation and to add realism to the Beer Game simulation, the standard linear supply chain model was extended to a more complex supply network. The "Network Beer Game Simulation" (NBGS) (Macal 2003a) consists of the five stages considered in the original Beer Game simulation but with the additional feature that the agents are connected in a dense network configuration as shown in figure 5.18. Each agent is connected to all upstream agents, excluding factory agents that do not have an upstream, and to all downstream agents, excluding customer agents that do not have a downstream. The agent-based modeling approach easily extends the supply chain model to this more realistic supply network structure. All that is required is to add more relationships to the agent model, each relationship corresponding to a link in the supply network.

There are several factors to consider in modeling supply chain agents and their decision processes and behaviors. These factors include (1) the sophistication of the agents' decision models, (2) the extent of the information currently available that is considered in making decisions, (3) the amount of information recalled from previous decisions, and (4) whether agents have internal models of how the supply chain works in the large, which could include, for example, models of other agents' decision processes that could be used for strategic planning purposes. Agents must make decisions within a limited amount of time and available resources and so must use heuristics or best guesses to process information and make decisions. The sophistication of the decision rules employed by the agents, in terms of processing load and memory requirements, may vary by agent. In addition, supply chain agents are necessarily social agents.

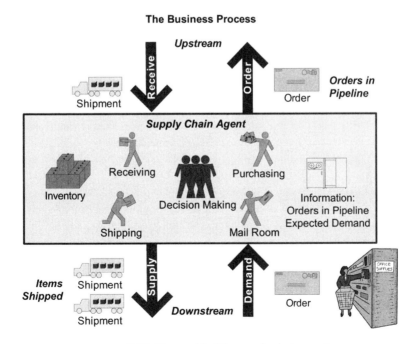

FIGURE 5.17 The world of the supply chain agent.

Time : 70

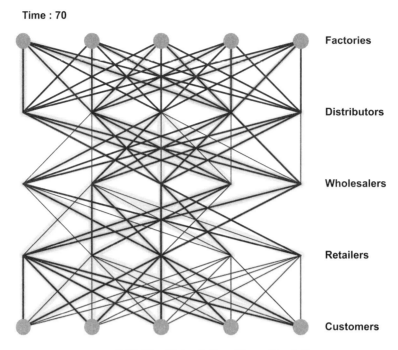

FIGURE 5.18 The Network Beer Game Simulation.

They seek sources for their supply from other supply chain agents, they seek outlets for their products, and they negotiate on pricing, delivery, and information sharing as well as other dimensions of interaction and exchange. The ABMS perspective allows one to capture the full range of the agents' environment and behaviors.

As shown in figure 5.19, in the supply chain model each agent carries the following minimal set of information:

- Inventory level and desired inventory.
- Orders in the pipeline and the desired level of orders in the pipeline.
- Current demand, coming from downstream agents.
- Expected demand or the demand forecast from downstream agent for the next period.

Agents also remember their previous decisions and the previous demand forecasts they made for the current period. This allows them to compare and adjust their demand forecasts.

Additional agent decision rules are needed for the network version of the supply chain simulation to account for additional decisions that have to be made in going from a chain to a network. For example, not only does the upstream agent have to decide on how much to supply in total to all downstream agents, but now also has to decide on the share of its supply or shipments that should be made to the various downstream agents. Agents now have a supply allocation rule, which answers the question of "Which downstream agents should get priority in filling backorders?," and an order allocation rule, which answers the question of "Which upstream agent or agents should receive my order?"

FIGURE 5.19 Supply chain agent representation.

Several alternatives rules could be considered concerning supplies and orders. For example, supplies could be allocated on the basis of supplying the downstream agents having the smallest backorder first, with the idea of satisfying the most customers. Alternatively, supplies could be allocated on the basis of supplying the downstream agents having the largest backorder first, with the idea that the customers who have been waiting the longest should be served first. The agent-based modeling approach allows for explicit testing of a variety of alternative rules. Taking the ABMS perspective, moving from the supply chain to the supply network means focusing first and foremost on expanding the rules of agent behavior to make them coincide with what agents would be expected to do in a real supply network.

As in the supply chain model that was introduced earlier in this chapter, network supply chain agents access only locally available information for making decisions. Information on orders (i.e., demand) and shipments (i.e., receipts) is obtained only as the result of interactions with other agents. In the agent-based network version of the supply chain model, the assumption of local information is relaxed to allow investigations into the value to an agent of having more than locally available information. Would it be helpful for an agent to know what the demand for its

product will be in two or three periods? After all, this information already exists in the supply chain in terms of orders already placed and in transit between agents. Would knowing this additional information allow agents to make better decisions—to better manage inventory and reduce costs? To answer this question, the modeler can simply allow the agents to access information at numerous points in the supply network and include this additional information in their ordering, forecasting, and shipping decisions as shown in figure 5.20. The modeler can then systematically vary the amount of information available to the agents, first allowing agents to "see" demand one period ahead, then two periods, three periods, and so on, as the orders work their way upstream. To study the benefits of the additional information, the modeler simply includes more references to the additional information within the agent models. To make the exercise more realistic, the model can also include costs associated with acquiring information. For example, information costs can be directly proportional to the amount of information acquired. Nonlinear information cost policies are also possible.

Results from a linear information cost simulation run are shown in figure 5.21. As can be seen from the figure, initially, more information results in lower costs, as agents are better able to anticipate incoming

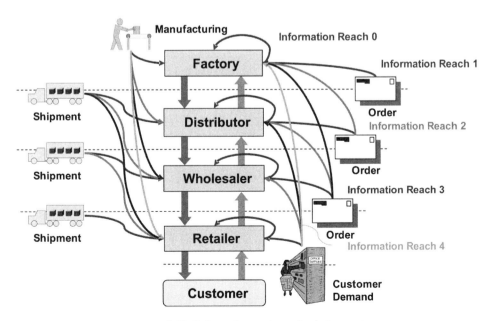

FIGURE 5.20 Information and supply chain agents.

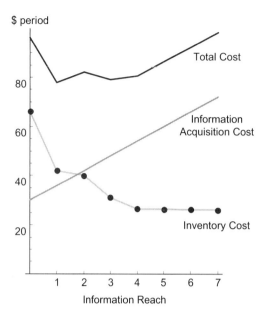

FIGURE 5.21 Results of information simulation experiments.

orders and shipments in the future and adjust their ordering and shipment strategies accordingly. In effect, more information allows the agents to mitigate the cyclic boom and bust patterns observed when only local information is available. However, more information has its benefits only up to a point. Information is costly to obtain, and eventually the additional benefits in terms of cost reduction are mitigated. In effect, the marginal value of information becomes negligible as more and more information is available.

Using Agent-Based Models

Agent-based modeling and simulation is widely used to understand systems composed of many interacting individuals. One way to think of it is that ABMS applies the concept of a wave in a crowd to allow business leaders to use their knowledge of consumers, employees, and business processes to discover strategic solutions for their enterprises. Consumer markets are an example. The need is to quantify the complex effects that corporate choices have on market outcomes. The agents are heterogeneous consumers and companies. Electric power markets are another example. The need is to assess possible outcomes of deregulated power markets. The agents include power generation companies, consumers, demand brokers, and others. Industrial supply chains are a good

example, as has previously been discussed. The need is to locate the synergies hidden in complex systems of autonomous decision-making units. The healthcare industry is yet another example. The need is to develop comprehensive and detailed assessments of the demands on healthcare providers. The agents are patients, doctors, and healthcare units. For modeling financial markets as consisting of interacting agents, the need is to estimate prices and price volatility under future scenarios concerning agent strategies and actions. The agents are traders. Another example is that of ecosystems. The need is to quantify how the individual members and species within an ecosystem contribute to the overall health of the system. The agents are individuals, species, hives, flocks, and other groups.

The most important benefit of agent-based modeling is the agent perspective that it takes. Agent modeling does not begin with the black-box approach as in statistical modeling—details and causal factors are important in agent modeling. Agent modeling does not begin at the process level, as in discrete-event simulation. Nor does agent modeling begin at the whole-system level, in which the approach is to aggregate system variables as in systems dynamics models. Agent-based modeling begins at the level of the decision-making individual or organization and builds upward from there. It may be straightforward to describe and model what everyone does in a group, but impossible to predict in advance what the behavior of the system will be. That is what agent modeling does: ABMS takes the agents and their interactions at whatever level of complexity is appropriate and puts them into a computational framework. The computer does what it does best—runs through the many thousands of agent interactions, building up the complexity of the whole from the ground up.

What is the attractiveness of agent modeling? Anecdotally, people are able to relate to the notion of agents in ways that go beyond how they are able to relate to other types of models. People can easily take on the roles of agents and hypothesize from afar on how they would behave in those roles. For example, it is much easier for people to imagine how they would go about running a distribution center if they were put in charge of one, than it is to design a distribution center in which they do not see themselves as a participant. This is a matter of perspective. People can put themselves quite naturally into the role of an agent, whether the agent is an individual or an organization, whatever role that agent might have.

In this respect, agent modeling can draw people into it as no other modeling technique can.

When should ABMS be used? An agent-based model shows how a system could evolve through time in ways that are often difficult to predict from knowledge of the behaviors of the individual agents alone. Use ABMS when there is a need to understand system behavior that results from the complex interactions of individuals. Use ABMS to explore the formation of structure. An ABMS discovers structures at the system or macro-level that are not directly included within the agents' programmed behaviors. Complex interdependencies among agents can generate nonlinear, counterintuitive, and unpredictable system behaviors. Feedback loops can amplify small variations and disturbances. Agents can also incorporate or discover substantial learning and adaptation capabilities.

One of the advantages of ABMS is that it allows an explicit representation of space and spatial relations. Agent models often incorporate agents that move in space as with cellular automata. Spatial modeling of agents is not restricted to the two-dimensional grid as in cellular automata. Networks and more general spatial structures that specify which agents can interact with other agents are also easily modeled in ABMS architectures.

ABMS models provide a testing platform to see what possible system and agent configurations might evolve as a result of the rules employed. The models can show how the repeated application of diverse individual processes results in both system-level and individual-level outcomes, providing a link between the micro- and macro-behaviors of the system.

When to Use Agents?

When are agent-based models appropriate to use? Apply agent-based modeling:

- When the problem has a natural representation as consisting of interacting agents.
- When there are decisions and behaviors that can be defined discretely, that is, with well-defined boundaries.
- When it is important that agents adapt and change their behavior.
- When it is important that agents learn and engage in dynamic strategic behavior.
- When it is important that agents have dynamic relationships with other agents, and agent relationships form and dissolve.

- When it is important that agents form organizations, and adaptation and learning are important at the organization level.
- When it is important that agents have a spatial component to their behaviors and interactions.
- When the past may be a poor predictor of the future.
- When scaling up is important, and scaling up consists of adding more agents and agent interactions.
- When process structural change needs to be a result of the model, rather than an input to the model.

Blended Modeling Approaches

All of the modeling approaches discussed in this chapter were originally developed to address specific types of problems: optimization for finding the best solution, discrete-event simulation for understanding the effects of uncertainty in a process, systems dynamics for understanding system interconnectedness, and so on. Experience has shown that each modeling approach is the "best" approach for the specific purpose for which it was originally intended and may also be very effective for closely related problems as well. But no single modeling approach can be said to be the best approach for addressing all types of problems. There is no "generic" modeling technique.

In developing a complex model for a given situation, it often is useful to combine one or more modeling approaches, employing each technique for that part of the model where it makes the most sense to do so, considering the unique capabilities and recognizing the limitations of each modeling approach. Agent modeling is a process and it borrows much from traditional modeling. The converse is not necessarily true, however. In this sense, agent-based modeling can be thought of as a more general, or more inclusive, modeling approach than traditional modeling techniques. Borrowing from other approaches, ABMS offers a full, end-to-end, package for how to go about building, applying, and analyzing models and results. This section shows how an agent-based modeling framework can combine several modeling techniques for maximally effective modeling. Agent-based modeling can either provide an overarching framework for model components based on other modeling techniques, or it can provide agent models that are embedded into larger systems. Using agent-based models in combination with other techniques is an approach that can be called model blending, and is the topic of this section. Consider several common situations where it might be desirable to combine ABMS with other modeling techniques:

ABMS and systems dynamics: Systems dynamics is extremely useful for identifying the important variables and causal linkages in a system and for structuring many aspects of model development. Many ABMS modeling projects can benefit greatly by beginning with a systematic identification and analysis of the important variables in the system and their causal relationships.

ABMS and discrete-event simulation: Discrete-event simulation offers methods for taking a process view of the system. To the extent that agents are engaged in processes and move through a system, for example, the steps of the process that a consumer engages in when moving through a store, DES techniques can be usefully employed in developing an agent model.

ABMS and participatory simulation: Participatory simulations are extremely useful activities to engage in as a prelude to developing an agent model, especially when the agents are people. How much information are people able to process in the given amount of time for making decisions? What key factors and indicators do people consider in making their decisions? How do people's past experiences enter into their decision-making process? Which strategies do people employ that are most effective? Participatory simulations are extremely helpful for discovering realistic agent rules, behaviors, and strategies.

ABMS and statistical models: Often, it is not realistic to develop a comprehensive agent model in which all the causal factors and relationships leading to an agent's decisions can be fully specified. The alternative is to use statistics for estimating behavioral decision rules for agents. These are essentially simple "thin" agent models relating situations the agents find themselves in to their decisions and actions. It is also possible to go the other way—from the complex or "thick" agent models to simpler statistical relationships between just a few of the key variables that govern most of the agent behaviors. Sophisticated statistical techniques such as principal component analysis can be used for this purpose.

ABMS and risk analysis: In traditional risk analysis, there is little apparent connection to agent-based modeling. However, as considered in the risk analysis discussion, sometimes risk is a property of a system as a whole, an "emergent" property. Then a comprehensive, system-wide assessment of the causal factors that lead to risk throughout the system needs to be addressed. In this case, agent-based modeling is a natural approach to representing the diverse characteristics and decision-making behaviors of companies or individuals that comprise the system or industry.

ABMS and optimization: As has been shown, optimization is a technique designed to model optimal individual and organizational decision-making. It has also been shown how agent-based modeling can be used in conjunction with agents that optimize on an individual basis, or how the agents can be collectively used to search for optimal system states.

Summary

This chapter set the stage for the practical application of agent-based modeling and simulation and created the context for agent-based modeling by answering the question, "Why does business engage in modeling and simulation?" This question is answered in the broader context for modeling beginning with systems analysis, then the need for modeling and simulation in general, and finally by taking a close look at the traditional types of modeling approaches that have been widely used in practical business applications. This chapter focused on the most widespread modeling techniques in use today in terms of their intended purposes, their capabilities, the kinds of applications for they are most appropriate, and the limitations or drawbacks in their application. This discussion created a context for agent-based simulation, emphasizing the unique capabilities of ABMS and the "value added" from its application and use. This chapter described agent-based modeling within the same framework as the other modeling approaches, comparing and contrasting the capabilities of ABMS. This chapter then proposed a new approach to modeling systems, called blended modeling, which provides a framework for ABMS to be most effectively applied and used together with the traditional modeling approaches.

In conclusion, agent-based modeling represents a new frontier in combining novel and traditional modeling approaches in ways that have not previously been possible. ABMS offers the possibility of providing new and better information on complex business systems and the impacts of decision-makers' strategies and actions than ever before, because more realistic representations of agents, agent behaviors, and interactions are now becoming possible. The current state of affairs also presents new challenges in terms of combining the different modeling approaches, but most importantly in demonstrating that the information obtained from such combinations truly represents "value added" to business decision-making.

Note

1. According to the *Algorithms and Theory of Computation Handbook*, a Monte Carlo algorithm "is a randomized algorithm that may produce incorrect results, but with bounded error probability" (CRC Press 2000). In contrast, according to the *Handbook*, a Las Vegas algorithm "is a randomized algorithm that always produces correct results, with the only variation from one run to another being its running time" (CRC Press 2000). An Atlantic City algorithm combines these features by having both the possibility of inaccurate results and variable runtime.

References

Ahn, H. J., H. Lee, and S. J. Park et al. (2003). A Flexible Agent System for Change Adaptation in Supply Chains. *Expert Systems with Applications* **25**(4): 603–618.

Apt, K. (2003). *Principles of Constraint Programming.* Cambridge, U.K.: Cambridge University Press.

Aristotle (1973). Poetics. In *Introduction to Aristotle*, trans. Ingram Bywater. Chicago: University of Chicago Press.

Bonabeau, E., M. Dorigo, and G. Theraulaz (1999). *Swarm Intelligence: From Natural to Artificial Systems.* Oxford: Oxford University Press.

Brugali, D., G. Menga, and S. Galarraga (1998). Inter-Company Supply Chain Integration via Mobile Agents. In G. Jacucci (Ed.), *Globalization of Manufacturing in the Digital Communications Era of the 21st Century: Innovation, Agility and the Virtual Enterprise.* Norwalk, Mass.: Kluwer, pp. 43-54.

Carson, Y. and A. Maria (1997). Simulation Optimization: Methods and Applications. *Proceeding of the 1997 Winter Simulation Conference.* Piscataway, N.J.: Institute of Electrical and Electronic Engineers.

Checkland, P. B. (1981). *Systems Thinking, Systems Practice.* Chichester, U.K.: Wiley.

Chen, F., Z. Drezner, J. K. Ryan, and D. Simchi-Levi (2000). "Quantifying the Bullwhip Effect in a Simple Supply Chain: The Impact of Forecasting, Lead Time, and Information. *Management Sciences* **46**(3): 436–443.

CRC Press (2000). *Algorithms and Theory of Computation Handbook.* Boca Raton, Fla.: CRC Press, pp. 15–21

Dantzig, G. (1982). Reminiscenses About the Origins of Linear Programming. *Operations Research Letters* **1**: 43–48.

Eckhardt, R. (1987). Stan Ulam, John von Neumann, and the Monte Carlo Method. *Los Alamos Science*, Special Issue 15: 131–137.

Forrester, J. W. (1958). Industrial Dynamics. A Major Breakthrough for Decision Makers. *Harvard Business Review* **36**(4): 37–66.

Forrester, J. W. (1959). Advertising: A Problem in Industrial Dynamics. *Harvard Business Review* **37**(2): 100–110.

Forrester, J. W. (1969). *Urban Dynamics.* Cambridge, Mass.: MIT Press (currently available from Pegasus Communications, Waltham, Mass.).

Forrester, J. W. (1971). *World Dynamics.* Cambridge, Mass.: Wright-Allen Press (currently available from Pegasus Communications. Waltham, Mass.).

Fourer, R. (1999a). 1998 Linear Programming Software Survey. *OR/MS Today* **26**(4).

Fourer, R. (1999b). Linear Programming. *OR/MS Today* **26**(4).

Fu, Y., R. Piplani, R. da Sousa, and J. Wu (2000). Multi-Agent Enabled Modeling and Simulation Towards Collaborative Inventory Management in Supply Chains. *Proceedings of 2000 Winter Simulation Conference.* Orlando, Fla.: Society for Computer Simulation International, pp. 1763–1771.

Gable, S. (2003). Welcome. *Agent 2003: Challenges in Social Simulation.* Chicago: University of Chicago, Argonne National Laboratory, pp. 151–152.

Garcia-Flores, R. and X. Z. Wang (2002). A Multi-Agent System for Chemical Supply Chain Simulation and Management Support. *OR Spectrum* **24**: 343–370.

Garcia-Flores, R., X. Z. Wang, and G. E. Gitz (2000). Agent-Based Information Flow for Process Industries' Supply Chain Modeling. *Computers and Chemical Engineering* **24**(2–7): 1135–1141.

Gilbert, N. and K. G. Troitzsch (1999). *Simulation for the Social Scientist.* Buckingham, U.K.: Open University Press.

Guetzkow, H., P. Kotler, and R. L. Schultz, Eds. (1972). *Simulation in Social and Administrative Science.* Englewood Cliffs, N.J.: Prentice-Hall.

Harmantzis, F. C. (2003). Operational Risk Management. *OR/MS Today* **30**: 31–36.

Helbing, D. (2003). Modeling and Optimization of Production Processes: Lessons from Traffic Dynamics. Santa Fe, N.M.: Santa Fe Institute.

Holland, J. H. (1992). Genetic Algorithms. *Scientific American* **267**: 66–72.

Holweg, M. and J. Bicheno (2002). Supply Chain Simulation—a Tool for Education, Enhancement and Endeavour. *International Journal of Production Economics* 78(2): 163–175.

isee systems inc. (2005). STELLA. Lebanon, N.H.: isee systems.

Jones, R. D. and J. Casti (2000). Insurance World: A Process for Understanding Risk Flows Due to Catastrophes in the Insurance/Reinsurance Industry. *Euroconference on Global Change and Catastrophic Risk Management*. Laxenburg, Austria: IIASA.

Karmarkar, N. (1984). A New Polynomial Time Algorithm for Linear Programming. *Combinatorica* 4: 373–395.

Koza, J. (1993). *Genetic Programming*. Cambridge, Mass.: MIT Press.

Law, A. M. (2007). *Simulation Modeling and Analysis*, 4th ed. New York: McGraw-Hill.

Lee, C. B. (2003). *Demand Chain Optimization: Pitfalls and Key Principles*. San Francisco: Evant, Inc.

Macal, C. M. (2003a). A Network Version of Sterman's Beer Game Supply Chain Simulation Model. Argonne, Ill.: Argonne National Laboratory.

Macal, C. M. (2003b). Supply Chains as Complex Adaptive Systems. Santa Fe, N.M.: Santa Fe Institute.

Macal, C. M., M. J. North, E. P. MacKerrow, G. E. Danner, and O. Densmore (2003). Information Visibility and Transparency in Supply Chains: An Agent-Based Simulation Approach. Santa Fe, N.M.: Santa Fe Institute.

McClave, J. T. and P. G. Benson (1994). *Statistics for Business and Economics*. Englewood Cliffs, N.J.: Prentice-Hall.

Melymuka, K. (2002). What If? *Computerworld*, online at www.computerworid.com, Feb.4, 2002.

Metropolis, N. and S. Ulam (1949). The Monte Carlo Method. *Journal of the American Statistical Association* 44(247): 335–341.

Miser, H. J. and E. S. Quade, Eds. (1985). *Handbook of Systems Analysis*. New York: North-Holland.

Mosekilde, E., E. R. Larsen, and J. D. Sterman (1991). Coping with Complexity: Deterministic Chaos in Human Decision Making Behavior. In J. L. Casti and A. Karlqvist (Eds.), *Beyond Belief: Randomness, Prediction, and Explanation in Science*. Boston: CRC Press, pp.199–229.

Nance, R. E. (1995). Simulation Programming Languages: An Abridged History. *Proceedings of the 27th Winter Simulation Conference*. Arlington, Va.: ACM Press, pp. 1307–1313.

Nash, S. G. (1998a). 1998 Nonlinear Programming Software Survey. *OR/MS Today* 25(3).

Nash, S. G. (1998b). Nonlinear Programming. *OR/MS Today* 25(3).

Powersim Software AS (2005). Powersim Studio. Bergen, Norway: Powersim Software, AS.

Pritsker, A. A. B. (1986). *Introduction to Simulation and SLAM II*. New York: Halsted Press.

Roberts, E. B., Ed. (1978). *Managerial Applications of System Dynamics*. Cambridge, Mass.: Productivity Press.

Schulte, C. (2002). *Programming Constraint Services: High-Level Programming of Standard and New Constraint Services*. Berlin: Springer.

Senge, P. M. (1990). *The Fifth Discipline: The Art and Practice of the Learning Organization*. New York: Doubleday/Currency.

Simon, H. A. (1955). A Behavioral Model of Rational Choice. *Quarterly Journal of Economics* 69: 99–118.

Simon, H. A. (1969). *The Sciences of the Artificial*. Cambridge, Mass.: MIT Press.

Simon, H. A. (1979). Rational Decision Making in Business Organizations. *American Economic Review* 69: 493–513.

Simon, H. A. (1982). Theories of Bounded Rationality. In *Models of Bounded Rationality: Behavioral Economics and Business Organization*. Cambridge, Mass.: MIT Press.

Sterman, J. D. (1987a). Expectation Formation in Behavioral Simulation Models. *Behavioral Science* 32: 190–211.

Sterman, J. D. (1987b). Testing Behavioral Simulation Models by Direct Experiment. *Management Science* 33(12): 1572–1592.

Sterman, J. D. (1989a). Misperceptions of Feedback in Dynamic Decision Making. *Organizational Behavior and Human Decision Processes* 43(3): 301–335.

Sterman, J. D. (1989b). Modeling Managerial Behavior: Misperceptions of Feedback in a Dynamic Decision Making Experiment. *Management Science* 35(3): 321–339.

Sterman, J. D. (1992). Teaching Takes Off; Flight Simulators for Management Education "The Beer Game." *OR/MS Today* 20(5): 40–44.

Sterman, J. D. (2000). *Business Dynamics: Systems Thinking and Modeling for a Complex World*. Boston: Irwin McGraw-Hill.

Sterman, J. D. (2003). The Beer Distribution Game: An Annotated Bibliography Covering its History and Use in Education and Research, available at http://www.solonline.org/pra/tool/bibl.html.

Swain, J. J. (2003a). 2003 Simulation Software Survey. *OR/MS Today* 30(4).

Swain, J. J. (2003b). Simulation Reloaded. *OR/MS Today* 30(4).

Ventana Systems Inc. (2000). VENSIM. Harvard, Mass.: Ventana Systems Inc.

6

Discovering Agents and Agent Behaviors

Agents Are What They Do

This chapter shows how to decide which agents should be used to model a given situation, how to determine which agent implementation approach to apply for modeling, and how to document the choices that are made. The computational agent implementation appproaches considered in this chapter were described in detail in chapter 3. Chapters 3 and 6 are presented separately because of the way the present chapter depends on the background provided by chapters 4 and 5.

Agent behaviors are the heart of agent-based modeling and simulation (ABMS). In many ways, the other issues such as agent environments and data are only addressed to set a stage for the agent activities. Properly specified agent environments are critical for correct agent operation and otherwise good models with bad data have little value. However, this said, finding and representing realistic agent behaviors is what agent modeling is all about. This quest begins with a consideration of behavioral examples.

Social Agents

Representing social systems such as corporations and customer bases is an important application of agent-based modeling. This kind of agent modeling, social ABMS, applies one or more of a variety of social theories to represent the behavior of individuals and groups. Social agent modeling has been used for both research and applications (Epstein and Axtell 1996; Carley 2001; Cederman 2002; North et al. 2003).

One need only consider a short list such as friendship, war, family, and governance to see that social phenomena are exceptionally diverse. As such, social scientists use a large number of theories to address the various observable phenomena. Several of these theories have been used to develop agent models. One of the more commonly used of these theories, the theory of rational individual behavior, will be discussed here as an example. Of course, this theory is just one of many. Which one should be used for a given social agent model depends on the question to be addressed by the model.

Examples of Behavioral Theories

The theory of rational individual behavior postulates that individuals collaborate with others when it is in their best economic interest to do so, and collaboration allows them to survive. The theory of rational behavior is known by several names, including rational expectations theory, rational choice theory, or colloquially as "rat choice" theory. This theory predicts that individuals will make choices on a logical, economic basis and often leads to analytically solvable models.

Rational expectations theory has widespread applications. Some agents such as large corporations or certain government organizations really can behave rationally. Rational choice theory is an excellent tool to model these types of entities. The challenge in modeling these agents is to ensure that the selected decision-making mechanisms have sufficient power to represent fully rational choices. Other agents, such as people, may not behave rationally but their behavior may be estimated to be rational under some circumstances. For these agents, rational choice theory may provide a first approximation to the actual behavior. For some applications, this approximation may be sufficient. For other applications, this approximation may be iteratively expanded or enhanced with refinements such as bounded rationality.

The main weakness of rational choice theory is that research strongly indicates that people rarely make purely rational decisions (Tversky and Kahneman 1981; Henrich et al. 2001; Gintis et al. 2003). Thus, it may be said that rational choice economics is mathematical beyond its means: it is often more concerned with being rigorous than being right! According to Henrich et al. (2001):

> One problem appears to lie in economists' canonical assumption that individuals are entirely self-interested: in addition to their own material payoffs, many experimental subjects appear to care about fairness and reciprocity, are willing to change the distribution of material outcomes at personal cost, and are willing to reward those who act in a cooperative manner while punishing those who do not even when these actions are costly to the individual. These deviations from what we will term the canonical model have important consequences for a wide range of economic phenomena, including the optimal design of institutions and contracts, the allocation of property rights, the conditions for successful collective action, the analysis of incomplete contracts, and the persistence of noncompetitive wage[s].

An interesting recent example is the ultimatum game described by Gintis et al. (2003):

> In the ultimatum game, under conditions of anonymity, two players are shown a sum of money, say $10. One of the players, called the "proposer," is instructed to offer any number of dollars, from $1 to $10, to the second player, who is called the "responder." The proposer can make only one offer. The responder, again under conditions of anonymity, can either accept or reject this offer. If the responder accepts the offer, the money is shared accordingly. If the responder rejects the offer, both players receive nothing.

Since the game is played only once and the players do not know each other's identity, a self-interested responder will accept any positive amount of money. Knowing this, a self-interested proposer will offer the minimum possible amount, $1, and this will be accepted.

In splitting $10, rational choice theory predicts that the first player will offer $1 and the second will accept. This is driven by the fact that the second player will be better off accepting the offer and will therefore accept it. The first player knows this and can see that they do not need to give up more than this to be successful. However, a question remains: do people really act this way? Gintis et al. (2003) provide an initial answer:

> The ultimatum game has been played around the world, but mostly with university students. We find a great deal of individual variability. For instance, in all of the above experiments a significant fraction of subjects (about a quarter, typically) behave in a self-interested manner. But, among student subjects, average performance is strikingly uniform from country to country.

According to Gintis et al. (2003), "when actually played, the self-interested outcome is never attained and never even approximated." University students are one thing. How does everyone else act? Henrich et al. (2001) conducted a global study in 15 different small-scale societies in 12 countries spread apart on four continents. They conclude that the "canonical model of the self-interested material payoff-maximizing actor is systematically violated." "In all societies studied," the game offers are "substantially in excess of the expected income-maximizing offer" (Henrich et al. 2001).

In reality, people rarely offer or accept less than specific focal points. For example, in Western cultures half or 50% is a common focal point. In other cultures the focal points vary, but are usually well above the rational choice prediction. When left to themselves, people tend not to offer less than one of their culture's focal points. This implies that people are making decisions using more than simple rational reasoning.

Bounded rationality refines rational choice theory by including decision-makers that have limited knowledge and finite cognitive abilities (Simon 1982). The strictly rational individual behavior focuses on perfect choices, while the bounded rationality focuses on merely reasonable choices. This affirms that attention is a finite resource and that agents have bounded ability and restricted time to consider any given alternative (Simon 1982). Furthermore, the effort and time invested in one decision is generally not available to make other decisions, so that decision-making is itself a resource that must be rationed. Related work includes that of 2002 Economics Nobel Laureates Daniel Kahneman and Vernon Smith (Royal Swedish Academy of Sciences 2002).

Kahneman "integrated insights from psychological research into economic science, especially concerning human judgment and decision-making under uncertainty" (Royal Swedish Academy of Sciences 2002). He demonstrated that human decisions are often reasonable but are not necessarily rational in the standard economic sense.

Smith "established laboratory experiments as a tool in empirical economic analysis, especially in the study of alternative market mechanisms" (Royal Swedish Academy of Sciences 2002). His work on experimental economics is not strictly agent modeling, but it is a natural fit with ABMS in general and participatory simulation in particular (Smith 1962, 1982, 1994).

Bounded rationality is a good fit for many kinds of human, and nonhuman, decision-making. The challenge in modeling using bounded rationality is to ensure that the approximations that result from time and effort rationing are a good match with the actual approximations made by the real agents. These approximations include the consideration of limited sets of possible options out of much larger sets, the use of simple rules of thumb to solve complicated problems, and the use of social mechanisms such as imitation. Smith (1994) states the following:

> That economic agents can achieve efficient outcomes which are not part of their intention was the key principle articulated by Adam Smith, but few outside of the Austrian and Chicago traditions believed it, circa 1956. Certainly I was not primed to believe it, having been raised by a socialist mother, and further handicapped (in this regard) by a Harvard education, but my experimental subjects revealed to me the error in my thinking. In many experimental markets, poorly informed, error-prone, and uncomprehending human agents interact through the trading rules to produce social algorithms which demonstrably approximate the wealth maximizing outcomes traditionally thought to require complex information and cognitively rational actors.

Dominated strategies are choices that are, from a rational perspective, completely inferior to one or more alternatives. Strict rational choice theories or game-theoretic analysis predicts that dominated strategies will not be chosen by rational agents. However, according to Smith (1994), "it is commonly argued that dominated strategies should never rationally be played, and thus can be eliminated in game-theoretic [rational choice] analysis. But players in [real] repeated games do sometimes play dominated strategies and there are sound reasons why."

Smith (1994) goes on to say that one of the main reasons to select otherwise inferior choices is the need to communicate "in ways that will be clearly understood." In some cases, strategies that are rationally superior, but complicated, can end up sending confusing messages to the other players. In these situations, inferior but simple strategies that send clear messages may be a better choice. An example is the selection of a simple "tit-for-tat" strategy that shows a willingness to stand up for oneself over a sophisticated schedule of measured responses that guarantees a moderate long-term payoff. It has been demonstrated by others that tit-for-tat is not necessarily a winning strategy. However, when dealing with a bully, a sophisticated response may be theoretically superior, but simply trading blows on an "eye for an eye" basis may be more practical.

Agents that are boundedly rational are often called satisficers. These satisficing agents do not seek perfect solutions. Instead, they look for solutions that are good enough or simply better than many other alternatives. When faced with extremely complicated situations for which there may be no best solution or for which the best solution may be impossible to find, satisficing may be more reasonable than rational choices!

It is interesting to note that the approximations used by boundedly rational agents have much in common with the heuristics discussed previously. As with heuristics, boundedly rational approximations are not guaranteed to find the best answer. These approximations only provide an answer that may or may not be good relative to some stated objective. In return, boundedly rational agents can often make decisions much more quickly and at much lower cost. Furthermore, boundedly rational agents can more effectively factor in apparently irrational factors such as cultural focal points, emotions, and the social implications of decisions. Moreover, complex "downward causation" feedback loops that flow from agents to social groups and institutions and then back to agents can also occur. Both the shopper spreadsheet proto-agents and the electric power consumer proto-agents presented in chapter 8 are primitive satisficers that implement a simple form of bounded rationality.

Is No Theory a Better Theory?

So, is no theory a better theory? Simply put, every social agent model, and every other agent model for that matter, implements some theory or set of theories regardless of the designer's intent. The only two questions are as follows:

1. What theory has been selected?
2. Why was this theory selected?

The selection of a theory to underpin a given model design is frequently difficult, and the ultimate choice is often debatable. However, the developers of good models can provide clear, if not perfect, answers to both of these questions when asked.

The Emergence of Organizations

One question that is raised by the interaction of social agents is how do organizations emerge? Even though there are many partial answers, the full question itself has not yet been completely answered. However, even with simple rules, agent-based modeling can be used to study how organizational structures form and evolve. An example is the use of cellular automata to investigate pattern formation in groups.

Cellular automata use extremely simple agents interacting in local "neighborhoods" that are typically embedded on a square checkerboard-like lattice. Two types of checkerboards are typically used. Checkerboards with "von Neumann neighborhoods" consider each square to have four neighbors. These neighbors are located above, to the left, to the right, and below each square as shown in figure 6.1. Checkerboards with "Moore neighborhoods" consider

each square to have eight neighbors. These neighbors surround each square in all directions as also shown in figure 6.1. To remember the difference in conversation, note that "Moore has more" neighbors.

Patterns such as hexagonal lattices that are more complex than simple checkerboards can be used for cellular automata, but this is relatively rare. These varying patterns and neighborhoods represent differing patterns of connections. The resulting structures of agent "connectedness" are often important determinants of system behavior.

In cellular automata models, each square takes on a state chosen out of a global list. This state is normally associated with a color that is used to display the square. An example is shown in figure 6.2. In this example, each square is shaded if it is in the "active" state and black if it is in the "passive" state. The rules for each square determine the next state for the square based on the square's current state and the current states of each of the neighbors. All of the checkerboard squares normally use the same rules. Cellular automata simulations are usually time-stepped such that the rules for all of the checkerboard squares are executed and the resulting state colors are all refreshed at each step.

As with other types of agent-based modeling, cellular automata often produce patterns and trends that are not necessarily implied or even consistent with the objectives of the individual agents. The basic cellular automata approach has been used to model everything from financial markets to environmental impacts.

Unlike simple cellular automata, social network models normally have complex neighborhood patterns. Instead of a square or hexagonal grid, social network model agents normally each have their own list of neighbors. This allows nearly any pattern to be formed, including approximations to social networks (Axtell and Epstein 1999; Dibble 2000; Contractor and

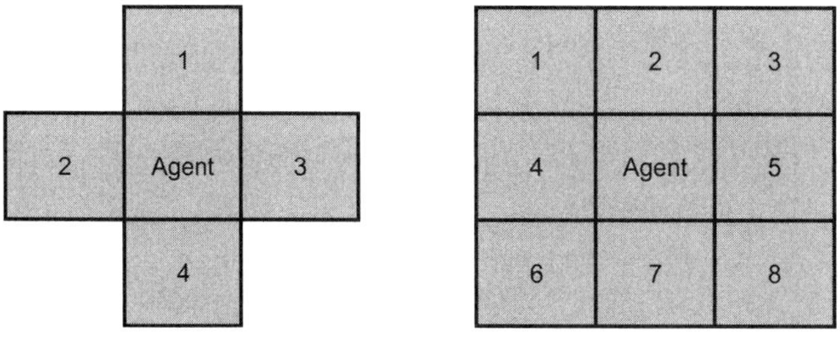

FIGURE 6.1 Examples of von Neumann and Moore neighborhoods.

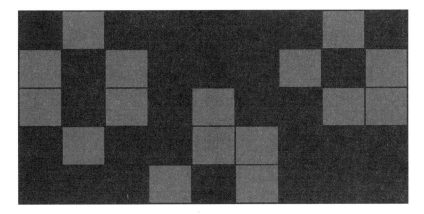

FIGURE 6.2 Example of cellular automata.

Monge 2003). The individual agents can represent specific, named people and the neighbors can represent the people's actual friends. People can even be friends with someone who does not return the favor by being a friend in return! An example is shown in figure 6.3. Rules that are more complex can also be used to study how organizational structures form and evolve.

Agent Diversity

Diversity among agents can lead to self-organization and system structure. While it is possible to have identical agents, normally each individual agent within an agent-based simulation is unique in some way. This individuality is what gives rise to the fundamental strength of agent modeling, namely the ability to model systems with many interacting heterogeneous components. This individuality may be expressed in terms of differing behaviors, capabilities, resources, positioning, or knowledge.

Other Agents

ABMS agents are different from the typical agents found in mobile systems models or artificial intelligence models. Mobile agent modeling focuses on the development of proxies for users. Artificial intelligence modeling focuses on creating human emulations to directly interact with actual people or parts of the real world. ABMS focuses on the development of representations of systems such as markets based on an understanding of the component parts.

Multi-Agent Systems

Mobile agent research develops proxies for users (Thomsen and Thomsen 1997). In the best case, these proxies are expected to act as representatives or agents for their users. This is the cause of the confusion in the use of the word "agent." Some techniques used in mobile agent research can be applied with ABMS, but there is a strong difference in emphasis. Mobile agent research produces individual agents that interact directly with users or other agents that

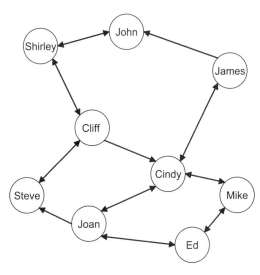

FIGURE 6.3 Example of social network friendship model with asymmetric relationships.

in turn represent users. These agents are intended to conduct transactions, monitor systems, or operate systems in place of a human user. ABMS produces agents that primarily interact with other agents, although user interactions can occur as well. ABMS agents are intended to represent the behavior of real system components to reproduce the behavior of a system as a whole.

Artificial Intelligence

Artificial intelligence research focuses on the creation of synthetic representations of individual human beings or major functions of individual human beings (Ginsberg 1993). These behaviors include solving complex problems, choosing reasonable actions in the face of high ambiguity, or participating in ordinary conversations. Of course, in the real world, this is an ambitious goal and even small steps represent progress. Naturally, many artificial intelligence techniques can be used within agent-based models. Details on appropriate techniques are presented throughout this book.

ABMS is different from artificial intelligence research. While artificial intelligence research emphasizes the development of artifacts that in some sense appear to be human, ABMS emphasizes the development of models that reproduce critical features of complex systems using component-level rules.

Discovering Agents

Properly identifying agents, accurately specifying their behavior, and appropriately representing the agent interactions are the keys to developing useful models. However, as has been previously discussed, agents are normally diverse and heterogeneous. As such, modelers must carefully consider what the agents will be in a given model. This leads to the need to discover suitable agents. So, what are agents in real systems?

Agents are generally the decision-makers in systems. These include traditional decision-makers such as managers as well as nontraditional decision-makers such as complex computer systems. Even broad groups can be considered agents for some modeling purposes.

The fundamental features that make something a candidate to be modeled as an agent are the capability of the component to make independent decisions, some type of goal to focus the decisions, and the ability of other components to tag or individually identify

the component. This in some ways follows Holland's seven properties and mechanisms for complex adaptive systems, which were discussed in chapter 4 (Holland 1995). The first feature requires the agent candidate to be active rather than purely passive and in some sense autonomous. The exact nature of the required autonomy is not fully agreed upon among agent-based modelers.

There is no universal agreement on the definition of an agent. Some modelers consider any type of independent component to be an agent (Bonabeau 2001). The behaviour of independent components can range from complex adaptive intelligence down to primitive reactive decision rules. These modelers focus on the independence of a component as the key ingredient that makes an agent. Other modelers insist that a component's behavior must be adaptive in order for a component to be considered an agent (Mellouli et al. 2003). These modelers still include reactive components in their models. However, simple reactive rules alone are not enough for these modelers to consider a component an agent. That label is reserved for components that can in some sense learn from their environments and change their behavior in response. Casti (1997) argues that agents should contain both base-level rules for behavior as well as a higher-level set of "rules to change the rules." The base-level rules provide responses to the environment while the "rules to change the rules" provide adaptation (Casti 1997).

It is important to emphasize that the definitions of the term "agent" agree on more points than they disagree. In fact, both groups often produce similar models and mostly just disagree on the terms used to describe the resulting products. This book uses a pragmatic definition of "agent" that embraces the full range of designs and implementations from the simple to the complex. This book refers to agents without adaptation as "proto-agents," as discussed in chapter 3. Using these definitions, modelers should look for labeled, autonomous decision-makers within the systems they are modeling and consider these the agents.

Discovering Agent Behaviors

Once the agents are defined, discovering the key agent behaviors becomes the next critical challenge. After the relevant behaviors are discovered, computational agents can be implemented using any of the techniques discussed in chapter 3. How can agent behaviors be discovered? Knowledge engineering can be used to answer this question.

Knowledge Engineering

Knowledge engineering is a discipline of software engineering that focuses on the development of clear descriptions of complicated systems and their interactions. Knowledge engineering itself is a collection of techniques for eliciting and organizing the knowledge of experts while accounting for reporting errors and situational biases (Wilson 1993). Knowledge engineering originally arose from the study of expert systems in artificial intelligence.

Knowledge engineering uses structured interviews to elicit information on agent behaviors. The interviews have between two and at most seven participants. One or two of the participants are the knowledge engineers who ask the other participants a series of focused questions. The other participants are domain experts who understand the various parts of the system to be modeled. Limiting the number of participants is critical since it tends to reduce wasted time and simplifies the flow of communication. If more than a few participants possess the needed information, then a series of separate interview sessions can be used. The details of how to conduct a successful knowledge engineering session are discussed later in this chapter.

Once a knowledge engineering session is completed, the results should be documented for later review. These documents must be clear enough for guided review by the domain experts and precise enough for ultimate implementation in software. Specifics on how to document knowledge engineering sessions are presented later in this chapter.

Like all human processes, knowledge engineering must deal with reporting errors and situational biases. It is a well-known fact that people, including experts, do not always accurately report information even when they are trying to. Knowledge engineering attempts as much as possible to recognize and compensate for these biases and imperfections. The results are not guaranteed to be free of errors or biases, but are often useful nonetheless. This chapter takes a pragmatic approach that takes advantage of the many useful products of knowledge engineering, while simultaneously acknowledging the potential imperfections.

Knowledge engineering is founded on goodwill. Domain experts are first and foremost people. As such, domain experts will only help others when they want to. Being on bad terms with domain experts is a sure route to project failure. Inaccurate information is far from the only threat.

As discussed further in chapter 14, successful agent-modeling projects have a champion that supports the simulation effort. The champion is a leader that strives to protect and nurture the project within an organization. Champions are critical to the long-term viability of any modeling project. Champions often encourage domain experts to participate in projects.

Being on good terms with domain experts is obviously essential. First, the experts will be motivated to provide accurate and complete facts as well as clear opinions. This motivation is particularly valuable when the questions to be answered are complex and detailed, as they often are with well-thought-out modeling efforts. Second, they will tend to speak highly of the modeling project as it proceeds both to management and to potential users. This positive word of mouth is invaluable in maintaining and growing modeling efforts as well as recruiting long-term model users. Third, they are much more likely to provide fair and constructive evaluations of the model as it is developed. This positive feedback often makes the difference between projects that are choked to the point of suffocation and projects that are allowed enough resources to shine.

How can knowledge engineers get and stay on good terms with domain experts? A variety of techniques that can be used will be mentioned later in this section. Most of these approaches are founded on four simple ideas. First, domain experts are not containers of information but rather are people who deserve respect. Second, domain experts are doing modelers a favor when they participate in knowledge engineering sessions. Third, it is important to sell domain experts on modeling. Fourth, each person has their own way of communicating.

The fact that domain experts are knowledgeable people instead of storage bins filled with interesting information is obvious but sometimes forgotten. One reason that it is forgotten is that people misunderstand knowledge engineering's focus on effectiveness. The knowledge engineering interview process is intended to be efficient rather than inhumane.

Modeling requires good information. Domain experts have this information. They also typically have something else, namely other demands on their time. If modelers consider domain experts' time valuable, then they have a chance to consider modeling to be worth their time.

Related to respect for domain experts' time is reminding them why modeling is being done in the first place. It helps to talk to them about what modeling is and why it matters to their organization. You can discuss how the model they are helping to build will benefit their organization. You can let them know that they will be credited with helping to bring these benefits to their organization. The project champion can also play an influential role here.

Every person has their own communication style. For example, some people find knowledge engineering to be a threatening process. These people need plenty of warning before they attend knowledge engineering sessions as well as lots of positive feedback during the sessions. It may also help to hold the sessions in their offices or somewhere else that is comfortable for them as well as to run a larger number of shorter sessions rather than a few longer ones. Other people feel the need to carefully check information before they make statements. These people may need multiple short sessions for questions to be posed, answers to be privately checked, and the results to be provided. Still other people require group support to be comfortable. Sessions with these people usually require the simultaneous attendance of several domain experts.

Language can also be an issue not only in terms of detailed domain nomenclature, but also general speaking style. Some domain experts are comfortable answering questions and will reply with positive word choices. Others perceive repeated questioning as a challenge to their expertise and will often reply with statements intended to remind everyone of the domain expert's knowledge or reputation. In this case, it helps to regularly and openly acknowledge the expertise of the advisor and note that the questions are being asked to help the knowledge engineer come to understand a challenging and complicated subject.

The Knowledge Engineering Interview

Knowledge engineering sessions themselves revolve around a series of questions structured in the form of interviews. Normally the general topic, agenda, and time limit for the interview are agreed upon in advance with the domain experts. Having an agreement will give them time to collect information and will allow the effectiveness of the meeting to be assessed.

Traditional knowledge engineering follows a day-long cycle. Interviews are completed in the morning. During the afternoon, knowledge engineers write up the results from the morning interview. These results are presented by the knowledge engineer and reviewed by the domain expert at the opening of the next morning session, if more than one day of interviews is scheduled. This daily cycle can be repeated as needed.

The knowledge engineering interviews generally begin with a short set of opening remarks from the modelers and then some open thoughts from the experts. The modeler's comments are intended to focus the meeting, review expectations, and quickly describe the interview process if this is the domain expert's first session. The domain expert's comments are intended to provide an overview and overall framework of the topic to be discussed from a domain perspective. Once these preliminaries are completed, the core interview can begin.

The knowledge engineering core interview involves a series of exploratory and probing questions. These questions are directed toward bounding and then refining the knowledge engineer's understanding of the topic of interest. The goal is not to make the knowledge engineer an expert on the domain. Normally, the domain expert can be consulted if follow-up questions are needed. The goal is for the knowledge engineer to extract the facts and opinions needed to build a suitable model.

Questions are the heart of a knowledge engineering session. These questions borrow from object-oriented software engineering (Booch 1993). Usually the questions proceed from the general to the specific. Initially, questions are asked about broad concepts such as what components are typically found in the system. Later, questions are asked about the interactions among these components. The repeatedly referenced nouns are good candidates to be agents or critical environmental features. Regularly mentioned verbs are good contenders to be the behaviors of the agents and the reactions of the environment. This follows the object-oriented design approach discussed later in this chapter along with the Unified Modeling Language (UML). In particular, UML Class Diagrams can be used to record the results during interviews. Interestingly, most domain experts relate well to Class Diagrams if the complex technical adornments are eliminated and only the raw classes and class relationships are shown. Class Diagrams are discussed in detail later in this chapter.

As the picture of the system becomes established, the interview questions normally become more detailed. Instead of asking the domain expert to name some types of system components, the knowledge engineer can ask about differences between and within groups of components. In place of open questions about the nature of the component interactions, the knowledge engineer can inquire about the exact rules that govern the interplay. Continually ask increasingly detailed versions of the following questions:

1. What changes the system? These are the best candidates for agents.
2. What are the changes? These are the best contenders for agent behaviors.
3. When do the changes happen? These are the activation conditions for the agent behaviors.
4. How do the changes happen? These are the mechanics of the agent behaviors.
5. Who are and what is affected by the changes? These are the consequences of the agent behaviors.

Looping through these questions with growing levels of specificity is the fundamental dynamic of the knowledge engineering interview.

At first, the answers to these questions will be quite general. Furthermore, the answers will likely seem to change and be contradictory. This is usually because there are several ways to understand and describe complex systems. Each of these differing viewpoints is usually correct for some purposes and inaccurate for others. In principle, many of these perspectives represent approaches to modeling varying parts of the system. Of course, each of these viewpoints necessarily includes observational biases. In the early stages of knowledge engineering, it is helpful to identify these different approaches and then begin to determine which of them or which combination of them seems best suited to modeling each part of the system.

For example, consider a connection-oriented viewpoint that describes the system in terms of who knows whom or what works with what. This perspective may be extremely useful for modeling information flows or resource distribution. This perspective might not be as helpful for modeling the activities that occur inside a given component. Conversely, a viewpoint that describes the system in terms of who has what may not be as helpful for modeling the connections.

However, this second viewpoint might provide exactly the details that are required to model the detailed behaviors within components. Selecting various viewpoints to provide information for modeling different parts of the system can be extremely effective. Over time, sophisticated agent-based models that capture all of these factors can be built. In fact, the ability to represent multiple scales and viewpoints is one of the key advantages of agent simulation. The keys are to consider observational biases and to match the perspective to the appropriate part of the system.

As time progresses, it is normal to focus on one of the viewpoints. The other viewpoints can be discussed later in the session or at another meeting. Once one viewpoint is selected, then both the questions and answers tend to become much more self-consistent. If this does not happen after a series of questions, then the domain expert may not be the right type of person to help specify the modeling requirements. This is discussed later in this chapter. Eventually, the selection of a viewpoint and the completion of an iterative set of questions about this perspective should lead to a relatively clear description of the system components and their basic behaviors.

When it comes to knowledge engineering, knowing who to interview is as important as knowing how to interview them. It is worth noting that merely having a large number of domain experts contributing to a model by itself is rarely helpful. The authors' experience suggests that about one in ten experts in any given domain has or can find nearly all of the information required to understand the process and design a model. Despite the recognized expertise of the other nine out of ten, they do not and will never have the information needed for model design. Most of these people are genuinely experts and often they can function quite effectively in their fields. They simply cannot help with modeling. The best response to these people is to politely thank them for their help and then move on. The time that might be spent trying to force these experts to provide the required knowledge is better spent looking for advisors that are more suitable. Table 6.1 summarizes the differences between domain experts that can help modeling projects and those that cannot.

Few domain experts have the knowledge required to build models. This appears to happen because the knowledge needed to be an effective expert on a topic and that required for modeling are in fact substantially different. Most experts tend to understand the

TABLE 6.1 Traits of domain experts that can help modeling projects and those that cannot

Domain experts that can help	Domain experts that cannot help
Listen to questions	Do all of the talking
Have a systems perspective	Are only interesting in tiny parts of the problem
Want to know how and why things work	Want to know simply that things do work
See a system as something to be explained	See a system as something to be defended or attacked
See a system as something that is	See a system as something that is right or wrong
Recognize that every system has at least some insignificant minutiae and understand the need to approximate such details of a system	Believe that their system has no minutiae and insist that all of the details of their system must be modeled in full
Understand the difference between social conventions or personal habits and physical requirements	Think that social conventions or personal habits are physical requirements
Are willing to say when they do not know something	Are interested in saying when the interviewer does not know something
Are willing to check into things that they do not know but could understand	Are focused on ignoring things that they do not know but could understand
Are aware that everyone has observational and memory recall biases, including themselves	Are convinced that they are perfectly objective, unlike everyone else

inputs and outputs of their domain but do not bother to delve deeper into the mechanisms that connect these factors. The one in ten experts who take the time to develop this deeper understanding are the key to effective model design. Spending the time to find and work with these rare experts is a highly recommended investment. These invaluable people can usually be found by canvassing the available experts and then repeatedly asking them about how things work at deepening levels of detail. The rare deep experts can provide clear answers. Shallow experts rapidly resort to hand-waving arguments to the effect of "it just works that way" or "that's just the way we do it" without being able to explain how or why. If these people are all that is available, modelers are advised to put their effort into finding experts who are more knowledgeable rather than trying to fruitlessly wring information from what they have. It should be said that a lack of the right domain experts is one of the more common causes for the failure of modeling projects. If suitable domain experts cannot be found, then the situation may not be suitable for modeling!

Documenting Knowledge Engineering Results

Knowledge engineering depends on effective interviews with domain experts to get results. However, knowledge engineering itself does not stop with question sessions. The process extends all the way into a fully specified model. As previously mentioned, this requires that the results of the knowledge engineering session be documented in a form that is simple enough for guided review by domain experts and specific enough for implementation by software developers. Knowledge-modeling tools such as the UML can be used to do exactly this (Devedzic 2001).

Knowledge modeling is the process of representing information in a documented form that is suitable for later modeling efforts (Devedzic 2001). The information for knowledge modeling is discovered during knowledge engineering sessions, knowledge engineering session follow-up reviews, model design sessions, and model implementation meetings. Knowledge-modeling tools are used to organize the results for both review and implementation.

A variety of knowledge-modeling approaches exist, including flowcharts, structure charts, data dependency diagrams, and UML (Devedzic 2001; Object Management Group 2004). Most knowledge management tools are visual in natural and thus they attempt to rely on pictures as much as possible to convey information. All of these tools have potential value for knowledge modeling. However, unlike the other techniques, UML is flexible and general enough to support the entire modeling process from initial conception to final coding (Object Management Group 2001). Furthermore, UML is widely supported by a wide range of software development environments (Object Management Group 2004).

UML is a special type of knowledge-modeling tool. UML is particularly useful since it is flexible, general, and easy to access. Furthermore, UML is independent of particular programming languages. If a prospective modeler has time to learn only one knowledge-modeling tool, then UML is definitely the best choice. In fact, UML is the only knowledge-modeling tool most modelers need to know.

UML can be used to produce written descriptions that are precise, if not complete. These descriptions can be progressively updated and refined as increasing levels of detail become available. Furthermore, UML can depict what is, or is to be, implemented, without being limited by how it is to be implemented (The Economist 2001):

Perhaps the closest thing today to a language that expresses the architecture of a program is UML. . . . UML was introduced in 1996 by Grady Booch, James Rumbaugh and Ivar Jacobson, who founded Rational Software of Cupertino, California, to exploit their invention. Originally, UML was conceived as a way of standardizing existing tools used to design computer programs. It is a "big picture" modeling language, and it has been embraced by many computer programmers, even though it is not restricted to programming.

UML allows the programmer to "declare" the desired state of a software application, mapping out relationships between different classes of objects. Tools associated with UML then help programmers to generate code in an object-oriented language such as Java. So far, these tools do not translate directly into a complete working program. Programmers still have to fill in many blanks themselves, and some cynics scoff that UML is just fancy flow charts.

Nerds who measure success in terms of lines of written code are unlikely to be sympathetic to such a new way of developing programs. It will take a generation of youngsters, raised on the likes of UML, before such "declarative" languages pose a significant threat to "imperative" ones. However, a generation change can happen awfully fast in the Internet age, as the switch to Java has shown. At a conference on UML applications in Genoa this spring, the buzz in the coffee breaks was about

industrial programmers completing major software development projects using just UML and related tools—without recourse to programming in more conventional languages.

Clearly, UML is gaining widespread acceptance as a software design tool. This standard defines several types of diagrams that together provide a powerful and widely accepted approach to knowledge modeling and software design. The UML is in fact a collection of ten diagram types (Object Management Group 2001). Several of these diagram types are particularly useful and usable for agent modeling, including Use Case Diagrams, State Diagrams, Activity Diagrams, Class Diagrams, and Object Diagrams. A combination of these diagram types can be used to fully document both the underlying knowledge and the resulting designs of agent-based models. The UML diagram types are as follows (Object Management Group 2001):

Use Case Diagrams represent how software or other systems are actually used as shown in figure 6.4. Use Case Diagrams are essentially scenarios showing how a user approaches a piece of software, invokes the software, interacts with the software, and then ultimately finishes using the software. Each use case follows the story of one or more uses of a particular piece of software or a set of software programs. Fundamentally, use cases are formalized stories about how the software will be used. In this sense, Use Case Diagrams can be considered software storyboards, with UML providing a formal diagramming notation. An example is a user that starts a model, inputs the initial parameters, runs the model, and then examines the results. Unfortunately, users are drawn as stick figures in Use Case Diagrams. Be warned, presenting a Use Case Diagram to a user and telling them that they are represented by a stick figure requires both parties to have good attitudes. Despite the standard, it is perfectly reasonable to leave the stick figures to the software engineers and to put an alternative symbol on the diagram presented to users. The software or other systems are drawn as labeled boxes. The interface components that the user interacts with or the activities that the user engages in are drawn as suitably labeled ovals. Lines represent invocations of the components or performance of the activities. Components and activities are normally shown within the boxes in their activation order.

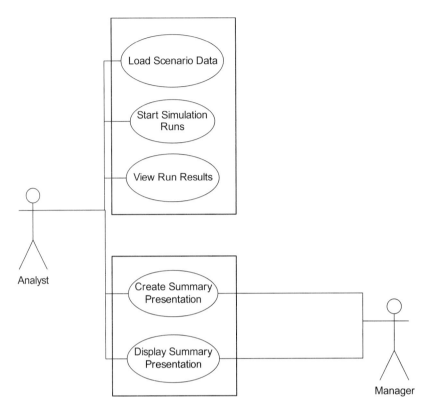

FIGURE 6.4 Example of a Use Case Diagram.

State Diagrams, more formally known as State Machine Diagrams, represent transition patterns within software components or other systems as shown in figure 6.5. A state is the current status of an object or system. State Diagrams show how an object or system moves between states over time in response to both external inputs and internal events. The initial state is represented by a filled black circle. Intermediate states are represented as rounded rectangles and are labeled to indicate the meaning of the state. The final state or states are represented by hollow circles containing smaller filled black circles. Lines with arrows represent transitions between one state and another. These transitions are labeled with the event that causes the transition. State Diagrams are quite useful for designing the inner workings of agents. For example, a State Diagram showing how consumers make impulsive purchase decisions could show the transitions between browsing, becoming aware of the product, becoming

interested in the product, product price checking, and the final purchase of the product before leaving the store.

Activity Diagrams represent work flows between software components or other systems as shown in figure 6.6. They are similar to State Diagrams in that they show how a system transitions from state to state over time. They are somewhat different in that they can document parallel actions and they explicitly include the flow of time. UML Activity Diagrams are read from top to bottom. As with State Diagrams, the initial state is represented by a filled black circle and the final states are represented by hollow circles containing smaller filled black circles. However, intermediate states are represented as ovals labeled to indicate the meaning of the state and transitions are represented as arrows without labels, since the cause is given by the attached states. Note that Activity Diagram states are specifically actions expressed as verbs rather than State Diagram statuses. Activity Diagrams

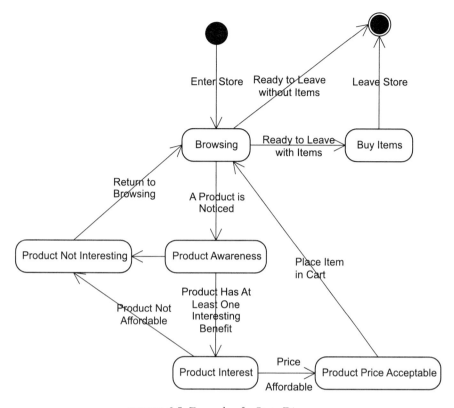

FIGURE 6.5 Example of a State Diagram.

have two extra symbols. The first is the swimlane, which is drawn as a set of three lines in an upside-down "U" shape labeled at the top with the name of an actor. Swimlanes represent the activities of one specific component in the system being specified. An example is a customer swimlane that shows how a customer behaves on a retail sales floor. The second extra symbol is the synchronization bar, which is drawn as a thick black horizontal line. Synchronization bars represent organization points for simultaneous activities. Transition lines branch or fork out of synchronization bars and can merge or join back into them. Synchronization bars are normally drawn in the swimlane of the coordinating party. An example is a retail customer synchronization bar that follows a purchase decision. The bar could have transitions that lead to the sales person being informed about the decision and simultaneously to the customer preparing to pay for the order.

Class Diagrams represent static structures as shown in figure 6.7. Classes specify the available properties and potential behaviors of objects. Different classes are connected by inheriting properties and behaviors from other classes. The inheritance sources are called parent classes or superclasses. The recipient classes are called child classes or subclasses. Inheritance is commonly used to specialize or refine classes. For example, a generic "person" class could be the parent of a "consumer" class and a "salesperson" class. The "person" class can provide basic attributes such as demographic details and essential behaviors such as movement and communications. The "consumer" class could use the demographic details and movement behavior to select items of interest in a retail store. The "salesperson" class could use the demographic details, movement behavior, and communication behavior to encourage consumers to buy specific items in the retail store. Classes are represented

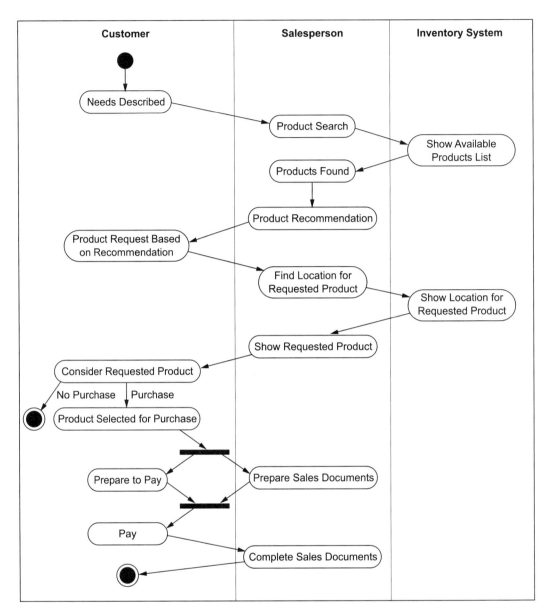

FIGURE 6.6 Example of an Activity Diagram.

by boxes in Class Diagrams. The name of the class is shown at the top of each box. Properties and behaviors can be optionally listed below the class name. Lines between classes with an arrow on one end represent inheritance. To the chagrin of many beginners, the arrow points to the parent class, not the child class, Clearly, standards are not always perfect! Classes can also have associations with other classes. Associations represent references between classes. For example,

the consumer class might have an association with the salesperson class. This association could represent the fact that each consumer can have a preferred salesperson. As stated previously, domain experts who are unfamiliar with UML often appreciate Class Diagrams if the complex technical adornments are eliminated and only the raw classes and class relationships are shown.

Object Diagrams represent dynamic structures as shown in figure 6.8. Classes statically represent the

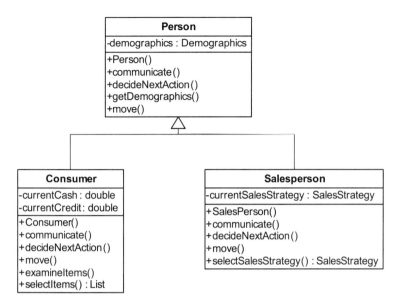

FIGURE 6.7 Example of a Class Diagram.

properties and behaviors of objects. Objects are actual instances of classes. There is normally only one class of a given kind. There can be any number of objects of a given class. Each object will have its own specific values assigned to its properties and can have its behaviors invoked. An example is a group of three consumer objects that move within a retail store and communicate with a salesperson object. The three consumer objects might represent a family that is considering a major purchase. Objects are draw as boxes in Object Diagrams and are labeled with the class name. The key properties and their values are normally listed below the class name. Solid lines in object diagrams represent specific associations and are often labeled with the meaning of the association. An association example is a consumer that has a "favorite" salesperson. Dashed lines are often used to represent flows of information.

Collaboration Diagrams represent communication flows between cooperating people or systems. Collaboration Diagrams show the detailed flow of messages coming from the interactions of system components. If needed, Collaboration Diagrams can be created after Activity Diagrams are completed. In most cases, though, Activity Diagrams are sufficient.

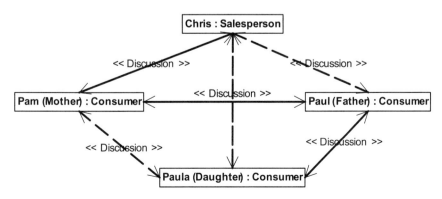

FIGURE 6.8 Example of an Object Diagram.

Sequence Diagrams represent the time-phased execution of stepwise processes. They show how objects behave in the context of other objects and the overall system. Sequence Diagrams have specialized usages, but for practical purposes they are substantially similar to Collaboration Diagrams.

Package Diagrams represent the internal layout of large-scale software packages. Packages are named sets of software components that are grouped together because they perform related functions.

Component Diagrams represent system architectures. They are most useful for managing the design of large-scale software architectures.

Deployment Diagrams represent software installation configurations or layouts. They represent how system or software modules are organized and grouped after the software is installed on a user computer. They are most useful for planning large-scale software installation routines.

Discovering Uncertain Behaviors

Despite the best efforts of informed domain experts and skillful knowledge engineers alike, some agent behaviors may remain uncertain for several reasons, including missing knowledge and imperfect conventional wisdom. For many systems, individual-level activities have never been fully considered. In this case, the modeling effort represents a significant opportunity to revolutionize an organization's ability to understand and thereby control critical systems. The individual interactions commonly assumed to take place within a given system may turn out to be poor descriptions of how the components actually behave. In this case, agent-based modeling presents a powerful tool to test and improve the consistency of conventional wisdom.

So, how can uncertainty in agent behaviors be resolved? The answer is quite simple. Agent-based models are testing platforms, so use them as such! Despite the cause of the uncertainty in agent behaviors, an incremental testing approach should be used when agent behaviors are not clear.

Incremental testing of possible agent behaviors has several steps. First, list possible candidate behaviors. Second, begin incrementally testing the behaviors against samples of real data using the simplest or most likely first. Third, add to the behaviors list as required and then repeat the process.

The candidate behaviors list should be as broad and as inclusive as possible. In particular, attempt to consider alternative behavioral descriptions that are as far apart as possible as opposed to a range of slight variations on the same basic theme.

When incrementally testing candidate behaviors against real data samples, it is possible that the results will not be unique. In other words, there may be more than one potential agent behavior that produces the observed system behavior. In fact, for many systems it is possible that several agent behaviors can or actually do cause the resulting system outcomes, so requiring uniqueness is not necessarily productive. However, for systems that require unique mechanisms, more detailed testing can usually narrow the set to the most likely behaviors.

It is possible that the actual behaviors in a given system are more complex than those that were proposed as candidates. As previously discussed, varieties of approaches are available to represent complex agent behaviors once they are defined. However, even if a given system appears to require complex rules, be sure to start with the simplest possible candidates and work upward in complexity from there. In the end, starting simple and grudgingly adding detail saves time, increases understanding, and enhances the quality of models.

A Market Example

Electricity markets are complex adaptive systems (CAS) that operate under a wide range of rules that span a variety of time scales. These rules are imposed from both above and below. The Electricity Market Complex Adaptive Systems Model (EMCAS) example started in chapter 3 will be continued. In particular, the detailed behavior of generation companies will be discussed.

Rules and norms encourage electricity market participants to behave in specific ways. The inputs run the gamut from rules that define the market's overall organization to those that structure individual interactions. For example, regulations that define settlement processes enumerate how market participants are paid for their inputs to electricity systems.

In addition to government and industry influences from above, the laws of physics constrain the operation of electricity market participants from below. Clearly, the power plants, transmission lines, consumer distribution wiring, and end-user electrical loads that make up the physical infrastructure of an electricity market all confine the choices available to electricity market participants. All of these complex physical influences must be taken into account by market participants.

Consider the EMCAS electric power market simulation discussed in the previous chapter. EMCAS represents the behavior of an electric power system and the producers and consumers that work within it. The EMCAS model itself contains the following main features as shown in figure 3.15. The components include an electric power grid, electrical generators, generation companies, transmission companies, distribution companies, and consumers. The electric power grid in the EMCAS model transfers electric power between the various agents and passive components within the system. The grid provides a high-power backbone for bulk energy transfers. The electricity grid is not considered an agent since it is a purely passive component. As previously stated, many of the components connected to the grid are agents.

The model has generators and several other active physical components. The model also has electric power production companies. These firms own and operate individual portfolios of generators.

Generation companies can bid parts or all of their generation capacity into several different markets. Each of these markets operates according to different rules. The first option is the bilateral contract market. This market with different rules is privately negotiated between individual buyers and sellers. Final contracts generally require approval from the independent system operator (ISO) to ensure system stability. The second option is the "spot" energy futures market. This market is centrally cleared by the ISO. The third option consists of the four backup generation options markets or "ancillary services" markets. Like the spot market, these markets are each centrally cleared by the ISO. Each of the four ancillary services markets varies in the required backup response time and the duration for which the associated options can be exercised. The faster response time ancillary services markets generally have higher prices. These faster response time markets also typically have smaller options windows.

Generation companies face a complicated situation since their commodity product, namely electric power, cannot be stored and the electric grid follows known, but complicated, physical laws. To make matters worse, generation companies have quite limited information about the other market participants.

To deal with their situation, generation companies balance the relative payoffs from successes against losses from failures. The anticipated return rates are based on individual historical records of events that include a log of past decisions and the perceived results of those decisions. The results are only perceived rather than strictly real since each company has its own standard of success and it is difficult to separate out the consequences of decisions from the noise caused by varying supply and demand conditions. Publicly available data such as aggregate power demands, system outages, and market prices are posted on the ISO's bulletin board.

Each company's decision-making is shaped by its willingness to take risks. Conservative companies with lower risk tolerances generally seek reliable incomes at the expense of profits. Aggressive companies with higher risk tolerances tend to choose strategies with greater profit potential and consequently higher chances for failure. Of course, not all companies choose good strategies. Some conservative companies can leave money on the table by selecting strategies that reduce profits without reducing risks. Likewise, some aggressive companies can follow strategies that increase risks without returning proportionate rewards. Just as in real life, the agent decisions do not have to be rational, but are usually reasonable.

The generation companies can consider several business choices. The company can partition its capacity between the privately negotiated contracts and the pool markets. If the pool markets are included in the bidding portfolio, then the company must further partition their pool capacity between the energy market and the four ancillary services markets.

Once companies have decided on their market portfolio, they can adjust or change their bid-pricing strategy. Examples of choices include bidding production cost, bidding low to ensure acceptance, withholding capacity, bidding high on the last portion of capacity, and submitting complex probing bids. Many of these choices can be significantly tuned once they are selected.

For many model usages, generation companies can be created based on the actual firms present in a given market. As discussed in chapter 3, these highly active decision-making entities are modeled

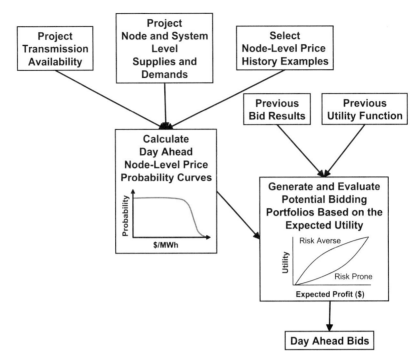

FIGURE 6.9 Selected generation company day-ahead decision rules.

as adaptive agents. The adaptive capabilities include the use of nonlinear multivariable regression and heuristic optimization techniques. The heuristic optimizations in particular make the model stochastic. This means that the model is generally run many times to produce a range of possible outcomes for analysis. Stochastic model runs are discussed in detail in chapter 13.

Generation company agents make decisions on multiple nested time scales. These time scales cover hourly, daily, weekly, monthly, yearly, and multiyear decision-making. Some of the decision rules for the generation company day-ahead decision-making are shown in figure 6.9. As mentioned in chapter 3, generation companies' adaptive features include the use of complex statistics to project potential future market prices and the use of heuristics to develop bidding portfolios. These approaches will be discussed in detail in later chapters.

Acting Up

As has been shown, realistic agent behaviors are the key to agent-based modeling. A variety of techniques

for discovering agent behaviors have been discussed including knowledge engineering. In the end, agent behaviors are found by carefully examining a situation, repeatedly asking questions, closely listening, testing proposed designs, and then repeating the process as indicated by the test results.

References

Axtell, R. L. and J. M. Epstein (1999). Coordination in Transient Social Networks: An Agent-Based Computational Model of the Timing of Retirement. In H. J. Aaron (Ed.), *Behavioral Dimensions of Retirement Economics*. Washington, D.C.: Brookings Institution, p. 280.

Bonabeau, E. (2001). Agent-Based Modeling: Methods and Techniques for Simulating Human Systems. *Proceedings of the National Academy of Sciences of the USA* 99(3): 7280–7287.

Booch, G. (1993). *Object-Oriented Design with Applications*, 2nd ed. Reading, Mass.: Addison-Wesley.

Carley, K. M. (2001). On the Evolution of Social and Organizational Networks. In D. Knoke and S. Andrews (Eds.), *Research on the Sociology of Organizations*. Stanford, Conn.: JAI Press.

Casti, J. L. (1997). *Would-Be Worlds: How Simulation Is Changing the World of Science*. New York: Wiley.

Cederman, L.-E. (2002). Endogenizing Geopolitical Boundaries with Agent-Based Modeling. *Proceedings of the National Academy of Sciences of the USA* **99**(3): 7296–7303.

Contractor, N. S. and P. R. Monge (2003). Using Multi-Theoretical Multilevel Models to Study Adversarial Networks. *Dynamic Social Network Modeling and Analysis: Workshop Summary and Papers*. Washington, D.C.: National Research Council.

Devedzic, V. (2001). Knowledge Modeling—State of the Art. *Integrated Computer-Aided Engineering* 8(3): 257–281.

Dibble, C. (2000). Geographic Smallworlds: Agent Models on Graphs. *Proceedings of the Workshop on Agent Simulation: Applications, Models, and Toolkits*. Chicago: Argonne National Laboratory.

Epstein, J. M. and R. Axtell (1996). *Growing Artificial Societies: Social Science from the Bottom Up*. Cambridge, Mass.: MIT Press.

Ginsberg, M. L. (1993). *Essentials of Artificial Intelligence*. San Francisco: Morgan Kaufmann.

Gintis, H., S. Bowles, R. Boyd, and E. Fehr (2003). Explaining Altruistic Behavior in Humans. *Evolution and Human Behavior* 24: 153–172.

Henrich, J., R. Boyd, S. Bowles, C. Camerer et al. (2001). In Search of Homo Economicus: Behavioral Experiments in 15 Small-Scale Societies. *American Economic Review* **91**(2): 73–78.

Holland, J. H. (1995). *Hidden Order: How Adaptation Builds Complexity*. Reading, Mass.: Addison-Wesley.

Mellouli, S., G. W. Mineau, and B. Moulin (2003). Laying the Foundations for an Agent Modelling Methodology for Fault-Tolerant Multi-Agent Systems. *Fourth International Workshop on Engineering Societies in the Agent's World*. Imperial College, London, U.K.

North, M., P. Thimmapuram, R. Cirillo, C. Macal, E. Conzelmann, V. Koritarov, and T. Veselka (2003). EMCAS: An Agent-Based Tool for Modeling Electricity Markets. *Proceedings of Agent 2003: Challenges in Social Simulation*. Chicago: University of Chicago, Argonne National Laboratory.

Object Management Group (2001). OMG Unified Modeling Language Specification Version 1.5. Needham, Mass.: Object Management Group.

Object Management Group (2004). Object Management Group UML Home Page. Needham, Mass.: Object Management Group.

Royal Swedish Academy of Sciences (2002). Press Release: The Bank of Sweden Prize in Economic Sciences in Memory of Alfred Nobel 2002. Stockholm, Sweden, Oct. 9.

Simon, H. A. (1982). Theories of Bounded Rationality. In *Models of Bounded Rationality: Behavioral Economics and Business Organization*. Cambridge, Mass.: MIT Press.

Smith, V. (1962). An Experimental Study of Market Behavior. *Journal of Political Economy* 70: 111–137.

Smith, V. (1982). Microeconomic Systems as an Experimental Science. *American Economic Review* 72: 923–955.

Smith, V. (1994). Economics in the Laboratory. *Journal of Economic Perspectives* 8(1): 113–131.

The Economist (2001). A Lingua Franca for the Internet. *The Economist Technology Quarterly*, Sept. 20, pp. 12–16.

Thomsen, L. L. and B. Thomsen (1997). Mobile Agents—the New Paradigm in Computing. *ICL Systems Journal* 12(1): 14–27.

Tversky, A. and D. Kahneman (1981). The Framing of Decisions and the Psychology of Choice. *Science* **211**: 453–458.

Wilson, M. (1993). Knowledge Engineering. *Proceedings of 20th Czech-Slovak Conference on Computer Science (SOFSEM '93)*. Hrdonov, Sumava, Czech Republic: Czech Society for Computer Science.

7

Office ABMS

In the Office

Basic agent-based modeling and simulation (ABMS) can be applied directly in an office setting. This chapter surveys the range of implementation environments that can be used to do office ABMS and then presents integrating criteria that can be used to determine which implementation environment to apply. The following three chapters provide details on each of the major implementation environments, namely, desktop ABMS, participatory ABMS, and large-scale ABMS. The environments themselves are presented based on increasing levels of organizational investment. Desktop ABMS can be done by an individual person in their spare time. Participatory ABMS generally requires a group for a short period of time. Large-scale ABMS often requires a group for a longer time. A variety of ABMS implementation environments will be presented in this and the following chapters. Beginning modelers commonly ask which implementation environment is best. The answer of course is that it depends.

The classic statement that a "Jack of all trades is a master of none" applies to ABMS environments. An ABMS environment may be perfect for one task but a poor fit for another based on the match between the approach's strengths and the model's needs. As each category of environment is presented, its strengths and potential weaknesses will be discussed.

Project needs vary over the life cycle of a model. No one ABMS implementation environment meets all needs equally well. Thus, there is a tendency to move from one ABMS environment to another over time.

This transition process can be quite constructive if it is properly timed. The most effective project stages in which to use each ABMS environment will be detailed.

Progressive Development

The development of agent-based models normally proceeds in a progressive fashion. The resulting interwoven design, implementation, and testing tasks are typically repeated in a cyclical manner as ABMS projects unfold. Each cycle typically builds on the last either directly or indirectly.

The ABMS environment remains the same between some development cycles. In this case, the model that was completed in one stage can be directly used in the following stage. The later development stage normally adds details and refines concepts created in earlier stages.

Prototyping

ABMS prototypes have several advantages that save time and money. Prototype models serve as proof-of-concept tools that have the basic structure or backbone of the final model since they are intentionally smaller in scale and scope and therefore relatively easy to construct. To achieve this, prototype models normally have simple rules and boundaries. The goal is to get at the core problem without the details or extras. The resulting model should be simple enough to make it relatively easy to track individual agent behaviors and identify model artifacts. As such, they can be used to verify basic ABMS concepts and approaches in a given domain as well as to check simple behaviors and potential interactions among the agents.

Prototypes should be small enough to be inexpensive to redo, rethink, and refine. Prototypes can also be used to focus on individual subproblems. These subproblem prototypes can be used as building blocks to address larger problems.

Prototype models can take several different forms. Spreadsheets, mathematical scripting environments, and dedicated ABMS prototyping tools such as Repast Py, NetLogo, and StarLogo can all be used to test out simple agent reactions and interactions. Participatory simulations can also be used to explore and document agent strategies and tactics.

Developing a series of prototype agent models is highly recommended. Fortunately, office ABMS tools are natural choices to implement the early prototypes.

ABMS Environments

Different ABMS environments have varying advantages and disadvantages. This creates a need to change environments between some development cycles. In this case, the overall agent design remains the same but the ABMS environment is changed. This change may occur for a variety of reasons, including the need to simulate much larger numbers of agents than before, the need to execute simulations for longer times than before, and the need to ensure compatibility with organizational standards. The reasons to move between ABMS implementation environments are discussed in detail later in this chapter.

Sometimes just moving from one ABMS implementation environment to another is not enough. In this case, the design of the agent model itself changes. This is often driven by the need to add additional agents to the simulation, the need to add more details than can be supported with the existing design, or the need to add new layers of interaction between agents.

New agents commonly are added to models over time as the range of questions to be addressed by the models expands. The new agents support simulation of an increasingly wide scope of behaviors.

The Four Model Growth Paths

The effort required to add new features to an agent model depends on the current model and the type of change to be made. So what types of changes are commonly made to agent models and how hard are they? In general, candidate model changes can be broken up into several basic categories, including adding behaviors that do not affect existing behaviors, adding behaviors that require modifications to existing behaviors, adding new agents that can interact with the existing agent's current behaviors, and adding new agents that require new responses from the existing agents. Each of these changes carries its own requirements.

Adding Compatible Behaviors

Model changes that add behaviors without affecting existing behaviors are usually the simplest to make. This is one of the strengths of agent modeling. This strength is derived from the factored or separated nature of agent designs. The act of defining individual agents and then implementing them in separate modules results in models that are nicely divided into independent components. Typically, this natural division allows changes to be isolated to a limited number of modules. This avoids a domino effect where one change rapidly leads to a whole series of modifications to the entire model. This sort of domino effect is common with many other modeling techniques. One thing to note, though, is that many small enhancements can accumulate over time into a substantial amount of overall change. Sometimes adding large numbers of individually simple details can eventually cause major design changes. When this happens, the raw amount of details essentially overwhelms an existing design.

Adding details or behaviors without affecting existing behaviors is quite common. A useful variation of this type of change occurs when existing behaviors are temporarily removed from a simulation. Why would this be done? A lot may have been invested in the model. Should this investment be wasted?

Appearances to the contrary, it can be wasteful to run every agent behavior in a simulation all of the time. First, almost every behavior consumes runtime resources but not every behavior contributes to output results. Some behaviors only make marginal contributions and some are canceled out by other factors. Second, some behaviors are limited by the environment and thus are not actually activated during a typical run. Executing simulations with these behaviors activated can make it more difficult to identify which behaviors are actually influencing the simulation. Third, understanding the consequences of specific behaviors can be one of the most useful outcomes from ABMS. Selectively activating behaviors allows consequences to be tested. This leads to a simple conclusion. At least in principle, most major agent behaviors should be designed and implemented with an option for easy deactivation.

Disabling or deactivating agent behaviors leads to the more general notion of the dependence of model outputs on inputs. Determining the influence of a given input on the results of a model is called sensitivity testing. Sensitivity testing is discussed in detail in chapter 13.

Adding Contentious Behaviors

Model changes that add behaviors that require modifications to existing behaviors are generally more difficult than the first category of enhancements. By their very nature, these changes ripple outward from the new behavior into many other locations. Even here, though, the modular simulations produced with ABMS are generally easier to update than the less modular products of other techniques. The fact that plainly recognizable behavioral modules, namely agents, are defined, both limits the outward ripple of modifications and channels it in predictable directions.

Adding Compatible Agents

Model changes that add new agents that can function with the existing agents' behaviors are usually quite easy once the appropriate agents are built. These changes take particular advantage of the way ABMS separates agent decision-making from agent communication. Almost any new type of agent can be added to an agent model if the new agents all generate the same types of messages as the existing agents. This works because the existing agents are capable of processing the current group of messages and the new agents produce these same communications.

Much like adding new behaviors without affecting existing ones, adding new agents without disturbing the current agents suggests a question. Can agents be removed from a simulation without affecting the existing agents? Clearly, the modular nature of agent models makes this type of change quite easy.

Why would someone make this type of change? There are two basic reasons. First, a given situation may not require a given type of agent. Second, the agent type might be no longer required for or be compatible with a model's anticipated future uses.

Sometimes certain types of agents do not appear in a given situation. In this case, the agent would not be removed from the model design or implementation. It would only be removed from the input data for the model runs of interest.

Sometimes certain types of agents will never appear again for the questions of interest or they might actually conflict with these new questions. An example of the former is a tax collection agent in a real-estate model where the model will only be used to study new home sales rather than occupancy and pricing trends of all types of homes. In this example, it may be decided that only the tax rate matters and that the tax collection process no longer needs to be modeled. The tax collection agent might then be removed to simplify the model design and streamline input data preparation. An example of the latter is a system-level accounting agent in a model of a financial market where the market is about to decentralize its clearing operations. In this example, it may be decided that the system-level accounting agent conflicts with the new decentralized approach enough to warrant removal. Note, however, that much of the implemented behavior of the existing accounting agent might be leveraged to speed up implementation of the decentralized model. In these cases, the agent would normally be removed from the model's design and implementation, but many of the agent's behaviors might be reused.

Adding Contentious Agents

Model changes that add new agents that require new responses from the existing agents are the most complex type of enhancement. As previously mentioned, the modular nature of agent-based modeling makes these changes manageable. Still, many would say that this development effort sounds expensive. Read on.

Leveraging Change

The preceding list describes many different ways to change a model. Why are there so many ways to change a model? What stops agent model designers from just getting things right in the first place? Perhaps most importantly, how much is this all going to cost anyway?

It should be noted that redesigning a model is not necessarily a bad thing nor is it automatically a negative comment on the work that went into the existing design. It may even be a good thing! Consider the advice of Frederick Brooks (1975, 1995):

> Chemical engineers learned long ago that a process that works in the laboratory cannot be implemented in a factory in one step. An intermediate step called the pilot plant is necessary. . . . In most projects, the first system is barely usable. It may be too slow, too big, awkward to use, or all three. There is no alternative but to start again, smarting but smarter, and build a redesigned version in which these problems are solved. . . . The management question, therefore, is not whether to build a pilot system and throw it away. You will do that. The only question is whether to plan in advance to build a throwaway, or to promise to deliver the throwaway to customers. Seen this way, the answer is much clearer. Delivering the throwaway to customers buys time, but it does so only at the cost of agony for the user, distraction for the builders while they do the redesign, and a bad reputation for the product that the best redesign will find hard to live down. . . . Hence, plan to throw one away; you will, anyhow.[1]

The reasons to redesign a model mirror the types of model output variations discussed in chapter 2. Variability is the natural variation in system outcomes caused by unpredictability in the system itself (Berleant et al. 2003). Uncertainty is the variation in system outcomes caused by incomplete information (AIAA 1998; Copas and Eguchi 2003). Error is the variation in system outcomes caused by recognized or unrecognized mistakes (AIAA 1998). Each of these can lead to model redesign.

Variability

Variability is driven by variations within the system being modeled. However, modelers can choose what to model. One cause of model redesign is restructuring to remove sources of variability or reduce their influence. Consider the electric power model we have been discussing throughout the book. One large source of variability in the price of power is weather conditions. In particular, extreme heat tends to increase loads such as air conditioning and thus tends to drive up prices. Weather has a huge impact on electric power production costs (Keener 1997). Prices are similarly affected (Mount 2002). Clearly, weather is a major issue for this type of model. There is just one problem. Weather is notoriously difficult to predict (Allen et al. 2002).

Precisely predicting weather is extremely difficult at best. Modeling both the weather and the market performance that results from weather is extremely daunting. It is also unnecessary. Modelers can choose what to model. The goal of the modeling effort was to provide quantitative insights into electric power market performance. Weather influences specific power market results but it is independent of individual markets. Modeling weather as an independent input allows the effects of temperature and other factors to be represented without requiring detailed forecasts. In the example modeling effort, sets of highly detailed weather traces prepared by a professional meteorologist were used. The sets were carefully selected to reflect the range of possible weather conditions. Separately running the model for each weather condition allowed the effects of weather to be taken into account without the need for explicit weather modeling.

Uncertainty

Uncertainty is the variation in system outcomes caused by incomplete information (Copas and Eguchi 2003). Fundamentally, uncertainty is caused by missing information. Ideally, this information can be found through consultations with experts or through focused data searches. However, the real world is far from ideal. In reality, there will always be some uncertainty in every model, or anything else in business for that matter. Short of real-world experimentation, one of the best ways to reduce uncertainty is to use the agent simulation itself to answer questions. The approach is to design, implement, and test run a possible answer to an uncertainty. If the answer fails to produce the expected results, then it is unlikely to be correct. If it does match the expectations, then it is a candidate solution. At first glance, a successful result may also seem to indicate that the candidate is actually the unique solution. This is not necessarily the case. In some situations, multiple candidate solutions can produce the expected system behavior. To guard against this, several other potential solutions should be tested. There are several possible outcomes.

When testing possible answers to uncertainties using an agent model, there is usually a range of outcomes.

Sometimes only one answer is found. If only one solution seems to produce the expected results, then it becomes increasingly likely to be the unique answer, as more solutions that are possible are tried and fail. An example is an energy market model where only one consumer reaction to weather seems to reproduce real-world behavior. If a small to moderate number of successful solutions appear, then these solutions are probably members of some related class of answers. An example is a power market model where some, but not all, bidding approaches can reproduce the actual recorded bids. The agent simulation can be used to categorize the successful solutions. If most possible solutions work, then it may not matter what answer is used in the model. An example is an electricity market model where the details of the customers' reactions to prices seems to have little if any effect as long as they buy less when prices rise. In this case, almost any reasonable answer can be used. Some might say that this sounds like sensitivity analysis for behaviors. Of course, it is. Agent-modeling sensitivity analysis is discussed further in chapter 13.

Error

Error is the variation in system outcomes caused by recognized or unrecognized mistakes (AIAA 1998). Recognized or acknowledged mistakes are a normal part of model development that can be effectively managed. Unrecognized or unacknowledged mistakes pose certain dangers to model development projects. Fortunately, these errors can also be dealt with. Each of these situations can lead to model redesign in the long term.

All models are necessarily approximations. As detailed in chapter 2, this is caused by many factors including limited model development resources. These approximations are errors. Thus, in this sense all models have errors. As statistician George Box famously observed, "all models are wrong, but some models are useful." The issue is to identify what the errors are and to use the models in a way that is compatible with the errors. No model, agent-based or otherwise, can include every decision-making process used in complex situations. Fortunately, they do not need to. Modeling the dominant processes and some moderately common alternatives may be enough to represent the vast majority of interactions. However, models cannot be used to investigate the effects of esoteric or unusual behaviors without accounting for these behaviors.

Acknowledged errors are known mistakes. These errors should be documented as soon as they come to light. This documentation should be in the form of updates to the user's guide if available, additions to the release notes for the resulting new version, and source code comments. Naturally, mistakes can be recognized before or after they are made.

Mistakes that are recognized before they are made are usually conscious expediencies needed to keep a model project on time, on budget, and focused on the questions at hand. This is a normal part of model development, since no model can or should contain every possible detail of the real world. The iterative approach to model development described throughout this book shows how to make good decisions about what to include in models and what not to include. Naturally, these decisions should be documented.

Mistakes that are recognized after they are made are usually the results of unintentional accidents or are created by system evolution. Unintentional accidents occur during model design, development, and maintenance while divergences caused by system evolution can occur at any time.

In the case of unintentional accidents, model developers need to assess the level of effort needed to fix the error and the effect of the error on model results. Comparing the cost of the repair with the benefit of the change gives a good indication of what should be done. Sometimes certain errors are simply not worth fixing. If this is the decision, then the effects of the error on the simulation outputs should be clearly documented to prevent later confusion about model results. A contrary example is the use of dollars per unit rather than cents per unit in one part of a price negotiation behavior. If the rest of the related behaviors use cents per unit, then the interactions between the behaviors will not be correct. While apparently basic, unit conversion problems are one of the most common sources of unintentional modeling errors. Using a common set of units throughout a model is highly recommended. If decision-makers like to see more than one type of unit for output, then these values should be calculated in a reporting module outside of the simulation itself. Clearly, this unit conversion omission must be corrected before the model can be used. Unintentional accidents can be discovered using the processes detailed in chapter 11.

Real-world systems that are being modeled change over time. Some of these changes are captured by models and can be tracked by models over time. However, some of these changes are not included in the modeling framework, either by conscious choice or by oversight. In either situation, models can get out of synchronization with reality. When this starts to happen, the model's current fit to the world needs to be reassessed and a decision about updating the models should be made. Sometimes the model can be updated to include the new behaviors. Sometimes the current design has simply outlived its usefulness and needs to be reworked.

Unacknowledged errors are mistakes that are made but not recognized. They are one of the key issues to be dealt with during model verification and validation. Unacknowledged errors are problematic since they can bias model results without being known to the model users.

Returning to the Questions

So what about the questions posed above? Why are there so many different ways to change agent models? What prevents agent modelers from just doing things once and then stopping? Most important of all, how much will it all cost?

There are many ways to change a model because there are many directions for model development. Agent modeling can be used to represent the behavior of nearly any complex adaptive system. This means that effective modeling is all about setting appropriate boundaries. These boundaries separate that which will be modeled from that which will not. Over time these boundaries can be moved, usually outward to include new factors in models. There are so many ways to change models since there are so many directions to expand any model's boundaries. Stepping back for a moment, this is actually a long-term strength of agent-based modeling. Imagine developing a model and then being faced with a new set of questions to answer. Imaging having to say that the new questions cannot be addressed without abandoning the old model and starting again from scratch. Of course, this occasionally needs to done with any type of modeling, but imagine having to do this every time the questions change. The extensibility of agent models offers a way out of this common modeling trap.

The question about "What stops agent model designers getting things right in the first place?" might be better phrased, "Is anyone willing to pay for a long-term effort with no results until the final day?" Hopefully, the answer is no. Certainly, any type of modeling is complicated by uncertainties and all modeling needs to take advantage of the simplifying advantages of carefully chosen acknowledged approximations. Developing a design may allow current developers and even domain experts to learn about the system being modeled. However, the larger issue is intermediate feedback. Getting things right in the first place really means that the model will not be ready for use until it is entirely complete. A model that is perfectly correct is a model that has all of the required features, all of the needed components, and every specified option. It is a finished model. This model only exists at the end of a development project. Making acknowledged approximations allows models to be tested along the way to the final results. These tests are the exact kind of feedback that managers of modeling projects need most. The tests indicate how the project effort is faring. Do the currently implemented parts of the model work? If so, how well? If not, how far off are the results and what can be done about them? This type of feedback can be expected from the iterative development process detailed throughout this book.

The changes listed above are not arbitrary. When properly done, these changes fit into a set of common model development stages. First, simple prototypes are constructed to demonstrate the potential of ABMS in a particular application. Second, participatory simulations may be completed. Third, initial desktop models are created to produce outputs for verification and validation. Finally, large-scale agent models may be developed if needed. The key is to start small and grow in simple incremental steps.

Ultimately, the question is how much will the development effort cost and how much more will iterative development add to the bill? Imagine for a moment how much a project might cost without iterative development. The questions to be addressed by the model are identified. The model is designed using the questions. The design is implemented. The implementation is tested, again using the questions. It sounds like an efficient process. There is only one issue. The system being modeled is highly nonlinear, poorly understood, brand new, or just plain complex. All of a sudden, the design is not so obvious. The implementation is not quite as easy and the testing is even harder. A large amount of development effort might be invested before design problems are found. The final tests may not be so final if they uncover deep issues in the model.

In addition, whoever said that the system being modeled would be kind enough to stop changing while the model is being developed? Things can change and do change while modeling processes proceed. Oh yes, and by the way, who really believes that the questions will actually remain constant? The questions to be answered by models often are one of the fastest changing things on modeling projects. As E. V. Berard has said, "walking on water and developing software from a specification are easy if both are frozen." Of course, some managers insist that they will hold the line and keep the questions from changing. This can be done. However, the usual price is irrelevance. After all, managers can hold questions constant but the topics of interest to upper management will change on their own. Imagine saying to senior management, yes, our new model addresses the questions it was designed for and, no, none of these questions is of interest today. Iterative development offers a path out of this trap. In the end, iterative development is less expensive because it limits modeling efforts to only those tasks that are actually necessary, supports progress tracking with detailed feedback, and allows models to remain relevant as both the world and management needs change.

Office ABMS Architectures

ABMS architectures have three basic components as shown in figure 7.1. The simulation engine performs the simulation work. The interface collects input data and displays output data. The data storage system provides persistence for agents and their environments.

The core ABMS architectural components are conceptual. The ABMS architectural components define core architectural functions. These core functions can be provided by a huge range of software tools. These core functions can be implemented in many different combinations. Some ABMS tools unify the user interface and simulation engine functions into a single package. Other agent modeling tools use completely different mechanisms for input collection and output reporting. These components are not intended to define a single rigid ABMS architecture, but rather they are intended to provide a solid conceptual framework for later learning and ABMS tool selection.

Several ABMS architectural styles are commonly used. These styles include tightly coupled architectures, loosely coupled architectures, and distributed architectures.

Tightly Coupled Architectures

Tightly coupled architectures confine the user interface and simulation engine components into a single

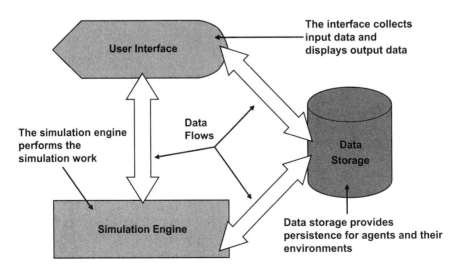

FIGURE 7.1 The core ABMS architectural components.

process space or program. Examples include mono-lithic C programs and basic Java[2] console applications. Tightly coupled architectures tend to be easier to work with but less scalable than the other architectures.

Tightly coupled architectures tend to be simpler than the other styles. They tend to have fewer required modules than the other styles, since modules can simultaneously handle display, simulation, and storage. They tend to have simpler communications between modules than the other styles, since direct function calls are usually sufficient. Since they tend to be sim-pler, systems with tightly coupled architectures are usually easier to develop and maintain than those designed using one of the other architectures. However, since these architectures are not as well factored, they tend to be less scalable than the other architectures. Tightly coupled architectures are well suited to small-scale ABMS. In this context, small-scale means tens of agents to a few thousand agents, depending on the complexity of the agent rules and the amount of data needed by each agent. Tightly coupled architectures generally are not well suited to medium- or large-scale ABMS. Medium-scale begins at about a few thousand agents, depending on the same factors as before.

Loosely Coupled Architectures

Loosely coupled architectures divide the user inter-face and simulation engine components into separate process spaces or programs. Examples include a Java program with a Java Servlet interface and a Microsoft Visual C++[3] program with a Visual Basic[4] interface.

Loosely coupled architectures tend to sit between the other styles in terms of development challenge and scalability. Loosely coupled architectures tend to be more complex than tightly coupled architectures. They tend to have more required modules, since display, simulation, and storage are separated for each program function. They also tend to have more complex communications between modules since direct function calls alone are often not sufficient.

Loosely coupled architectures tend to be simpler than distributed architectures. They tend to have fewer required modules, since a single module usually pro-vides the simulation engine functions. They also tend to have less complex communications within the simulation module since direct function calls are usu-ally sufficient. However, since the simulation engine is not as well factored as in distributed architectures, loosely coupled architectures tend to be less scalable

on the high end. Loosely coupled architectures are generally well suited to medium-scale but not large-scale ABMS. Medium-scale begins at about a few thousand agents and ends at about a few hundred thousand agents. As before, this depends on the agent rule complexity and the volume of data accessed by each agent.

Distributed Architectures

Distributed architectures spread the user interface and simulation engine components across separate processes on many computers. Examples include a Java Remote Method Invocation (RMI) program with a Java Servlet interface and a Visual C++ Distributed Component Object Model (DCOM) program with an Active Server Pages (ASP) interface.

Distributed architectures tend to be the most scalable but also the most challenging to develop. Distributed architectures tend to be more complex than loosely coupled architectures. They tend to have even more modules than loosely coupled architec-tures since they have many more simulation engine components. They also tend to have much more complex communications between the modules within the simulation engine. However, since the simulation engine is better factored than in loosely coupled architectures, distributed architectures tend to be much more scalable. Distributed architectures generally are well suited to large-scale ABMS. Large-scale begins at about a few hundred thousand agents, depending as before on the agent complexity and the data used by each agent.

The Office ABMS Continuum

The iterative development process suggests a contin-uum of modeling tools. Managers can begin with spreadsheets and other desktop software, then incre-mentally move up to participatory ABMS when they are comfortable. The key is to start small and move upward in size and complexity.

Prototypes are the stuff of iterative development. Prototypes are valuable to business for a variety of reasons, including their capacity to be used for intermediate feedback and their ability to be used as development milestones. In many ways, every model produced following the iterative process described in this book is a prototype for the next model that may be developed. This is as true for an operational model that is used for detailed daily operations as it is for a new proof-of-concept model that demonstrates the potential of modeling in a given area. It is expected that many prototypes will be extended to produce next-generation models. However, occasionally prototypes reach the end of their useful lives and the next generation of model needs to be implemented from the ground up. Reimplementation is normally needed when new computing platforms, such as a transition from a spreadsheet to a high-level language, are required for the modeling effort. Fortunately, the extensibility of agent models makes rebuilding a rare event. Furthermore, even when rebuilding is needed, the modular nature of agent models allows learning from the previous prototype to be directly applied to the new model.

The simple prototypes that are implemented at the start of an ABMS project are intended to prove the capabilities of agent modeling in a specific context. These proof-of-concept models typically include only enough detail to allow the simulation to be checked against basic facts about the application domain. This scoping allows modeling approaches and even modeling itself to be tested with small investments before larger investments are made. Later versions of the model can become increasingly focused on operational concerns.

Agent modeling usually starts with common desktop tools such as spreadsheets. However, depending on the organization and the individual modelers, it is also possible to start with participatory ABMS. In either case, the more demanding behavioral complexity requirements, agent counts, and data volumes typical of operational simulations are usually met using more sophisticated tools such as those described in chapter 10.

Tradeoffs

The office ABMS continuum is based on several key tradeoffs. The decisions include trading off agent count and complexity, trading off availability of development skills, trading off ease of development and flexibility, trading off synchronous and asynchronous execution, and trading off structured, object-oriented, functional, and constraint-based construction.

Agent count and complexity compete since larger agents require more resources. This limits the number of agents that can be modeled on a fixed-capacity computer system. Following the definitions presented earlier in this chapter, small-scale means tens of agents to a few thousand agents, depending on the complexity of the agent rules and the amount of data needed by each agent. Medium-scale begins at about a few thousand agents, depending on the same factors as before. Large-scale begins at about a few hundred thousand agents. Each of the major types of environments for office agent simulation targets different modeling scales.

Naturally, the availability of development skills is critical throughout the life cycle of a model. This is particularly an issue during initial model development when resources are usually most limited. The long-term success of the modeling effort can often depend on the selection of modeling tools for which development skills are readily available. As will be discussed later, this is one of the driving factors for beginning most initial modeling projects with spreadsheets or participatory ABMS.

Ease of development and flexibility are to some extent mutually contradictory. Certainly, some office ABMS tools are better designed than others. Better tools are both easier to use and more flexible. However, in the end there are usually tradeoffs between these two goals. This is caused by the fact that ease of development ultimately comes from focus. Tools that are easier to use in a given area usually are more focused on the given area. These tools provide an overall structure as well as built-in functions that support the area of interest. Unfortunately, this strength becomes a weakness when the tool is applied to a significantly different area. When this happens, the mismatched structure and built-in functions begin to get in the way of development efforts. It is much like the differences between a hammer, a screwdriver, and a multifunction penknife. A hammer is the easiest to use for driving nails but can also be used as a marginal substitute for a screwdriver. Conversely, the screwdriver is the easiest to use for turning screws but can also be forced to act as a hammer. What about a multifunction penknife with a small built-in hammer and a built-in screwdriver? Of course, it is not as specialized as the hammer or the screwdriver. It cannot drive a nail as well as a dedicated hammer nor can it turn a screw as well as a specialized screwdriver. However, it does a better job of both driving nails and turning screws than either of the dedicated tools does alone. It is the same with ABMS tools.

Development Tools

As detailed in chapter 10, there are several overall styles of agent development tools. Structured environments allow functions to be defined but do not directly support the identification of individual components such as agents. All of the tracking of which property, such as current net assets or age, belongs to which agent must be done manually. The advantage is the potential for moderate performance optimizations at the expense of much greater development time and higher development skill requirements needed to take advantage of these optimizations. Examples include the C programming language and the core scripting languages in most spreadsheets (Kelley and Pohl 1987). Tools that are merely structured are not recommended for long-term modeling, although they can be useful for initial prototyping. This is particularly true for spreadsheets.

Object-oriented tools extend structured tools by adding explicit tracking of individuals, such as agents, among other features. Examples include Java, C++, and C#[5] (Kruglinski 1998; Foxwell 1999; Archer 2001). Object-oriented tools are a good long-term choice for large-scale agent-based modeling.

Functional and list-based tools use a recursive or nested approach to specifying programs. They define activities in terms of items that are evaluated based on their contents such that the item contents are themselves items to be evaluated. Examples include MATLAB, Mathematica, and the Prolog language (Bratko 1990; The MathWorks Inc. 2004; Wolfram Research Inc. 2004). These tools are useful for prototyping but are less useful for large-scale modeling, since the formulas can become increasingly difficult to manage and calculate.

Constraint-based approaches use groups of variables with possible values that are progressively narrowed to find solutions. Variables are initially defined to have broad sets of potential assignments and then limits or constraints are placed on these assignments. Over time, the accumulating limits restrict the variables' values to specific solutions. Examples include the ILOG Solver[6] and Oz/Mozart (Roy and Haridi 1999, 2004; ILOG Inc. 2004). Constraint-based approaches are useful for prototyping complete models and are a good choice for implementing agent behaviors within large-scale models. The use of constraint-based approaches to implement agent behaviors is discussed in chapter 3.

Desktop ABMS

The office ABMS tool continuum begins with desktop ABMS. Desktop agent modeling can be used to begin exploring the potential of ABMS with minor time and training investments. Desktop agent modeling allows the investigation of key agents and their basic behaviors. Desktop agent modeling tools are generally limited to small-scale simulations in terms of the number of agents that can be modeled and the complexity of the agent rules. Spreadsheets and other desktop software such as Repast Py, NetLogo, StarLogo, Mathematica, or MATLAB can be used for desktop ABMS.

Spreadsheets are in many ways the simplest approach to modeling. They allow easy interactive changes and are available nearly everywhere in business environments. Spreadsheets such as Microsoft Excel[7] can be used for basic prototyping and simple research. Spreadsheet ABMS prototypes use tightly coupled architectures. Spreadsheets have several major advantages. They are immediately familiar to most business people. Furthermore, most business people are comfortable performing "what if" analysis with spreadsheets. In many cases, the interfaces that result from spreadsheet models can be directly used by decision-makers. Several ABMS researchers, including Derek Bunn and John Bower, have even published highly regarded agent models based on spreadsheets (Bower and Bunn 2000).

It is easier to develop models with spreadsheets than with many of the other tools. However, the resulting models generally have extremely limited agent diversity, exceedingly restricted agent behaviors, and poor scalability compared to many of the other tools. Spreadsheets generally use synchronous execution and structured programming. Agent modeling with spreadsheets is discussed and specific examples are provided in chapter 8.

Repast Py, NetLogo, StarLogo, and related tools provide special-purpose facilities that are focused on agent modeling. In particular, Repast Py is the entry point for larger-scale Repast J modeling while NetLogo and StarLogo are targeted to support complexity education. Repast Py has the unique advantage of being upwardly compatible with the large-scale Repast J modeling toolkit. Skills in these tools are less available than spreadsheets, but are relatively easy to acquire. All of these tools make it much easier to develop agent models than do larger-scale toolkits, but they also tend to be far less flexible. These tools are generally used to develop synchronous object-oriented models. All of these tools use tightly coupled architectures. They are all discussed in chapter 8 along with examples.

Participatory ABMS

Participatory ABMS employs people to play the role of agents. Participatory ABMS can be used to continue the exploration of the potential of ABMS with a modest time and training investment. As with desktop ABMS, participatory ABMS allows the central agents and their basic behaviors to be investigated. The skills for participatory ABMS are usually readily available in a business environment. Participatory ABMS models are usually the easiest to develop and have the most flexibility of the major development approaches. However, participatory ABMS is usually quite limited in the number of agents or people that can be included in a model and the precision of the agent rules. Furthermore, the agent rules usually need to be quite simple or the people will tend to unintentionally ad lib their own interpretations. As such, participatory ABMS is extremely useful for rapid prototyping but is generally limited to extremely small-scale ABMS with short time horizons. Participatory ABMS can be asynchronous and is in some very broad sense object-oriented in terms of design.

Two important architectural issues for live simulation are information privacy and time management. The first issue is, how will the privacy of information and communication be maintained to ensure that players only know what their corresponding agents would know? The second issue is, how will the flow of time be managed to ensure that the live simulation matches the corresponding agent environment? These questions are addressed in chapter 9 along with specific examples.

Large-Scale ABMS

Large-scale ABMS focuses on the development of models with a few hundred thousand or more agents, depending as before on the agent complexity and the data used by each agent. Large-scale ABMS is usually done with computer-based ABMS environments. These environments must meet several requirements, including the need for sophisticated time schedulers, the need for agent communications tools, and the need for mechanisms to store agents. Examples of large-scale agent-modeling tools include Repast and Swarm (Minar et al. 1996; Tobias and Hofmann 2004; North et al. 2006). These environments and

the large-scale ABMS development processes are discussed in detail in chapter 10.

The lack of available large-scale ABMS development skills can be a limiting factor. Fortunately, the selection of a large-scale modeling platform that is based on a widely used language such as Java can greatly widen the pool of potential developers. These tools generally have the most difficult development processes and have higher flexibility that most of the other techniques. These platforms usually support asynchronous execution and object-oriented development. Many also include special support for hybrid development that combines object-oriented construction with functional programming, constraint-based programming, or both. Large-scale ABMS is discussed in chapter 10 along with specific examples.

Examples

Two simple examples of office agent models will be briefly discussed. The first example uses a spreadsheet to model consumers and producers in an electric power market. The second example is a participatory simulation where people play the role of various agents including electricity consumers, generation companies, and power system operators.

A Spreadsheet Example

The spreadsheet shown in figure 7.2 is a power market model with two types of agents, namely consumers and generation companies. This simple spreadsheet is not intended to be a model of an actual electric power market and is not related to the EMCAS model discussed earlier. Rather, it is intended to be a demonstration of one way spreadsheets can be used for agent modeling. The example agents compete in a simplified open daily electric power commodities market. A third agent, the independent system operator (ISO), manages the flow of payments in the overall daily market.

Each consumer agent has a unique initial demand for electricity and places a specific value on the power that they purchase. This personal value measures the benefit that the consumers get from consuming one marginal unit of power. If power prices rise above this point, then consumers will slowly resort to conservation measures.

Each generation company agent has a fixed number of units that are bid into the market. Each generation company bids all of its capacity at each time step.

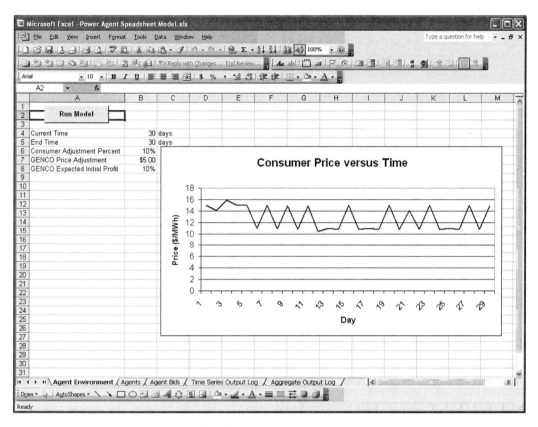

FIGURE 7.2 The power market environment.

Bids can be accepted in whole or in part. Each company has a different amount of capacity and a different production cost per unit of power generated. Naturally, companies attempt to make profits by having their prices exceed their production costs. The challenge is getting bids with high enough prices accepted.

Each company has a target share of their production capacity that they are seeking to sell. Generation companies use a two-part strategy in forming their bids. First, they lower their prices until their target market share is achieved. Once they reach their desired market share, they consider their profit levels. If their profit level is falling from one period to the next, companies raise their prices. Otherwise, if profit levels are constant or rising, the companies maintain their prices and enjoy their success, albeit temporarily. The model does not address bankruptcies, so variable production cost sets a lower bound on prices. Clearly, this simple behavior is purely for illustrative purposes. The generation company agents can be extended to represent additional corporate behavior as needed.

Consumer electric power use is measured by the ISO for each day of the simulation. The ISO attempts to match power consumers with power producers. When the final matches are found, generation companies are each paid what they bid while all consumers pay one uniform price. The consumer price is the weighted average price for all of the accepted generation bids, so total buyer and seller payments exactly match for each period. In this model, ISOs are separately funded as third-party market managers. The ISO logs the daily power price results as the simulation run proceeds.

The consumer, generation company, and ISO agents jointly form a power market. The details of the agent behaviors, as well as the full model implementation, are presented in chapter 8.

A Participatory Simulation Example

The Electricity Market Complex Adaptive System (EMCAS) model introduced in chapter 3 was prototyped using several techniques, including participatory simulations. Three types of agents were identified for one of the participatory simulations. The identified agent types were consumer agents, generation company agents, and ISO agents. Consumer agents draw power or load from a virtual grid and curtail demand when electricity becomes very expensive. Generation company agents own and operate power plants, submit power bids to the ISO, generate electricity to meet loads, and strive to maximize profits. The ISO agent accepts and rejects generation company agents' bids, dispatches operational units according to market rules, posts day-ahead weather and load forecasts, computes and posts market clearing prices, and posts unit outages. It was determined that people would play the roles of some of the agents in the virtual marketplace.

Once the agents were specified, the market rules and regulations were defined. This included the agent bidding structure, the available agent resources, the costs, and the payment rules. The information to be distributed to the agents and the publicly available environmental variables were also determined.

The participatory market simulation allowed the EMCAS designers to explore agent behavioral strategies and observe adaptive agent behavior. Some of these behaviors are discussed in chapter 6. The EMCAS participatory simulation is described in detail in chapter 9.

Back at the Office

As has been shown, ABMS can be done in an office setting. Several office ABMS implementation environments were reviewed. These environments will be discussed in more detail in the chapters that follow, along with several specific examples of applications. Ultimately, the opening question remains. Which implementation environment is best? This chapter has shown that the answer depends on the situation and has provided recommendations on the best uses for each environment.

Notes

1. Brooks has revised his "build one to throw away" idea as he now explicitly supports incremental development versus the waterfall model (Brooks 1995). He also credits Winston Royce with the original "build one to throw away" idea (Brooks 1995).

2. Java is a trademark of Sun Microsystems, Inc.
3. Visual C++ is a registered trademark of Microsoft Corp.
4. Visual Basic is a registered trademark of Microsoft Corp.
5. C# is a registered trademark of Microsoft Corp.
6. ILOG and ILOG Solver are registered trademarks of ILOG Inc.
7. Microsoft Excel is a registered trademark of Microsoft Corp.

References

AIAA (1998). *AIAA Guide for the Verification and Validation of Computational Fluid Dynamics Simulations.* Reston, Va.: American Institute of Aeronautics and Astronautics.

Allen, M. R., J. A. Kettleborough, and D. Stainforth (2002). Model Error in Weather and Climate Forecasting. *Proceedings of the 2002 European Centre for Medium-Range Weather Forecasts Predictability Seminar.* Reading, U.K.: European Centre for Medium-Range Weather Forecasts.

Archer, T. (2001). *Inside C#.* Redmond, Wash.: Microsoft Press.

Berleant, D., M.-P. Cheong, C. Chu, Y. Guan, A. Kamal, S. Ferson, et al. (2003). Dependable Handling of Uncertainty. *Reliable Computing* 9: 1–12.

Bower, J. and D. Bunn (2000). Model-Based Comparisons of Pool and Bilateral Markets for Electricity. *The Energy Journal* 21(3):1–29.

Bratko, I. (1990). *Prolog Programming for Artificial Intelligence.* Wokingham, U.K.: Addison-Wesley.

Brooks, F. P. (1975). *The Mythical Man-Month: Essays on Software Engineering.* Boston: Addison-Wesley.

Brooks, F. P. (1995). *The Mythical Man-Month: Essays on Software Engineering, 20th Anniversary Edition.* Boston: Addison-Wesley.

Copas, J. and S. Eguchi (2003). Model Uncertainty and Incomplete Data. *ISM Research Memorandum* (Institute of Statistical Mathematics, Japan) 884: 45.

Foxwell, H. (1999). Java 2 Software Development Kit. *Linux Journal* (online at http://www.linuxjournal.com/).

ILOG Inc. (2004). ILOG Home Page (http://www.ilog.com/). Gentilly, France: ILOG, Inc.

Keener, R. N. (1997). The Estimated Impact of Weather on Daily Electric Utility Operations. *Workshop on the Economic Impacts of Weather.* Boulder, Colo.: University of Colorado Center for Science and Technology Policy.

Kelley, A. and I. Pohl (1987). *C by Dissection: The Essentials of C Programming.* Menlo Park, Cal.: Benjamin Cummings.

Kruglinski, D. J. (1998). *Inside Visual C+*. Redmond, Wash.: Microsoft Press.

Minar, N., R. Burkhart, C. Langton, and M. Askenazi. (1996). The Swarm Simulation System: A Toolkit for Building Multi-Agent Simulations. Working Paper 96-06-042. Santa Fe, N.M.: Santa Fe Institute.

Mount, T. D. (2002). Using Weather Derivatives to Improve the Efficiency of Forward Markets for Electricity. *Proceedings of the 35th Annual Hawaii International Conference on System Sciences*. Hilton Waikoloa Village, Hawaii: IEEE.

North, M. J., N. J. Collier, and R. J. Vos (2006). Experiences Creating Three Implementations of the Repast Agent Modeling Toolkit. *ACM Transactions on Modeling and Computer Simulation* 16(1): 1–25.

Roy, P. V. and S. Haridi (1999). Mozart: A Programming System for Agent Applications. *The European Network of Excellence for Agent-Based Computing (AgentLink) Newsletter*. 4 (online at www.agentlink.org/admin/docs/1999/1999-022.txt)

Roy, P. V. and S. Haridi (2004). *Concepts, Techniques, and Models of Computer Programming*. Cambridge, Mass.: MIT Press.

The MathWorks Inc. (2004). The MathWorks Home Page. Natick, Mass.: The MathWorks Inc.

Tobias, R. and C. Hofmann (2004). Evaluation of Free Java-Libraries for Social-Scientific Agent Based Simulation. *Journal of Artificial Societies and Social Simulation* 7(1) (online at jasss.soc.survey.ac.uk/7/1/6.html)

Wolfram Research Inc. (2004). Wolfram Research Home Page. Champaign, Ill.: Wolfram Research, Inc.

8

How to Do Desktop ABMS

ABMS on the Desktop

Agent-based modeling and simulation (ABMS) can be done on the desktop with a standard office computer. Desktop ABMS can be used to learn agent modeling, test agent modeling design concepts, and perform some types of analysis. Standard computers can also be used to run many of the more sophisticated products of chapter 10. Unlike that chapter, this chapter focuses on agent models simple enough to be designed and developed in a period of a few days by one person as well as on tools that can be learned in a few days or weeks by computer-literate business analysts. The desktop tools considered in this chapter include spreadsheets, dedicated prototyping environments, and computational mathematics systems.

Spreadsheets are natural tools for most business analysts. Fortunately, spreadsheets can be used for basic ABMS. As such, spreadsheets are an excellent starting point for developing desktop agent models. Two complete examples of agent spreadsheet models are detailed in this chapter. The first example models the spatial flow of consumers in a retail store. This example is covered in the section on agent spreadsheets. The second example models a commodity market. This example is part of the market model coverage that runs throughout the book. The example is included in the last section.

There are several alternatives to spreadsheets on the desktop. These alternatives include dedicated ABMS prototyping environments as well as computational mathematics systems. In general, these environments trade off generality and specialization. ABMS prototyping environments tend to offer ready-to-use simulation components and are consequently less flexible than general-purpose spreadsheets. Several examples of ABMS prototyping environment models are briefly covered in the prototyping environments section. Computational mathematics systems tend to offer better mathematical modeling libraries and output routines than conventional spreadsheets. However, these environments are harder to learn and use in return. The advantages and disadvantages of each of these environments will be discussed in more detail in the following sections.

Examples of ABMS prototyping environments are shown in figures 8.32 through 8.37 while examples of computational mathematics systems are shown in figures 8.38 and 8.39. These examples will be discussed in the following sections along with the advantages and disadvantages of the environments.

Agent Spreadsheets

Any modern spreadsheet program can be used to do basic agent-based modeling. A spreadsheet program is considered modern for the purposes of this book if it supports multiple worksheets within a given workbook and has a simple scripting language. For the purposes of this book, the term "workbook" refers to a data file that can be loaded into a spreadsheet program independently of other files. A "worksheet" is one set of rows and columns within a workbook that can be independently addressed. The intersection of each row and a column forms a "cell." Each cell contains one number, text item, or formula. Cells normally can be color coded as well. The scripting language must include branching "if then" instructions and must be able to execute any basic command that could otherwise be entered with the keyboard. A few other features are highly useful but not strictly required, including support for "named ranges," "subroutines," and "code comments." Most modern spreadsheets support these features.

Named ranges are specially marked sets of spreadsheet cells that are associated with a shorthand name. Once a range of cells is named, spreadsheets can use the named range as if it was the cells themselves. In particular, changes to a named range cause immediate updates to the referenced worksheet cells. An example of a named range is the "Current Time" value shown in the Microsoft Excel[1] spreadsheet in figure 8.1. In case the range is named [Current_Time]. The corresponding spreadsheet cell is visible on the right side of the figure and

contains the value 11,640. This cell is located immediately to the right of the cell with the contents "Current Time." Excel named ranges are denoted with square brackets "[]". In this book, named ranges are being used anywhere bracketed text is seen in the code. The named ranges discussed in this book are defined in the text as well as labeled so that their purpose is clear.

Subroutines are small named sets of code that can be invoked at will. Subroutines are used to group commonly used code into a single location for easy reuse and also to break up long sections of code into smaller and more readable chunks. This book uses subroutines extensively to make the presentation of the example spreadsheet models easier to digest.

Similar to participatory simulation, spreadsheets are an excellent way to begin the iterative agent-based modeling process. Starting with participatory simulation allows simpler specifications to be used and immediately engages other people. However, starting with spreadsheets allows independent exploration and creates a more rigorous initial model. Spreadsheets are

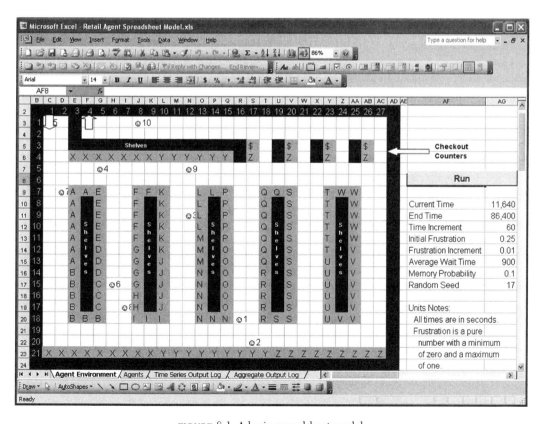

FIGURE 8.1 A basic spreadsheet model.

also a natural follow-up to participatory simulations. Spreadsheets allow the initial results from participatory simulations to be formalized and documented in an executable form. Either way, spreadsheets provide a good framework for early explorations with agent-based modeling as well as an approachable path for presenting agent-based modeling to senior managers.

Regardless of whether they are used before, after, or in place of participatory simulations, spreadsheets can be used for a variety of agent-modeling purposes. Spreadsheet ABMS can be used to develop business insights, to demonstrate agent-modeling concepts to business stakeholders, and also to initially test ideas for further ABMS development.

Business insights can be derived from agent-modeling spreadsheets through several mechanisms. The process of designing and developing usually deepens the modeler's understanding of the domain being modeled. The act of specifying and writing the spreadsheet encourages modelers to think in new ways about their domain. This new thinking is documented in the resulting spreadsheet. The spreadsheet model itself also provides many new opportunities for business insights. Since the spreadsheet is an agent model, it can be used to both explore and answer questions about the domain being modeled.

Agent spreadsheets have both strengths and weaknesses compared to the other ABMS tools. Agent spreadsheets tend to be easy to build, but they also tend to have limited capabilities. This balance makes spreadsheets ideal for agent-based model exploration, scoping, and prototyping. Simple agent models can be implemented on the desktop using environments outside of spreadsheets as well.

Spreadsheets are an ideal environment for simple agent-based modeling. However, simple environments dedicated exclusively to agent-based modeling are available. Several such environments will be discussed later in this chapter. Many of these prototyping environments are freely available without charge and can be immediately obtained from the Internet.

Dedicated ABMS prototyping environments tend to feature ready-to-use simulation components at the cost of reduced flexiblity compared to general-purpose spreadsheets. It should be noted that many of these environments are in fact educational tools specifically designed to introduce people to agent-based model design and development. This focus on education makes the tools easier to learn for beginners and also means that there are a variety of materials available to support learning.

Agent spreadsheets have several advantages, including the fact that they can be easy to build, quickly developed, and low cost to write. Furthermore, agent spreadsheets can use many of the built-in calculation and output functions provided by modern spreadsheet environments. The built-in calculation functions can be used to develop spreadsheet agents with behaviors based on relatively sophisticated mathematical functions. The advanced graph-plotting and statistical tabulation functions found in modern spreadsheets can be used to create high-quality output reports and graphs for agent spreadsheets.

In addition to several notable strengths, agent spreadsheets also tend to have specific limits. These limits include complexity constraints, size bounds, and diversity restrictions. While not an issue for initial models, these limits can be problematic for more advanced modeling efforts.

In principle, it is possible to write nearly any function using the advanced scripting capabilities found in many modern spreadsheet packages. Furthermore, since the code for every desktop computer programming environment runs on the same underlying processor, nearly anything that can be done in one programming environment can be done in any other. In practice, the amount of effort required to complete a given task in different programming environments can vary enormously. Even the most modern spreadsheets have relatively simple internal structures compared to more advanced environments such as full-featured programming languages. This simplicity is why spreadsheets are much easier to use than full-featured programming languages. The simplicity of spreadsheets comes from specialization. Spreadsheets are highly specialized to provide an interactive environment for basic business calculations and analysis. This is why they can be used to quickly create simple agent-based models. For example, it is relatively easy to create market bidding agents that remember commodity prices from previous days. However, this simplicity comes at a price. The specialization of spreadsheets limits the range of computational activities that can be easily performed. This is why the complexity of agent rules within agent spreadsheets is usually quite restricted compared to the other computational environments to be discussed later. In principle, any behavior can be programmed into a spreadsheet agent. In practice, only behaviors based on row- and column-oriented mathematical functions are easy to program. Behaviors become increasingly difficult and awkward to program as their specifications diverge from numeric grid-oriented mathematics. Continuing the example of market bidding agents, it is relatively difficult to create agents that maintain variable-sized trading networks of sources and clients. The specialization of spreadsheets introduces limits on other things in addition to the complexity of agent behaviors.

The number of agents allowable in ABMS spreadsheets is usually small compared to the other computational environments. This is caused by a combination of two factors. First, even advanced modern spreadsheets usually have strict constraints on both the allowable number of rows and the permitted number of columns. Usually the maximum row count is in the upper tens of thousands and the maximum column count is in the hundreds. Second, most spreadsheet model implementations require at least one row and several columns for each agent. The result is an upper bound on the number of agents that can be instantiated in a spreadsheet simulation. As discussed previously, the emphasis that spreadsheets place on data storage in rows and columns makes them easier to work with but also has other consequences as well.

Row- and column-oriented storage tends to make it difficult to create a large number of structural differences between agents. This difficulty stems from the need to create custom scripts to work with each of the different agent types. Thus, agent diversity within ABMS spreadsheets is usually lower than that found in the other computational environments discussed in this book.

One mixed blessing that comes with spreadsheet models is that by default the code and data are stored together. This feature is shared by most computational mathematics systems. The advantage of this feature is that it makes reproducing model runs easier since restoring the data automatically restores the code. However, this can also be problematic since code updates need to be propagated to all of the spreadsheets containing the underlying data. In general, it is possible to break up the code and data into separate workbooks. This is not recommended for prototyping since having the data with the code simplifies testing and speeds initial development. Breaking up the code and data is recommended for operational models since this makes code updates more reliable.

Example of a Retail Store Spreadsheet Model

Developing spreadsheet models involves more than simply copying and pasting one or more agents into a spreadsheet environment. As will be discussed, a variety of issues must be considered, including time management, input data setup, output results collection, and stochastic run specification. These operations will be illustrated with a specific example, which is a basic retail store spreadsheet model. This illustrative example model[2] was inspired by John Casti's SimStore model (Casti 2001):

> The starting point for SimStore is a real supermarket in the Sainsbury chain, one located in the London region of South Ruislip. The agents are individual shoppers who frequent this store. These electronic shoppers are dropped into the store, and then make their way to the various locations in the store by rules such as "wherever you are now, go to the location of the nearest item on your shopping list," so as to gather all the items they want to purchase.

This subsection will discuss the conceptual design of the simple spreadsheet example. The remaining subsections in this section will detail the implementation of the conceptual design using Microsoft Excel for concreteness, although the approach presented here can be used with any modern spreadsheet.

The goal of the project is to represent the flow of retail customers on a department store sales floor at about a 4-foot resolution on a rectangular grid to test the effects of different floor plans on the percentage of trips with successful purchases, the volatility of trips with successful purchases, the average customer frustration level, and the customer frustration volatility level. The consumers will be boundedly rational for simplicity. The agents in the model are retail shoppers who are buying items in a store. The retail store has items placed on shelves located throughout the store. The shelves contain a group of each type of item. Shoppers can select any item from the appropriate group. Once they select an item, shoppers head to the checkout counters to purchase the item and then leave the store.

Each shopper agent has one item they are shopping for. This limit was chosen to keep the exposition that follows simple. This limit can be extended as needed. However, for some department stores this may be quite reasonable, particularly if impulse buying is excluded. The model can be easily modified to include impulse buying by modifying the shopper's shelf-checking behavior to periodically check for and pick up unexpected items of interest. This can be done with just a few lines of code. The implementation of the shelf-checking behavior is discussed in detail later in this chapter.

Shoppers begin their trip at the front door of the store. Each shopper may or may not remember where their individual item is located in the store. The first time a shopper visits the store they do not know where their item is located. Once they find the item, they may remember the location on their next visit but their memories are not perfect.

To find an item, each shopper either moves toward the remembered location of their item or they mill through the store from the front to the back. If they know the location they head roughly in the correct direction. If they do not remember the location then they mill through the store. Again, none of the shoppers has perfect knowledge of the store, so their movements are only approximately in the right direction. Furthermore, the movements of shoppers are complicated by the need to avoid bumping into other shoppers and the store shelves.

Once a shopper finds their item of interest, they head to the checkout counters. As before, shoppers have limited knowledge of where the counters are and which counters have shorter lines until they get near the counters. Shoppers leave the store through the main exit once they have visited a checkout counter to purchase their item. Shoppers return to the store for another purchase trip on a periodic basis.

What about shoppers who have a hard time finding their item of interest? Simply put, they become frustrated and eventually leave the store without purchasing an item. Shoppers can become frustrated due to a lack of knowledge of their item's location, crowds slowing their progress, or a complex store layout. Any of these factors will drive the shopper out of the store. Shoppers remember their frustration with previous trips when they return to the store. There is some good news, though: shoppers' frustration drops when they quickly find their item of interest. These good experiences are also remembered.

There are several important measures of interest. These include the percentage of trips with successful purchases, the volatility of trips with successful purchases, the average frustration level, and the frustration

level volatility. These measures can be used to evaluate the effectiveness of various store layouts.

How to Design Agent Spreadsheets

Spreadsheets are intended to be used in a highly interactive and iterative fashion. This springs from their original purpose of supporting basic "what if" reasoning. This focus is a natural fit for desktop ABMS. Following this line of reasoning, an obvious question is "Should agent spreadsheets be designed at all?" Why should they not simply be built up interactively in stages from the simplest components? The answer is that in many cases they should be built this way. So why have a section on spreadsheet agent design?

Thinking about spreadsheet agent design for a few moments has some substantial benefits. First, it allows new modelers to get a better handle on their goals. One of the biggest challenges with desktop agent modeling is limiting the problem description to something manageable. This is just like writing a paper. Pick a problem too large and the paper will be difficult to write. Pick a problem of an appropriate size and direction and the paper will almost write itself. Considering the design of an agent spreadsheet for a few minutes allows the problem to be bounded to a workable scale. Second, considering spreadsheet agent design will allow the reader to better understand the detailed model presentation that begins in the next section. In particular, the discussion of the spreadsheet design will introduce the design decisions and modeling approximations made in creating the spreadsheet. These choices will be detailed in the sections on the model code that follow. Third, covering spreadsheet agent design will build fundamental knowledge that will be useful later in chapter 10. Fourth, covering spreadsheet agent design will provide extra examples of the techniques discussed in chapter 6.

There are a variety of approaches to agent spreadsheet design. The informal techniques include hand-drawn diagrams, presentation graphics diagrams, and simple text descriptions. The formal techniques include Unified Modeling Language (UML), which is detailed in chapter 6. It is recommended that designers start simple with basic diagrams and then refine their ideas using more structured techniques. UML is often not necessary. The most common path is to begin with a few hand-drawn diagrams and then supplement this with a short written description of the agent behaviors. A detailed example that shows each of the stages in designing a model of retail shopping will make these steps clear.

Like most spreadsheet agent designs, the design used for the example of a retail shopping model is relatively simple. Figure 8.2 shows an informal thumbnail sketch of the retail agent spreadsheet design. The fact that the sketch is hand drawn onto a napkin reinforces the informality of this design stage. The diagram on the right shows that each shopper moves through a store shown on the left following a regular cycle shown on the right. The store layout on the left seems to be relatively clear. The implementation details certainly remain, but these will be discussed later. The behavioral cycle on the right seems to need some clarification. This leads to the second description of the model. This description uses informal text to extend, clarify, and correct the original diagram. In particular, note that the text control flow is significantly different from the original sketch. This occurred because the process of adding details highlights missing issues in the original sketch. This text describes the design from the point of view of the shopper:

1. The shopper checks to see if they are waiting outside the store between shopping trips. If they are waiting, then they determine if it is time for another trip to the store.

2. The shopper checks to see if they are at the store exit. If they are, then they leave the store and begin to wait for their next trip. While exiting, they record that they have completed another trip. This record is used by the environment for simulation results logging.

3. The shopper checks to see if they have found the target they are seeking. The target can be either the item of interest or the checkout counters, depending on the shopper's current situation. If either target is found, the shopper checks the type of target found and then selects the appropriate next goal. If the target is an item to be purchased, then the shopper records that they have found another item of interest. As with the trip count, this record is used by the environment for simulation results logging.

4. The shopper checks to see if they are trying to leave the store after passing the checkout counters. If they are, then they move toward the door.

5. The shopper checks to see if they are currently feeling frustrated or are momentarily distracted. If they are, then they mill about randomly for a moment.

6. Finally, if none of the other choices are made, then the agent moves toward their current target.

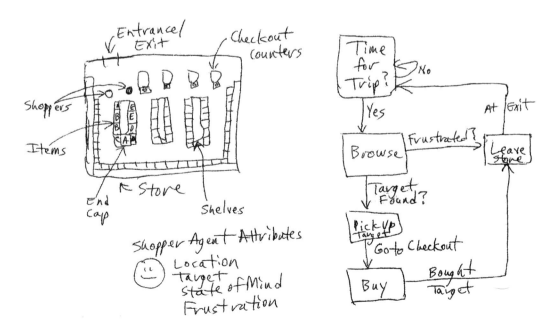

FIGURE 8.2 Informal retail agent spreadsheet sketch with a store layout on the left and the shopper behavioral cycle on the right.

As before, the target can be either the item of interest or the checkout counters. The shopper moves by picking the neighboring cell that is closest to the remembered target location using the Manhattan distance or taxicab metric. The Manhattan distance is the number of rows and columns in a rectangular path between the shopper and the goal. An example is shown in figure 8.3. Notice that this approach of minimizing Manhattan distance can cause shoppers to get trapped as shown in figure 8.4. These traps are escaped by the frustration-induced random movements in step 5. This simple approach seems to work reasonably well based on the fact, later, that a substantial percentage of shoppers are able to find their targets.

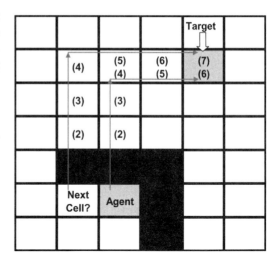

FIGURE 8.4 A shopper trapped by a barrier (black cells) due to Manhattan distance minimization.

Each attempt to move leads to a check of the selected cell. The shopper moves to the selected cell if it is empty. This slightly reduces their frustration level. Frustration is a pure number with a minimum of zero and a maximum of one. The shopper stays put if the selected cell is occupied by another shopper or if the cell is a wall or shelf. Shoppers who are unable to move forward slightly increase their frustration level. If the frustration level rises far enough, then the shopper gives up and heads toward the checkout counters and then the door without buying. The trigger point for leaving the store is a frustration level of one.

The simple behaviors discussed here are not intended to be a complete representation of all retail shopper behaviors. Rather, they are intended to provide a simple and understandable example of how to design and later build a basic spreadsheet agent model. Of course, real shopper behavior is more detailed than this and the specifics of shopper behavior depend on the type of retail establishment. Furniture stores have different traffic patterns than discount grocery stores. The model presented here simply shows how agent modeling can be done with spreadsheets. Furthermore, it must be remembered that this is a spreadsheet model. More sophisticated behaviors can be implemented using spreadsheets, but this tends to become progressively more difficult. The recommended approach is to move to the more scalable tools presented in chapter 10. For now, the grocery store model is a proto-agent simulation as can be seen from the shopper's minimally adaptive behavior. Figure 8.5 shows a UML State Diagram for our basic spreadsheet shopper agent.

Each shopper determines their own behavior when they get activated. So how do the shoppers get activated in the first place? This is the ABMS environment's job. Figure 8.6 shows the UML State Diagram for the agent spreadsheet environment. The figure shows the following basic steps:

1. The model is initialized. This allows the agents to reset their agent attributes and lets the environment clear its output logs.
2. A time loop is started. The loop is repeated for each time step until the simulation end time

FIGURE 8.3 Example of a Manhattan distance calculation yielding a distance of six squares between an agent and the agent's target.

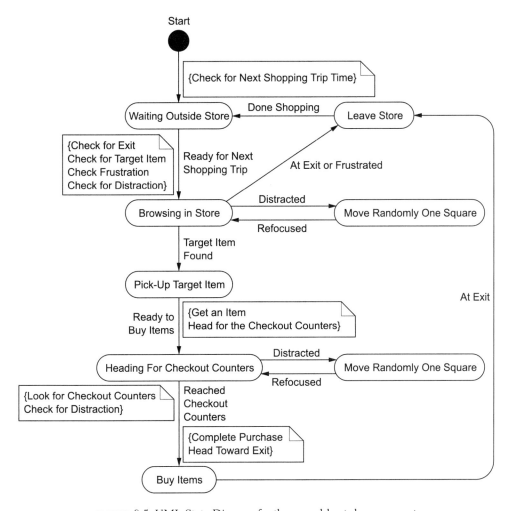

FIGURE 8.5 UML State Diagram for the spreadsheet shopper agent.

is reached. Each pass through the loop involves the following activities:

(a) Each of the agents is sequentially activated. Each activation cycle follows the previously discussed steps.

(b) The two main output logs are updated. The time-series output log records and graphs the current average frustration. The aggregate output log records the current averages and standard deviations for the number of items found, the number of trips, and the frustration level. The percentage of successful trips is also recorded.

How to Organize Agent Spreadsheets

There are a variety of approaches to implementing agent models using spreadsheets. These approaches vary in the complexity of their designs and the sophistication of the resulting agents. The simplest approach associates a spreadsheet row with each agent. More complex approaches assign multiple rows or even whole worksheets with each agent.

The most basic approach to developing an agent model using spreadsheet software is to factor the model implementation into three major components along functional lines. The main components are the agent list, the agent environment, and the model output logs.

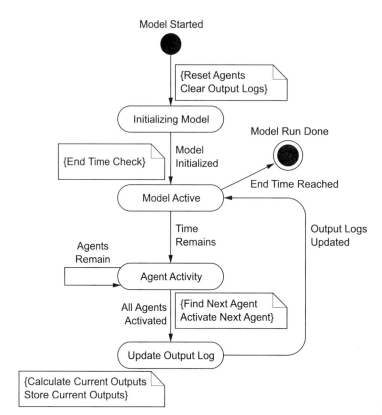

FIGURE 8.6 UML State Diagram for a basic spreadsheet ABMS environment.

Each of these modules implements a separate critical task as shown in the retail consumer agent model example in figure 8.1. These elements are normally placed into different worksheets within basic spreadsheet models to simplify development and maintenance. These separate worksheets can be seen along the lower tabs labeled "Agent Environment," "Agents," "Time Series Output Log," and "Aggregate Output Log" in the figure.

The first basic spreadsheet component is the agent list. Naturally, this list contains all of the agents in the model. In the simplest spreadsheet models, the agents all have the same number and kind of properties with varying values. Each row in the worksheet is associated with one agent. Each column in the worksheet is associated with an agent property. Each cell contains the value of a given property in the selected column for a given agent in the selected row. An example is shown in figure 8.7. Each agent is a retail store shopper who is looking for one item in the store. Slightly more sophisticated implementations can include optional agent properties by leaving blank the cells for

agents that lack a given property. The consumer market spreadsheet model presented at the end of this chapter uses this more sophisticated structure to represent multiple agent types each of which has different properties.

The second component is the agent environment. The agent environment represents the container or context that surrounds the agents. Agent environments normally show or post status information that is intended to be available to most, if not all, agents residing within a given environment. Because of this, agent environments are sometimes called "blackboards" or "bulletin boards." A simple example is shown in figure 8.1. The foundational concepts underpinning agent environments are discussed in more detail in chapter 10. This chapter will discuss how they are structured and implemented.

Agent environments can contain a range of content. Example content includes hourly clearing prices within commodity market models, global weather within a transportation model, and changing government worker protection requirements within

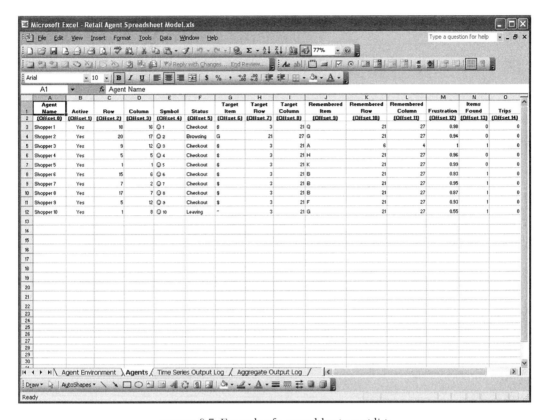

FIGURE 8.7 Example of a spreadsheet agent list.

human resources models. This content is structured to be available to all of the agents within the environment. Normally this is achieved within spreadsheet models by placing the content in a special worksheet that is available to all of the agents in the system.

It is possible to have more than one agent environment by placing the appropriate values in more than one worksheet. Agents can interact with more than one environment or move between environments using indexing to name the environment worksheet they are using at any given time. An example is a business simulation with agents that can choose to bid into one of several markets at any given time. Each market represents a separate environment that the agents can move between over time. While it is possible to have more than one agent environment within a spreadsheet model, this is not commonly done in practice. This is mainly driven by the fact that once a model becomes complex enough to require multiple agent environments, it has usually outgrown the limits of spreadsheet modeling.

The third component is the model output log. An example to be discussed later is shown in figure 8.30. This log records critical values over time. As can be seen by comparing figures 8.29 and 8.30, model output logs normally contain two types of data. The first are time-series data and the second are aggregate outputs. Time-series data stores data in a list that is indexed by time. Aggregate data combines data from many agents across time periods into a much smaller set of data. Time-series and aggregate data are discussed in chapter 12. Techniques for managing, understanding, and presenting both kinds of data are discussed in chapter 13.

How to Develop Spreadsheet Environments

Agent spreadsheet environments consist of three major components. The first is the environment variables, the second is the agent world, and the third is the output logs. All of these components are visible in figure 8.1.

The environment variables section contains storage for constants such as the [Time_Increment] named range and variables such as the [Current_Time] named range. One key value is the named range for the random seed, [Random_Seed]. A variable of this type is needed in every model that uses random numbers as explained in chapter 13. All of the constants and parameters used in the model should be collected into the environment variables worksheet or worksheets to clearly document the contents of the model and to simplify model parameter changes. The environment variables for the retail model are listed in table 8.1. In addition to the variables list, the other major environmental component is the agent world.

Agent worlds house the agents in the spreadsheet model. In contrast to the relatively simple structure of the environment variables worksheets, agent worlds can vary greatly in complexity. There are in fact a large number of different options for agent worlds. The simplest worlds have no spatial structure at all. An example is the market model presented near the end of this chapter. In this model, the agents compete in a commodities market without a notion of space. There is no grid or map. All that is present are agents sending bids into the market and receiving responses in return. This is in fact the most common structure for spreadsheet agent worlds. Other arrangements are possible, however.

In contrast to the simple nonspatial market example at the end of this chapter, the retail shopping model has a full store floor plan. This floor plan is shown in figure 8.8. The floor plan is composed of a set of cells that are marked with colors and text content. The colors are used to identify walls and shelves. Specifically, the walls are cells with a black background and the shelves and other special content are denoted with gray cells. The gray special content cells each contain one character that determines what the cell contains.

The letters A through Z represent items for sale. Items are stocked throughout the store, sometimes in multiple places. The U.S. dollar sign ("$") represents checkout counters. The numbers that count down the far right column and across the top row represent the coordinates of the intersected cells. An example is the cell at relative row seven and relative column three (Excel cell E9) that contains item A. Relative locations are used in the model since they simplify many of the calculations and allow stores to be described in their own natural coordinates. The arrows in the upper left of the store around Excel cells C3 and F3 represent the entry and exit doors respectively. Finally, the agents in the store are visible in the figure. An example agent, in this case agent number 4, can be found at the relative location given by row five and column five (Excel cell I19).

Store navigation uses the [Environment] named range. [Environment] identifies the upper left corner of the store. This named range is located at relative row zero column zero (Excel cell B2). All of the location information in the store discussed above

TABLE 8.1 ABMS spreadsheet environment variables

Environmental variable	Default value	Meaning
Current time	0 seconds	The simulation time counter in seconds
End time	86,400 seconds	The simulation stopping time in seconds
Time increment	60 seconds	The number of seconds to add to the current time for each shopping group time step
Initial frustration	0.25	The shopper's current mental state. Frustration is a pure number with a minimum of zero and a maximum of one
Frustration increment	0.01	The value to add to the frustration level every time things get worse and to subtract every time things get better
Average wait time	900 seconds	The average number of seconds between separate shopping trips
Memory probability	0.1	The probability that the shopper will remember a located item the next time they return to the store
Random seed	17	The value used to choose a random number sequence for simulation execution. Each new value produces a new stochastic run.

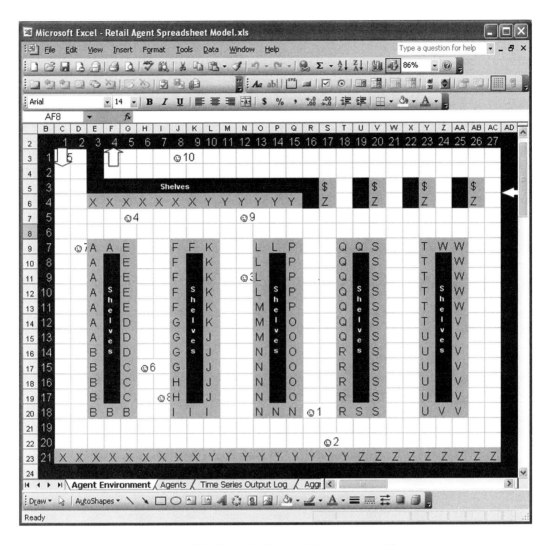

FIGURE 8.8 Example of a spreadsheet agent world.

is relative to this point. As will be shown later, offsets from the named [Environment] range are used to move agents and sense items in the store.

Agent worlds and the associated environmental variables are often placed in the same worksheet if they can be fit together onto about one screen. More complex agent models break them up over several worksheets if visibility or complexity become issues. The current agent model supports end caps, displays, and features but only allows one level of shelves. Of course, shelf height placement is a major issue for retailers and product manufacturers alike. The current model could be extended to represent multiple

shelves of goods by separating the different floor elevations into separate worksheets. The main floor plan worksheet would contain the black wall markings, the gray shelf markings, and the customer locations. Each of the other store worksheets would contain one shelf level such as floor level, below eye level, eye level, above eye level, and top. The extra worksheets can be easily made by creating new worksheets, copying the current floor plan, and then updating the contents. The only required code change is to the shopper's "LookAround" subroutine that is detailed near the end of this section. The needed change is outlined along with the discussion of the current code. Many readers can guess the next sentence. This straightforward extension is left as an exercise for the reader.

Agent spreadsheets normally operate by using a simple time-stepped approach. As described in chapter 6, time-step scheduling counts forward in time and allows each agent to execute exactly once during each time step. This is normally accomplished using a double loop approach. The outer loop counts time. The inner loop scans down the list of agents and allows each agent to execute once per time step.

An example of an outer loop for a retail consumer model written using Microsoft Excel Visual Basic for Applications[3] is shown in figure 8.9. This subroutine includes a variety of code comment lines marked with a leading single quote (" ' "). These comment lines are not executed and can contain any desired text. As shown in the example, comments are used to clarify the meaning of code.

This code is assigned to the "Run" button visible in figure 8.1. To execute the model, open up the spreadsheet, move to the "Agent Environment" worksheet if it is not already open, size the Excel window so that both the store layout on the left and the "Run" button on the right are visible, and then press the "Run" button. Shoppers will begin to move around the store. Excel prevents workbooks from being modified while the model is running. The current simulation time and end time are shown immediately below the "Run" button. The simulation will automatically stop when the current time reaches the end time. Shorter runs can be requested by setting the end time to a smaller value. The model can be stopped at any time by pressing the "Escape" key and selecting "End" from the resulting interruption notification window.

The code begins by executing an initialization routine named `Initialize` that resets the agent environment and assigns the initial values of the agent variables. It then sets the current simulation time (the [Current_Time] named range) to zero. The [Current_Time] simulation time variable is taken to be in seconds. Once the simulation time is set to zero, the `Run` routine begins a time loop that increments the current simulation time until it exceeds the selected simulation end time.

As previously discussed, the simulation time loop repeats three basic activities. The first activity is letting

```
' This is the main simulation routine.
Sub Run()

  ' Initialize the model.
  Call Initialize

  ' Reset the current simulation time.
  [Current_Time] = 0

  ' Check the current simulation time (Note that this is a
  ' synchronous model).
  Do While ([Current_Time] < [End_Time])

    ' Let the shoppers shop.
    Call ActivateShoppers

    ' Note the average customer frustration level.
    Call RecordAverageFrustration

    ' Step the current simulation time forward.
    [Current_Time] = [Current_Time] + [Time_Increment]

  Loop

End Sub
```

FIGURE 8.9 The environment's main routine.

the agents shop in the store. The second is to log the customer frustration level. The third is to increment the time variable. In this case, the time variable is incremented by [Time_Increment] = 60 units since each time step represents one minute of activity and the underlying simulation counter is in seconds.

The initialization routine is presented in figure 8.10. The routine begins by declaring a variable to point to the current shopper. It then sets the random seed value using the [Random_Seed] named range to ensure that simulation runs can be reproduced. Random seeds and run reproduction issues are discussed in chapter 11. Two lines are used to set the random seed due to a quirk in Excel (Gile 1999). Next, the output log graphing information is cleared. Several lines are used to ensure that the data is left in the proper state for later model execution. Finally, the environment initialization routine gives each agent a chance to initialize itself.

The environment's shopper initialization loop begins by setting the shopper variable declared earlier to point to each of the agents in the model. The agents are found using the [Shoppers] named range, which points to the names of each of the agents. Thus, the [Shoppers] named range references column A of the "Agents" worksheet as shown in figure 8.7. As will be detailed in the next subsection, each row in the [Shoppers] list represents one shopper agent.

The attributes of each shopper are contained in the columns of the shopper's row. In the Initialize routine the Offset(row, column) function is used to individually address one agent attribute at a time. The Offset function finds the cells that contain shopper agent attributes in the given column. The Offset function is discussed in detail in the next subsection on developing spreadsheet agents.

```
' This is the initialization routine.
Sub Initialize()

  ' Declare the local variables.
  Dim shopper As Range

  ' Set the random seed.
  Rnd (-1)
  Randomize ([Random_Seed])

  ' Reset the graph.
  [Frustration].Offset(1, 1) = 0
  [Frustration].Offset(2, 1) = 0
  [GraphLabels].Clear
  [GraphValues].Clear

  ' Initialize all of the shoppers.
  For Each shopper In [Shoppers]

    ' Complete the basic shopper initialization.
    Call InitializeShopper(shopper)

    ' Reset the items found counter.
    shopper.Offset(0, 13) = 0

    ' Reset the trip counter.
    shopper.Offset(0, 14) = 1

    ' Start with a moderate frustration level.
    shopper.Offset(0, 12) = [Initial_Frustration]

  Next shopper

End Sub
```

FIGURE 8.10 The environment's initialization routine.

```
' The shopping shopper initialization routine.
Sub InitializeShopper(shopper As Range)

    ' Remove the shopper from the store.
    Call ClearShopper(shopper)

    ' Reset the shopper's state.
    shopper.Offset(0, 5) = "Browsing"

    ' Set the shopper's starting location to the door.
    shopper.Offset(0, 2) = 1
    shopper.Offset(0, 3) = 1

    ' Have the shopper start by looking through the
    ' store from the door to the back corner.
    shopper.Offset(0, 10) = 21
    shopper.Offset(0, 11) = 27
    shopper.Offset(0, 6) = shopper.Offset(0, 9)
    shopper.Offset(0, 7) = shopper.Offset(0, 10)
    shopper.Offset(0, 8) = shopper.Offset(0, 11)

    ' Place the shopper in the store.
    Call DrawShopper(shopper)

End Sub
```

FIGURE 8.11 The shopper initialization routine.

The shopper initialization loop begins by calling the `InitializeShopper` subroutine which is discussed later and is shown in figure 8.11. The example subroutine can take a parameter, in this case the `Shopper` itself. In this example, the parameter's values can be changed and these changes are returned to the calling routine. The subroutines used in this book rely on the ability to change the values of parameters to simplify the model code. This subroutine allows shoppers to set their starting location, starting state, and opening goal as detailed in the next subsection. The `Initialize` subroutine loop resets the counters used to track the number of items the shopper has found and the number of trips the shopper has completed. Finally, the shopper's initial frustration level is set based on the environment's default frustration level as given by the `[Initial_Frustration]` named range.

The main shopper activation routine, `Activate Shoppers`, is shown in figure 8.12. This routine simply declares a shopper variable and then uses it to sequentially activate each shopper for the current time step. Shopper activation is accomplished by calling the `Shop` routine for each shopper.

Once the shoppers have been activated, the environment logs the results. The data recording preformed by the aggregate output log and the time-series data logged by the `RecordAverage Frustration` routine are detailed in the "How to Log Spreadsheet Output" section after the underlying agent data to be stored is discussed.

How to Develop Spreadsheet Agents

The spreadsheet environment is simply the stage for the shopper agents. The agents are the real purpose of the spreadsheet model. Agents in spreadsheet models are normally associated with a row in an agent list worksheet. The first column typically contains a name or tag that identifies that agent and the remaining columns represent the agent properties. The second column usually represents the agent type for models with more than one kind of agent. The retail shopper example has only one kind of agent, so a type column is not present. The example market spreadsheet presented near the end of this chapter uses two types of agents. In this case, the agents have different sets of attributes so the properties columns used by the agents are different. It is a good idea to sort the agent list by type to separate different kinds of agents with varying column definitions. It is also

```
' The main group shopping routine.
Sub ActivateShoppers()

    ' Declare the local variables.
    Dim shopper As Range

    ' Allow all of the shoppers to execute.
    For Each shopper In [Shoppers]

        ' Allow the next shopper to shop.
        Call Shop(shopper)

    Next shopper

End Sub
```

FIGURE 8.12 The shopper activation routine.

advisable to divide different agent types into separate worksheets if the agent properties are widely divergent. The example market model agent types have different, but closely related, properties so they fit reasonably well into one worksheet.

Ultimately, there are many potential ways to store agents in spreadsheets. Some are better than others. The retail shopper example (figure 8.8) provides a concrete illustration of a highly recommended approach for spatial agents. The market model presented later provides the same sort of example for agents that function without space.

The attributes of each shopper are contained in the columns of the shopper's row. In the Initialize routine the Offset(row, column) function is used to individually address one agent attribute at a time. The Offset(row, column) function starts with a cell, such as the shopper range, and then accesses the cell that is in the row given by (shopper + row) and column given by (shopper + column). Notice that offsets are one less than the row or column number since offsets are relative values (e.g., offset zero refers to the original row itself). The Excel Offset function is regularly used to access cells relative to named ranges and variables. The offsets for each shopper attribute are shown in the second row of figure 8.7 and are reproduced in table 8.2 for reference. The offsets are used throughout the discussion of the model details.

The ClearShopper subroutine removes the shopper from the display. This subroutine is shown in figure 8.13. It is used in conjunction with the DrawShopper subroutine to animate the shopper as they walk around the store. DrawShopper places the icon for the given shopper at the location in the store given by the row and column parameter. DrawShopper is shown in figure 8.14. The icon for each shopper is in the fifth column (or fourth offset). By default, shoppers are represented by smiling face symbols with the shopper number to the right. These icons are used for both animation and to mark cells as occupied to prevent shoppers from colliding. For this model, collisions are defined as two shoppers occupying the same cell at the same time. Such collisions are not allowed. The underscore ("_")

TABLE 8.2 The shopper attribute offsets

Offset	Shopper attribute
0	Agent name
1	Active
2	Row
3	Column
4	Symbol
5	Status
6	Target item
7	Target row
8	Target column
9	Remembered item
10	Remembered row
11	Remembered column
12	Frustration
13	Items found
14	Trips

```
' This is the shopper clearing routine.
Sub ClearShopper(shopper As Range)

  ' Clear the shopper from the display.
  [Environment].Offset(shopper.Offset(0, 2), _
    shopper.Offset(0, 3)) = ""

End Sub
```

FIGURE 8.13 The shopper clearing routine.

character indicates the continuation of a statement onto the following line.

Both the ClearShopper and the DrawShopper subroutines use the [Environment] named range for their work. As previously stated, this named range is located in the upper left corner of the store at relative row zero, column zero (Excel cell B2). The clearing and drawing subroutines use offsets from [Environment] to modify the contents of the store floor. In both cases the offsets used represent the shopper's current row at offset 2 and current column at offset 3. These offsets are given in table 8.2 and the corresponding columns can be seen in figure 8.7.

The main shopper shopping subroutine is shown in figure 8.15. This routine represents the heart of the agent shopping behavior. This is the principal subroutine to update if different shopping behavior is desired.

The shopping behavior subroutine allows the shopper to determine their current state and then act on the results that are found. The subroutine takes the form of a cascading set of conditional checks followed by actions. Each of the checks allows the shopper to compare their current attributes to status markers (i.e., "Waiting," "Found," or "Leaving"), a location (i.e., the door), or a derived value (i.e., a random draw for frustration). Each of the actions allows the shopper to respond appropriately to its situation.

The shopper's shopping behavior subroutine follows the UML State Diagram shown in figure 8.5. The actual internal states the shopper goes through are shown in figure 8.16. Note that one of the effects

of the agent behaviors in figure 8.5 is to drive the shopper through the internal states shown in figure 8.16. Other effects include moving, picking up items, and purchasing items. The steps are as follows:

1. The shopper checks to see if they are waiting outside the store between shopping trips as given by the shopper. Offset(0, 5) = "Waiting" check. Offset 5 is the shopper status column that is used several times in this routine. The possible shopper values of the shopper status column are itemized in table 8.3. If they are waiting, then they call the CheckWait subroutine to determine if it is time for another trip to the store. The shopper's row and column location are not changed by the subroutine so the shopper stays put.
2. The shopper checks to see if they are at the store exit, which is located at relative row one, column four (i.e., shopper.Offset(0, 2) = 1 and shopper.Offset(0, 3) = 4). If they are at the exit, then they leave the store using the FinishTrip subroutine. After FinishTrip the shopper will begin waiting to return to the store.
3. The shopper checks to see if they have found the target they are seeking (i.e., shopper. Offset(0, 5) = "Found"). The target can be either the item of interest or the checkout counters. If either target is found, the shopper checks the type of target found and then selects the appropriate next goal by calling

```
' This is the shopper drawing routine.
Sub DrawShopper(shopper As Range)

  ' Draw the shopper.
  [Environment].Offset(shopper.Offset(0, 2), _
    shopper.Offset(0, 3)) = shopper.Offset(0, 4)

End Sub
```

FIGURE 8.14 The shopper drawing routine.

```
' The main shopper shopping routine.
Sub Shop(shopper As Range)

  ' Check to see if we have found the target.
  If (shopper.Offset(0, 5) = "Waiting") Then

    ' Check to see if our wait is over.
    Call CheckWait(shopper)

  ' Check to see if the shopper is at the door
  ' and ready to leave the store.
  ElseIf ((shopper.Offset(0, 2) = 1) And _
    (shopper.Offset(0, 3) = 4)) Then

    ' Note the finished trip.
    Call FinishTrip(shopper)

  ' Check to see if we have found the target.
  ElseIf (shopper.Offset(0, 5) = "Found") Then

    ' Check the target item.
    Call CheckTarget(shopper)

  ' Check to see if the shopper should leave the
  store.
  ElseIf (shopper.Offset(0, 5) = "Leaving") Then

    ' Move toward the door.
    Call MoveTowardTheDoor(shopper)

  ' Check to see if we are frustrated or distracted.
  ElseIf (shopper.Offset(0, 12) > Rnd()) Then

    ' Move randomly.
    Call MoveRandomly(shopper)

  Else

    ' Move toward the target using the
    ' Manhattan distance.
    Call MoveTowardTheTarget(shopper)

  End If

  ' Check to see if what we are looking for is
  nearby.
  Call LookAround(shopper)

End Sub
```

FIGURE 8.15 The main shopper shopping routine.

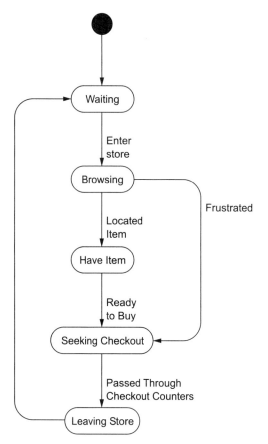

FIGURE 8.16 Shopper status UML State Diagram.

TABLE 8.3 The shopper status values

Status value	Meaning
Browsing	This value marks shoppers who are in the store and are looking for their item of interest. This is the initial value at the start of a model run and it is the first value when shoppers enter a store.
Found	This value marks shoppers who have just found what they are looking for. Shoppers enter this state either because who found their item or because they found the checkout counters. Shoppers who found what they are looking for have the item as their "Target Item" (i.e., the value of "Agents" worksheet column G or `shopper.Offset(0, 6)`).
Checkout	This value marks shoppers who are heading toward the checkout counters
Leaving	This value marks shoppers who have passed through the checkout counters either because they purchased an item or have given up shopping in frustration
Waiting	This value marks shoppers who are waiting outside the store between shopping trips

the `CheckTarget` subroutine. The shopper's row and column location are not changed by the subroutine.

4. The shopper checks to see if they are trying to leave the store after passing the checkout counters (i.e., `shopper.Offset(0, 5)` = "Leaving"). If they are leaving, then they move toward the door using the `MoveToward TheDoor` subroutine. The shopper's row and column locations are updated to move the shopper one cell closer to the door each time `MoveTowardTheDoor` is called.

5. The shopper checks to see if they are currently feeling frustrated or are momentarily distracted (i.e., `shopper.Offset(0, 12) > Rnd()`). This line works by comparing the shopper's current frustration level at offset 12 against a random number generated by Excel's built-in `Rnd` function. As previously discussed, the frustration level is a number between zero and one, with one representing the greatest aggravation. The `Rnd` function generates a new number between zero and one from the uniform distribution every time it is called. The uniform distribution is a flat line that assigns all of the values between zero and one an equal probability of being drawn. If the current frustration level is greater than the randomly generated number, then the shopper mills about randomly for a moment using the `MoveRandomly` subroutine. The shopper's row and column locations are updated to move the shopper to a randomly selected neighboring cell each time `MoveRandomly` is called.

6. Finally, if none of the other choices is made, then the agent moves toward their current target using the `MoveTowardTheTarget` subroutine. When shoppers move, they update their row and column location to be one cell closer to the target cell.

Once the above-mentioned steps are called, the shopper calls the `LookAround` subroutine to see if the target being sought is nearby. The target is either a shelf item if the shopper's status is "Browsing" or a checkout counter if the status is "Checkout." In the other statuses the `LookAround` subroutine is called but the results are not used. As described later, the `LookAround` subroutine checks the Moore neighborhood of the shopper for the shopper's target item

```
' This is this wait checking routine.
Sub CheckWait(shopper As Range)

    ' Check to see if our wait is over.
    If (Rnd() < 1 / [Average_Wait_Time]) Then

        ' Our wait is over.
        shopper.Offset(0, 5) = "Browsing"

        ' Note the trip.
        shopper.Offset(0, 14) = shopper.Offset(0, 14) + 1

    End If

End Sub
```

FIGURE 8.17 The shopper's waiting routine.

as given by the value of "Agents" worksheet column G or shopper.Offset(0, 6).

The CheckWait subroutine in figure 8.17 determines when shoppers return to the store after finishing their previous trip. The subroutine draws a random number using Excel's built-in Rnd function and then compares this number to the one from the [Average_Wait_Time] named range. Inverting the [Average_Wait_Time] causes larger values of the variable to produce smaller probabilities of exiting the waiting condition. The result is a simple function that causes the shoppers to wait based on the average value given by the named range. If the shopper's number is up, then their status is changed to "Browsing" and subroutine increments the value of the trips counter located at Offset (0, 14). This will cause them to begin shopping on the next time step.

The FinishTrip subroutine shown in figure 8.18 is called by shoppers when they reach the store's exit door. This routine is used by shoppers to end their current shopping trip and set the agent up for the next trip. Next the InitializeShopper subroutine is called to clear the shopper's cells of temporary values. Finally, the shopper sets its status to the "Waiting" state.

Shoppers use the CheckTarget subroutine shown in figure 8.19 when they find something of interest using the LookAround subroutine. CheckTarget determines if the shopper has found an appropriate item on a shelf or if they have found an available checkout counter. The target item value in shopper offset 6 (i.e., the value of "Agents" worksheet column G) gives the item being sought. If the value is a U.S. dollar sign ("$"), then the shopper was seeking a checkout counter. After checking out, the shopper status is updated to "Leaving" and the shopper stops looking for items (i.e., the target item is updated to the otherwise unused "~" value). If any other value is present in the target item column, then the shopper was seeking an item available for sale on a shelf. In this case, several things happen.

```
' This is the trip completion routine.
Sub FinishTrip(shopper As Range)

    ' Reinitialize the shopper.
    Call InitializeShopper(shopper)

    ' Wait to return to the store.
    shopper.Offset(0, 5) = "Waiting"

End Sub
```

FIGURE 8.18 The shopper's trip completion routine.

```
' This is the target checking routine.
Sub CheckTarget(shopper As Range)

  ' Check the target item.
  If (shopper.Offset(0, 6) = "$") Then

    ' A checkout counter was found so we should
    ' leave the store.
    shopper.Offset(0, 5) = "Leaving"

    ' Not that nothing is being sought.
    shopper.Offset(0, 6) = "~"

  ' A regular item was found.
  Else

    ' Note that an item was found.
    shopper.Offset(0, 13) = shopper.Offset(0, 13) + 1

    ' Check to see if we will remember where we
    ' found the item.
    If (Rnd() <= [Memory_Probability]) Then

      ' Remember where we found the item.
      shopper.Offset(0, 10) = shopper.Offset(0, 2)
      shopper.Offset(0, 11) = shopper.Offset(0, 3)

    End If

    ' Select the checkout counter area as the
    ' next target.
    shopper.Offset(0, 5) = "Checkout"
    shopper.Offset(0, 6) = "$"
    shopper.Offset(0, 7) = 3
    shopper.Offset(0, 8) = 21

  End If

End Sub
```

FIGURE 8.19 The shopper's target-checking routine.

First, the "item found" counter at offset 13 is incremented to account for the new find. This counter is used later to determine the average number of items found in the store.

Second, the shopper determines if they will remember the location using the [Memory_Probability] named range. By default [Memory_Probability] is set to 0.1, meaning that shoppers have a 10% chance of remembering where they found an item the next time they return to the store. If the uniform random number generated by the Rnd function is less than or equal to the [Memory_Probability] value, then the shopper remembers the location. Otherwise they stick with their current knowledge. The default 10% value assumes that shopping in this store is a either a very low involvement situation or that the shopper visits the store infrequently. This value can be easily changed by modifying it in the agent environment variables list. The location is remembered by storing the current row and column information into the shopper columns with offsets 10 and 11.

Third, the counter area is selected as the shopper's new target. This is accomplished by setting the shopper's status to "Checkout," the target item to the U.S. dollar sign ("$"), and the location being sought to the approximate center of the checkout counters. Setting this location assumes that the shopper either remembers or can see roughly where the counters are. This is reasonable under the circumstances. To simulate extremely complex store layouts or highly confused shoppers, it is relatively straightforward to modify the model to work with the same memory mechanisms used for finding items on shelves.

The `MoveRandomly` behavior begins by selecting a candidate cell for the next move. The relative coordinates of the candidate cell are stored in `nextRow` and `nextColumn`. The default values for `nextRow` and `nextColumn` are zero. Therefore, in the absence of changes to these values, the shopper stays put. The majority of the agent movement behaviors select nonzero values for `nextRow` and `nextColumn`. `MoveRandomly` is no exception. The subroutine opens by declaring the `nextRow` and `nextColumn` variables and then uses the `Rnd` function to select a nearby row and column. The `Rnd` function produces a new real number between zero and one every time it is called. Multiplying this by two and subtracting one yields a number between negative

one and positive one. The new candidate row and column are calculated by adding the newly generated numbers to the shopper's current row (i.e., `shopper.Offset(0, 2)`) and column (i.e., `shopper.Offset(0, 3)`). The result is a new cell in the Moore neighborhood of the shopper's current cell. Finally, this candidate cell is evaluated using the `CompleteMove` subroutine. As detailed later, the shopper uses `CompleteMove` to check the given candidate cell to make sure that it is empty. If the cell is empty, the shopper also uses `CompleteMove` to move to the new cell. The `MoveRandomly` subroutine is shown in figure 8.20.

The shopper uses the `MoveTowardTheTarget` subroutine to step cell by cell toward their remembered target location. The remembered target row and column are stored in agent offsets 6 and 7 in the "Agents" worksheet (Excel columns K and L). As discussed previously, the Manhattan distance is the number of rows and columns in a rectangular path between the shopper and the goal as shown in figure 8.3.

The `MoveTowardTheTarget` subroutine shown in figure 8.21 begins by declaring the `nextRow` and `nextColumn` variables along with a `delta` variable. The `delta` variable is used to hold the horizontal and vertical distances between the shopper and their goal. To select the new row, `delta` is set to the difference between the shopper's remembered target row (i.e., `Offset(0, 7)`) and the shopper's current

```
' This is the routine that moves us in a random
' direction.
Sub MoveRandomly(shopper As Range)

    ' Declare the local variables.
    Dim nextRow As Integer
    Dim nextColumn As Integer

    ' Move randomly.
    nextRow = Round((shopper.Offset(0, 2) + _
        2 * Rnd() - 1), 0)
    nextColumn = Round((shopper.Offset(0, 3) + _
        2 * Rnd() - 1), 0)

    ' Try to complete the proposed movement.
    Call CompleteMove(shopper, nextRow, nextColumn)

End Sub
```

FIGURE 8.20 The shopper's random motion routine.

```
' This is the routine that moves us toward the
' target using the Manhattan distance.
Sub MoveTowardTheTarget(shopper As Range)

  ' Declare the local variables.
  Dim nextRow As Integer
  Dim nextColumn As Integer
  Dim delta As Integer

  ' Select a neighboring row.
  delta = shopper.Offset(0, 7) - shopper.Offset(0, 2)
  If (delta > 0) Then
    nextRow = shopper.Offset(0, 2) + 1
  ElseIf (delta = 0) Then
    nextRow = shopper.Offset(0, 2)
  Else
    nextRow = shopper.Offset(0, 2) - 1
   End If

   ' Try to complete the proposed movement.
   Call CompleteMove(shopper, nextRow, nextColumn)

  ' Select a neighboring column.
  delta = shopper.Offset(0, 8) - shopper.Offset(0, 3)
  If (delta > 0) Then
    nextColumn = shopper.Offset(0, 3) + 1
  ElseIf (delta = 0) Then
    nextColumn = shopper.Offset(0, 3)
  Else
    nextColumn = shopper.Offset(0, 3) - 1
  End If

  ' Try to complete the proposed movement.
  Call CompleteMove(shopper, nextRow, nextColumn)

End Sub
```

FIGURE 8.21 The shopper's goal-seeking routine.

row location (i.e., Offset(0, 2)). If the value is positive, then the shopper needs to move up one row so delta is set to one. If the value is zero, then the shopper is in the correct row so delta is set to zero. Finally, if the value is negative, then the shopper needs to move down one row so delta is set to negative one. Once a candidate cell is identified, then the shopper evaluates it using the CompleteMove subroutine. As discussed later, the shopper uses CompleteMove to check the given candidate cell to make sure that it is empty and if so to move there. The process of cell identification is repeated for the column. Rows and columns are considered independently to allow shoppers to move freely to any of the surrounding eight cells. If the row and column were both evaluated at the same time, then shoppers blocked on one axis would be prevented from moving along the other axis as well.

Shoppers use the MoveTowardTheDoor subroutine shown in figure 8.22 to head directly toward

```
' This is the routine that moves us toward the door.
Sub MoveTowardTheDoor(shopper As Range)

  ' Declare the local variables.
  Dim nextRow As Integer
  Dim nextColumn As Integer

  ' Move toward the door.
  nextRow = shopper.Offset(0, 2)
  nextColumn = shopper.Offset(0, 3)
  If (nextRow > 1) Then
    nextRow = nextRow - 1
  End If
  If ((nextRow = 1) And (nextColumn > 4)) Then
    nextColumn = nextColumn - 1
  End If

  ' Try to complete the proposed movement.
  Call CompleteMove(shopper, nextRow, nextColumn)

End Sub
```

FIGURE 8.22 The shopper's door-seeking routine.

the door once they have passed the checkout counters. As with the other movement, MoveTowardTheDoor begins by declaring the nextRow and nextColumn variables. These variables are initially set to the shopper's current row (i.e., shopper.Offset(0, 2)) and column (i.e., shopper.Offset(0, 3)). The row is then decremented as long as the shopper is away from both the store wall (nextRow > 1) and the door ((nextRow = 1) And (nextColumn > 4)). Since the shopper is leaving at the checkout counters near row 3 and column 21, decrementing the row and column moves the shopper closer to the door located at row 1 and column 4. Once the next cell is identified, then the shopper checks it and moves there using the CompleteMove subroutine.

The CompleteMove subroutine shown in figure 8.23 finalizes the movement process. It is used by shoppers to check for occupied cells and to move to cells that are empty. The subroutine parameters include the shopper as well as the shopper's candidate row and column. The subroutine begins by declaring the variables used to check the color of the candidate cell. As discussed before, background colors are used to mark walls and shelves. The floorColor variable is set to the color (i.e., RGB(255, 255, 255) or bright white) used to mark floors. The nextCellColor

variable is set to the background or interior color of the candidate cell. If the next cell has the same color as the floor (nextCellColor = floorColor) and there are no occupants in the cell ([Environment]. Offset(nextRow, nextColumn) = ""), then the candidate cell is empty. The shopper icon is then cleared from the old location using ClearShopper, the new location is accepted, the shopper is drawn at the new location using DrawShopper, and the shopper feels better since they could make progress (FeelBetter). Note that marking the cells with DrawShopper serves both to provide a useful simulation animation for the user and to mark cells as occupied to avoid shopper collisions. If the location is a wall or is occupied, then the move is rejected and the shopper's frustration rises using the FeelWorse subroutine.

The FeelBetter subroutine shown in figure 8.24 is quite simple. Shoppers use the FeelBetter subroutine to reduce their frustration when they are able to move toward their target. The frustration level is a pure number between zero and one. The subroutine is used to subtract the environment's [Frustration_Increment] parameter from the shopper's current frustration level. The frustration level is stored in shopper offset 12 in the "Agents"

```
' This is the routine that completes the proposed
' movement.
Sub CompleteMove(shopper As Range, _
  nextRow As Integer, nextColumn As Integer)

  ' Declare the loal variables.
  Dim floorColor As Long
  Dim nextCellColor As Long

  ' Note the floor color.
  floorColor = RGB(255, 255, 255)

  ' Check for walls and other shoppers to avoid bumping.
  nextCellColor = [Environment].Offset(nextRow, _
    nextColumn).Interior.Color
  If ((nextCellColor = floorColor) _
    And ([Environment].Offset(nextRow, nextColumn) = "")) _
    Then

    ' There is nothing in the way so move the next
    ' location.

    ' Clear the current shopper location.
    Call ClearShopper(shopper)

    ' Assign the new location.
    shopper.Offset(0, 2) = nextRow
    shopper.Offset(0, 3) = nextColumn

    ' Move the shopper to the new location.
    Call DrawShopper(shopper)

    ' Become less frustrated every time we can move.
    Call FeelBetter(shopper)

  Else

    ' Become more frustrated every time we are blocked.
    Call FeelWorse(shopper)

  End If

End Sub
```

FIGURE 8.23 The shopper's movement completion routine.

worksheet (Excel column M). If the subtraction causes the frustration level to drop below zero, then the level is set back to zero.

The FeelWorse subroutine shown in figure 8.25 works similarly to the FeelBetter subroutine. The two differences are that the shoppers use FeelWorse

to add the [Frustration_Increment] to their frustration level and to check to see if they have reached their boiling point. If the shopper's frustration level has reached or exceeded its upper bound of one (shopper.Offset(0, 12) >= 1) and they are browsing for an item (shopper.Offset

```
' This is the routine that makes us feel better
' every time we can move forward.
Sub FeelBetter(shopper As Range)

    ' Become less frustrated every time we can move.
    shopper.Offset(0, 12) = shopper.Offset(0, 12) - _
      [Frustration_Increment]
    If (shopper.Offset(0, 12) < 0) Then
      shopper.Offset(0, 12) = 0
    End If

End Sub
```

FIGURE 8.24 The shopper's frustration reduction routine.

```
' This is the routine that makes us feel worse
' every time we are blocked.
Sub FeelWorse(shopper As Range)

    ' Become more frustrated every time we are blocked.
    shopper.Offset(0, 12) = shopper.Offset(0, 12) + _
      [Frustration_Increment]
    If (shopper.Offset(0, 12) >= 1) Then

      ' Give up if we have not found what we are
      ' looking for.
      If (shopper.Offset(0, 5) = "Browsing") Then

        ' Abandon the shopping without finding the item.
        ' Select the checkout counter area as the next
        ' target.
        shopper.Offset(0, 5) = "Checkout"
        shopper.Offset(0, 6) = "$"
        shopper.Offset(0, 7) = 3
        shopper.Offset(0, 8) = 21

      End If

      ' Note that there is a limit to our frustration.
      shopper.Offset(0, 12) = 1

    End If

End Sub
```

FIGURE 8.25 The shopper's frustration increase routine.

(0, 5) = "Browsing"), then the shopper starts looking for the checkout counters on the way to the door. Finally, if the shopper's frustration level was too high, then the shopper sets their frustration to one to stay within the stated limit.

The LookAround subroutine shown in figure 8.26 is used by shoppers to check their Moore neighborhood for items of interest. Items of interest are either store shelves or checkout counters depending on the shopper's status. In both cases, the items of interest are stored in shopper offset 6 in the "Agents" worksheet (Excel column G). The routine uses two nested "For...Next" loops to scan each of the nearby cells. The Exit For statement is used to leave the inner loop early after something is found. To simplify the loop, the shoppers also check their own location. Since the shoppers are not seeking themselves, they never find an item of interest at their own location. At least the shoppers are not too self-centered! If an item is found, then the shoppers change their status

in offset 5 to "Found" (i.e., shopper.Offset (0, 5) = "Found").

Obviously, shelf height placement is a major issue for retailers and manufacturers. As previously discussed, the current model can be extended to represent multiple shelves of goods by separating the different floor elevations into separate worksheets. The main floor plan worksheet would continue to contain the background color markings along with the customer locations. The new floor plan worksheets would each contain one shelf level. The extra worksheets can be easily made by creating new worksheets, copying the current floor plan, and then updating the contents. The only required code change is to replace the "LookAround" subroutine's [Environment] check with a set of checks for each level. The checks could be ordered to give preference to the most visible shelves. The Rnd function could also be used to give shoppers a nonzero chance of looking on the less visible shelves, just as it is used to determine

```
' This is the nearby area scanning routine.
Sub LookAround(shopper As Range)

    ' Check the eight neighboring squares to see if our item
    ' is nearby.
    For row = -1 To 1

        ' For simplicity we will check our own square too,
        ' but do not expect to find the item we seek.
        For column = -1 To 1

            ' Check the next nearby spot for our item.
            If ([Environment].Offset(shopper.Offset(0, 2) + row, _
                shopper.Offset(0, 3) + column) = _
                shopper.Offset(0, 6)) Then

                ' Note that we have found the item of interest.
                shopper.Offset(0, 5) = "Found"
                Exit For

            End If

        Next column

    Next row

End Sub
```

FIGURE 8.26 The shopper's shelf- and counter-checking routine.

shopper frustration. In fact, the probabilities could easily be set using real data on the likelihood of shoppers looking at each shelf.

How to Set Up Spreadsheet Input Data

The input data setup for agent spreadsheets is relatively simple since the spreadsheet itself can be used. Normally the environmental variables are set and then input data for individual agents is entered into the appropriate rows. Examples of environmental parameters are shown in figure 8.27. These parameters were discussed in detail in the "How to Develop Spreadsheet Environments" subsection. The example agent input data discussed in the previous subsection is shown in figure 8.28. This is all that is typically needed for models that do not involve spatial interactions, such as the market example to be discussed later in this chapter. Models that require spatial inputs, such as the store layout in the retail example, require slightly more work.

Spatial data can be represented in spreadsheets using the cell-based technique discussed in the previous subsections. Using this approach, individual cell contents are used to represent movable items such as agent locations and store stock. Immobile items such as store shelves and walls are marked using background colors. Note that this approach allows both movable and immobile items to coexist in the same cell. This might be used to add a parking lot with sidewalks to the model. The sidewalks could be marked with a special background color that the shoppers can walk on but automobile agents cannot. With this approach, creating new maps is as simple as painting a new background color pattern and moving some cell contents. For example, the store layout can be changed at any time by painting the new layout on top of the present floor plan. One disadvantage of the spreadsheet approach is the relatively low resolution of spreadsheet cells. However, this resolution may be sufficient for many purposes. Furthermore, the resolution can be increased since

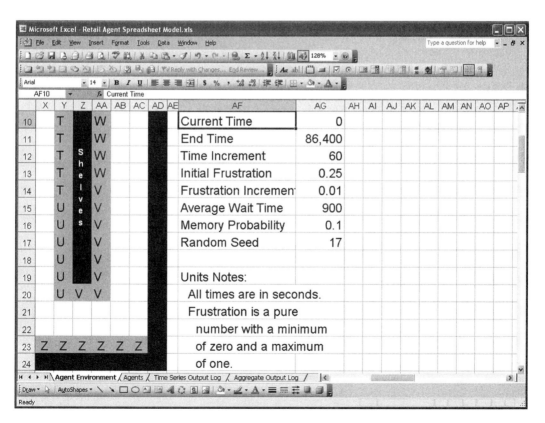

FIGURE 8.27 Examples of environmental variables.

FIGURE 8.28 Agent spreadsheet input data setup.

	Agent Name (Offset 0)	Active (Offset 1)	Row (Offset 2)	Column (Offset 3)	Symbol (Offset 4)	Status (Offset 5)	Target Item (Offset 6)	Target Row (Offset 7)	Target Column (Offset 8)	Remembered Item (Offset 9)	Remembered Row (Offset 10)	Remembered Column (Offset 11)	Frustration (Offset 12)	Items Found (Offset 13)	Trips (Offset 14)
3	Shopper 1	Yes	10	7	☺1	Checkout	$	3	21	Q		21	27	0.99	0	1
4	Shopper 2	Yes	1	1	☺2	Waiting	G	21	27	G		21	27	0.76	0	2
5	Shopper 3	Yes	4	21	☺3	Leaving	~	3	21	A		21	27	0.87	3	2
6	Shopper 4	Yes	1	1	☺4	Waiting	H	21	27	H		21	27	0.67	0	1
7	Shopper 5	Yes	1	1	☺5	Waiting	K	21	27	K		21	27	0.6	0	2
8	Shopper 6	Yes	1	1	☺6	Waiting	B	21	27	B		21	27	0.71	1	2
9	Shopper 7	Yes	17	17	☺7	Checkout	$	3	21	B		21	27	0.96	1	0
10	Shopper 8	Yes	5	3	☺8	Checkout	$	3	21	B		21	27	0.93	1	0
11	Shopper 9	Yes	3	2	☺9	Checkout	$	3	21	F		21	27	0.97	1	1
12	Shopper 10	Yes	1	1	☺10	Waiting	G	21	27	G		21	27	0.72	1	2

modern spreadsheets can support worksheets with thousands of rows and columns. Even if this is not sufficient, there are alternatives. For example, large-scale ABMS environments can easily accommodate layouts that are much bigger than this.

How to Log Spreadsheet Output

As with input data, spreadsheets make output results collection relatively simple. There are two major types of spreadsheet model logs, namely aggregate logs and time-series logs. Aggregate logs capture data that summarizes a number of time periods, often covering the entire simulation run. Time-series logs capture data from selected individual steps in time.

Spreadsheet aggregate logs are usually calculated using either running totals or summary statistics on time-series data. Figure 8.29 shows several running totals calculated for the retail shopper model. These values are based on running totals maintained by the individual shoppers. For example, the "Average Number of Items Found" formula (`"=AVERAGE(Agents!N3:N12)"`) finds the mean value of the "Items Found" column in the "Agents" worksheet (Excel column N). The other values are calculated similarly.

Note that the average percentage of successful trips simply divides the average number of items found by the average number of trips. This is not strictly correct since the shoppers who have just found an item will increment the number of items before they increment the number of trips. Thus, the reported

average percentage of successful trips may be slightly overestimated. For large numbers of shoppers the inaccuracy will be quite small. Of course, this is a simple prototype model designed to explore concepts rather than provide perfect results. Furthermore, all models are approximations and no system is perfect. The important point is to clearly document these types of issues so that modeling project managers and users can make informed decisions about the tradeoffs between model accuracy and implementation costs. If managers and users identify this approximation as problematic, then the issue can be corrected by extending shoppers to write their intermediate results to a temporary location. Thorough testing during development as described in chapter 11 can be used to identify these issues.

Spreadsheet time-series logs are normally maintained during the simulation by the agents themselves and their environment. The agents should do the logging if the items being logged pertain to the agent level. Otherwise, the environment should do the logging. In either case, the logging can occur for every time period or only for selected moments. If the logging is done every period, then the agents or the environment should be activated to complete the work. Selective logging is typically done for every nth time step, where n is an integer greater than one, or when interesting events occur. For both situations the logging is normally performed after all of the simulation activity for the period has been completed.

Figure 8.30 shows an example of an "Average Frustration" time-series log. Since the logged

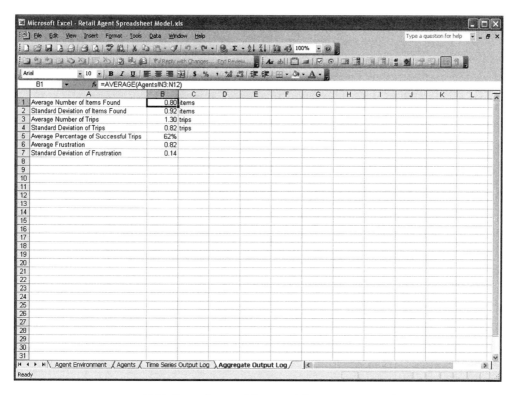

FIGURE 8.29 Example spreadsheet model aggregate output log.

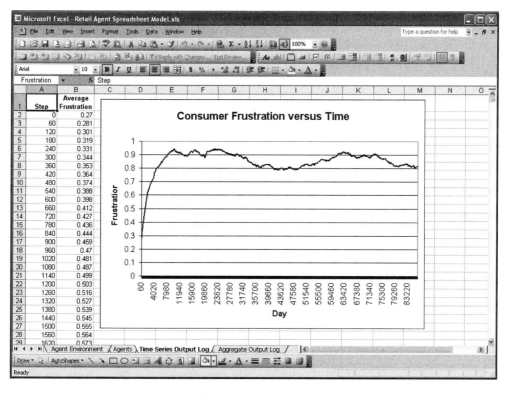

FIGURE 8.30 Example spreadsheet model time-series output log.

```
' This is the average frustration recording routine.

Sub RecordAverageFrustration()

    ' Record the average customer frustration level.

    [Frustration].Offset([Current_Time] / _

      [Time_Increment] + 1, 0) = [Current_Time]

    [Frustration].Offset([Current_Time] / _

      [Time_Increment] + 1, 1) = [Average_Frustration]

End Sub
```

FIGURE 8.31 The environment's time-series data recording routine.

values span agents, the log is maintained by the environment. The main recording subroutine is `RecordAverageFrustration`. As shown in figure 8.31, `RecordAverageFrustration` uses the `[Frustration]` named range to locate the storage area on the "Time Series Output Log" worksheet. The environment uses this subroutine to record the current time (`[Current_Time]`) and the average frustration (`[Average_Frustration]`) in "Time Series Output Log" worksheet (Excel columns A and B, respectively). The "Time Series Output Log" worksheet also contains a dynamically updated graph that shows the values recorded in the log.

How to Use Spreadsheet Models

Spreadsheet ABMS can be used for several purposes, including learning ABMS, prototyping model concepts, developing proof-of-concept models, and developing simple operational models. Each of these applications leads to a different pattern of model use.

Models intended for learning are used in an exploratory manner. The example retail agent simulation is such a model. With these types of models, the user essentially performs a type of undocumented "what if" testing. During this process the model is not only used but it is typically changed, often dramatically, since tweaking existing models is one of the best ways to learn practical ABMS.

Proof-of-concept models are used in a demonstration mode. The goal is to show that the model can reproduce basic features of a situation of interest. Typically the features are chosen such that representing them

has been especially challenging for the previously applied approaches. During this process, basic model verification and validation is performed as detailed in chapter 11 and the model results are interpreted at a basic level as described in chapter 13.

In many ways, operational models start where proof-of-concept models leave off. The goal is to use the model to reproduce important features of a situation of interest and then to use this knowledge to support better informed decision-making.

Of course, the way spreadsheet models are used depends on the type of model. As discussed in chapter 13, there are two fundamental types of models. These two types are deterministic models and stochastic models. Deterministic models always produce the same outputs when they are repeatedly run with identical inputs. An example is a simple reactive market model with bidding agents that raise prices by a fixed amount when their last bid was accepted and lower prices by another fixed amount when their last bid was rejected. Stochastic models can and often do produce different outputs when they are repeatedly run with identical inputs, excluding the random seed. An example is a market model with bidding agents that raise prices by a randomly chosen amount when their last bid is accepted and lower prices by a randomly chosen amount when their last bid was rejected. Stochastic models can produce different outputs because they include behaviors based on random or probabilistic elements. Because of this, stochastic models are said to be nondeterministic.

Most agent-based models include random or probabilistic elements. Thus, most agent-based models are stochastic. These probabilistic elements are often used to represent complicated behaviors that need to be included in the model but do not by themselves need to be modeled in detail. These elements are typically implemented using random draws from probability distributions.

As previously discussed, individual random draws from probability distributions are called variates (Law 2007). The fully specified probability distributions from which the variates are drawn are called random variables. The use of variates drawn from random variables makes a model inherently stochastic. Almost any modeling situation that uses variates drawn from random variables requires stochastic or repeated runs to derive general conclusions. However, the individual runs may also have substantial value since they may represent possible event sequences. These potential sequences can be used as examples for detailed investigation and as narratives for training.

The example retail shopper spreadsheet model is stochastic due to its use of the Rnd function. The random seed can be adjusted using the "Agent Environment" worksheet. This feature can be used to complete stochastic runs with the model. In contrast, the market model presented near the end of this chapter is deterministic and therefore does not require a random seed.

Dedicated ABMS Prototyping Environments

Spreadsheets are not the only method for performing desktop agent-based modeling. Dedicated ABMS prototyping environments can also be used. Many of these prototyping environments are available free of charge. All of the examples discussed in this book are free for many uses. Even better, the source code is freely available for some of these tools! Modelers can see a variety of ways to implement agent-based modeling components by looking through the source code for these environments.

ABMS Prototyping Environments

A variety of dedicated ABMS prototyping environments are available. All of the examples of prototyping environments discussed in this book are available for free learning through the Internet. The examples presented in this section were selected based on this factor as well as ease of use, breadth of features, and user community size. There are many differences between these environments. However, they all tend to have several key traits in common.

The most directly visible common trait shared by the various prototyping environments is that they are designed to get first-time users started as quickly as possible. This trait manifests itself in several ways. A visual orientation pervades these tools. They tend to use point-and-click inputs as much as possible. When they resort to text input they use simple and intentionally streamlined dialects. Many basic modeling components are available ready for use. In fact, most of the support mechanisms needed to execute an agent-based model, such as activity schedulers and data trackers, are automatically created and connected to the user's model without manual intervention. The cumulative effect of these features is a greatly reduced initial learning curve compared to most other alternatives. However, the learning curve for most prototyping environments tends to top out fairly quickly. This occurs because the very features that make these environments easy to learn ultimately tend to limit their flexibility.

An important and generally expected trait of prototyping environments is direct support for agent development. These environments normally have individual icons, specialized lists, and dedicated storage reserved for agents. These reserved resources are normally managed on the agent level. This means that, instead of allocating memory and then assigning agent properties to the free space, developers simply create agents and let the environment handle the digital details. This is quite different from ABMS spreadsheets that require developers to explicitly manage ranges of rows and columns for each agent. The price is that the environments naturally have bounds on the kinds of agent details they can manage. This in turn places limits on the types of agent designs that the environments can realistically support. Once again, there is a tradeoff between focus and flexibility.

The ABMS prototyping environments all share the trait of being easy to learn. Since they are intended to help new modelers learn ABMS, they are designed to automatically provide most of the common components and functions found in basic agent-based models. For example, prototype agents with simple built-in capabilities and generic agent environments are usually available. These tools are also arranged to maintain an extremely close correlation between the design of models and the visual presentation of those designs. For example, adding a new agent type to a model usually causes new markers to be added to the environment display for the model as well as new topics to be added in the appropriate places to the commonly supported model outline view. This clearly simplifies both learning and using the tools. Unfortunately, the tools achieve this simplification by assuming quite a lot about the model's structure. These assumptions tend to restrict the long-term scalability of these tools.

Most ABMS prototyping environments have limited mathematical functions and coarse output facilities. This is driven by several factors. Naturally, sophisticated mathematical functions and output facilities require more effort to learn than simpler systems. It is quite difficult to shield new modelers from this sophistication. The mere presence in the documentation of otherwise hidden functionality makes tools more challenging to learn. Furthermore, the simplicity of these tools owes much to the automation of common tasks. This automation is normally achieved by assuming that the model developers want to use the most common designs or options in their models. It is hard to develop systems that automate tasks yet also allow full manual intervention. The creators of most ABMS prototyping environments typically resolve this dilemma by restricting the allowed level of manual intervention for most tasks. If a model matches the common automated choices embedded in the tools, then the modeler is in luck. An ABMS prototyping environment might be used for the full model. If not, then the modeler will probably need to eventually have the model implemented using one of the other platforms described in this book. Even in this case, one or more of the prototyping environments may be extremely useful for hands-on learning of ABMS and for initial model prototyping.

Several dedicated ABMS prototyping environments will be described in the following sections. These tools are excellent for learning the fundamentals of agent model development, for testing basic model design directions, and for creating simple simulations. Some also have special features such as migration paths to large-scale toolkits or built-in support for participatory ABMS. These features are discussed along with the details on the individual tools.

Repast for Python Scripting

The REcursive Porous Agent Simulation Toolkit (Repast) is the leading free and open-source large-scale agent-based modeling and simulation toolkit (North et al. 2006). Repast seeks to support the development of extremely flexible models of agents with an emphasis on social interactions, but it is not limited to social modeling alone. Repast is maintained by the Repast Organization for Architecture and Design (ROAD) (ROAD 2004). More information on Repast, as well as free downloads, can be found at the Repast home page, http://repast.sourceforge.net/.

There are four Repast platforms. Together they form a complete agent-based modeling portfolio. The members of the Repast portfolio are Repast for Python Scripting (Repast Py), Repast for Java (Repast J), Repast for the Microsoft.NET framework[4] (Repast.NET), and Repast Simphony (Repast S). Repast Py is described in this section. The other versions are discussed in chapter 10.

Repast Py is a cross-platform visual model construction system that allows users to build models using a graphical user interface and write agent behaviors using a subset of the Python scripting language (Lutz and Ascher 1999). All of the features of the Repast J system are available in Repast Py, but Repast Py is designed for rapid development of prototype agent models. Repast Py models can be automatically exported to Repast for Java for large-scale model development.

The Repast Py interface running a simple social network model called the "Uniform Reinforcement Past Noise Linker" is shown in figure 8.32. This example is an implementation of a basic social network model from Skyrms and Pemantle (2000). The lines in the lower display window indicate social ties between the connected agent points. Agents form ties over time based on individually maintained lists of partner preferences. These preferences change over time as links form and are maintained. Agents with ties increase their preferences for the agents that they are tied to with occasional interfering noise. This agent model and several other examples are included with Repast Py.

Repast Py code that is equivalent to the Excel LookAround subroutine is shown in figure 8.33. The Repast Py code finds retail components that are in the Moore neighborhood of the agent (i.e., self.getMooreNeighbors()), then loops through the resulting list (i.e., neighbors). The variable self refers to the current agent. The type (neighbor.type) of each list element is compared to make sure that the element is not a shelf

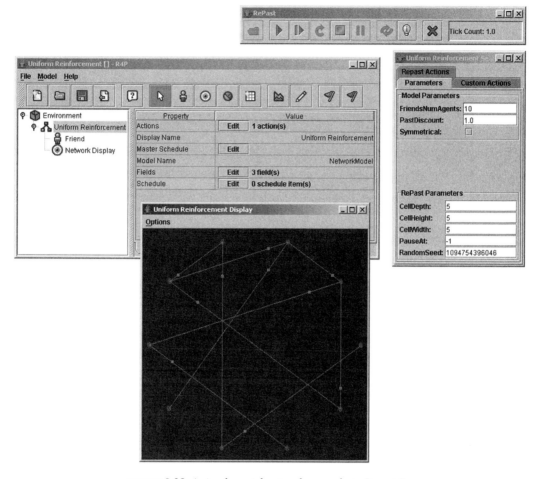

FIGURE 8.32 A simple social network example in Repast Py.

(neighbor.type == "shelf") and is the target item (shelf.targetItem.equals(neighbor.item)). If it is, then the item is considered to be found (self.status = "Found"). The Repast Py code in the figure is more streamlined than the corresponding Excel code shown in figure 8.26. This is possible due to Repast Py's specific focus on agent modeling. However, Repast Py has far fewer output analysis features than Excel and it requires users to learn an additional, although relatively simple, development environment.

Repast Py is relatively easy to use but has more limited functionality than the other ABMS prototyping environments. The major reason to use Repast Py is that it is the only prototyping environment that provides a direct migration path to a large-scale agent-modeling environment, in this case Repast J. The migration path allows models to be initially developed in Repast Py and then easily exported to be used with Repast J. The Repast J toolkit is discussed in chapter 10. Repast Py can be downloaded from http://repast.sourceforge.net/.

NetLogo

NetLogo is an educational ABMS environment (Wilensky 1999a). The NetLogo language uses a modified version of the Logo programming language (Harvey 1997). NetLogo uses a tightly coupled architecture. NetLogo is designed to provide a basic computational laboratory for teaching complex adaptive systems concepts. NetLogo was originally developed

FIGURE 8.33 The Repast Py version of the Excel LookAround subroutine.

to support teaching, but it can be used to a develop a wide range of applications. NetLogo provides a graphical environment to create programs that control graphic "turtles" that reside in a world of "patches" that is monitored by an "observer." NetLogo is particularly well suited for artificial life projects.

NetLogo includes an innovative participatory ABMS feature called HubNet (Wilensky and Stroup 1999). HubNet allows groups of people to interactively engage in simulation runs alongside of computational agents. The use of HubNet and other tools to support participatory ABMS is discussed in chapter 9. The NetLogo interface has many commendable features including visual development tools and a code editor with syntax highlighting. NetLogo was developed by Uri Wilensky, Seth Tissue, and others at Northwestern University's Center for Connected Learning and Computer-Based Modeling. NetLogo can be downloaded from http://ccl.northwestern.edu/netlogo/.

The NetLogo interface running a simple model called "Gridlock" is shown in figure 8.34 (Wilensky 1999b). This model simulates the traffic movement in a simple set of city blocks. In this example, the cars move forward under the direction of traffic lights. The model allows users to experiment with traffic light

placement and signal timing strategies. This agent model and an impressively large number of other examples are included with NetLogo. These examples are well documented and are nicely organized in the built-in models library.

NetLogo code that is equivalent to the Excel LookAround subroutine is shown in Figure 8.35. The procedure begins by defining a local variable (i.e., target-item) to match the current target item for later reference. This variable is used with the "any?" function to query the local "neigbors" that have the same color (i.e., pcolor) as the target item (i.e., target-item). Here patches are used to represent shelves and walls while turtles are used to model shoppers. Individual colors are used to differentiate specific shelf items and walls. If any elements are found, then the shoppers status (i.e., found-item?) is set to found (i.e., set found-item? true). As with the Repast Py code, the NetLogo code in the figure is more streamlined than the equivalent Excel code in figure 8.26. As before, this is achieved through NetLogo's focus on agent modeling. In exchange, NetLogo has far fewer output analysis features than Excel. Of course, NetLogo also requires users to learn an additional, albeit simple, development environment.

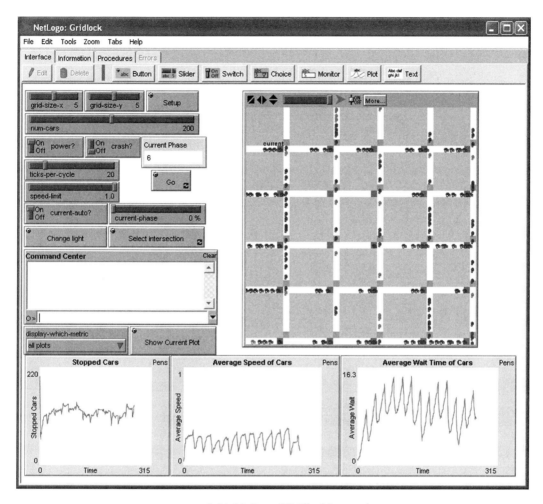

FIGURE 8.34 NetLogo "Gridlock" example.

NetLogo is a good choice for learning the fundamentals of agent-based modeling, for prototyping basic modeling concepts, and for supporting participatory ABMS. However, NetLogo only supports models with moderate agent counts and has practical limits on the possible sophistication of agent behaviors. Therefore, it is not recommended for large-scale model development.

StarLogo

StarLogo is an educational ABMS environment that is similar to NetLogo (Resnick 1997). Like NetLogo, the StarLogo language is a modified version of the Logo programming language (Harvey 1997). As before, StarLogo uses a tightly coupled architecture

that is designed to provide a basic computational toolkit for teaching concepts in complexity. StarLogo uses the same overall turtle- and patch-based graphical approach as NetLogo. As such, it is also particularly well suited for artificial life projects. Similarly to NetLogo, StarLogo was originally developed for educational uses, but it can support a wider range of applications. StarLogo was developed by Mitchel Resnick, Andrew Begel, and others, initially at the Massachusetts Institute of Technology Media Laboratory. It can be downloaded from http://www.media.mit.edu/starlogo.

The StarLogo interface running a simple model called "Sugarscape" is shown in figure 8.36. This model is a partial implementation of Epstein and Axtell's Sugarscape artificial society model (Epstein and

```
▶ LookAround - NetLogo                                    _ □ X

File   Edit   Tools   Zoom   Tabs   Help

Interface | Information | Procedures

  🔍 Find...    |   ✓ Check   |    Procedures ▼

;; This is the nearby area scanning routine.      ▲
to look-around

    ;; Note the type of item being sought.
    locals [ target-item ]
    set target-item item-color

    ;; Check the nearby cells.
    if (any? neighbors with [pcolor = target-item])
      [
        ;; Note a discovery.
        set found-item? true
      ]

end                                                ▼

◄                                                      ►
```

FIGURE 8.35 The NetLogo version of the Excel `LookAround` subroutine.

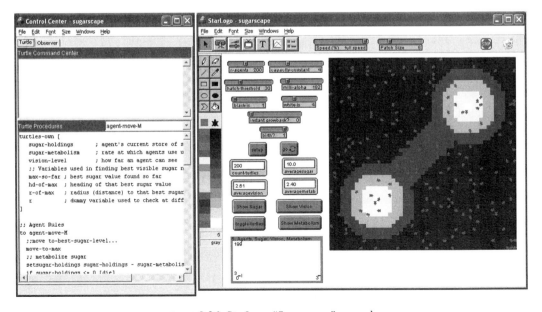

FIGURE 8.36 StarLogo "Sugarscape" example.

Axtell 1996). In this example, the small turtles in the graph on the right side of the figure represent members of a simple society. They live on a landscape, called the Sugarscape, with hills and valleys that are covered with varying amounts of sugarcane. The higher sugar levels are indicated by lighter landscape shading. The sugar grows over time and is consumed by the agents. The agents move about and reproduce over time based on sugar availability. Agents with limited access to sugar eventually die of starvation. The Sugarscape model was originally implemented using the Ascape toolkit. The StarLogo version includes a limited set of the core features of the original model. This agent model and quite a few other examples are included with StarLogo.

StarLogo code that is equivalent to the Excel LookAround subroutine is shown in figure 8.37. As with NetLogo, patches are used to represent shelves and walls while turtles model shoppers. Again, individual colors are used to identify shelf items and walls. The procedure begins by defining three local variables (i.e.,: `row, :column, and :temp-color`) for later reference based on the current turtle location. These variables are used with the "`count-patches-with`" function to count the items that are the same color (i.e., `pc`) as the target item (i.e., `temp-color`) and less than one unit from the current patch (i.e., `(distance: row: column) < 1.5`). Like NetLogo, if any elements are found, then the shopper's status (i.e., `found-item?`) is set to found

(i.e., `set found-item? true`). As with Repast Py and NetLogo, the StarLogo code is more streamlined than the related Excel code in figure 8.26. In fact, parts of the StarLogo and NetLogo code look similar due to their common origin in the Logo language. Significant differences in syntax can also be seen, however. As with NetLogo and Repast Py, StarLogo has far fewer output analysis features than Excel.

As with NetLogo, StarLogo is a good choice for learning the fundamentals of agent-based modeling as well as prototyping basic modeling concepts. However, it only supports models with moderate numbers of agents and has limited ability to implement extremely complex agent behaviors. Therefore, it is not recommended for large-scale model development.

Computational Mathematics Systems

Dedicated computational mathematics systems are a desktop alternative to spreadsheet ABMS and ABMS prototyping environments. With appropriate preparation, computational mathematics systems can be used to develop moderately complex agent-based models. As has been discussed, prototyping environments in general have the advantage of being more specialized than spreadsheets but also tend to be more limited in their long-term scalability. Computational mathematics systems usually have greater scalability than prototyping environments and even spreadsheets but can be comparatively more difficult to learn and use.

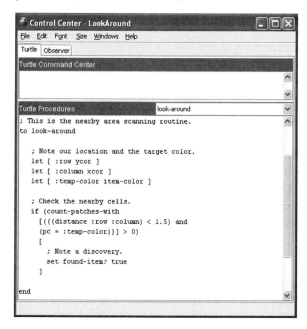

FIGURE 8.37 The StarLogo version of the Excel `LookAround` subroutine.

Which computational mathematics systems are suitable? Almost any general-purpose desktop computational mathematics system with an integrated development environment can be used. The basic requirements are full scripting combined with array or list-processing capabilities. Current examples include MATLAB and Mathematica. Many others exist. One or more of these environments or a similar environment might already be familiar. If so, this is a good place to start agent-based modeling!

Computational mathematics systems have some advantages compared to the other options. These advantages are derived from both the mathematical and interactive orientations of these tools.

All of these environments have rich mathematical functions. Nearly any mathematical relation, map, or function that can be numerically calculated is available within these tools or their add-on libraries. In many cases these tools even support symbolic mathematical processing for systems of equations that can be solved analytically. Clearly, all of this power has a cost in terms of learning curves and development time. These tools offer far more options that the other desktop environments. This increases the time and effort required to learn these tools. Development time for a given agent-based model can vary significantly compared to the other desktop environments, depending on the mathematical orientation of the model's design. If the model tends to rely on the types of advanced mathematics supported by these tools, using these tools to implement the model will likely save a large amount of time compared to the other desktop options. If the model does not take advantage of the mathematical sophistication of these environments, the use of these tools may actually increase the time required to build the model.

In some cases, these environments can be fast, efficient, and easy for prototyping. Simple to moderately complex agent-based models with mathematically oriented behavioral rules can often be quickly developed in these environments. Furthermore, if the modeler is already familiar with one of these environments, then only a small amount of learning is required to apply their existing knowledge. These environments also typically have rather sophisticated editors or integrated development environments. These editors normally have features such as syntax highlighting, popup function documentation, runtime model tracing, and automatic incremental model compilation without user intervention. Syntax highlighting color codes a script based on its contents. This makes complex lists of instructions much easier to read. Popup function documentation displays the definitions of mathematical notations immediately on the screen in real time as scripts are input. This saves the user from having to check manuals while editing scripts. Automatic incremental model compilation checks the structural correctness of scripts while they are being edited. This reduces the accumulation of errors and provides the user with more timely feedback on errors than full manual compilation. All of these highly recommended features can be found in many computational mathematics systems. Be sure that these features are present in whatever computational mathematics system is chosen, if any.

Computational mathematics systems can be useful in supporting a multiphase model development strategy that starts simple and then builds in complexity. In some cases the resulting models may in and of themselves be sufficient to meet an organization's needs. In the remaining cases, these environments can at least be used to test basic design concepts and even core implementation approaches. They can also be used to demonstrate the potential of agent-based modeling and to explore the requirements of larger-scale efforts. In this light, these environments can fit quite well into the overall model development approach recommended throughout this book.

Computational mathematics systems usually have sophisticated output facilities, such as graphics that are fully integrated with the program. These facilities allow agent-based models to immediately present advanced charts and graphs in a wide range of formats. Many of these outputs can even be considered to be publication quality. The output facilities of these tools are often so powerful and useful that these packages are often used in combination with the large-scale modeling techniques presented later in the book. In these situations, the agent models are implemented using large-scale ABMS toolkits or native code and the model output results are imported into a mathematical prototyping environment for final display. Depending on the scripting environment, the linkage between the agent-based model and the output system can even be live. This means that model results are immediately made available to the scripting tool without the need for an explicit importing step.

One size rarely fits all equally well. Similarly, a given agent-modeling environment may be perfect for a specific model, but none is perfect for all models.

As with all toolkits, computational mathematics systems have some disadvantages compared to the other options. These drawbacks include a lack of built-in agent functionality, substantial learning curves if the environment is unfamiliar, and limited long-term growth potential.

These environments usually lack agent-oriented features, although these features can be programmed. As stated previously, one of the most important features of computational mathematics systems is their ability to easily yield high-quality outputs. From one perspective, the additional effort required to add agent-oriented features to one of these environments needs to be weighed against the benefit of having extremely high-quality output tools readily available. From another perspective the question is, how much effort will be needed to produce high-quality outputs from an agent toolkit? The same question can be asked about the complex mathematical functions, such as numerical integration, that are readily available within computational mathematics systems but which are more difficult to access using other tools. There are many answers for either of these questions, but one of the best is usually to mix agent toolkits and computational mathematics systems incrementally depending on the demands. Early in a project, all of the work can be completed in a computational mathematics system. As the project grows, the agent-modeling portion can be moved or ported to a specialized agent-simulation toolkit. The result is a hybrid model that mixes the strengths of both agent toolkits and mathematical environments along a continuum that is appropriate to the project's incremental demands.

Many people who regularly use computational mathematics systems report that these environments are easy to use. Many experienced pilots claim the same thing about jet airplanes. Don't be fooled. The power of these environments comes at a price. These environments have substantial learning curves, if the user is not already familiar with them. If a computational mathematics system has already been mastered, then extending this mastery to agent-based modeling can be a good approach. However, learning how to do agent-based modeling, how to use a computational mathematics system, and how to apply the system for agent simulation all at once is quite a challenge. In this case, using a specialized agent-based modeling toolkit as discussed earlier may reduce the amount that needs to be learned. Be sure to factor in the current level of knowledge when considering the use of a computational mathematics system.

As has been previously mentioned and as is continually advertised, it is easy to start writing scripts in a mathematical environment once the environment itself is mastered. This book provides instructions on how to build agent models with the same ease. Growing the size of models within a computational mathematics system is another story. Initial increases in the number and complexity of agents within a given model beyond a small default size typically have little effect on the model's manageability and execution performance. Unfortunately, there are usually critical thresholds beyond which the code becomes difficult to maintain and beyond which the model runtime memory and time requirements become inhibiting. The code becomes difficult to maintain because, for the most part, these environments were never intended to support tens of thousands of functions being updated by several simultaneous developers. This simple fact is that these environments tend to be limited in their long-term growth potential and scalability. This makes them well suited for initial work and possibly long-term output presentation, but poorly suited for large-scale long-term agent simulation.

It is important to note that computational mathematics systems do have several attractive features that are highly desirable for agent simulation. Foremost among these features is high-quality output and the ready availability of complex mathematical functions as has been previously described. As has also been discussed, it is possible to use these environments for specialized functions in collaboration with the ABMS systems detailed in chapter 10.

Note that the same mixed blessing of shared code and data storage that comes with spreadsheet models also is the default for most computational mathematics systems. As detailed in the agent spreadsheet section, this feature makes reproducing model runs easier but makes updating code harder. Therefore it is recommended that initial prototypes combine code and data but that operational models break code and data up into separate files.

Mathematica and MATLAB are examples of computational mathematics systems that can readily be used to supplement agent-based modeling efforts. The reasons for this are twofold:

1. Mathematica and MATLAB are powerful, consisting of fully integrated development environments that combine capabilities for

programming, graphical display, data import and export, and linkages to external programs.

2. Mathematica and MATLAB are convenient to use, are mature, and provide immediate results and feedback to users.

Computational mathematics systems provide a wide range of built-in functions and algorithms. Computational mathematics systems are structured in two main parts: (1) the user interface that allows dynamic user interaction, and (2) the underlying computational engine, or kernel, that performs the computations according to the user's instructions. The underlying computational engine is written in the C programming language for these systems, but C coding is unseen by the user. The interpreted nature of these systems avoids the compilation and linking steps required in traditional programming languages.

with enormous integrated numerical processing capability (The MathWorks Inc. 2004). An example of a MATLAB agent model is shown in figure 8.38. MATLAB uses a scripting-language approach to programming. MATLAB is a high-level matrix/array language with control flow, functions, data structures, input/output, and object-oriented programming features. The primary data type is the double array, which is essentially a two-dimensional matrix. Other data types include logical arrays, cell arrays, structures, and character arrays. The user interface consists of the MATLAB Desktop, which is a fully integrated and mature development environment. There is also an application programming interface (API) that allows programs written in C, FORTRAN, or Java to interact with MATLAB. There are facilities for calling routines from MATLAB (dynamic linking) and routines for reading and writing specialized MATLAB files.

MATLAB

MATLAB, originally the "Matrix Laboratory," is a commercially available numeric processing system

Mathematica

Like MATLAB, Mathematica is a commercially available numeric processing system with enormous

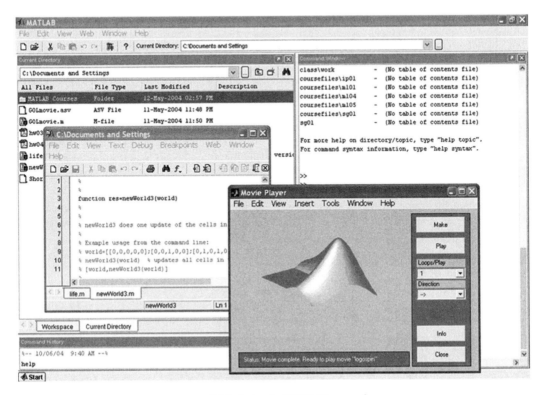

FIGURE 8.38 A simple MATLAB example.

integrated numerical processing capability (Wolfram Research Inc. 2004). An example of a Mathematica agent model is shown in figure 8.39. Mathematica is a fully functional programming language. Unlike MATLAB, Mathematica is also a symbolic processing system that uses term replacement as its primary operation. Symbolic processing means that variables can be used before they have values assigned to them; in contrast, a numeric processing language requires that every variable must have a value assigned to it before it is used. In this respect, although Mathematica and MATLAB may appear similar and share many capabilities, Mathematica is fundamentally very different than MATLAB, with a much different style of programming and which ultimately results in a different set of capabilities for developing agent-based models and simulations.

A Market Example

This section discusses an example of an Excel agent spreadsheet[5] that models a simplified electric power market for pedagogical purposes. This simple example model is not related to the EMCAS model presented earlier. The main worksheet for this spreadsheet is shown in figure 8.40. This model uses two types of agents that compete in an open commodity market for electric power. The agents represent consumers and generation companies. These power market agents can be seen in figure 8.41. Note that

the consumer and generation company agents each have different kinds of properties. A third agent, the independent system operator (ISO), manages the flow of payments in the overall daily market. A full-scale model of this kind might seek to address questions about market volatility, dynamics, and participation. The agents in this example will be boundedly rational for simplicity.

This model is executed using the same procedure used for the retail shopper model. To execute the model, open up the spreadsheet, move to the "Agent Environment" worksheet if it is not already open, size the Excel window so that both the "Run" button on the left and the daily price graph on the right are visible, and then press the "Run" button. The price graph will change to reflect each day's market activity. As before, Excel prevents workbooks from being modified while the model is running. The current simulation time and end time are shown immediately below the "Run" button. The simulation will automatically stop when the current time reaches the end time. Shorter runs can be requested by setting the end time to a smaller value. The model can be stopped at any time by pressing the "Escape" key and selecting "End" from the resulting interruption notification window. The model also includes a set of environmental parameters as detailed in table 8.4. The parameters can be changed as desired.

Each consumer agent has an independently assigned initial demand for electricity and a value that they assign to the power they purchase. This value

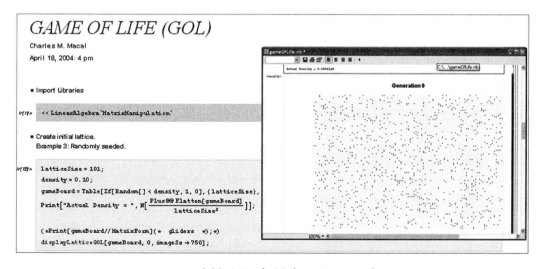

FIGURE 8.39 A simple Mathematica example.

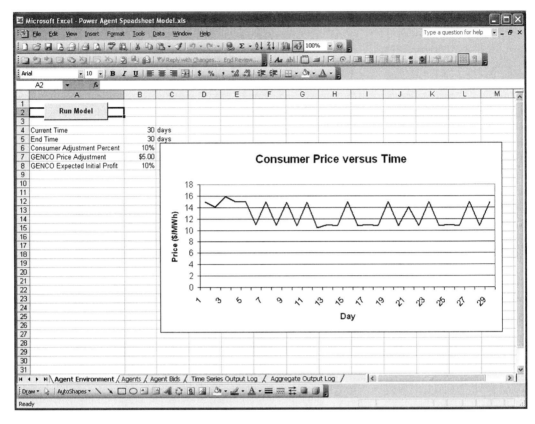

FIGURE 8.40 The power market environment.

measures the maximum amount that consumers are willing to pay for power before they will resort to conservation measures. The reality of most power markets is that even in the face of outrageous prices, consumers can only reduce, but not eliminate, their demand for power. Furthermore, the habit of turning off the lights in empty rooms can form quickly, but getting more energy-efficient homes takes much more time. Therefore, electricity demand tends to adjust slowly. Power markets thus are said to be highly price inelastic. To model this effect, the model's consumers slowly reduce their power demand when the price of power exceeds the value that they place on it. The converse is also true. The model's consumers slowly increase their demand for power when it is worth more to them than what they pay for it. Consumers are full participants in the marketplace. They only know the previous prices and always pay the current day's prices for their consumption. To deal with this, consumers must use previous prices

as future estimates to set their current demand. Obviously, this behavior at best captures the most basic features of electric power consumer behavior and is intended to be used for educational purposes only. The consumer agents can be enhanced to exhibit more sophisticated and realistic behavior if required. As with the retail shopper example, this is a proto-agent simulation to make the model clear enough to be understandable in the available limited space.

The consumer code uses the same offset calculations previously introduced with the retail shopper spreadsheet model. Table 8.5 shows the consumer offsets and their associated attributes. Some columns are used only by the generation companies. The other columns are used by both types of agents.

The generation company agents each have a fixed number of units that they bid into the electric power market. Each generation company bids all of its capacity at each time step. Each company has a different amount of capacity and a different production

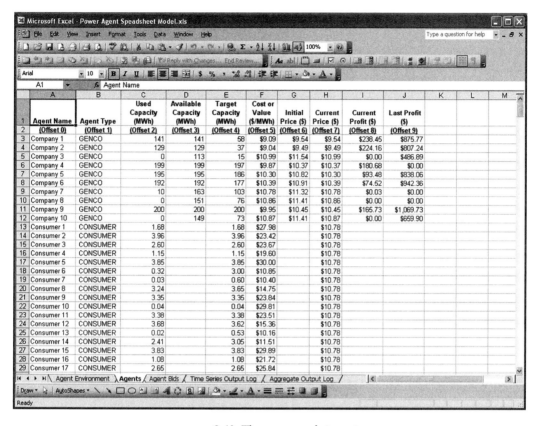

FIGURE 8.41 The power market agents.

TABLE 8.4 The consumer model environmental parameters

Environmental variable	Default value	Meaning
Current time	0 days	The simulation time counter in days
End time	30 days	The simulation stopping time in days
Consumer adjustment	10%	The percentage by which consumers adjust their demand up or down
Generation company (GENCO) price adjustment	$5.00	The dollar amount by which generation companies adjust their prices up or down
Generation company expected initial profit	10%	The percentage profit added to the production cost to set the initial bid price

TABLE 8.5 Consumer offsets and associated attributes

Offset	Consumer attribute
0	Agent name
1	Agent type
2	Used capacity (MWh)
3	Not used
4	Target capacity (MWh)
5	Cost or value ($/MWh)
6	Initial price ($)
7	Current price ($)
8	Not used
9	Not used

cost per unit of power generated. Naturally, companies attempt to make profits by having their prices exceed their production costs. The challenge is getting bids with high enough prices accepted.

Bids can be accepted in whole or in part. Each company has a target share of their production capacity that they are seeking to sell. Electricity generators typically take many years to build, so the total amount of production capacity is fixed in the model. Thus, the target capacity can be approximately related to a target market share. The generation company bids worksheet is shown in figure 8.42.

Generation companies use a two-part strategy in forming their bids. First, they lower their prices until their target market share is achieved. Once they reach their desired market share, they consider their profit levels. If their profit level is falling from one period to the next, companies raise their prices. Otherwise, if profit levels are constant or rising, then the companies maintain their prices and enjoy their success, albeit temporarily. These values are calculated based on

the generation company offsets and their associated attributes as shown in table 8.6. The model does not address bankruptcies so the variable production cost sets a lower bound on prices. Clearly, this simple behavior is purely for illustrative purposes. The generation company agents can be extended to represent more realistic corporate behavior as needed.

Consumer electric power use is measured by the ISO for each day of the simulation. The ISO attempts to match power consumers with power producers. When the final matches are found, generation companies are each paid what they bid while all consumers pay one uniform price. The consumer price is the weighted average price across all of the accepted generation bids, so total buyer and seller payments exactly match for each period. ISOs normally are separately funded as third-party market managers. The ISO stores the daily power price results into the "Time Series Output Log" worksheet shown in figure 8.43 and stores the overall results to the "Aggregate Output Log" worksheet shown

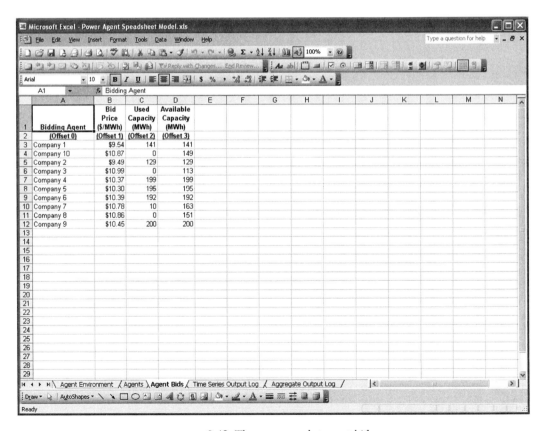

FIGURE 8.42 The power market agent bids.

TABLE 8.6 Generation company offsets and associated attributes

Offset	Generation company attribute
0	Agent name
1	Agent type
2	Used capacity (MWh)
3	Available capacity (MWh)
4	Target capacity (MWh)
5	Cost or value ($/MWh)
6	Initial price ($)
7	Current price ($)
8	Current profit ($)
9	Last profit ($)

in figure 8.44. These logs follow the same approach as the examples of retail shopper model time-series and aggregate logs discussed in previous sections. The one exception is that the dynamic times-series graph is now in the "Agent Environment" worksheet. The construction process is similar, however.

The main spreadsheet environment subroutine is shown in figure 8.45. This subroutine works similarly to the retail model Run subroutine except that there are now two agent types to activate rather than just one.

The environment's Initialize subroutine shown in figure 8.46 is much like that for the retail model Initialize subroutine except that there are now two agent types referenced by [Generation_ Companies] and [Consumers] rather than just one. The comments in the code describe the detailed program flow. Note that individual agents are often initialized using their own unique values, such as when each generation company's current price is set from their own initial price (i.e., genco. Offset(0, 7) = genco.Offset(0, 6)). Also note that no random seed is being set. This is important because, unlike the retail model, this is a deterministic model.

The time-series output logging routine is shown in figure 8.47. LogPrices uses the same approach as RecordAverageFrustration except that the time step is now fixed at one day.

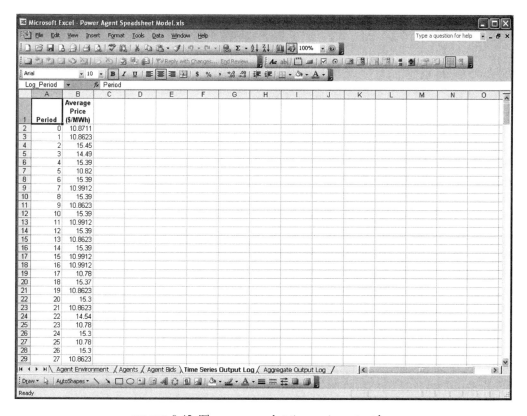

FIGURE 8.43 The power market time-series output log.

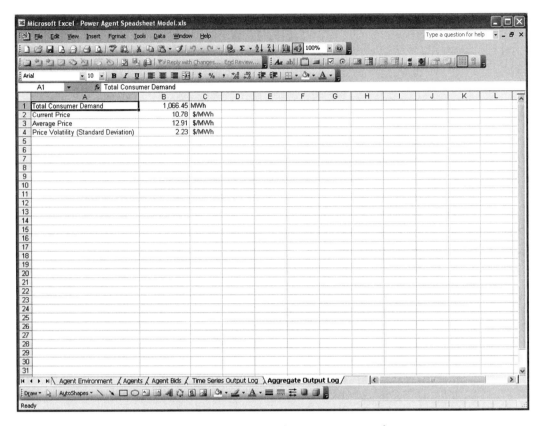

FIGURE 8.44 The power market aggregate output log.

The `StepGenerationCompanies` subroutine shown in figure 8.48 activates each generation company. This allows them to prepare their bids following the previously discussed strategy. First, each company checks to see if it missed its market share goal (i.e., `genco.Offset(0, 2) < genco.Offset (0, 4)`). If it failed to achieve its goal, then it reduces its prices to increase its share (`genco.Offset(0, 7) = genco.Offset(0, 7)-[GENCO_Price_Adjustment]`), with a minimum price given by the company's variable production cost (`genco.Offset(0, 5)`). If the market share goal was achieved, then the company checks to see if profits have fallen since yesterday (`genco.Offset(0, 8) < genco.Offset (0, 9)`). If they have, then the company raises its prices in the hope of selling the same amount of power for more money. If profits have stayed the same or increased since yesterday, then the company keeps the same price. Finally, the company updates its previous price tracker once it has completed the current day's biding. As before, the code comments help to detail the program flow. Note here that the main loop (`For Each genco`) scans across the generation companies and directly includes the agent behavior rather than calling a separate subroutine. This is often seen in simple agent spreadsheets since it reduces the number of modules. This "inline" looping is fine for smaller models. It is recommended that subroutines be used for each major behavior in more complex agent spreadsheets since this makes reading and testing the code much easier and enhances the code's extensibility.

Consumers are activated using the `Step Consumers` subroutine shown in figure 8.49. This subroutine scans across each consumer and lets them adjust their demand based on the last power price and the value they place on the power. If the price is less than the value (`consumer.Offset(0, 7) < consumer.Offset(0, 5)`), then consumers feel

```
' This is the main simulation routine.
Sub Run()

  ' Reset the current simulation time.
  [Current_Time] = 0

  ' Initialize the model.
  Call Initialize

  ' Check the current simulation time (Note that
  ' this is a synchronous model).
  Do While ([Current_Time] < [End_Time])

    ' Allow all of the generation companies to
    ' execute.
    Call StepGenerationCompanies

    ' Allow all of the consumers to execute.
    Call StepConsumers

    ' Allow the ISO to execute.
    Call StepISO

    ' Log the current average price.
    Call LogPrices

    ' Step the current simulation time forward.
    [Current_Time] = [Current_Time] + 1

  Loop

End Sub
```

FIGURE 8.45 The environment's main routine.

that they are getting a good deal and increase their demand (consumer.Offset(0, 2)) by a small fixed adjustment percentage ([Consumer_Adjustment_Percent]). Otherwise they reduce their demand. Note that this subroutine uses the same inline looping approach as StepGeneration Companies. Again, this is fine for smaller models but can become ungainly for larger projects.

The final consumer model routine is the ISO's activation subroutine as shown in figure 8.50. The ISO uses this subroutine to perform market clearing following the previously discussed procedure. The subroutine works by sorting the bids in the "Agent Bids" worksheet by the bid price column ([Bid_Price]) and then scanning down the list. Bids are accepted in order of increasing price until all of the demand stored in the remaining_demand

variable is met. The last bid might only be accepted in part. In the last step the bids are resorted by company name to make it easier for the generation companies to look up their results in the next time period. As with the other subroutines, the code comments detail the program flow.

This example has demonstrated the detailed design and development of a simple agent-based consumer market spreadsheet model. This model is differentiated from the retail shopper spreadsheet model in that it is deterministic, it is not spatial, there is more than one agent type, and the agent types include larger entities such as corporations rather than just individual people. As previously mentioned, the model is intended to be simple enough to be illustrative rather than to reproduce real phenomena.

```
' This is the initialization routine.
Sub Initialize()

  ' Declare the local variables.
  Dim genco As Range
  Dim consumer As Range

  ' Reset the graph.
  [Log_Period].Offset(1, 1) = 0
  [Log_Period].Offset(2, 1) = 0
  [GraphLabels].Clear
  [GraphValues].Clear

  ' Initialize all of the generation companies.
  For Each genco In [Generation_Companies]

    ' Copy the initial price to the current price as
    ' follows:
    '   [Current Price] = [Initial Price]
    genco.Offset(0, 7) = genco.Offset(0, 6)

    ' Clear the last profit as follows:
    '   [Last Profit] = 0
    genco.Offset(0, 9) = 0

  Next genco

  ' Initialize all of the consumers.
  For Each consumer In [Consumers]

    ' Copy the target capacity to the used capacity
    ' as follows:
    '   [Used Capacity] = [Target Capacity]
    consumer.Offset(0, 2) = consumer.Offset(0, 4)

  Next consumer

End Sub
```

FIGURE 8.46 The environment's initialization routine.

```
' The time series output price logging routine.
Sub LogPrices()

  ' Log the current price.
  [Log_Period].Offset([Current_Time] + 1, 0) = _
    [Current_Time]
  [Log_Period].Offset([Current_Time] + 1, 1) = _
    [Current_Price]

End Sub
```

FIGURE 8.47 The environment's average price logging routine.

```
' This is the generation company time step routine.
Sub StepGenerationCompanies()

  ' Declare the local variables.
  Dim genco As Range

  ' Allow all of the generation companies to execute.
  For Each genco In [Generation_Companies]

    ' Calculate the direction to change prices.
    ' Check the market share as follows:
    '   if ([Used Capacity] < [Target Capacity]) then
    '     Reduce Our Prices
    '   else
    '     Check Our Profit Goal
    If (genco.Offset(0, 2) < genco.Offset(0, 4)) Then

      ' Reduce our prices in an attempt to increase
      ' sales back to our target as follows:
      '   [Current Price] = [Current Price] -
      '     [GENCO Price Adjustment]
      genco.Offset(0, 7) = genco.Offset(0, 7) - _
        [GENCO_Price_Adjustment]

      ' We will never sell for less than the production
      ' cost as follows:
      '    if ([Current Price] < [Cost] then
      '       [Current Price] = [Cost]
      If (genco.Offset(0, 7) < genco.Offset(0, 5)) Then
          genco.Offset(0, 7) = genco.Offset(0, 5)
      End If


    Else

      ' The sales target was met so consumers are buying
      ' our electricity. If profits are down we must not
      ' be charging enough for our power so check our
      ' profit goal as follows:
      '   if ([Current Profit] < [Last Profit]) then
      '     Increase Our Prices
      '   else
      '      Do Nothing
      If (genco.Offset(0, 8) < genco.Offset(0, 9)) Then

        ' We did not charge enough, so increase our
        ' prices as follows:
        '   [Current Price] = [Current Price] +
        '     [GENCO Price Adjustment]
        genco.Offset(0, 7) = genco.Offset(0, 7) + _
          [GENCO_Price_Adjustment]

      Else

        ' Our sales target was met and our profits are
        ' increasing, so keep our prices the same and
        ' enjoy the success for now!

      End If

    End If

    ' Copy the current profit to the last profit.
    genco.Offset(0, 9) = genco.Offset(0, 8)

  Next genco

End Sub
```

FIGURE 8.48 The generation company's bidding routine.

```
' This is the consumer time step routine.
Sub StepConsumers()

  ' Declare the local variables.
  Dim consumer As Range

  ' Allow all of the Consumers to execute.
  For Each consumer In [Consumers]

    ' Check the current price to see if we are paying
    ' more than the power is worth to us as follows:
    '   if ([Current Price] < [Value]) then
    '      Increase Our Demand
    '   else
    '        Reduce Our Demand
    If (consumer.Offset(0, 7) < consumer.Offset(0, 5)) _
      Then

      ' The power is worth more to us than what we pay
      ' for it. Check to see if we are conserving power
      ' as follows:
      '   if ([Used Capacity] < [Target Capacity]) then
      '      Increase Our Power Usage
      If (consumer.Offset(0, 2) < consumer.Offset(0, 4)) _
        Then

        ' We are conserving electricity, so we will
        ' increase our power usage as follows:
        '   [Used Capacity] = (100% +
        '     [Consumer Adjustment Percent]) *
        '     [Used Capacity]
        consumer.Offset(0, 2) = (1 + _
          [Consumer_Adjustment_Percent]) * _
          consumer.Offset(0, 2)

      End If

    Else

      ' The power is worth less to us than what we pay
      ' for it so we will conserve power and reduce our
      ' usage as follows:
      '   [Used Capacity] = (100% -
      '     [Consumer Adjustment Percent]) *
      '     [Used Capacity]
      consumer.Offset(0, 2) = (1 - _
        [Consumer_Adjustment_Percent]) * _
        consumer.Offset(0, 2)

    End If

  Next consumer

End Sub
```

FIGURE 8.49 The consumer's consumption routine.

```
' This is the ISO time step routine.
Sub StepISO()

  ' Declare the local variables.
  Dim bid As Range
  Dim remaining_demand As Double

  ' Clear the market by sorting and then assigning the
  ' bids. First, sort the bids by price.
  [Bids_for_Sorting].Sort key1:=[Bid_Price], _
    order1:=xlAscending

  ' Second, assign the bids.
  remaining_demand = [Total_Consumer_Demand]
  For Each bid In [Bids]

    ' Check to see if all of the demand has been met as
    ' follows:
    '    if (remaining_demand <= 0) then
    '       Reject All Remaining Bids
    '    else
    '       Accept At Least Part of the Next Bid
    If (remaining_demand <= 0) Then

      ' Reject all the remaining bids as follows:
      '    [Used Capacity] = 0
      bid.Offset(0, 2) = 0

    Else

      ' Accept at least part of the next bid.
      ' Check the next bid to see if we will accept all
      ' of it as follows:
      '    if (remaining_demand >=
      '       [Available Capacity]) then
      '          Accept All of the Offered Power
      '    else
      '          Accept Only Some of the Offered Power
      If (remaining_demand > bid.Offset(0, 3)) Then

        ' Accept all of the offered power by accouting
        ' for the power and then assigning the
        ' consumption.

        ' Account for the purchased power as follows:
        '    remaining_demand = remaining_demand -
        '       [Available Capacity]
        remaining_demand = remaining_demand - _
          bid.Offset(0, 3)

        ' Assign the consumed power level as follows:
        '    [Used Capacity] = [Available Capacity]
        bid.Offset(0, 2) = bid.Offset(0, 3)

      Else

        ' Accept only some of the offered power by
        ' assigning the consumption and then accouting
        ' for the power.

        ' Assign the consumed power level as follows:
        '    [Used Capacity] = remaining_demand
        bid.Offset(0, 2) = remaining_demand

        ' Account for the purchased power as follows:
        '    remaining_demand = 0
        remaining_demand = 0

        ' Note the current market wide price.
        [Current_Price] = bid.Offset(0, 1)

      End If

    End If


  Next bid

  ' Resort the bids by company name.
  [Bids_for_Sorting].Sort key1:=[Bids], _
    order1:=xlAscending

End Sub
```

FIGURE 8.50 The ISO's market-clearing routine.

Summary

The chapter has shown that agent-based modeling and simulation can be done on the desktop with standard office computers. This approach can be used to learn agent modeling, test agent-modeling design concepts, and perform some types of analysis. Two complete examples of agent models were detailed in this chapter. The first example used a spreadsheet to model the movement of consumers in a retail store. The second example used a spreadsheet to model consumers and producers in a commodity market.

Notes

1. Microsoft and Microsoft Excel are registered trademarks of Microsoft Corp.
2. This simple spreadsheet is not intended to be a model of an actual retail store. Rather, it is intended to be a demonstration of one way spreadsheets can be used for agent modeling.
3. Visual Basic for Applications is a registered trademark of Microsoft Corp.
4. Microsoft.NET is a registered trademark of Microsoft Corp.
5. As with the retail market example, this simple spreadsheet is not intended to be a model of an actual electric power market. It is intended to be a demonstration of another way spreadsheets can be used for agent modeling.

References

Casti, J. L. (2001). BizSim: The World of Business—in a Box. *Complexity International* **08**: 6.

Epstein, J. M. and R. Axtell (1996). *Growing Artificial Societies: Social Science from the Bottom Up.* Cambridge, Mass.: MIT Press.

Gile, B. (1999). *RAND and Rnd in Excel.* Arlington, Va.: Casualty Actuarial Society.

Harvey, B. (1997). *Computer Science Logo Style.* Cambridge, Mass.: MIT Press.

Law, A. M. (2007). *Simulation Modeling and Analysis,* 4th ed. New York: McGraw-Hill.

Lutz, M. and D. Ascher (1999). *Learning Python.* Sebastopol, Cal.: O'Reilly.

North, M. J., N. T. Collier, and R. J. Vos (2006). Experiences Creating Three Implementations of the Repast Agent Modeling Toolkit. *ACM Transactions on Modeling and Computer Simulation* **16**(1): 1–25.

Resnick, M. (1997). *Turtles, Termites, and Traffic Jams: Explorations in Massively Parallel Microworlds.* Cambridge, Mass.: MIT Press.

ROAD (2004). Repast Home Page (http://repast.sourceforge.net/). Chicago: ROAD.

Skyrms, B. and R. Pemantle (2000). A Dynamic Model of Social Network Formation. *Proceedings of the National Academy of Sciences of the USA* **97**(16): 9340–9346.

The MathWorks Inc. (2004). The MathWorks Home Page (http://www.mathworks.com/). Natick, Mass.: The MathWorks Inc.

Wilensky, U. (1999a). *NetLogo.* Evanston, Ill.: Center for Connected Learning and Computer-Based Modeling, Northwestern University.

Wilensky, U. (1999b). *NetLogo Gridlock Model.* Evanston, Ill.: Center for Connected Learning and Computer-Based Modeling, Northwestern University.

Wilensky, U. and W. Stroup (1999). *HubNet.* Evanston, Ill.: Center for Connected Learning and Computer-Based Modeling, Northwestern University.

Wolfram Research Inc. (2004). Wolfram Research Home Page. Champaign, Ill.: Wolfram Research, Inc.

9

How to Do Participatory ABMS

Live and In Person!

With proper instruction and discipline, people can act as agents for conducting live agent-based modeling and simulation (ABMS). Participatory ABMS combines the agent-modeling paradigm with ideas from organization theory to achieve several specific goals. Participatory agent modeling can be used to develop business insights, to demonstrate agent-modeling concepts to business stakeholders, and to test ideas for further development. This chapter introduces the fundamental ideas behind participatory ABMS and details how participatory agent modeling can be efficiently conducted in an office environment.

In many ways, participatory ABMS is a natural follow-up to desktop ABMS. The concepts tested using participatory agent modeling are often initially explored on the desktop with spreadsheets, prototyping environments, or mathematical scripting tools. Once the ideas have been initially tested, they can be refined and scaled up using participatory ABMS. Of course, it is also possible to do participatory ABMS first and then follow up with desktop modeling. However, ordering things this way requires some experience with the agent-modeling process to ensure that the simulation participants are given productive guidance.

The Start of It All

Participatory modeling was one of the first forms of agent modeling. More recently, participatory simulation has become closely tied to experimental economics. Experimental economics adds a laboratory component to economics research (Smith 1982, 1994). Instead of demonstrating economic facts using theoretical mathematics or statistical analysis of historical events, experimental economists conduct controlled experiments using volunteer human subjects. Experimental economics has been pioneered by Vernon Smith, who won a Nobel Prize for Economics in 2002 for his groundbreaking contributions to this field (Smith 1962). Experimental economics provides a solid theoretical foundation for participatory simulation and offers specific methods for conducting such simulations. However, participatory ABMS is distinct from experimental economics due to a difference in focus. Participatory ABMS is in some ways broader than experimental economics in that participatory simulation is used to model noneconomic aspects of agent behavior in biology, ecology, sociology, psychology, and many other areas. In fact, the agents in participatory simulations do not even have to represent economic entities such as people or corporations at all. They can just as easily represent animals, computers, or factory equipment. Experimental economics is also more focused on strict scientific progress. Certainly, participatory simulation can be used for this purpose, but it is just as useful to help business people learn or even develop more effective applied management strategies.

Today, variations of participatory ABMS are commonly used in business and management training schools. Many of the management training exercises where students act as corporate executives for fictitious companies are essentially participatory agent simulations. These exercises have been found to be quite effective for teaching management concepts, particularly for ideas that are counterintuitive or complex. Participatory ABMS adds to these exercises by supplying a solid conceptual foundation for the work and by providing a natural progressive development path to grow these tabletop games into enterprise-level strategic modeling tools.

Strengths and Weaknesses

Like all modeling approaches, participatory ABMS has several strengths and some weaknesses. The strengths include the ease of setup and the clarity of the results. The weaknesses include limits on the number of agents, bounds on the length of simulation runs, certain kinds of constraints on the complexity of the rules, and the imperfect match between experiments and reality.

It Is Easy

Participatory ABMS tends to be easier to perform than other agent-modeling approaches since the participants can be given much higher-level instructions than programmable systems. This is why it can sometimes be good to start with participatory modeling and then move to desktop ABMS as the second step. However, the instructions for the simulation participants must still have the appropriate level of specificity, which is why beginning agent modelers are advised to gain some experience with desktop modeling before they involve a group of other people in the activities.

It Is Clear

Results from participatory ABMS are often easier to understand than results from other agent-based modeling techniques, since the simulation can often be directly observed. This transparency allows the participants to connect their individual actions and the actions of others around them to system-level consequences. The transparency of participatory ABMS also allows the participants to experiment in ways that are difficult if not impossible with real systems. For example, participants in a participatory consulting services marketing simulation can examine the differences in outcomes achievable through varying types and levels of communication with potential clients. The participatory ABMS approach allows the communication levels to be controlled by the simulation organizers in ways that are not possible in real systems.

Of course, participatory simulations are not the real thing. People can and sometimes do make different decisions in participatory simulations than they might in real situations. The reasons include greater involvement, heightened emotions, and a variety of observational biases that are inherent in real situations. However, participatory simulations can still be an extremely productive way to glimpse the inner workings of complex processes.

Is It by Invitation Only?

Except possibly for sports fans simulating waves with stadium crowds, participatory ABMS tends to be limited to smaller numbers of agents than the other approaches due to the typical number of people available to participate. Normally, in an office setting without special technical support, no more than about twenty or so people can meaningfully engage in participatory ABMS. The use of simulation automation and other techniques discussed later can increase the limit up to several thousand participants or more. However, making these techniques available usually requires significant resource commitments from the hosting organization. The limit on the number of participants in a live simulation is driven by a variety of factors, including time scheduling and costs.

The larger the group, the harder it is for the individual participants to connect their actions and the actions of those around them to the simulation results. As groups move above twenty or so participants, the connections between individual and system behaviors become difficult to track. This decline in transparency tends to reduce the personal value of participatory agent simulation. Depending on the goals of the participatory simulation, this reduction in transparency may not be a problem. If the goal is to train individuals on specific roles, then transparency, while helpful, may not be required. Simply being able to experience and learn about the demands of a specific assignment can be a valuable outcome. This is particularly true when the participatory ABMS focuses on unusual or extreme situations that are not commonly encountered but which occasionally occur. In addition, participatory agent simulation that introduces people to new roles can be extremely valuable even if the number of participants limits transparency.

Increasing amounts of time are spent on management and coordination of the simulation when group sizes rise. When groups start to move to over twenty participants it is often difficult to keep the simulation moving forward due to individual disruptions and distractions. One useful tool to deal with this is the automation of basic simulation tasks. The use of computers to handle the bookkeeping and detailed tracking can allow participatory simulation with several hundred or more participants.

The more people that take part in a participatory simulation, the more complex time scheduling becomes. At a certain point, it becomes difficult to arrange the required meetings. This is particularly true if the participatory simulation is run using a series of meetings spread out over a substantial period. When scheduling, don't forget "calendar gravity," that mystical force that seems to cause scheduled events to attract unrelated conflicting events in direct proportion to the number of events already on the calendar for that date and time. Running a single, intense, but short-duration participatory simulation can help to mitigate this problem. An example is an organization that holds a "participatory simulation day" where the assembled group focuses exclusively on the simulation. Asynchronous or Internet-based participatory ABMS such as that found in some online systems can also partially address these issues.

Of course, organizing larger groups of people usually costs more money than organizing smaller groups. Furthermore, taking groups away from regularly scheduled tasks has costs of its own in terms of forgone activities.

In addition to facing size constraints, participatory ABMS tends to be limited to shorter model runs than the other approaches due to the limited time availability of participants. The model runs may take place over substantial periods of time such as days, weeks, or even months, but the total simulated time is usually limited to at most a few hundred steps.

Participatory simulations that require a week or less of runtime can often be performed on a full-time or dedicated basis. An example is an intense participatory organizational management simulation that requires the full attention of managers at two teleconferencing sites for one day. The meeting rules require the managers to provide their responses to events, if

any, in real time. During the meeting, several simulation time steps or event cycles are to be completed during each hour of real time. The fact that all participants immediately receive and respond to messages makes this type of simulation synchronous. As detailed in chapter 10, synchronous simulations can represent both time-stepped and event-level situations. For example, a participatory management simulation can have the simulation time clock advance by one day for each cycle or it can simply have a series of events occur. In the latter case, each event may be separated from the previous one by a different simulation time interval. Thus, a simulated supplier parts delay starting on model day 3 might be followed by a simulated increase in raw material costs on day 10.

Participatory simulations that stretch over periods of real time longer than a week are generally run on a periodic or part-time basis. An example is a participatory commodity market simulation that requires a half-hour meeting on Tuesdays and Thursdays. This meeting is used by the participants to report their current decisions and receive feedback on the results. One time step is normally completed during each meeting. These simulations are often the easiest to run since they require less time commitment from the participants. The flexibility to work at convenient times and the ability to merge the activity into their regular calendar makes these simulations attractive to the participants. This flexibility comes from the independent work schedule of these participatory simulations.

However, there are challenges as well. First, the independent nature of these simulations generally limits them to fixed time steps. Theoretically, it is possible to run variable time step or event simulations in an independent environment. In practice, this is difficult to manage due to the need to keep all of the participants informed and to allow them to plan their simulation activities on a structured basis. This is particularly true for independent simulations with very little time coupling. An example is a participatory simulation that uses e-mail for communication. Including asynchronous events makes it difficult and frustrating for the participants to plan their simulation activity schedules since they do not know when the simulation clock will advance to a given point in time. Asynchronous scheduling is discussed in chapter 10. Third, the limited number of weekly meetings causes simulation time to advance slowly. This means that a large amount of real time is required to simulate moderate amounts of model time. For example, if each time step represents a day, then simulating a month of activity with biweekly meetings requires approximately four months of real time.

Periodic participatory simulations are often virtual. This means that they can often be run using e-mail messages, web pages, or files on network servers with only occasional group meetings. Returning to the participatory commodity market simulation example, it is possible that instead of two meetings a week the simulation uses daily e-mail messages and one-hour status meetings every other week. The daily e-mail messages are used to step the simulation forward in time. The status meetings are used to discuss the overall state of the simulation and keep the team focused. As before, these simulations are generally limited to fixed time step modeling.

Keep It Simple

Time and size bounds are not the only limits for participatory ABMS. Participatory agent modeling also tends to be constrained to fewer, simpler rules than the other approaches. This is caused by the limited ability of most people to repeatedly follow complicated instructions for substantial periods. If asked to perform highly detailed and extremely varied tasks over and over again, most people tend either consciously or unconsciously to make up their own rules after a while. This tendency to ad lib can be both destructive and productive. If the goal of the simulation is to test specific sets of agent rules, then participants who ad lib are undermining the process and will skew the results. In fact, one of the purposes of testing results from participatory simulations using computational tools such as large-scale agent-modeling environments is to ensure that the rules were properly implemented. However, if the goal is to explore possible behaviors, then this improvisation is ideal. The complexity limits on participatory agent rules can be converted into a strength by specifying the rules at a high enough level to allow for creativity. When properly employed, this can be used as a strength of participatory modeling.

Ultimately, there is a tension between following the rules and exploring new behaviors. Too much rote repetition closes the door to new possibilities. Too much creativity undermines testing of the rules. The answer is to balance these two issues using the opening directions and follow-up debriefings discussed later in this chapter.

Developing Strong Minds

Participatory agent modeling can be a powerful educational tool to train participants and observers on a variety of topics, including the relationships between local actions and system-level results, business-specific issues, and the value of agent modeling. This training is particularly valuable since it gives the participants a sense of having hands-on involvement with the system of interest rather than simply hearing or reading about it. It also gives participants an opportunity to test their thoughts about the system in a less structured environment than that commonly encountered in typical training situations.

Through these exercises, participants can begin to develop intuition for and experience with the relationships between local actions and system-level results that are common in complex systems. In particular, the ability of well-written agent-based models to minimize noise allows the participants to focus on the key relationships and avoid being confused by extraneous distractions. The ability of agent modeling to support unstructured and semistructured experimentation allows the participants to learn by trial and error as well as to investigate new and innovative solutions to challenges. The results of their experiences with simulated systems allow the participants to develop useful intuition for the behaviors of the system. Certainly, these exercises are not a substitute for experience, but they can help the participants learn faster than if they had to master these relationships through reading, lectures, and time spent with the full system.

Improved understanding of business-specific issues is a key outcome of participatory modeling. The ability to work with systems in a highly interactive format allows the participants to develop new and deeper intuition for complex systems.

Participatory agent modeling allows the participants to experience first hand both the value and the unique benefits of agent modeling. These experiences increase the participants' appreciation for ABMS and allow them to contribute to agent model development.

Participatory agent modeling can increase stakeholder buy-in by demonstrating the value of agent modeling in a highly tangible environment. Directly experiencing something live and in person is one of the most powerful means of persuasion. Giving stakeholders this type of personal experience with agent modeling can do more to convince people of its value then any amount of discussion.

Turning Over Rocks

Everyone has asked how something works and been given an answer only to discover later that things do not really work the way the answer suggested. Participatory ABMS can help to uncover such issues within organizations. The details of how the organization actually docs business at the most detailed level can be found, even when this understanding has not previously been articulated. Hidden assumptions, unstated procedures, and unwritten rules of practice can be and often are uncovered through participatory modeling.

This is possible with participatory ABMS since the ostensible procedures can be tested to see if things really work this way. Here the tension between accurate repetition of rules and creative interpretation is directly felt. If the goal is to uncover undocumented procedures, then, to highlight the missing facts, accurate repetition should be the focus of the simulation. However, the natural tendency of the participants may be to do things as they are actually done. Admitting the truth is always the first step to enlightenment. If the real procedures are hidden, then the best course is to show that the "by the book" rules just do not work. Once this is done, the real behaviors can be found. Clear rules, proper opening instructions, and good follow-up debriefings are the key as previously discussed. The debriefings can be particularly useful since they often point the way to the real rules.

Details, Details, Details

Participatory ABMS can be an inclusive exercise that can be conducted with a variety of people with different levels of experience, educational backgrounds, organizational rank, and skills. Participatory ABMS requires team-building skills and ideally can lead to team building and development of group cohesion.

The keys to participatory ABMS are clear guidelines and appropriate time allocations. Clear and specific guidelines for participants, in written form, are required so that participants understand the situation. These should include specific articulation of the expectations for participants. If the participants should be creative, tell them. If the participants need to follow the exact rules, tell them that instead. Appropriate time allocations are required for participants so that they can act within the simulation without undue distractions.

Practice

Practice sessions should be used to teach participants both the mechanics of the simulation and what each individual needs to do. Running the simulation under minimal conditions, with simplifying assumptions and minimal events occurring, is recommended for practice sessions. The practice sessions should include plenty of time for the inevitable participant questions to be answered by the simulation manager. No questions? A lack of questions often means that the participants do not even understand enough to ask!

The opening directions set the stage for the participatory simulation. These directions should be based on the goals of the simulation. Are rules being tested? Are new possibilities being sought? This needs to be clarified for the participants before the simulation begins.

The rules given to the participants also need to be clear and appropriate to the goals. If the goal is testing behaviors, then the rules should be written in the form of a step-by-step guide. These rules should be discussed with the participants and a dry run should be performed. Plan to take at least twice as long as expected with these exercises, knowing that these exercises are well worth the extra time!

Holding a discussion with the participants about the rules to be implemented in a participatory simulation often seems like a waste of time for many people. It is almost guaranteed that at least some if not all of the participants will feel this way. Then why bother? The answer is simple. Who reads directions? Think back to the last time some new software was installed or a package that required assembly arrived. Was the manual read? Was the installation guide read? Was anything really read? Probably not. It is natural to assume that highly educated adults will read directions, but the simple fact is that instructions are rarely read. In this regard, the authors are particularly grateful that the reader has gotten this far into this book! Of course, insist that the participants read the instructions ahead of time. However, no one should assume that every participant will do this. In simple terms, reading through the step-by-step instructions as a group may be boring, but it is necessary for there to be any hope of properly executing the simulation, regardless of the level of creativity being sought. The dry run is just as necessary too.

The dry run allows the participants to test and then demonstrate their understanding of the directions. The dry run should include at least three passes through the rules with enough environmental variation to cover the main cases.

The opening passes of the dry run are for the participants. During this time, the simulation managers should expect a large number of questions, much confusion, and some playfulness. Two of the main advantages of participatory simulation are that people often find such activities to be simultaneously entertaining and insightful. Yes, participatory simulation can bring out the inner child in some people. This is not necessarily a bad thing, but it helps to be aware of this ahead of time. Combining this tendency with the challenge of following rules in a group setting can lead to the need to restart the first trial pass several times to allow everyone to finish. Do not let this happen more than a few times or the participants may become too dependent on restarting the simulation when things get complicated.

The later passes of the dry run are for the simulation managers to make sure that everyone is properly trained. The managers should carefully observe the individual participants to make sure that they properly understand the rules. Of course, since the participants are often adults, at least chronologically, this observation needs to be performed with a light touch.

Be sure that everyone knows that the dry run is just for learning. This is often not as obvious as it should be, particularly with simulations that involve some form of competition. In addition, printed instructions or other handouts are highly recommended. Be sure to bring enough copies for everyone because someone always forgets to bring their copy, even with advance warnings. Assuming that everyone will print out directions and bring them is guaranteed to add at least five minutes and quite a bit of unnecessary confusion to the meeting!

During the Run

Once the rules are well understood, then the simulation itself can begin. There should be at least one person who is available to answer questions about the rules. This official simulation authority should be clearly identified to the group before the meeting so that everyone knows where to get answers to their questions. Whenever there are no questions, this person should try to observe people's behavior to make sure that the rules are being followed. Politeness is a definite virtue here. Few things offend people more than being corrected in front of a group! Be sure

that the observer knows how to be tactful with their monitoring and feedback!

Finding a knowledgeable and experienced person to take on the role of the simulation authority is required. The authority's job is to answer questions about the simulation, make immediate decisions, and provide ongoing feedback to participants. The authority is entrusted with providing the pace at which the simulation progresses and ensuring the proper flow or synchronization among the participants. They also should provide system-level measures of performance back to the group as the simulation proceeds. These requirements mean that the authority is often the designer of the simulation or else is very experienced with the simulation design.

Many people see the simulation end time as the end of the simulation. To experienced simulationists, the end is only the beginning! Even though it is natural to complete the simulation, quickly review the results, and move on, this misses one of the most valuable learning opportunities, the debriefing.

Debriefing

The results produced during the simulation run and the participants' learning are important outcomes from a participatory simulation. Of course, these results are driven by the participants' behavior during the simulation. The debriefing is intended to reveal this behavior either to understand the divergences from the stated rules or to bring creative thinking to the larger group.

Debriefings are best done individually. Group debriefings have some value, but they can lead to groupthink where people converge on shared conclusions that are typically unfounded. This is often driven by the participants' fear of embarrassment, their identification with the group, and the convenience of agreeing rather than disagreeing with others.

When possible, the individual debriefings should follow a reasonably standard format and detailed written notes should be taken. It is best for the interviewer or a third party to take the notes to allow the interviewee to focus on the situation. Normally the interview should begin by allowing the participant to mention any outstanding issues that they feel are important. Examples include questions about the rules, questions about the simulation results, questions about the behavior of others, and descriptions of the creative ideas that they discovered. Next, ask the participant to step through one or two examples of their behavior during the simulation. Not all behaviors need to be recreated and memories can be short, but it is good to see roughly what the participant was doing. Going through a few example steps often jogs the participant's memory and leads to further useful observations. It is recommended that one average situation and one exceptional situation be observed. During these examples, be sure to ask questions if unexpected or creative behaviors are observed. Also, be kind about the details. It is hard to remember minutiae from a previous meeting run by someone else! If the simulation steps were time-consuming or required complicated operations, then allow the interviewee to abbreviate these long or difficult steps. The length of the interviews depends somewhat on the details of the simulation and the interviewee's talkativeness, but 30 minutes is usually sufficient.

Ideally, all of the simulation participants should be debriefed, but if there are a large number then sampling the group is workable. Once the debriefings are completed, then a short summary report should be prepared. The goal of the summary report is to collect the results of the individual debriefings with an eye toward both the commonalities and the differences. The commonalities are the observations that come up repeatedly in the interviews. The differences are the unusual comments made by only one or two interviewees. Ask these people why they felt the way they did. Finally, the most interesting results are often found in moderate size clusters within a larger group. In this case, a sizable subgroup, but less than a majority of the participants, may have observed something significant. These clusters of observations are often worth substantial investigation.

Computer Support

Participatory ABMS can be done with or without computer support. Without computer support there is a reason, or perhaps an excuse, to bring the participants to a single location. Even better, there is a reason to make this location remotely isolated from the participants' normal work environment, which will help to focus them by minimizing the usual office distractions. Of course, this can still be done with computer support, but it is often harder to justify. All told, there are several practical benefits to working without computer support. Without computer support, the participants generally are forced to

be physically present. Physical presence often causes higher levels of engagement and causes the participants to be less prone to distractions. In addition, participants can more readily identify the component functions of the business process, more easily identify the decisions that are made, and more directly develop an appreciation for the constraints on those decisions.

There also are several shortcomings to working without computer support. Without computer support, the simulation process can take a long time, which limits the ability to explore many cases, alternative scenarios, and events. Also, without computer support, participants tend to focus on the specific aspects of the basic business process that they are manually managing rather than seeing the big picture. Finally, it may take some time to collect and tabulate information from participants on the performance of the system.

With computer support, participants can often remain in their normal work environments and participate in the simulation from their desktop. A computer system or server that is reliable and accessible to all participants is required. This server will contain the common data repository and will provide timely updates to all participants.

There are several benefits to working with computer support. Working with computer support can be faster because the computer can be used to perform many of the mechanistic tasks. In addition, computer support can allow immediate feedback on the state of the simulation to be provided to the participants.

There also are some issues with computer support. Working with computer support can open up participants to other distractions such as web browsing. Computer support mediates participant interaction so that participants may not receive the full benefits of learning from the interpersonal interactions. Working with computer support can also inhibit participants with limited computer literacy and comfort.

A variety of computer support tools are available. Useful tools include general-purpose technologies such as spreadsheets distributed via a network server or e-mail and web servers as well as specialized systems such as NetLogo or HubNet (Wilensky and Stroup 1999; Wilensky 1999).

Spreadsheets can be used to distribute data in support of participatory ABMS. Simple nonnumeric simulations can even use text files. However, for most purposes, spreadsheets are recommended since they are widely available, well understood, and can greatly simplify the simulation authority's tabulation work.

Typically, simulation support spreadsheets or other files are placed on a shared network server. Multiple files are normally used, one for each participant. The files can be named based on the agent to which they correspond. Depending on the simulation design and group trust level, the files can all be made available to the entire simulation group or the files can be assigned individual protections. File-level access is usually set up by network server administrators who can assign read and write privileges by user. The simulation authority is normally given full access to all of the files and the individual participants are given privileges that match the purview of their agents. If the number of files is constant during the life of the simulation, the simulation authority typically creates them and then lets the network administrators assign privileges. If files are to be created by the participants during the simulation, then the simulation authority should set up one network directory for each participant and have the network administrators assign privileges for each directory. Group access can work fine for small simulations with low stakes or in a situation where full visibility of the data is required by the rules. It is highly recommended that file-level access permissions be set up for larger or more competitive groups, particularly in situations where privacy of information is required by the rules. In these situations, the temptation to peek is just too great for some people and few things discourage creativity more than making it easy to steal good ideas. The use of spreadsheets to develop agent-based models is discussed in more detail in chapter 8. Examples showing the use of spreadsheets for a participatory market simulation are given later in this chapter.

E-mail is another option for distributing simulation support files. Compared to network files, e-mail has the advantage of providing automatic time stamping and being easy to access remotely for many people. Network files normally are marked with the date and time of the last update, but this is less obvious. E-mail has the disadvantages of being easily lost and making it more difficult for the simulation authority to track participants and automate activities. This is particularly true if participants are allowed to modify their submissions repeatedly before the next time step is executed. E-mail is used similarly to network servers with the direction of message flows replacing file read and write privileges.

Participatory simulation with web servers generally requires more setup work than spreadsheets but allows faster and larger simulations once things are configured. Web servers usually require more customized configuration than spreadsheets. This customized work includes the creation of specialized input forms and output reports. This work can pay off if there are a large number of participants, if there is a need to automate the simulation authority's tabulation tasks, or if the simulation will be run many times. However, unless a web-based collaboration system is readily available, it is recommended that most organizations start with spreadsheets distributed via network servers or e-mail before moving to web servers.

HubNet is an innovative component of the NetLogo agent-based modeling tool (Wilensky and Stroup 1999). HubNet allows participatory simulation to be performed using a group of networked computers or handheld calculators with wireless networking. The computers or calculators allow the participants to assume the role of agents alongside computational agents in a shared simulation. While NetLogo was originally developed for classroom use, it can support a wider range of participatory simulations. NetLogo itself is described in detail in chapter 8 along with several other useful prototyping environments. Because of the familiarity most business people have with spreadsheets, it is recommended that most teams start with spreadsheets distributed via network servers or e-mail before moving to specialized tools such as HubNet.

A Market Example

The electricity market example started in chapter 3 will be continued. As discussed in that chapter, power markets are composed of electricity consumers, generation companies, system operators, and various intermediaries. These participants were simulated using participatory ABMS in preparation for the development of the Electricity Market Complex Adaptive Systems (EMCAS) model. One of the participatory ABMS exercises assigned consumption, generation plants, or system management responsibilities to various people as shown in figure 9.1.

The participatory ABMS exercise used spreadsheets to distribute system information and collect participant responses. The spreadsheets were exchanged using a secure network server. Individual participants were allowed to read but not change the system information spreadsheet shown in figure 9.2. They were allowed to update their own response spreadsheet but not to read those that belonged to the

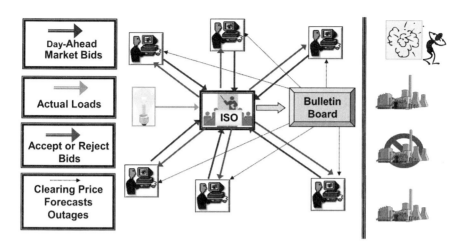

FIGURE 9.1 The participatory ABMS agents.

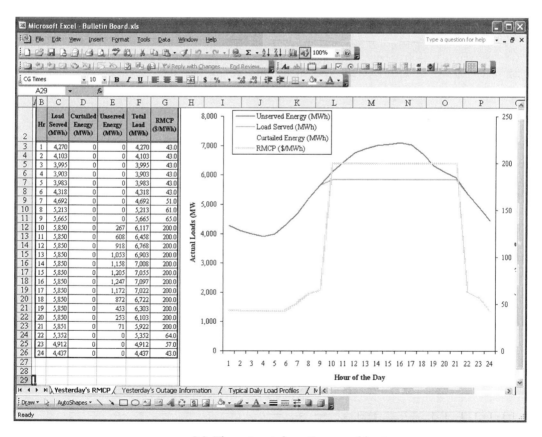

FIGURE 9.2 The system information spreadsheet.

Unit ID Number	Supply Source	Energy Sales Block ID	Bid Price ($/MWh)	Incremental Quantity (MWh)	Total Quatity (MWh)	Quantity Remaining (MWh)	Heat Rate (BTU/kWh)	Incremental Heat Rate (BTU/kWh)	Incremental Production Costs ($/MWh)
1	Baseload Coal	1	20	25	25	475	19,077	19,077	33.3
1	Baseload Coal	2	21	225	250	250	10,885	9,975	18.8
1	Baseload Coal	3	22	125	375	125	10,127	8,611	16.6
1	Baseload Coal	4	23	125	500	0	9,758	8,651	16.6
1	Baseload Coal	5	90	0	500	0	9,758	0	0.0
2	NGCC	1	63	75	75	175	11,030	11,030	62.2
2	NGCC	2	64	100	175	75	7,986	5,704	32.6
2	NGCC	3	65	50	225	25	7,681	6,612	37.6
2	NGCC	4	66	25	250	0	7,514	6,012	34.3
2	NGCC	5	40	0	250	0	7,514	0	0.0
3	Gas-Turbine	1	70	35	35	40	11,003	11,003	67.0
3	Gas-Turbine	2	85	20	55	20	9,631	7,230	46.0
3	Gas-Turbine	3	100	20	75	0	9,150	7,827	49.3
3	Gas-Turbine	4	30	0	75	0	9,150	0	0.0
3	Gas-Turbine	5	30	0	75	0	9,150	0	0.0

FIGURE 9.3 Example of a generation company response spreadsheet.

other participants. An example of a generation company response spreadsheet is shown in figure 9.3. Each of the response spreadsheets contains 24 hours' worth of operation instructions such as bids.

The simulation exercise operated on a 24-hour cycle. Each time step took 24 hours and happened to represent one day. At the start of each simulation cycle, the system information spreadsheet was updated by the simulation authority. The participants were then reminded about the update via e-mail. Participants had 24 hours from the receipt of the reminder e-mail to update their response spreadsheet. If they did not update their spreadsheet, then their previous spreadsheet was used at the participant's own peril. The participants were told that a group meeting would be held at the end of the simulation to discuss the results and that the most successful participants would receive special recognition. These two factors encouraged the participants to keep up the pace!

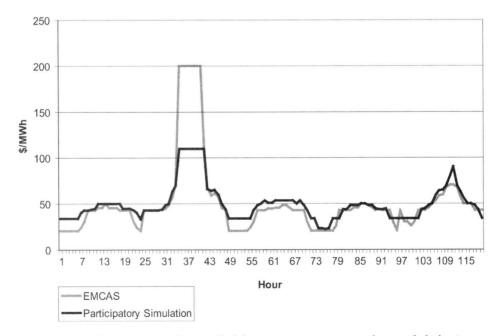

FIGURE 9.4 Human-generated prices (dark line) versus agent-generated prices (light line).

All of the rules were itemized for the participants. The goal for generation companies was to explore a wide range of possible strategies. This led to the need to keep the rules for these participants open-ended to encourage creativity on the part of the participants. On the other hand, consumer loads were based on factors such as the weather. The weather data for the simulations was prepared by a professional meteorologist. The rules for these agents were much more structured.

Once the participants submitted their spreadsheets, the simulation authority tabulated the results and updated the system information spreadsheet. In particular, locational marginal pricing was used to clear the market. This pricing approach assigns the highest accepted bid price to all of the accepted bids as discussed later. The updates also included random outages of specific components, in particular the electric power plants. The outage probabilities were developed by power systems engineers based on the known failure rates of electric grid components. These failures added a realistic level of uncertainty to the simulations. The updates to the system information spreadsheet started the next cycle of the simulation.

Several runs of the simulation exercise were performed. Debriefings followed each of the runs. The debriefing results from an example run with six players were eventually used to recreate a specific run using the EMCAS model. To do this, computational agents were programmed with the strategies of each of six people in the participatory simulation. Figure 9.4 shows the resulting market-clearing prices in the two cases. These results in general are very close.[1] The main difference occurs during the early price jump that happened during an unexpected shortage. There, the computational agents were more aggressive than the original people were. This occurred because the agents were programmed based on the debriefed strategies. It turned out that the people learned to become more aggressive during shortages by observing the results of the market. The computational agents were programmed with this strategy right from the start and therefore raised prices more quickly than the corresponding people.

Some interesting strategies were found during the debriefings. As an example, it was found that some of the participants learned to charge relatively low prices for most of their power except for the last few percent, which was assigned an extremely high price. It turned out that this technique yielded exceptional results since it allows for substantial profits with limited risk. Asking for low prices for most of the power ensures that almost all of the company's capacity will be sold. Under locational marginal pricing all of the accepted bids are paid the highest accepted prices. Therefore, the high prices for the last few percent guarantee that prices will be high in times of shortage. This bidding approach, labeled the "hockey stick strategy" due to the shape of the resulting bid curve shown in figure 9.5, has been seen in real markets (Hurlbut et al. 2004).

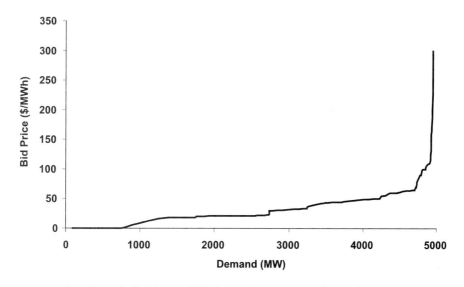

FIGURE 9.5 Example "hockey stick" bid curve like that noted by Hurlbut et al. (2004).

Summary

As this chapter has shown, people can act as agents in live agent-based models. Participatory ABMS can be used to develop business insights, to demonstrate agent-modeling concepts to business stakeholders, and to test ideas for further development. Of course, proper instruction and discipline are required. This chapter introduced the fundamental ideas behind participatory ABMS and showed how participatory agent modeling can be efficiently conducted in an office environment.

Note

1. For the statistically inclined, the correlation between the curves in figure 9.4 is 0.93. A correlation of zero indicates an extremely poor fit and a value of one indicates a perfect fit.

References

Hurlbut, D., K. Rogas, and S. Oven (2004). Protecting the Market from "Hockey Stick" Pricing: How the Public Utility Commission of Texas is Dealing with Price Gouging. *The Electricity Journal* (Apr.) 26–33.

Smith, V. (1962). An Experimental Study of Market Behavior. *Journal of Political Economy* 70: 111–137.

Smith, V. (1982). Microeconomic Systems as an Experimental Science. *American Economic Review* 72: 923–955.

Smith, V. (1994). Economics in the Laboratory. *Journal of Economic Perspectives* 8(1): 113–131.

Wilensky, U. (1999). *NetLogo*. Evanston, Ill.: Center for Connected Learning and Computer-Based Modeling, Northwestern University.

Wilensky, U. and W. Stroup (1999). *HubNet*. Evanston, Ill.: Center for Connected Learning and Computer-Based Modeling, Northwestern University.

10

How to Do Large-Scale ABMS

From Desktops on Up

Large-scale agent-based modeling and simulation (ABMS) extends agent modeling beyond simple desktop environments and allows thousands of agents or more to engage in sophisticated interchanges in complex arenas. Many large-scale agent models can be run using desktop computers, but their construction generally requires higher development skills and more development resources than the desktop environments discussed in the previous chapters.

Features Galore!

Large-scale agent modeling is usually done with computer-based simulation environments. These environments must support several specific features, including the availability of a time scheduler, the availability of communications mechanisms, the availability of flexible interaction topologies, a range of architectural choices, facilities for storing and displaying agent states, large-scale development support, and in some cases special topic support. Several standards are also available, including the Foundation for Intelligent Physical Agents' (FIPA) architecture specifications, the results of the Object Management Group (OMG) Agent Platform Special Interest Group (AP SIG) Agent UML, and the Knowledge-able Agent-oriented System architecture (KAoS) (Bradshaw 1996, 1997; Object Management Group 2001, 2004; FIPA 2003).

Schedulers

Large-scale ABMS environments require a scheduler to control the flow of time. Schedulers are the heart of the simulation engine in large-scale toolkits. Schedulers allow individual agents to synchronize their activities over time. They allow agents to determine the current time, either globally or locally, and then schedule their activities relative to the current time. The general requirements for schedulers are discussed in more detail in the "Scheduler Design Pattern" subsection later in this chapter.

There are two major approaches to time scheduling. The first approach, time-step scheduling, is easy to use for simple tasks but becomes unwieldy for tasks of realistic complexity. The second approach, discrete-event scheduling, requires more sophistication on the part of designers and developers than time-step scheduling, but allows complex event sequences to be intuitively represented.

Time-Step Simulation

Time-step simulation uses an integer counter to track the flow of time. Time thus steps from zero to one to two to three and so on. These time steps are normally assigned a time unit for each model. This time unit is generally set to the period of the fastest behavior. Agent behavioral actions must occur at one of these integer time steps. For example, consider residential real estate sales. Records might show that the sale for a specific home closed on Tuesday, 7/6/2004. The records would probably not show that the sale closed on Tuesday, 7/6/2004 at 1:32:02.0393 A.M. CST. Even if the records technically stored a value this precise, few people in the market would actually use it. Therefore, a model for this market would probably use time steps to count days since homes contracts, home loans, and the other major activities are typically tracked at the daily level.

Time-step scheduling allows multiple agent behaviors to occur at a given time step. Thus, many homes may have closed in the model on Tuesday, 7/6/2004. It is expected that the individual events scheduled during a single time step will be executed in the order specified by the scheduler. By default, many schedulers assume that the events in a single time step will execute in the order that they were originally given to the scheduler. This can be good if this represents the actual ordering. However, it can be bad if it favors some agents over others. How could this happen? It is quite easy. Most events are given to the scheduler by the agents themselves. This is the whole point of agent modeling. If one agent happens to start before the other agents, then this leading agent will get to act first during a given time step. It will thus be able to schedule its next actions before the other agents. This process will continue and allow the leading agent to always act first. If acting first is an advantage or disadvantage, then this agent will always be ahead or behind. For models where this represents reality, this is certainly fine. But for most models this does not represent reality. The answer is to use more sophisticated scheduling that changes the order of agent execution. These new ordering rules include rotation and randomization. Rotation gives each agent a turn at leading the rest. For most models this is an improvement over a fixed ordering but can still result in biases, albeit more subtle ones. The most widely used solution is randomization. This technique uses a new random drawing each time step to define the event execution order. Time-step scheduling has the advantage of being simple to start with. Its three main disadvantages are its unintuitive time measurement, its lack of scalability, and the way it complicates the integration of multiple simulations.

Clearly, counting is a simple process. What is not so simple is remembering that day number 562 is in fact Tuesday, 7/6/2004. The use of counting numbers to represent time steps turns out to be interestingly inconvenient as models grow in size. This is one reason to use a more flexible method to measure time.

Returning to the daily time-step example, imagine the need to include the scheduling of home visits into the model. Imagine further that looking at visit scheduling conflicts is a major area of interest. In this case, the model should now operate at the hourly level. Moving to the hourly level will require all of the existing daily behaviors to be rewritten as complex nested scheduling work to be done for each day. It might be said that the model should have been hourly in the first place. In fact, it is highly recommended that time-step models use a time resolution at least one step finer than the expected speed of the behaviors. Thus, daily models should use hours and then schedule events to occur during only one selected hour of each day. The other 23 hours each day would not be initially used. This provides some padding in case finer-grained behaviors are required. However, the underlying need to move to finer-grained representations of time really cannot be completely addressed this way since it is always possible to need faster behaviors.

Integrating multiple agent models or adding selected agents from one model into another model should be relatively easy operations if the two models share compatible modeling goals. What if the models use time-step scheduling and each model has a different time step? The situation is similar to adding finer-grained behaviors to an existing model. Integration requires the slower model to be restructured to work with the faster model's time-step size. Things should not be this hard. Fortunately, there is a better way to schedule time.

Discrete-Event Simulation

Discrete-event simulation generalizes time-step scheduling by allowing events to occur at any time that can be specified by a real number (Law 2007). This allows events to occur at 1, 3, and 5 as before as well as at 1.5, 3.25, 5.737896, or any other arbitrary number. The "discrete events" referred to in the name are the events that are executed for each behavior. The events are discrete because in principle only one event executes at any one time. Events with different time stamps occur in the order of their time stamps. Events with the same time stamp are executed in some order determined by the scheduler. The process of selecting the order of events with the same time stamp is essentially the same as with time-step simulation. The constraint that only one simulation event can execute at any one time is often relaxed by parallel discrete-event schedulers. However, the basic concepts are the same for both sequential and parallel execution.

With discrete-event simulation, the underlying scheduler simply remembers all of the pending events and runs the next most imminent event whenever the current event finishes. The scheduler is said to use a "time wheel" to store the pending events. The wheel contains the events in increasing time order. The closest event on the time wheel is the one currently executing behavior. The next closest event is the next event to be scheduled. The current event can schedule new events at any time in the future, including ahead of the event that is currently next. When the current event ends, the time wheel is conceptually rotated forward until the next event is reached. This event is executed and the process continues.

Discrete-event simulation allows agents to schedule events at any time that suits them and allows simulation designers to pick whatever time scale makes the problem the easiest to solve. For example, in a residential real estate sales model each time step might represent a day. Hours can simply be one twenty-fourth of a day or about 0.041667 days each. Discrete-event simulation also allows arbitrarily fast events to be added to an existing simulation without requiring changes to the current model. If the existing real-estate model needs to include minute-level events, then behaviors can be scheduled every 0.000694 or so days. This allows different agent-based models to be merged simply by connecting the agent behaviors. As long as the models have a common time base, then the scheduler can be used to coordinate the flow of time.

Global and Local Time

Global time is maintained by a universal simulation scheduler that manages the overall flow of time. Virtually all agent simulations contain one universal simulation scheduler. Local time is managed by one or more local schedulers. These local schedulers normally synchronize their measurement of time with the universal scheduler on a periodic basis.

Local schedulers are used for several reasons. First, they can be used for modularity. Local schedulers are sometimes used in multiscale simulations to represent the flow of time within agents or groups of agents. In this case, the time intervals between the locally scheduled simulation behaviors is usually much smaller than the typical intervals in the behavior managed by the universal scheduler. The local "subschedule" thus allows the details of micro-behaviors to be hidden from the majority of the simulation. This hiding simplifies the connections between the macro- and micro-levels. An example is an organizational management model that measures the flow of time on the corporate level in intervals about the size of weeks, but models the behaviors of individuals within the corporation on a daily level.

Second, they can be used for compatibility. It is sometimes effective to use existing models to implement the behaviors of agents or parts of the agent environment. Legacy models often have extremely different notions of time than the agent-based models that are wrapped around them. This mismatch in time scales can be overcome by having local schedulers that relate time as viewed by the legacy models to time as measured by the agent simulation. An example is a petroleum refinery model that uses a legacy optimization package to model the yield from given production configurations. These production configurations are set by the agents representing managers and other plant employees. The production yields are in turn used by the agents to help determine their future choices. The legacy model operates at the level of minutes while the agent behaviors take place over hours. A local scheduler tracks minutes for the production yield optimization and relates this back to the hours that are flowing by at the agent level.

Third, they can be used to improve the efficiency of model execution. In particular, events are typically dependent on only a few other events. A universal scheduler holds all future events as pending until the current events are completed. However, what if some of the future events are independent of the currently executing events? In this case, these future events can be executed at the same time as the current events. In practice, there are usually a large number of independent events in agent models. This is caused by the fact that each agent usually has a limited ability to consider inputs. This is a consequence of bounded rationality and other theories of the individual that are discussed in chapter 6. This independence allows multiple events to be processed simultaneously. This implicit concurrency can be used to increase the execution speed of agent simulations. Large-scale agent models that run on computers with multiple processors or on distributed systems with multiple computers can particularly benefit from this parallelism. Some large-scale agent schedulers have built-in features to support this type of execution (North et al. 2006).

The concept of event independence must be defined carefully to produce correct results. Two events are independent if neither uses data that is required by the other. Consider two examples from an agent-based movie theater simulation. The agents are potential movie patrons throughout the United States. Each day every agent chooses whether to go to the movies. The agents coordinate their selections with neighboring agents that are part of the same social network. If a group of agents chooses to see a movie, then they have several movies at a few different local theaters from which to choose. They also have several times available for each movie. Of course, there are a certain number of screens in each theater and each screen can only show one movie at a time. This can lead to occasional competitions for tickets between groups of agents that want to see a popular movie in the same location at the same time.

Imagine two agents about to make their selections. The selections are independent events if the two agents are in different social groups and if they live far enough apart to avoid competing for tickets to shows that are likely to sell out.

Let movie distribution companies also be agents in the model. Consider two movie distribution companies vying to schedule screens. Two distribution contract signing events are potentially dependent if the two competing distribution companies are working with the same theater chain. The events are actually dependent if both contracts have some of the same screens in the same locations at the same time. With fully dependent events such as this one, only one of the events can ultimately be honored.

In some ways, there is an inherent conflict between the local focus of ABMS and the use of universal simulation schedulers. The use of local schedulers ameliorates this a bit, but it still leaves the question of why a bottom-up approach uses a universal scheduler. The answer is that universality of agent schedulers is an artifact of a barely recognized optimization to handle dependent events. In particular, a theoretically ideal agent simulation would have individual agents exchanging messages directly without a universal scheduler. Notice here that event scheduling and messaging are being used synonymously. This will be discussed in the next section. Having agents coordinate their own messaging events would be a fully bottom-up approach. In practice, having individual agents to coordinate the events they process would be extremely slow. The use of a universal scheduler that acts as a central coordination point for events makes event scheduling an efficient process. This small sacrifice is generally worth the substantial performance improvement.

Communications Mechanisms

Mechanisms to allow agents to communicate are required. These communications mechanisms commonly take the form of a message-queuing system. This system allows agents to send information to other agents on an asynchronous basis as well as to receive information in an ordered fashion.

Message-passing systems such as the Message-Passing Interface can be integrated into schedulers (Hansen 1998). When this occurs, the scheduler's ability to coordinate the flow of time is used to queue messages being passed between agents. This discipline is often a very effective way to manage messaging, especially when it is tied to automatic logging of events. More advanced tools such as the Globus grid computing system or specialized tools such as the High Level Architecture (HLA) can also be used (Lu et al. 2000; IEEE 2001a, 2001b, 2001c; Foster et al. 2002).

Flexible Interaction Topologies

Topology describes how things are connected (Lawson 2003). Agent interaction topologies describe the possible connections between agents. These connections may be permanent or they may be transient. The connections may be formed by the agents themselves or they may be externally specified. The critical point is that the large-scale agent-modeling toolkits must support a wide range of different connection options. This range includes soups, grids, irregular polygons, networks, active environments, and even real maps.

Soups

Soups are the simplest connection structure or interaction topology. They simply mix agents together on a random basis. Any time two or more agents need to interact, the appropriate number of agents is drawn at random from the available population and momentarily connected together. An example of a soup is shown in figure 10.1. Soups are easy to set up but lack the ability to represent lasting neighborhoods due to the transient nature of the connections. Soups are useful for representing situations that actually are randomly mixed, for representing more structured situations for which the patterns are unknown or extremely

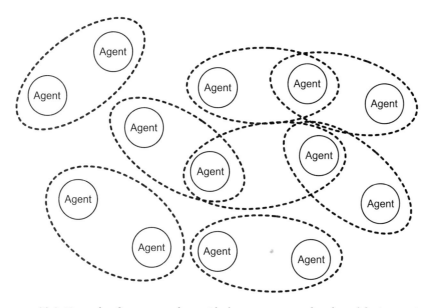

FIGURE 10.1 Example of a soup topology with the agents currently selected for interaction.

complicated, and for initial prototyping of more sophisticated topologies.

Networks

Networks are point-to-point connections between agents. Networks generalize soups by allowing agents to remember the other agents to which they are connected. Networks are normally represented as graphs as shown in figure 10.2. Networks are extremely useful for representing nonspatial connections such as business and social relationships. An example is a network that represents a supply chain in which each link between agents indicates a customer relationship. Tools for manipulating and visualizing networks are especially helpful when dealing with large and complex agent graphs. Finding the average, maximum, and minimum number of connections between agents in the supply chain example along with the average, maximum, and minimum shipping delays on each link might be useful for understanding the performance of the network. Networks are commonly used in conjunction with other interaction topologies such as the use of the example supply chain network on top of a map from a geographic information system.

Grids

Grids are arguably the simplest interaction topology that has a spatial component. The simplest grids are

rectangular checkerboard worlds as shown in figure 10.3. Grids that consider every square to have four neighbors are said to have von Neumann neighborhoods as shown in figure 10.3. Grids that consider every square to have eight neighbors are said to have Moore neighborhoods. The phrase "Moore is more" is an easy way to remember this difference. Grids that are more sophisticated can have hexagonal neighborhoods as shown in figure 10.4. Grids are useful for introducing basic spatial relationships into models. Rectangular grids are the simplest way to model basic spatial interactions. However, hexagonal grids are more uniform than rectangular grids, since all of the neighboring cells are the same distance away. This makes hexagonal grids better for modeling situations for which spatial symmetry is important.

Grids can have borders on the edges that stop agents from leaving the space or grids can allow agents traveling off one edge to reappear on another edge. A torus is a special grid that has connected opposing borders. Thus, agents that cross a border of a torus immediately reappear at the opposite border. This is the familiar "Asteroids world" commonly seen in video games.[1] Tori are useful for representing infinite worlds with periodically repeated contents.

Irregular Polygons

Irregular polygons are arbitrarily shaped closed regions bounded by convex loops. An example

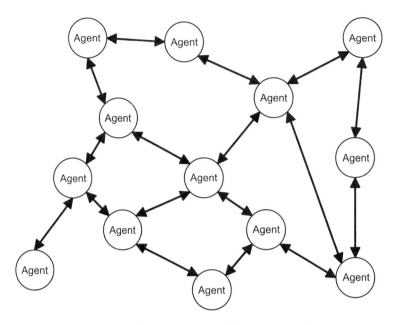

FIGURE 10.2 An agent network shown as a graph.

is shown in figure 10.5. Irregular polygons are a step toward true maps generated by geographic information systems. However, irregular polygons normally lack the high level of boundary and content details found in realistic maps. In exchange, irregular polygons are usually easier to work with than full-fledged maps. Irregular polygons are a good intermediate step between the simple worlds provided by grids and the complex worlds derived from geographic information systems.

Geographic Information Systems

Geographic information systems (GIS) are software tools for working with spatial or map data. Mature GIS tools are available both commercially and in free open-source form. Integrating GIS into agent-modeling

toolkits is a major new direction for large-scale agent-modeling environments. The overall goal is to allow agents to move on and interact with realistic maps. Two major types of agent representations are used to integrate GIS and agent-modeling toolkits, namely the Lagrangian and Eulerian representations (Brown et al. 2005).

Lagrangian representations associate specific features or discrete components with agents. These agent components can individually move through time. An example of a military communications model is shown in figure 10.6. The agents are vehicles that move and interact in a simulated combat area. Some agent-modeling environments use this type of representation to support varying levels of integration with GIS.

Eulerian representations associate agents with regions of higher or lower values in numeric grids as

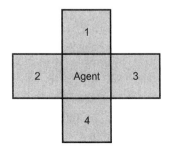

FIGURE 10.3 A rectangular grid with labeled von Neumann and Moore neighborhoods.

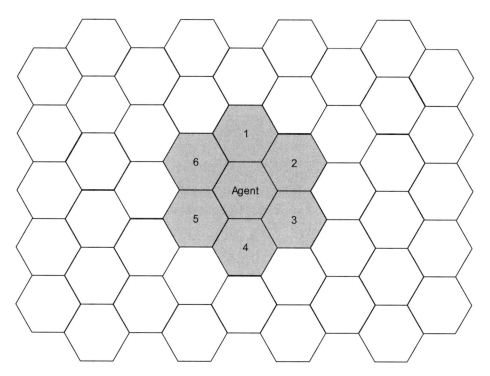

FIGURE 10.4 A hexagonal grid.

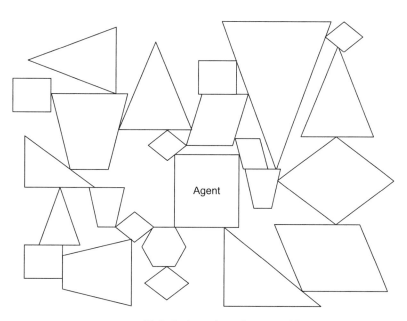

FIGURE 10.5 An irregular polygon world.

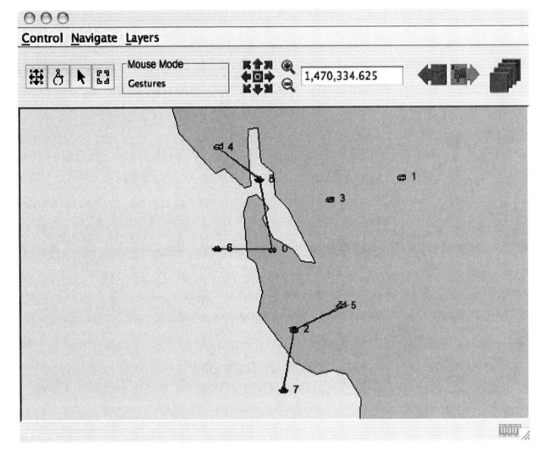

FIGURE 10.6 Example of an agent GIS environment.

compared to the surrounding locations. Thus, Eulerian systems represent agents using special types of waves. These numeric waves can move from grid region to grid region. An example is a vegetation-growth model that counts the height of the grass at each point in a dense grid. This type of GIS integration is also supported by some agent toolkits.

Active Environments

Active environments are worlds that are sophisticated enough to be considered agents in their own right. These worlds are often built by combining one or more of the other interaction topologies with specific behavioral rules for the environment itself. An example is a GIS-based shopping mall model that includes complex weather imposed by the environment. Active environments are commonly used when large-scale conditions such as weather need to be included in agent-based models.

Architectural Choices

Several ABMS architectural styles are commonly used as detailed in chapter 7. These styles include tightly coupled architectures, loosely coupled architectures, and distributed architectures. The ability to select the type of architecture and change this choice over time is a critical feature of agent-modeling environments.

Storing and Displaying Agent States

Mechanisms for displaying and saving the states of agents are required. State display is required to allow users to inspect and possibly modify agent properties. State saving is needed to allow agent properties to be examined outside the simulation and possibly stored for later reuse. This reuse most commonly takes the form of "hot starting" model runs or testing simulation alternatives from a common starting point.

Hot starts are commonly used to avoid having to spin up or warm up simulations. Warm-up periods are needed when the initial input data for a simulation does not place the resulting agents close enough to stable values to be useful. In this case, the simulation is normally run for an interval of time to allow the agent properties to stabilize. Hot starts are used to load these values directly and run forward from this point rather than recalculate the stable values every time the simulation is run. Testing alternatives originating from a common starting point is a kind of "what if" analysis. It is used to investigate possible outcomes that all share the same initial state. This initial state may represent the current condition of the system being simulated, it may represent a possible future state, or it may be based on a past state. If the current state is being considered, then the branching possibilities are usually alternative courses of action. If a future state is being considered, then the branches usually represent possible short- or long-term options. If the past is being considered, then the branches commonly represent alternatives that were available but not taken. In each of these cases, the goal is to investigate the possible consequences of alterative choices. Branching runs are discussed in more detail in chapter 13.

Facilities for storing and displaying agent states can be directly provided by the environment or they can be custom built using other more primitive features in the environment. Clearly, leveraging existing features can save development time and resources. This is particularly true if the organization creating the model has limited experience in agent-based simulation design and development. Furthermore, existing environments usually have support available. This support can come from the user community or from a commercial organization.

Reading inputs and generating outputs from sources commonly used by analysts helps with user buy-in and makes the use of the model more efficient. Common file sources include widely used word-processing programs, presentation programs, spreadsheets, databases applications, and GIS packages as well as XML, HDF, and netCDF.

Presentation Tools, Word Processors, Spreadsheets, and Desktop Databases

The ability to load spreadsheets, desktop databases, and GIS data directly into agent models is extremely helpful. This allows analysts to set up model inputs using tools that are comfortable and familiar. In some cases, it also can allow existing data sources to be directly used.

It is often convenient to have agent simulations automatically produce overview briefings and summary spreadsheets that describe the major outputs from model runs, along with supporting reports and detailed spreadsheets that trace the model execution steps. Moderate-scale databases for use with desktop database software and GIS outputs can also be automatically generated. When possible, the briefings should be stored in presentation software files and the reports should be stored as word-processing software files. Choosing an environment that can generate files in formats commonly employed by the model users is particularly helpful. In some cases, it is even possible to use presentation and report templates from the users so that the briefings are in an immediately recognized and instantly usable style. Ideally, the briefings and reports should be structured to match actual documents that the users have already read about the system being modeled. This makes the model results easier to understand and simplifies direct comparisons with real-world data.

XML

Extensible Markup Language (XML) is a highly flexible storage format that allows data to be easily exchanged between different programs. XML essentially wraps each data element in a document with a tag that describes the content of that element. This makes XML files in many ways self-describing. Anyone who has had to struggle to understand the contents of an undocumented file from an inaccessible source will appreciate the advantages of self-documented files. In some ways, XML is the data equivalent of the literate programming systems described later in this chapter. XML also allows data to be easily converted between formats using an XML-based transformation language called Extensible Stylesheet Language Transformations (XSLT). XSLT works with many widely available programs to complete XML document conversions. Configuring agent models to use XML input and output allows data to be easily moved into and extracted from large-scale models. Agent-modeling tools with direct support for XML can save substantial amounts of time.

Enterprise Databases

Most organizations maintain enterprise databases. Obtaining simulation data from these databases and storing simulation results back into them can provide several benefits for users. First, this type of integration allows users to apply existing data-mining tools to prepare model inputs and analyze model outputs. Second, integration allows models to be executed immediately using data as it arrives rather than requiring secondary processing before the data can be used. Third, integration simplifies sharing results with the rest of an organization. Of course, models must be well developed and carefully tested before they are connected to enterprise databases. Furthermore, enterprise database integration requires more sophistication on the part of model developers. As such, it is not recommended for early versions of models. However, enterprise database integration is highly recommended as a long-term model development goal.

HDF

The Hierarchical Data Format (HDF) from the National Center for Supercomputing Applications is used to store extremely large scientific and engineering datasets (NCSA 2004). HDF focuses on portability between computer systems and high-performance input and output for distributed execution. HDF is a good choice for storing data from large-scale distributed simulations. HDF and its supporting tools are free and open source.

netCDF

The network Common Data Form (netCDF) is a self-describing portable file format for storing large data arrays (Unidata 2004). Free and open-source libraries for reading and writing netCDF files are available for many languages. netCDF was developed by the Unidata Program Center in Boulder, Colorado, and has been extended by user contributions. Much like HDF, netCDF is an effective way to store data from large-scale distributed simulations. netCDF files are typically smaller than HDF files with the same content. netCDF file reading and writing is also usually simpler to program than HDF file access. However, HDF has more flexibility and can natively encode much more complex data structures than netCDF.

Visualization Support

Generating visualizations that show some of the inner workings of the model using domain-specific images that in some sense look like the real world being modeled can also help with user buy-in. Visualization is discussed in detail in chapter 13. The ability to develop user-editable prototype mockups can also be helpful. Model prototyping is considered in chapters 7, 8, and 9.

Large-Scale Development Support

Environments must support large-scale software development. This is often provided indirectly by using an enterprise language and development environment such as Java in Eclipse or Microsoft C# in Microsoft Visual Studio[2] (Foxwell 1999; Archer 2001; Eclipse 2004). Critical development environment features include object-oriented programming support, a fully integrated debugger, refactoring tools, version control support, and literate programming support.

Object-Oriented Programming

In general, object-oriented programming is quite helpful for large-scale model development since objects are a natural way to implement agents. In fact, agents can be considered self-directed objects as detailed in chapter 3. Object-oriented programming uses objects to represent discrete entities. Objects are created from templates called classes. Classes define the behaviors and properties of objects. Objects contain specific settings for each of their class's properties. As such, there can only be one class of a given kind, but there can be any number of objects of a given class. For example, there can be only one "Automobile" class in a car dealership model, but there can be many "Automobile" objects sitting on the simulated lot. Each of these cars can have unique behaviors such as acceleration, braking, and cornering as well as properties such as make, model, vehicle identification number, and price. Object-oriented programming support requires several key features, namely encapsulation, inheritance, and polymorphism (Booch 1993).

Encapsulation is the ability of classes to bind behaviors and properties together in one place and for each class to control how its behaviors and properties are accessed. The binding allows objects to be treated as discrete entities. The access control allows each behavior and property of a class to be marked with an access code such as "public" or "private." Public behaviors can be invoked by anyone. Public properties can be changed by anyone. Private behaviors and properties can only be manipulated by objects of the same class as the owner of the behaviors and properties. This access control allows developers to protect behaviors from being unexpectedly executed and to prevent properties from being unexpectedly changed. For example, "Automobile" acceleration may be a public property since any object can ask a car to accelerate. However, "fire spark plug" may be a private property since only the car itself should be requesting this. Most object-oriented programming languages include several other finer-grained access controls in addition to public and private.

Inheritance is the ability for classes to be specified starting with the behaviors and properties of existing classes. This allows hierarchies of classes to be formed. Each class in the hierarchy adds new behaviors and properties to those of its parent class. Child classes are called subclasses and parent classes are called superclasses. For example, the "Automobile" superclass could give rise to a "Sports Car" subclass and a "Sedan" subclass. There may be many "Sports Car" objects and "Sedan" objects available for sale. Each "Sports Car" and "Sedan" inherits the ability to accelerate, brake, and corner as well as the presence of make, model, vehicle identification number, and price properties. The "Sports Car" class might add properties indicating the presence of a spoiler and a turbocharger to those of "Automobile." The "Sedan" class might add properties indicating the presence of rear seat televisions to those of "Automobile."

Polymorphism is the ability of each class to provide its own implementation for each behavior. Thus, the way a "Sports Car" accelerates can be completely different from the way a "Sedan" accelerates, yet since "Automobile" implements acceleration, anyone can ask an "Automobile" to accelerate and get an appropriate response. The word "polymorphism" itself here refers to the ability of one message, namely "accelerate," to take many forms such as "Sports Car" acceleration and "Sedan" acceleration.

Visual Development

Visual development is the use of diagramming techniques such as the Unified Modeling Language (UML) to design and implement software using detailed pictures. UML is discussed in detail in chapter 6. The better development environments can automatically write code based on UML diagrams. This can be used to develop programs visually. The best development environments offer a "round trip" visual development feature that automatically writes code based on diagrams and then automatically keeps the diagrams up to date with any manual code changes. These features can greatly simplify and speed model development.

Integrated Debuggers

Integrated debuggers allow programmers to execute programs by stepping through code one line at a time. This allows code to be checked for correctness and greatly reduces the time needed to track down errors. Most development environments have some type of debugger. Better debuggers are directly connected into the development environment to allow debugging directly from file-editing windows without needing to change the code. The best debuggers can run extremely large programs without major slowdowns. Be sure that the development environments being considered for or used on a project can run programs at least as large as the simulations that are expected. This may seem trivial, but many managers miss this point and regret it later.

Refactoring Tools

Refactoring tools allow source code to be automatically reorganized with minimal human effort. For example, such tools allow developers to rename classes and automatically propagate the changes throughout the source code. Another example is moving pieces of code from one place to another to group related functions. Refactoring tools will automatically update all of the dependent code without human intervention. Refactoring tools simplify and speed up the normally time-intensive process of restructuring code. This makes code reorganization affordable and allows code to remain orderly as it is iteratively developed.

Version Control

Version control systems keep track of changes to code over time and automate the details of merging code changed by multiple developers. Version control systems typically log each code change along with the time of each change, the developer who made the change, and a note describing the reason for the change. They also track the development history of software and allow any previous version of the code to be recovered at any time. Such systems also allow the merging of code changes from several developers who are working simultaneously, even if the developers are working on the same code files. These systems normally run on a server that is accessible to all of the team members on a project. Most large-scale development environments can connect to several different version control systems. Such systems are essential for team development and can also be extremely helpful for individual developers looking for rigorous source code tracking.

Literate Programming

Donald Knuth, Professor Emeritus of the Art of Computer Programming at Stanford University, introduced literate programming by stating that "I believe that the time is ripe for significantly better documentation of programs, and that we can best achieve this by considering programs to be works of literature" (Knuth 1984). He eleborates as follows:

> Let us change our traditional attitude to the construction of programs: Instead of imagining that our main task is to instruct a computer what to do, let us concentrate rather on explaining to human beings what we want a computer to do.
> The practitioner of literate programming can be regarded as an essayist, whose main concern is with exposition and excellence of style. Such an author, with thesaurus in hand, chooses the names of variables carefully and explains what each variable means. He or she strives for a program that is comprehensible because its concepts have been introduced in an order that is best for human understanding, using a mixture of formal and informal methods that reinforce each other.

Literate programming systems also typically allow comments to be embedded in source code in a form that can be automatically converted into standalone documentation. For example, Java's JavaDoc standard allows developers to write special notes in code that can be extracted to form a set of web pages documenting how the code works. The ability to do literate programming is a language feature. The documents produced by literate programming systems are particularly useful for new developers who are trying to get up to speed on existing software.

Special Topic Support

Some modeling toolkits provide special support for specific modeling applications. For example, one of the toolkits to be discussed later includes special tools for modeling social networks. Leveraging existing support for a topic of interest can significantly reduce model development time. It is highly recommended that candidate toolkits be evaluated in part on the relevance of any special tools that they provide.

Community Support

Wandering alone in the dark is a tough way to get places. It is also a tough way to develop models. The availability of a vibrant user community or responsive commercial support is invaluable for practical model development. The availability of help from others is one of the strongest arguments against developing proprietary tools. Be sure to consider the level of activity on any available online discussion groups or the support commitments available from vendors when selecting a toolkit.

Current Toolkits

Where are ABMS toolkits and environments today? Thanks to substantial public and private research and development investments, many environments are now available for business use without charge, including Repast and Swarm. Proprietary toolkits are also used.

Repast

The REcursive Porous Agent Simulation Toolkit (Repast) is the leading free and open-source large-scale ABMS toolkit (North et al. 2005a, 2005b, 2006). Repast seeks to support the development of extremely flexible models of agents with an emphasis on social interactions, but it is not limited to social models alone. Repast is maintained by the Repast Organization for Architecture and Design (ROAD). More information on Repast, as well as free downloads, can be found at the Repast home page, http://repast.sourceforge.net/. According to ROAD (2004):

> Our goal with Repast is to move beyond the representation of agents as discrete, self-contained entities in favor of a view of social actors as permeable, interleaved and mutually defining, with cascading and recombinant motives. We intend to support the modeling of belief systems, agents, organizations, and institutions as recursive social constructions. The fuller goal of the toolkit is to

allow situated histories to be replayed with altered assumptions. To achieve this goal, it will be necessary for Repast to provide a feast of advanced features, and it is toward that objective that we work.

There are four members of the Repast agent-based modeling portfolio. The four portfolio members are Repast for Python Scripting (Repast Py), Repast for Java (Repast J), Repast for the Microsoft.NET framework (Repast.NET), and Repast Simphony (Repast S). Each of these portfolio members has the same core features. However, each provides a different environment for these features. Taken together, the Repast ABMS portfolio gives modelers a choice of model development and execution environments.

Repast Py is a cross-platform visual model construction environment that is described in chapter 8. Repast Py allows users to build models using a graphical user interface and to write agent behaviors using Python scripting. All of the features of the Repast system are available in Repast Py, but Repast Py is designed for rapid development of prototype agent models. Repast Py models can be automatically exported to Repast J for large-scale model development.

Repast J is a pure Java modeling environment. Repast J is designed to support the development of large-scale agent models. It includes a variety of features such as a fully concurrent discrete-event scheduler, a model visualization environment, integration with GIS for modeling agents on real maps, and adaptive behavioral tools such as neural networks and genetic algorithms. Neural networks and genetic algorithms are discussed in chapter 3.

Repast.NET is a pure C# modeling environment. Repast.NET brings all of the features of the Repast J system to the Microsoft.NET framework. Repast.NET models can be written in any language supported by the Microsoft.NET framework such as Managed C++, C#, Visual Basic, or even Managed Lisp or Managed Prolog.[3]

Repast S extends the Repast portfolio by offering a new approach to simulation development and execution. The Repast S runtime is designed to include advanced features for agent storage, display, and behavioral activation, as well as new facilities for data analysis and presentation. The Repast S development environment is designed to include advanced point-and-click features for agent behavioral specification and dynamic model self-assembly. A simple Repast S social network model is shown in figure 10.7. A simple Repast S predator–prey model is shown in figure 10.8.

All of the members of the Repast portfolio have sophisticated time schedulers that can do both time-step and discrete-event simulation as well as maintain both global and local views of time. Repast allows a wide range of communications mechanisms to be used with all of the major agent interaction topologies. Repast models can be built with any major architectural style and it works well with most large-scale development environments. Repast includes a full set of tools for displaying agents as shown in figures 10.7 and 10.8. Most versions of Repast include tools for integration with both commercial and free open-source GIS using both Lagrangian and Eulerian representations. The commercial GIS integration includes automated connectivity to the widely used ESRI ArcGIS GIS. Furthermore, all members of the Repast portfolio are fully object-oriented.

Swarm

Swarm is a free, open-source ABMS library (Minar et al. 1996). Swarm seeks to create a shared simulation platform for ABMS and to facilitate the development of a wide range of models. Users build simulations by incorporating Swarm library components into their own programs.

Swarm is a collaborative effort. It was launched in 1994 by Chris Langton at the Santa Fe Institute. Swarm's contributors include Chris Langton, Roger Burkhart, Nelson Minar, Manor Askenazi, Glen Ropella, Sven Thommesen, Marcus Daniels, Alex Lancaster, and Vladimir Jojic. Swarm is currently maintained by the Swarm Development Group (SDG). More information on Swarm, as well as free downloads, can be found at the SDG home page (www.swarm.org). The following is from Daniels (1999):

> Swarm is a set of libraries that facilitate implementation of agent-based models. Swarm's inspiration comes from the field of Artificial Life. Artificial Life is an approach to studying biological systems that attempts to infer mechanism from biological phenomena, using the elaboration, refinement, and generalization of these mechanisms to identify unifying dynamical properties of biological systems. . . . To help fill this need, Chris Langton initiated the Swarm project in 1994 at the Santa Fe Institute. The first version was available by 1996, and since then it has evolved to serve not

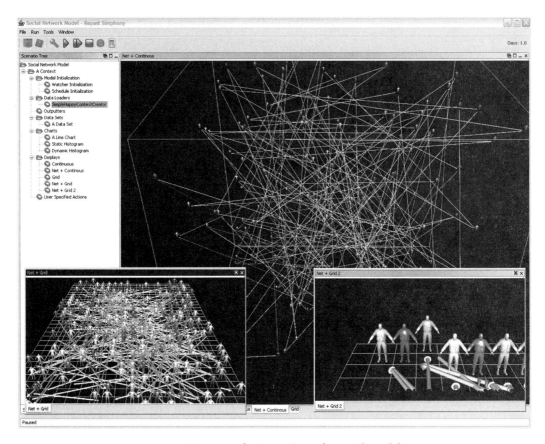

FIGURE 10.7 A simple Repast S social network model.

only researchers in biology, but also anthropology, computer science, defense, ecology, economics, geography, industry, and political science.

The Swarm simulation system has two fundamental components. The core component runs general-purpose simulation code written in Objective-C, Tcl/Tk, and Java. This component handles most of the behind-the-scenes details. The external wrapper components run user-specific simulation code written in either Objective-C or Java. These components handle most of the center-stage work.

Similarly to Repast, the Swarm interface uses probes to display and edit the properties of agents. Probes are normally activated by clicking on an agent in one of the display windows.

Unlike Repast, the Swarm scheduler only supports time-step scheduling, but it does so at a high level of resolution. The Swarm scheduler can maintain global and local time schedules. Swarm supports a full set of communications mechanisms and can model all of the major interaction topologies. Swarm models can be built following any major architectural approach. Swarm includes a good set of tools for storing and displaying agent states. Since Swarm is based on a combination of Java and Objective-C, it is object-oriented. However, this mixture of languages causes Swarm to have difficulties with some large-scale development environments. Swarm has support for GIS through the Kenge library. As a note, the annual Swarm users' conference, which is known as "SwarmFest," is an excellent way to get involved with the details of the Swarm toolkit.

Proprietary Toolkits

Proprietary toolkits are commonly used for agent modeling. These toolkits have the advantage of being custom designed for specific uses. They also can be modified without concern for remaining synchronized

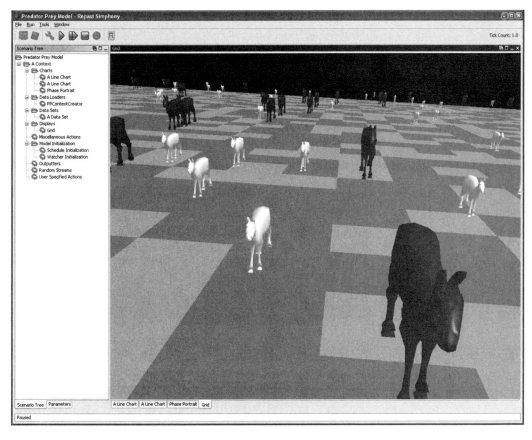

FIGURE 10.8 A simple Repast S predator–prey model.

with the public version of the toolkit. However, developing and maintaining such a toolkit can require substantial resources and a long-term organizational commitment. Furthermore, developing such toolkits causes projects to lack the community or commercial support often found with publicly available toolkits. This support can include online help, in-person help, code sharing, targeted conferences, and user meetings. The lack of availability of developers experienced with the toolkit is also an issue faced with proprietary toolkits.

The Large-Scale Modeling Life Cycle

There are certain core issues in applying any of these environments. Developing an agent-based simulation is just part of the more general software and model development process. The development timeline typically has several highly interleaved stages:

1. The concept development and articulation stage defines the project goals.
2. The requirements definition stage makes the goals specific.
3. The design stage defines the model structure and function.
4. The implementation stage builds the model using the design.
5. The operationalization stage puts the model into use.

In practice, successful projects typically iterate over stages 3 and 4 several times with increasingly detailed models resulting from each pass. Successful projects usually begin small, using one or more of the tools described in chapter 8, and then grow into the larger-scale tools in stages as detailed in chapter 14.

Designing Large-Scale Models for Use

There are a variety of issues to consider when designing large-scale models for practical use. These issues include simulation timing, system execution capacity, the model's guidance horizon, and the possibility of parallel execution.

Simulation Timing

Execution time requirements are a substantial component that determines the potential uses of a model. Execution time is the amount of clock time required to complete a deterministic simulation run or a full set of stochastic simulation runs. Execution times vary from faster to slower than actual clock time. Models that run fast enough can be used in a conversational mode. Surprisingly, even models that are slower than real time can have substantial business value.

Model Runtimes

Sub-real-time models run faster than actual time. These models can be used to gain insight into future events. An example is an agent-based manufacturing plant model that can simulate a day's worth of factory production activities in 15 seconds. Such models are natural candidates for tactical and operational applications since they can simulate events before they happen.

Supra-real-time models run slower that actual time. The events in these models take more time than real events. Most models are used in some way to "predict" the real world. However, supra-real-time models are slower than the real world. It has been said tongue-in-cheek that the real world can be used to predict the results of these models! How could such models have any value at all? The answer depends on how the models are applied.

Simulations that take longer to run than the events that they are modeling can be used to analyze historical occurrences and to prepare for possible future situations. Understanding what happened in previous events, why things happened in previous events, and how the outcomes might have been changed is related to the "trial and error" approach discussed chapter 2. This is certainly a legitimate use of agent-based

simulation and other types of modeling for that matter. However, by itself it fails to take advantage of some of the strengths of agent-based modeling. In particular, agent simulation can be used to investigate future events that have not yet been experienced and to generate descriptions of future occurrences that otherwise might not even be imagined. Clearly, supra-real-time requirements set bounds on how often a model can be used and for what purposes. Most agent-based business models run in sub-real time.

Conversational Modeling

Conversational models are models that are designed to run fast enough and be clear enough to be executed live during meetings with decision-makers. The idea is to allow decision-makers to ask "what if" type questions and then have model experts modify the model inputs, run the model, and show the results all in real time. Ideally, the model experts could be the decision-makers themselves, although this is rarely achieved or even necessary in practice. Naturally, conversational models must be kept relatively simple to allow all of this to be done quickly enough to fit into meetings with decision-makers. Furthermore, the decision-makers themselves need to understand that even though the models are fast, some time may be needed to complete each run and that every model has limits to the kinds of questions it can address.

Execution Capacity

Execution capacity requirements mirror execution time requirements. Some models need relatively few resources to run while others have substantial demands. Typically, there is a rough tradeoff of resource usage and execution time. The key resources for most agent-based models are computer memory, computer processing speed, and disk storage.

Computer memory is used to track the state of both agents and their environments. In modern computers, there are two basic kinds of memory, namely physical memory and virtual memory. Physical memory is what most people think of as computer memory. It consists of computer chips directly installed in computers. As such, it tends to be extremely fast compared to virtual memory. Virtual memory acts the same as physical memory but it is normally stored on a hard disk. The operating systems in modern computers move data from physical memory to virtual memory on hard disks and back again to allow running programs to use more memory than is physically available. This process is called "swapping" memory. Thus, a personal computer with one gigabyte of physical memory might be able to run programs that require two gigabytes of total memory. In fact, when businesses buy operating systems, the ability to maintain virtual memory is among the main features they are paying for.

Virtual memory is certainly advantageous, but it has a cost in terms of execution time. Each agent in a simulation takes memory. Large numbers of agents can require substantial amounts of memory. Of course, this memory can be either physical or virtual and is normally some continuously updated mixture of the two. Up to a certain limit, the more physical memory that is used, the faster the simulation will execute. The difference in speed between physical and virtual memory is usually at least a factor of ten. In the worst cases, swapping can become so extreme as to dominate the execution time of a program. When this happens, the program is said to be "thrashing." In the authors' experience, substantial swapping commonly causes models to take at least twice as much time to execute as would have been required without the swapping. Even worse, thrashing typically causes model execution to take at least ten times longer. The lesson is clear. Physical memory really speeds up medium to large simulation runs. Time is expensive. Memory is cheap. Buy lots of memory for simulation!

Performance Optimization

One common issue faced by model developers is the balance between extensibility and performance. Models that can be extended tend to have clear code that eschews special cases for performance and uses little caching. Fast models tend to have many special cases to reduce unnecessary processing and quite a lot of caching to reduce redundant data access. There are arguments in the software engineering community that extensible code can actually be faster and there can be some truth to this. However, as C. A. R. Hoare has said, "premature optimization is the root of all evil in programming." According to W. A. Wulf, "more computing sins are committed in the name of efficiency (without necessarily achieving it) than for any other single reason—including blind stupidity." Finally, consider M. A. Jackson's "Rules of Optimization":

Rule 1: Don't do it.
Rule 2 (for experts only): Don't do it yet.

Jackson was right!

The modular nature of agent models tends to reduce the conflict between extensibility and performance compared to traditional techniques. However, the underlying tension remains. Which is best depends on the model's life stage. Models that are being actively extended tend to fare best with minimal optimization. Models that are being heavily used often need at least some optimization. This optimization should be completed based on real performance results from actual model runs rather than supposition. Experts are regularly surprised by what actually causes performance problems. Avoid surprises. Use performance-profiling software to determine the actual causes of problems, once problems are found.

The Guidance Horizon

Operational models are typically used to answer day-to-day questions. These day-to-day questions focus on fine-tuning short-term details rather than major changes to fundamental directions. Clearly, all decisions no matter how sweeping are ultimately made in the near term. In the end, all actions no matter how large are executed in the present. However, operational decisions are made routinely on short time cycles. To make this practical, operational decisions are usually made within well-defined bounds.

For most businesses, operational models need to produce quantitative results that are within 3% to 5% percent of real-world values. This level of accuracy is usually sufficient to provide good guidance for near-term decisions. Tradeoffs are generally required to achieve this level of accuracy. The main factors are the model guidance horizon and the related range of allowed agent behaviors.

The simulation guidance horizon for operational models is generally small. This limit is imposed by the need to attain high output accuracy levels. It is important to differentiate the simulation guidance horizon from the simulation execution horizon. The simulation execution horizon is the total length of time simulated in a model run. The simulation guidance horizon is the subset of the simulation execution horizon that is used to assist decision-making.

The day-to-day time horizon typical of operational models is the simulation guidance horizon. It describes how the results are used rather than the time range simulated by the model. It might be necessary to simulate a month or more of activities to answer daily questions. For example, consider an energy market model that is used to determine bid prices for a generation company. To determine effective prices for tomorrow's bids it may be necessary to model the market conditions for the entire upcoming week.

The need to limit the simulation guidance horizon in operational models to a short time period is a direct function of the level of uncertainty in the agent behaviors. The more clearly defined the individual agent behaviors are, the longer the guidance time horizon can be. For example, consider an agent-based factory simulation. Say that the model includes only a small amount of adaptation on the part of the simulated plant operators. Further, say the individual production machinery has a low failure rate. This model will then have a long guidance horizon. On the other hand, if the factory has highly adaptable operators and unreliable machinery, then the uncertainty in the model's outputs will tend to grow fast enough to limit the operational guidance to a short time frame. Even with a short time horizon, stochastic runs may be needed for nondeterministic models. One of the causes of this limit is the high output accuracy expected from operational models. Longer guidance horizons can easily be obtained in exchange for correspondingly lower accuracies.

As has been discussed, the guidance horizon is intimately tied to the range of allowed agent behaviors. The more variable the behavior is, the shorter the guidance horizon will be. In addition to this basic tradeoff, the allowed range of agent behaviors sets limits on the range of output results that can be seen. Having strict limits on behaviors assumes that the agents in the system will not radically alter their strategies or plans during the simulation run. This may be quite appropriate for an operational model since high-level strategies often change slowly relative to the operational decisions. However, such limits are less suitable for tactical models and are generally not appropriate at all for strategic models.

Distributed Agent Simulation

We have described agents as the modularized, self-contained units within a simulation. This description applies to both how the agents are represented in the model and how they are treated in the actual execution of the software. In agent simulation, the agents are composed of recognizable segments of software code. The software representation includes the agent's attributes and behavioral decision rules. This view corresponds most readily to an object-oriented implementation of agent-based simulations in which each agent is a self-contained piece of software. With the growing popularity of multiprocessor computers and the increasing availability of distributed computing resources such as computing clusters, which consist of hundreds or potentially thousands of nodes, it is natural to seriously consider distributing the agents for computation purposes. This is the basis for distributed agent simulation (DAS).

Conceptually, each agent can have its own computer processor, dedicated to executing the rules and behaviors of that agent. The location of the computers is irrelevant. They could even be located around the world, only needing to be connected via a computer network. Distributed agent simulation offers the possibility of running larger-scale simulations, with millions of agents, and running more extensive exploratory simulation parameter sweeps, with millions of simulation runs, within reasonable lengths of calendar time. That is, although the same amount of computer processing time may be required, we can do more simulations in a shorter amount of real clock time, and presumably create information that will still be useful and responsive to decision-making.

Parallel and Distributed Execution

There are two fundamental approaches to executing agent models in parallel. The first or coarse-grained approach uses parameter sweeps. The second or fine-gained approach actually implements the models themselves in parallel.

Coarse-Grained Parallel Execution

Coarse-grained parameter sweeps work with ordinary sequential models. Parameter sweeps run one instance of a model on each available computer or processor. Each instance normally has a different input file such that there are varying parameters or at least different random seeds. Random seeds are discussed in chapter 13.

As can be seen, parameter sweeps are not sexy. As can be imagined, computer experts find parameter sweeps to be boring. In fact, they usually find parameter sweeps so numbing that they do everything they can to encourage the development of the full parallel implementations to be discussed next. There are only two problems. First, parameter sweeps are quite practical. Most models can benefit from using parallel computers for parameter sweeps, at least for testing varying random seeds. As discussed later, only some models can benefit from fine-grained parallel implementations. Many actually run slower. Second, parameter sweeps can usually be set up with only a little extra effort and few if any model changes. This is particularly true if the model uses a loosely coupled architecture with a separate simulation engine as discussed in chapter 7. Fine-grained parallel implementations take substantial additional resources to develop.

Fine-Grained Parallel Execution

Fine-gained parallel implementations take advantage of multiple computer processors to execute more than one agent behavior or environmental action at a time. These parallel implementations are distributed architectures as described in chapter 7. Concurrent agent-modeling implementations appear to act in parallel but may not actually do so because of computer hardware limitations. Neither of these approaches violates the requirement to avoid simultaneously modifying a single variable's value by careful simulation design. Properly designed parallel or concurrent agent models only allow simultaneous execution of actions that update different variables. If two or more actions within these models will update the same variable at the same time, then these actions will be run consecutively. Both types of simultaneous execution can be desirable for large agent models since they can reduce the total execution time required for a given simulation.

Some questions immediately present themselves when it comes to the possibilities that distributed computing offers for agent modeling. One could ask the following series of questions:

Q1: "If we have a million computers, can each computer be an agent?"
Q2: "If we have a million agents computing on a million computers, does that mean we can do a simulation in one-millionth the time that it would take to run the simulations sequentially?"
Q3: "If it only takes 0.1 second to run a simulation, does that mean we can do a million simulation runs in which we vary all the parameters or test all the different assumptions in the model within 24 hours?"

We would like to answer these questions in the affirmative, but the real answers are that "it depends."

As previously discussed, in standard discrete-event simulation there is a clock and the impact of the events are addressed sequentially as the clock ticks during the simulation. The clock is updated to the time of the next event, the event occurs, and this directly spawns more events that will occur in the future. The clock updates the simulation time, taking the next tick to the next scheduled event, and so on. The simulation scheduler is charged with managing the event clock. A simple scheduler in agent simulation can operate just as it does in event simulation, sequentially addressing each event, scheduling new events, ticking off time event by event, and so on. In distributed simulation, the scheduler must take on a new role. The scheduler is like the conductor of an orchestra, coordinating and synchronizing the interactions of the agents, sorting out conflicts and ties, and blending the results into a meaningful whole.

There are two ways to do fine-grained scheduling in distributed simulation:

- *Case 1: Compute and wait.* The agents complete their computation and wait until all the other agents have finished processing and interacting within a given time period before any of the agents advance in time.
- *Case 2: Compute and backtrack.* The agents each simulate forward in their own (local) time, making assumptions about the behaviors and interactions with the other agents, until it is discovered that an inconsistency has developed. An agent has made an assumption about the behavior of another agent in the interest of being able to proceed in its calculations, but later it turns out that that assumption was wrong and the agent has to retrace its steps.

In the case of the agents waiting until everyone is ready to proceed (case 1), the notion is that all the mechanisms of causality should be worked out in advance to be consistent, a quite logical approach. The disadvantage is that several agents, or processors, may be waiting quite a lot of the time, in effect wasting time and not realizing any benefits from distributed computing. In the case of all the agents going ahead over a certain amount of time (case 2), the notion is that most of the operations that an agent performs are not critically dependent on interactions with other agents and so they can productively proceed, computing in time until at a certain point this assumption is checked. At that point in time, the states of the agents are reconciled and any inconsistencies are identified. This may require that the simulation be set back to a previous time from which all agents begin again and be simulated forward, losing some of the computational effort that had been discarded. It turns out to be very much the case in many simulations that the latter approach is useful.

For example, consider a simulation of warehouse operations. A warehouse distribution agent may have placed a pallet on a loading dock for loading onto a truck, only to discover later (when agent behaviors are reconciled) in the simulation that the loading dock has not yet been built by the facility agent at the time the pallet was placed there. The warehouse agent has made a wrong assumption. Another example is of an agent moving through space only to discover later that the space along its path had been occupied by another agent, but that fact was discovered only after the other agent had updated its position.

The issue of maintaining coordinated behavior among distributed agents is central to distributed agent computation, and is currently an area of active development by ABMS researchers. Some of the widely used approaches turn out to be tailored to the specific application being modeled and have limited generality. More complex models, in which agents have planning functions that are concurrent with the process simulation (that is, agents plan for the future by simulating the operations of the system through time, possibly contradicting the planned course of events as unanticipated events occur), represent the greatest degree of complexity in agent-based models.

We can now answer the original questions.

Q1: "If we have a million computers, can each computer be an agent?"

Answer: Yes, if the agents are structured in the proper form, such as being based on object-oriented principles.

Q2: "If we have a million agents computing on a million computers, does that mean we can do a simulation in one-millionth the time that it would take to run the simulations sequentially?"

Answer: No, not necessarily. There will be gains that are sizable in many cases, which makes the distributed computing approach highly desirable, but some overhead will be incurred in accounting for the agent interactions across processes.

Q3: "If it only takes 0.1 second to run a simulation, does that mean we can do a million simulation runs in which we vary all the parameters or test all the different assumptions in the model within 24 hours?"

Answer: Yes. In this case the agent interactions do not have to be coordinated. Only the final results of the agent simulation need to be processed, assuming they are being collected and assembled as the simulation proceeds. The processing can be done independently of the distributed simulation, after the simulation has been completed.

When Is Distributed Computing Agent Computing?

Military simulations have relied on distributed computing to support elaborate military exercises in which the entire exercise occurs in a virtual world solely on the computer. People and/or computers are participants in the simulation. In fact, the participants may not be aware of who, or what, the other participants are. The Aggregate-Level Simulation Protocol (ALSP), the Distributed Interactive Simulation (DIS) standard, and the High Level Architecture (HLA) are examples of distributed computing architectures developed primarily for military purposes, but these frameworks are not necessarily agent-based or even object-oriented (Wilson and Weatherly 1994; IEEE 1995a, 1995b, 2001a, 2001b, 2001c).

Distributed simulation is not an invention of agent simulation. It is common to have a distributed system composed of software components that do not exhibit the characteristics of agent-based systems, namely agents that are autonomous, heterogeneous, and exhibit some form of learning and adaptive behavior. Further confusing the situation, we may have distributed computing architectures that are very general in terms of being frameworks for integrating objects of a general nature. Such an architecture does not preclude the development of agents as objects, but it offers no specific benefits or templates for developing agents within the framework.

Distributed simulation is not necessarily the same as agent simulation and, vice versa, agent simulation is not necessarily the same as distributed simulation. But agent simulation can make use of and benefit from distributed computing if the proper care is taken in design and implementation. Distributed computing is not currently the standard approach to agent simulation, but that will likely change in the future.

Architectural Choices

It is natural to consider parallel execution when designing agent-based models. The very concept of agents in some sense implies parallel behaviors. In practice, parallel implementations can either speed up or slow down model execution depending on the underlying model itself. Memory limits can also be addressed with parallel implementations. For example, agents in the Schelling model presented in chapter 4 simply count their neighbors and then compare the result to a constant ratio. These simple agents likely will execute more slowly in parallel than in sequential mode since there is a high dependency between the agents (Schelling 1971, 1978). Shared-memory architectures that reduce the communication time between processes can help with this. The Electricity Market Complex Adaptive Systems (EMCAS) generation company agents, introduced in chapter 3, do complex statistical calculations on large data sets and make repeated heuristic decisions with the results for every time step (North et al. 2003). This model can and does benefit from parallel execution since the agents can do quite a lot of independent computation.

A large number of formulas have been proposed to predict the potential gains, or losses, from distributed computing (Kumar et al. 1994; Foster 1995). However, applying these formulas and building the corresponding software is currently a sophisticated art (Kumar et al. 1994; Foster 1995). Expert intuition from an agent modeler experienced in parallel programming is the best way to chose a distributed computing strategy. If this sort of person is not available, then a thumbnail estimate can be made by the modelers that are on the project.

The potential improvements in memory availability from parallel execution are somewhat simpler than performance. In general, the larger the parallel machine, the more agents that can be run. Keep the potential performance issues in mind, though.

Of course, building efficient parallel models requires substantial sophistication and experience with ABMS. If this is to be undertaken, it is recommended that an individual experienced in parallel and concurrent programming be added to the project team.

Agent Patterns and Antipatterns

Patterns form a "common vocabulary" for describing tried and true solutions for commonly faced software design problems (Coplien 2001). Patterns were first introduced in architecture by Christopher Alexander in his book *The Timeless Way of Building* (Alexander 1979). According to Alexander, "each pattern is a three-part rule, which expresses a relation between a certain context, a problem, and a solution." The first part of a design pattern characterizes the situation in which the problem occurs. The second part defines the outstanding issue itself. The third part describes a resolution to the outstanding issue as well as its positive and negative consequences. Every pattern has both fixed and variable elements (Alexander 1979). The fixed elements define the pattern. The variable elements allow the pattern to be adapted for each situation. Alexander's pioneering work focused on urban planning and architecture, but was later applied by several others to software design.

The concept of software patterns, and more generally software pattern languages, was pioneered by Beck and Cunningham in a 1987 conference paper titled "Using Pattern Languages for Object-Oriented Programs." From Beck and Cunningham's paper (1987):

> The search for an appropriate methodology for object-oriented programming has seen the usual rehash of tired old ideas, but the fact is that [object-oriented programming] OOP is so different that no mere force-fit of structured analysis or entity-relationship methods will provide access to the potential inherent in OOP. . . . We propose a radical shift in the burden of design and implementation, using concepts adapted from the work of Christopher Alexander, an architect and founder of the Center for Environmental Structures. Alexander proposes homes and offices be designed and built by their eventual occupants. These people, he reasons, know best their requirements for a particular structure. We agree, and make the same argument for computer programs. Computer users should write their own programs. The idea sounds foolish when one considers the size and complexity of both buildings and programs, and the years of training for the design professions. Yet Alexander offers a convincing scenario. It revolves around a concept called a "pattern language."
>
> A pattern language guides a designer by providing workable solutions to all of the problems known to arise in the course of design. It is a sequence of bits

of knowledge written in a style and arranged in an order which leads a designer to ask (and answer) the right questions at the right time. Alexander encodes these bits of knowledge in written patterns, each sharing the same structure. Each has a statement of a problem, a summary of circumstances creating the problem and, most important, a solution that works in these circumstances. A pattern language collects the patterns for a complete structure, a residential building for example, or an interactive computer program. Within a pattern language, patterns connect to other patterns where decisions made in one influence the others (Alexander 1979).

Software patterns were later popularized by writers such as the software "Gang of Four" composed of Gamma, Helm, Johnson, and Vlissides through their book *Design Patterns: Elements of Reusable Object-Oriented Software* (Gamma et al. 1995). The software Gang of Four state (Gamma et al. 1995):

> A designer who is familiar with such [design] patterns can apply them immediately to design problems without having to rediscover them. . . . An analogy will help illustrate the point. Novelists and playwrights rarely design their plots from scratch. Instead, they follow patterns like "Tragically Flawed Hero" (Macbeth, Hamlet, etc.) or "The Romance Novel" (countless romance novels). . . . Once you know the pattern, a lot of design decisions follow automatically.

There are many software design patterns. An example is the "Memento" design pattern that can be used to store the state of programs to implement an "undo" command. Extensive lists of design patterns can be found in catalogs such as that by Gamma et al. (1995).

An antipattern "describes a commonly occurring solution to a problem that generates decidedly negative consequences" (Brown et al. 1998). Antipatterns usually express attempted solutions that fail in subtle or unobvious ways. Antipatterns are used to avoid common pitfalls. An example is the "Blob" antipattern in which one software module performs almost all of the tasks for a program.

Patterns and antipatterns are normally given catchy names to aid learning and increase long-term recall. Patterns and antipatterns are extremely useful to software developers since they allow highly successful and widely applied solutions to commonly encountered problems to be easily communicated to wide audiences. Three examples of agent patterns include the Agent-Based Model (ABM) pattern, the Scheduler Scramble pattern, and the Double Buffering pattern.

The Agent-Based Model Design Pattern

Name: Agent-Based Model.

Problem: The problem is representing complex systems containing many interacting components for the purpose of experimentation. How do you experiment with complex systems containing many interacting components when real experiments cannot be performed?

Context: A complex system containing many interacting components exists. Experiments need to be performed on this system. Real experiments on the actual system cannot be performed due to ethical, safety, cost, time, or other concerns.

Forces: You want to observe the interactions of individual components of the system and see how these components affect the whole. You also want to see if the whole exhibits behaviors that are not a simple sum of the component's behaviors. This is called "emergent behavior." We want to extend human expertise by allowing insights about component rules to be obtained and hypotheses to be tested.

Solution: Create a system of components called an "agent-based model" (ABM) that abstractly mirrors the components of the actual system. Components within the ABM that can modify their behavior are called "agents." For clarity, agents with simpler behaviors are generally preferred over those with behaviors that are more complex. However, agents must be complex enough to be useful representations. All other ABM components form the "environment." Validate the ABM by comparing both the agent rules and resulting system behaviors to the real system. Qualitative validation allows qualitative uses. Quantitative validation allows quantitative uses. Use the ABM as an experimental vehicle to gain insights and test hypotheses. In particular, vary agent behaviors to observe the effect on the agents and the system.

Resulting context: Sometimes an ABM cannot be validated or is insufficient to gain insights or test hypotheses. An ABM containing more detail can then be created.

Rationale: Experiments cannot be performed on many complex systems due to ethical, safety, cost, time, or other concerns. This pattern is intended to allow new insights about these systems to be derived and hypotheses about such systems to be tested.

The Scheduler Scramble Design Pattern

Name: Scheduler Scramble.

Problem: Two or more agents from the ABM pattern can schedule events that occur during the same clock tick. Getting to execute first may be an advantage or disadvantage. How do you allow multiple agents to act during the same clock tick without giving a long-term advantage to any one agent?

Context: Two or more agents from the ABM pattern may attempt to simultaneously execute behaviors during the same clock tick.

Forces: Two or more agents want to activate a behavior at the same time. Activating a behavior before other agents can be either an advantage or disadvantage for the agent that goes first. No agent should have a permanent advantage or disadvantage.

Solution: Schedule the competing behaviors in a single clock tick in a random order. Use a different random order for each clock tick with competing behaviors.

Resulting context: A sequential behavioral activation order is produced. Each of the behaviors can be executed sequentially.

Rationale: The ABM pattern should allow several agents to activate during the same clock tick. The Scheduler Scramble pattern is intended to allow this.

The Double Buffering Design Pattern

Name: Double Buffer.

Problem: Different agents from the ABM pattern often simultaneously view and change shared values during the same clock tick. The results of the updates and changes should not be dependent on the order of event execution. How do you allow different agents to use and change the same item during the same clock tick without introducing dependencies on the behavioral activation order?

Context: Two or more agents from the ABM pattern may need to simultaneously use and change shared items during the same clock tick while avoiding behavioral execution order dependencies.

Forces: You want to allow the competing agents to use or view a constant value while also allowing them make changes to the value. The changes should be visible after the tick has completed.

Solution: Use two storage locations for each value to be accessed. The first location is always used for reading or viewing. The second location is used for temporary storage of updates during a clock tick. The temporary value is copied to the reading location at the end of each clock tick.

Resulting context: Multiple storage locations are used for holding values. The copy operation requires

a special behavior to occur at the conclusion of each clock tick.

Rationale: The ABM pattern should allow different agents to simultaneously view and change shared values during the same clock tick. The Double Buffering pattern is intended to allow this.

Examples

Two examples of large-scale agent-based models will be presented. The first simulation models a market. The second simulation models a supply network.

A Market Example

The EMCAS electric power market simulation is an agent simulation that represents the behavior of an electric power system and the producers and consumers that work within it. EMCAS was introduced in chapter 3 and was discussed in the chapters that followed. EMCAS is a Repast model that contains a variety of major agents and other supporting environmental elements. These main agents and supporting environmental elements are shown in figure 3.15. The agents include generation companies, transmission companies, distribution companies, and consumers. The supporting elements include an underlying electric power grid and negotiation forums. EMCAS is detailed throughout this book.

EMCAS uses Repast's time scheduler, employs several kinds of complex agent communications mechanisms, has a multilayer network topology, was designed with a distributed architecture, uses a customized Java interface, and was developed using the Eclipse development environment (Eclipse 2004). Eclipse is one of several free and open-source development environments with all of the advanced features recommended earlier in this chapter. Eclipse is available from www.eclipse.org.

A Supply Chain Example

The supply chain model discussed starting with chapter 3 was extended to support a full supply network (North and Macal 2002). The interface for the new network model is shown in figure 10.9. This model was developed by the Santa Fe Institute Value Network Modeling group, which includes the authors.

The Value Network model was written using Repast J. The model includes producers that ship to

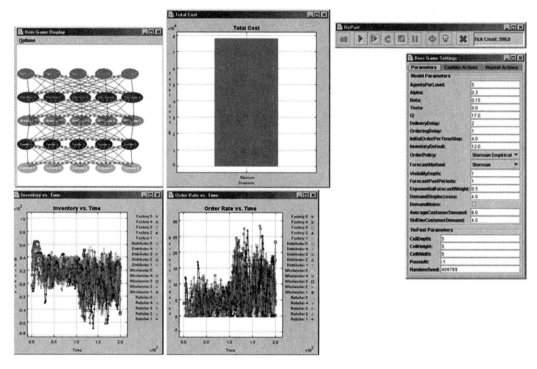

FIGURE 10.9 The supply network interface.

multiple consumers as well as consumers that select from multiple producers. Consumers place orders based on their previous experience. Producers ship to consumers based on orders and resolve conflicting demands with preferences for key customers. The model's UML Class Diagram is shown in figure 10.10. The Value Network model was designed to be used to explore the network effects in supply systems as well as to investigate the costs and consequences of increasing information visibility in networked supply chains.

The Value Network model used Repast's time scheduler, employed direct agent communications mechanisms, had a complex network topology, was designed with a tightly coupled architecture, and took advantage of Repast's probes to display agent states.

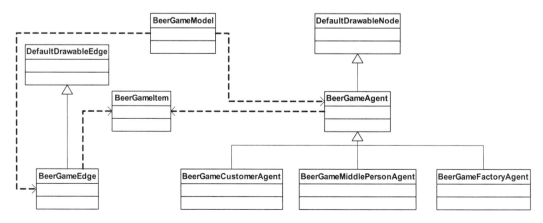

FIGURE 10.10 The supply network UML Class Diagram.

Summary

As has been shown, large-scale ABMS is usually done with computer-based ABMS tools. The criteria for selecting a good tool for a specific large-scale modeling task should include consideration of each system's time scheduler, communications mechanisms, interaction topologies, allowed architectural choices, capabilities for storing and displaying agent states, large-scale development support, and special topic support.

Notes

1. Asteroids is a trademark and registered copyright of Atari Interactive, Inc.
2. Microsoft, C#, and Visual Studio are registered trademarks of Microsoft Corp.
3. Managed C++ and Visual Basic are registered trademarks of Microsofts Corp.

References

Alexander, C. (1979). *The Timeless Way of Building*. Oxford: Oxford University Press.

Archer, T. (2001). *Inside C#*. Redmond, Wash.: Microsoft Press.

Beck, K. and W. Cunningham (1987). Using Pattern Languages for Object-Oriented Programs. Tektronix Technical Report CR-87-43. Presented at the 1987 Conference on Object-Oriented Programming, Systems, Languages and Applications (OOPSLA-87) Workshop on Specification and Design for Object-Oriented Programming.

Booch, G. (1993). *Object-Oriented Design with Applications*, 2nd ed. Reading, Mass.: Addison-Wesley.

Bradshaw, J. (1996). KAoS: An Open Agent Architecture Supporting Reuse, Interoperability, and Extensibility. *Proceedings of the 1996 Knowledge Acquisition Workshop*. Banff, Alberta, Canada: University of Calgary.

Bradshaw, J. (1997). An Introduction to Software Agents. In J. Bradshaw, *Software Agents*. Menlo Park, Cal.: AAAI Press, p. 480.

Brown, D. G., R. Riolo, D. T. Robinson, M. J. North, and W. Rand (2005). Spatial Process and Data Models: Toward Integration of Agent-Based Models and GIS. *Journal of Geographical Systems* 7: 25–27.

Brown, W. J., R. C. Malveau, H. W. McCormick, and T. J. Mowbray (1998). *AntiPatterns: Refactoring Software, Architectures, and Projects in Crisis*. Chichester, U.K.: Wiley.

Coplien, J. O. (2001). Software Patterns Page (available as http://hillside.net/patterns/).

Daniels, M. (1999). Integrating Simulating Technologies with Swarm. *Proceedings of the Agent 1999 Workshop on Agent Simulation: Applications, Models, and Tools*, ANL/DIS/TM-59, co-sponsored by Argonne National Laboratory and the University of Chicago, Oct. 15–16.

Eclipse (2004). Eclipse Home Page. The Eclipse Project, www.eclipse.org.

FIPA (2003). Foundation for Intelligent Physical Agents Standards Repository. Alameda, Cal.: FIPA.

Foster, I. (1995). *Designing and Building Parallel Programs*. Reading, Mass.: Addison-Wesley.

Foster, I., C. Kesselman, J. Nick, and S. Tuecke (2002). The Physiology of the Grid: An Open Grid Services Architecture for Distributed Systems Integration. Global Grid Forum Open Grid Service Infrastructure Working Group. Lemont, Ill.: Global Grid Forum.

Foxwell, H. (1999). Java 2 Software Development Kit. *Linux Journal* (online).

Gamma, E., R. Helm, R. Johnson, and J. Vlissides (1995). *Design Patterns: Elements of Reusable Object-Oriented Software*. Wokingham, U.K.: Addison-Wesley.

Hansen, P. B. (1998). An Evaluation of the Message-Passing Interface. *ACM SIGPLAN Notices* **33**: 65–72.

IEEE (1995a). IEEE Standard 1278.1-1995 (DIS V 2.0): *IEEE Standard for Distributed Interactive Simulation—Application Protocols*. Piscataway, N.J.: IEEE.

IEEE (1995b). IEEE Standard 1278.2-1995: *IEEE Standard for Distributed Interactive Simulation—Communication Services*. Piscataway, N.J.: IEEE.

IEEE (2001a). IEEE Standard P1516: *HLA Framework and Rules*. Piscataway, N.J.: IEEE.

IEEE (2001b). IEEE Standard P1516.1: *HLA Federate Interface Specification*. Piscataway, N.J.: IEEE.

IEEE (2001c). IEEE Standard P1516.2: *Object Model Template (OMT) Specification*. Piscataway, N.J.: IEEE.

Knuth, D. E. (1984). Literate Programming. *Computer Journal* **27**(2): 97–111.

Kumar, V., A. Grama, A. Gupta, and G. Karypis (1994). *Introduction to Parallel Computing: Design and Analysis of Algorithms*. Redwood City, Cal.: Benjamin Cummings.

Law, A. M. (2007). *Simulation Modeling and Analysis*, 4th ed. New York: McGraw-Hill.

Lawson, T. (2003). *Topology: A Geometric Approach*. Oxford: Oxford University Press.

Lu, T., C. Lee, W. Hsia, and M. Lin (2000). Supporting Large-Scale Distributed Simulation Using HLA. *ACM Transactions on Modeling and Computer Simulation* 10(3): 268–294

Minar, N., R. Burkhart, C. Langton, and M. Askenazi (1996). The Swarm Simulation System: A Toolkit for Building Multi-Agent Simulations. Working Paper 96-06-042. Santa Fe, N.M.: Santa Fe Institute.

NCSA. (2004). Hierarchical Data Format 5 Home Page. Champaign, Ill.: National Center for Supercomputing Applications.

North, M. J. and C. M. Macal (2002). The Beer Dock: Three and a Half Implementations of the Beer Distribution Game. Presentation at SwarmFest 2002, University of Notre Dame, South Bend, Ind.

North, M., P. Thimmapuram, R. Cirillo, C. Macal, G. Conzelmann, V. Koritarov, and T. Veselka (2003). EMCAS: An Agent-Based Tool for Modeling Electricity Markets. *Proceeding of Agent 2003: Challenges in Social Simulation*. Chicago: University of Chicago, Argonne National Laboratory.

North, M. J., T. R. Howe, N. T. Collier, and J. R. Vos (2005a). Repast Simphony Development Environment, in C. M. Macal, M. J. North, and D. Sallach (Eds.), *Proceedings of the Agent 2005 Conference on Generative Social Processes, Models, and Mechanisms*, ANL/DIS-06-01, co-sponsored by Argonne National Laboratory and the University of Chicago, Oct. 13–15.

North, M. J., T. R. Howe, N. T. Collier, and J. R. Vos (2005b). Repast Simphony Runtime System, in C. M. Macal, M. J. North, and D. Sallach (Eds.), *Proceedings of the Agent 2005 Conference on Generative Social Processes, Models, and Mechanisms*, ANL/DIS-06-01, co-sponsored by Argonne National Laboratory and the University of Chicago, Oct. 13–15.

North, M. J., N. J. Collier, and R. J. Vos. (2006) Experiences Creating Three Implementations of the Repast Agent Modeling Toolkit. *ACM Transactions on Modeling and Computer Simulation* 16(1): 1–25.

Object Management Group (2001). OMG *Unified Modeling Language Specification Version 1.5*. Needham, Mass.: Object Management Group.

Object Management Group. (2004). *Object Management Group UML Home Page*. Needham, Mass.: Object Management Group.

ROAD (2004). Repast Home Page (http://repast.sourceforge.net/). Chicago: Repast Organisation for Architecture and Design.

Schelling, T. C. (1971). Dynamic Models of Segregation. *Journal of Mathematical Sociology* 1: 143–186.

Schelling, T. C. (1978). *Micromotives and Macrobehavior*. New York: Norton.

Unidata (2004). netCDF. Boulder, Colo.: University Corporation for Atmospheric Research.

Wilson, A. L. and R. M. Weatherly (1994). The Aggregate Level Simulation Protocol: An Evolving System. *Winter Simulation Conference*. Orlando, Fla.: Association for Computing Machinery.

11

ABMS Verification and Validation

Model verification and validation (V&V) are essential parts of the model development process if models are to be accepted and used to support decision-making. One of the very first questions that a person who is promoting a model is likely to encounter is "Has the model been validated?" If the answer to this critical question is no, experience has shown that the model is unlikely to be adopted or even tried out in a real-world business setting. There is a sense that a model that has not been validated is not ready for prime time. As a result, often the model and the modeler are sent back to the drawing board. The challenge for V&V then becomes one of being able to say yes to this critical question.

Even before a model can be validated, it must be verified that it works correctly. The aim of model verification is to make the model usable, by ensuring that the model works as intended. The ultimate goal of model validation is to make the model useful in the sense that the model addresses the right problem and provides accurate information about the system being modeled.

Verification and validation and data collection and cleaning are the most time-consuming parts of ABMS since they are where models most directly touch the real world. This chapter explores what model V&V means in practical terms and describes how to reach the milestones of verifying and validating a model. The chapter addresses the V&V of models in general and of agent-based models in particular. V&V terminology is defined, procedures are discussed, and experiences with the V&V of agent-based models are described. A case study of validating ABMS for an electric power market model is described.

V&V Overview

Verification and validation work together by removing barriers and objections to model use. After all, if a model runs perfectly well and correctly reflects the workings of an important real-world system, why wouldn't someone want to use the model?

Verification refers to whether a model performs as the model developers and programmers intended the model to operate by matching a model against its intentional design specification. Verification is done to ensure that the model is programmed correctly, that the algorithms have been implemented properly, and that the model does not contain errors, oversights, or bugs. Model verification does not ensure that the model solves an important problem, meets a specified set of model requirements, or correctly reflects the workings of a real-world process. These latter issues are the province of model validation and related topics such as certification and accreditation.

Validation matches a model against its "real world" subject as indicated in figure 11.1. According to many modelers, V&V is the single most important step in the model development process. The following thought captures the essential importance of V&V: "Before appropriate V&V, models are toys; after appropriate V&V, models are tools."

V&V can be a complex process, involving many steps and iterations. The difficulties of V&V and the resources required for V&V are often underestimated. The following sections discuss the basic ideas of V&V. An excellent reference on V&V for traditional

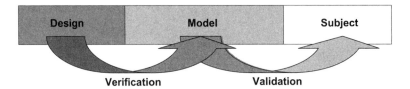

FIGURE 11.1 Verification and validation in context.

simulation models is the book by Law (2007). ABMS presents additional challenges to traditional modeling V&V, namely the V&V of agent behaviors, agent interaction mechanisms, and the processes and structures that emerge from ABMS at varying scales.

Verification

Verification consists of ensuring that a model does what it is intended to do from an operational perspective — that the model performs the correct calculations according to its intended design and specification. In other words, verification ensures that the specification is complete and that mistakes have not been made in implementing the model. Accordingly, the model's intended design and specification must be well specified in advance of developing the model.

The Goal of Verification

No model using ABMS or any other computational technique will ever be fully verified, guaranteeing 100% error-free code. A high degree of statistical certainty is all that can be realized for any model. Statistical certainty is increased as more and more important cases are identified and tested. With a properly structured testing program, the level of certainty that is achievable for verifying models is acceptable for virtually all business applications (Jackson 2006).

In principle, all possible cases for which a model could be exercised (for example, all possible parameter settings and branching points in the model) could be enumerated and tested to ensure that the model works properly. It is even possible to automate the testing process so that the tedium of systematically constructing and analyzing numerous model runs is placed on the computer — a task that computers are well equipped to handle. Model verification proceeds as more tests are performed, errors are identified, and corrections are made to the underlying code, often

resulting in retesting requirements to ensure code integrity. The end result of verification is technically not a verified model, but rather a model that has passed all the verification tests!

Practical Verification

Practical model verification involves covering as many test cases as possible with the model. A variety of techniques can be used to cover cases where the operation of the code is compared to the expectations stated in the design documents. These techniques include structured code walk throughs, structured debugging walk throughs, unit testing, formal methods, and test cases and scenarios.

Documentation for Verification

The purpose of verification is to ensure that, however a model was built, the resulting system works as described in its design documents. Design documents should be created when the model design process begins. This can be accomplished based on the management specifications, or reference to standards such as IEEE 1012-1998 on software V&V, or the detailed project requirements plan. Ideally, design documents should be included as part of the statement of work written before the modeling project begins. Design documents can take many forms, including plain text documents or more structured specifications such as those provided by UML (Unified Modeling Language) diagrams. To be meaningful, model verification requires that model design documents be periodically expanded to reflect the ongoing discovery of more detailed model requirements as the development process moves into the implementation phase.

Structured Code Walk Throughs

Many people have experienced the embarrassment of having a typographical error in a document that, despite careful checking, is not discovered until after the document is printed and distributed. (Hopefully this book will be a happy exception!) Adding to the pain is the fact that such typographical errors are often obvious in hindsight. Structured code walk throughs work on this principle, without the public pain. Structured code walk throughs are designed to match the computer code against the intended design for the purpose of identifying errors. Structured code walk throughs are group meetings where the code developers present the code they have written and then manually trace through examples of execution sequences. The audience is expected to include independent developers who are tasked with critiquing the code and auditing the execution sequences for correctness. The fundamental principle is simple: few things bring errors to light faster than a fresh pair of eyes during a presentation.

The goal of the walk through is for the code developer to show how the code is supposed to work and then to allow the audience to determine if the code actually works as described. At no time during the meeting should code actually be changed or executed! Furthermore, the auditing developers in attendance should not suggest modifications to the code. Suggesting changes to code or making actual modifications creates an inherent conflict of interest for the auditing developers by making them contributing authors of the code. Executing the code leads to a second approach, namely structured debugging walk throughs.

Structured Debugging Walk Throughs

Structured debugging walk throughs build on structured code walk throughs by executing the code for a set of test cases. The term "debugging" here refers to the use of automated tools that allow programs to be traced line by line while allowing the values of program variables to be interactively examined. As discussed in chapter 10, most modern development environments have built-in support for this kind of work.

Compared to structured code walk throughs, structured debugging walk throughs allow direct confirmation or denial of the existence of errors. Structured debugging walk throughs also allow immediate examination of values that are difficult to calculate, such as large sums. However, structured debugging walk throughs often cannot cover as many cases as structured code walk throughs since real input data or appropriate unit tests must be configured for each test.

Unit tests are covered in the next section. Furthermore, the use of automated tools to execute the code can reduce the audience's need to track the activities since they can simply rely on the output of the debugger. This can decrease the effectiveness of the testing.

In general, structured code walk throughs and debugging walk throughs are both useful for verification. Most commonly, structured code walk throughs are used to initially verify code and structured debugging walk throughs are used for later verification work when more complex cases need to be and can be investigated. This complementary usage is highly recommended.

Unit Testing

Unit testing is based on a bottom-up approach to code testing. The idea is to individually test each function, then individually test each module, then individually test each area, and finally test the entire system. The notion is that each software component, be it a function, module, or whatever, should have well-defined inputs and outputs that can be used for testing. Following this approach, verification testing is reduced to providing defined inputs to a component and then making sure that the expected output is received.

Following the unit testing approach, software changes involve these activities:

- The software is modified.
- The unit tests for the software are updated to reflect the modifications.
- All of the unit tests are rerun.

The final stage of rerunning all of the units is particularly critical since it allows many "regression" errors (i.e., errors where the modified software is worse than its predecessor) to be caught. This fact causes the test rerun process to be labeled "regression testing." The fact that the unit tests need to be run again and again suggests that they should be automated. Tools such as JUnit have been developed to automate these common repetitive tasks and to determine how well unit tests cover given sections of code (Beck and Gamma 1998). The use of coding to test code has even led to the suggestion that unit testing can help to make programming "fun" (Beck and Gamma 1998):

Sometimes you just won't feel like writing tests, especially at first. Don't. However, pay attention to how much more trouble you get into, how much more time you spend debugging, and how much more stress you feel when you don't have tests. We have been amazed at how much more fun programming is and how much more aggressive we are willing to be and how much less stress we feel when we are supported by tests. The difference is dramatic enough to keep us writing tests even when we don't feel like it.

Regardless of how exciting unit testing may or may not be, it can be a powerful way to test and retest code. As such, unit testing is highly recommended.

Formal Methods

The methods previously discussed may seem formal in the sense that there are well-defined processes for structured walk throughs and unit testing. However, from a broader perspective, such processes are informal in the sense that they do not result in proofs of correctness. For example, even the best unit testing does not prove that code is correct. It only provides an argument that a large number of thorough tests did not uncover any errors. There are a variety of methods that can go farther and provide at least some type of proof that a given piece of code is correct. See Dijkstra (1976) and Gries (1981) for pioneering examples.

One way to think about proving the correctness of code relates to geometry. Many readers remember taking geometry classes where they were asked to prove statements such as "a triangle with three equal length sides also must have all three interior angles as equal." (Readers might remember that this type of triangle is an equilateral triangle.) The geometry students then used a series of explicit assumptions (i.e., axioms) and previously proven rules (i.e., theorems) to prove the given statement. At heart, formal methods for proving the correctness of software work similarly. In practice, formal methods-based approaches often use automated tools to speed the code development process and prove that the code works correctly.

Formal methods can be extremely useful for certain mission-critical and high-risk applications. However, the cost and expense of formal methods can in some practical cases outweigh the benefits. Donald Knuth, Professor Emeritus of the Art of Computer Programming at Stanford University, once commented on some code as follows: "Beware of bugs in the above code; I have only proved it correct, not tried

it" (Knuth 1999). He has also noted the following (Woehr 1996):

> I try to clean up all bugs and I try to write in such a way that, aware of the formal methods, I can be much more sure than I would be without the formal methods. But I don't see any hope of proving everything in these large [commercial] systems, because the proof would be even more likely to have bugs!

Formal methods are not recommended for most agent-modeling applications.

Test Cases and Scenarios

Before verification tests can be performed, model results must be recorded and possibly archived for later use. This is especially an issue with agent-based models because their detailed nature tends to produce a great deal of information at the system level as well as at the agent level in terms of agent behaviors and interactions.

Model Logging

Agent-based models generate a myriad of data pertaining to system and agent behaviors. Capturing this information in a form that one can work with requires the creation of a model output log for the time-series data generated by the model. The model output log reflects the states of specific agents, the aggregate states of collections of agents, and the specific states of the environment over time. This data is stored as a set of values indexed by time for each variable of interest. Examples include hourly bid and ask prices in a futures market simulation, daily factory output in an agent-based manufacturing model, and weekly temperature in an agricultural crop model.

Logging model results comes at a cost, owing to the sheer volume of information that agent models can produce. On the up side, increasingly large logs allow model results to be analyzed in progressively greater detail. Many modelers are attracted to the concept of storing most if not all of the time-series data generated by a given model. This often leads modeling projects down into the proverbial darkness. Consider for a moment the volume of time-series data produced by even the simplest agent-based models. For example, take an hourly market model with fifty agents, each with their own supply or demand curve and a straightforward bidding strategy. The model

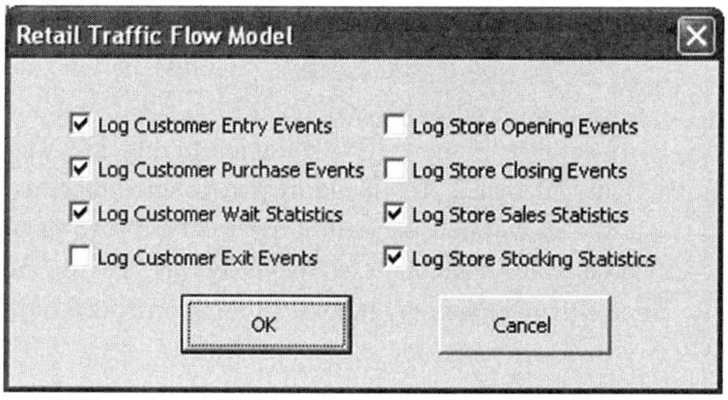

FIGURE 11.2 Retail store traffic model topical logging selection window.

itself will easily fit into a spreadsheet. Now, imagine executing the simulation to model a full year of market activity. There are 8,760 hours in a standard year. Storing all of this agent data for one year will therefore require 8,760 times the storage requirement for one hour. This mass of data is enormous. Extending the model runs from one year to several years makes the storage requirements even more daunting. Increased storage space usage is not the only cost of detailed logging. Creating and accessing large model output logs can require substantial computer-processing capabilities as well. Thus, maintaining large logs will often greatly increase both model execution time and the time required for analyzing the results.

The potentially high space and time requirements inherent in detailed model logging is not a problem with agent-based modeling per se, but rather is a more general problem of output storage prioritization. Just like people living in a small city apartment, modelers can't keep everything they ever owned around forever. Some things, in fact many things, need to be thrown away. Put another way, not all output data is equally valuable. When collecting this data, it is important to be sure that the cost required to collect the data is worth the investment required to collect, store, and process it. Identifying up front what data is required and what data is not as important is the solution. The idea then is to clearly define the required time-series output data and store only these results. This basic concept can be supplemented with user-selectable logging and controllable randomness.

User-selectable logging allows model operators to select the type of logging to be performed before each model run is executed. This allows the user to trade off the benefits of more logging with the greater execution time and storage space requirements of more detailed outputs. The two most common and effective logging methods are the topical approach and the level-of-detail approach.

The topical approach allows model users to log items by content. An example from a retail store traffic model is shown in figure 11.2. The agents in this example are customers moving through retail stores. The customers can enter, exit, wait for various events within the store, and purchase goods. Stores open and close each day as well as manage inventory and make sales. In figure 11.2, the check boxes allow the user to request logs by topic for the various types of events that can occur. Note that the user can select any combination of the options presented. The topical approach has the advantage of allowing users to tailor the content of the outputs to suit their needs. However, it does not allow them to control the relevance or volume of output within a given topic. This is particularly important for models that can generate large amounts of data that need to be stored and sifted.

The level-of-detail approach allows model users to log results by output specificity. A level-of-detail log selection window for the retail store is shown in figure 11.3. Here the user can decide on the classes of items to be logged and thus control the volume of outputs. Note that the options are mutually exclusive. The level-of-detail approach allows users to select output relevance and volumes. With this approach, users only need to store and sift through the types of model output items that they are most interested in. However, users cannot select the topics for the output types.

Combining the topical and level-of-detail approaches gives model users the maximum flexibility to choose the content, relevance, and volume of model outputs. An example is shown in figure 11.4. Here the user can independently select the level of

FIGURE 11.3 Retail store traffic model detail-level logging selection window.

detail for each available topic. This is the preferred logging selection approach, but it also requires somewhat more sophistication on the part of the model developers as well as additional development time. The time invested in attaining this extra flexibility is well worth the cost for all but the simplest models.

An important adjunct to logging selection is ensuring that models have controllable randomness. This allows model runs and the resulting output logs to be reproduced at a later date. Controllable randomness is accomplished through random number seeding, as discussed in chapter 13.

At least in principle, individual values can be summarized to produce aggregate outputs. Aggregate outputs are summaries or synopses of individual agent behaviors and environmental states. As such, they can be derived from low-level agent behavioral time-series data. In practice, finding appropriate methods for aggregation is critical to fully understanding model results.

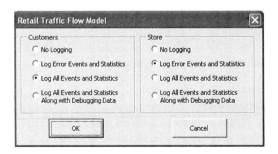

FIGURE 11.4 Retail store traffic model combined logging selection window.

Rapid Prototyping

As stated above, the model's intended design and specification must be well specified in advance of the model development. The exception to this rule is for a model that is developed as part of an exploratory research and development program or part of a rapid prototyping development process. For these cases, the process of identifying the model requirements is built into the model development process itself. The notion is that people may not be able to articulate complete and detailed design requirements up front, but can constructively react to mockups (user interfaces without functionality or prototypes with minimal functionality) of system design—that is, they "will know it when they see it." These are high-risk cases for which it is generally understood from the beginning that the model development process may instead conclude that developing a model to answer the specific questions at hand is not feasible due to time, cost, or other technical reasons such as the unavailability of the necessary data.

ABMS, since it is a relatively new approach, is often done under an exploratory, rapid prototyping development process. ABMS design is often iterative. Most substantial designs undergo major revisions before they are completed. The revisions often occur in stages in which a design concept is considered, tested in a prototype form, and then adjusted as needed. Prototyping is often done using live simulations, with simple tools such as Repast Py, NetLogo, StarLogo, or even Excel spreadsheets.

ABMS design is often evolutionary. The model designers learn more about the model (and possibly the underlying system) during each design iteration. This learning can be used to improve the design during successive steps. The rapid prototyping approach brings the added requirement that model design documents need to be developed and maintained in parallel with requirements definition and model implementation.

Validation

Validation generally refers to whether a model represents and correctly reproduces the behaviors of a real-world system. In effect, a validated model allows one to learn about aspects of the real world through performing "what if" computational experiments with the model. The standard approach is to take a selected number of cases from the real-world system and attempt to reproduce them using the model. Then the model is used to study additional cases that cannot be performed on the real-world system. This approach immediately leads to some important questions about model validation that are of particular concern for ABMS:

- If the real-world system that is being modeled does not currently exist, how can the model be validated?
- If only one or a few cases exist for the real-world system (for example, a single historical data set), how can we know that the model will perform well for cases that are far away from the range of historical experience?
- If the model is not deterministic and has random or stochastic elements, that is, each run of the model produces a different result due to the modeled random effects, how can the model be validated?
- How can agent behaviors and interaction mechanisms be validated?

Not all of these questions currently have completely satisfactory answers in all cases. However, various techniques and approaches have been developed to gain enough credibility for models to be accepted by users and supportable as decision-making aids.

The Goal of Validation

Similarly to model verification, no model using ABMS or any other computational technique will ever be fully validated. A high degree of statistical certainty is all that can be realized for any model using ABMS or other computational techniques. Unlike model verification, however, the level of certainty that is achievable for validating models is highly variable, subject to judgment, and must be carefully considered relative to the business application requirements for the model. Statistical certainty with respect to validation is increased as more and more important cases are identified, run, and analyzed.

Validation exercises really amount to a series of attempts to invalidate a model. In fact, one recently developed V&V technique, active nonlinear tests (ANTs), explicitly formulates a series of mathematical tests designed to "break the model" (Miller 1998). Presumably, once a model is shown to be invalid by any validation exercise, the model is salvageable with further work and results in a model having a higher degree of credibility and confidence. The end result of validation is technically not a validated model, but rather a model that has passed all the validation tests as well as a better understanding of the model's capabilities, limitations, and appropriateness for addressing a range of important questions.

Practical Validation

Model validation consists of validating the model's inputs (data), the model's outputs, the processes included in the model, and for ABMS in particular, agent behaviors and interaction mechanisms as well as emergent structures or properties. There are several perspectives one can take in approaching model validation:

- *Requirements Validation*: To be meaningful, model validation requires the clear definition of requirements and the questions about the real world that are to be answered by the model. Is the model solving the right problem? Has the problem changed or shifted in its importance?
- *Data Validation*: Have the data used in the model been validated?
- *Face Validation*: When looked at in a systematic way, do the assumptions upon which the model is based seem plausible? Do the model results look right?
- *Process Validation*: Do the steps in the model and the internal flows of what is being modeled correspond to the real-world process?
- *Model Output Validation*: If the real-world system is available for study, do the model outputs match the outputs of the real-world system?
- *Agent Validation*: Agent-based models include an additional aspect of model validation due to the presence of agents in the model. Agent behaviors, agent relationships, and agent interaction processes are all additional aspects of agent models that require validation. Do agent behaviors and interaction mechanisms correspond to agents in the real world?
- *Theory Validation*: What theory is included in the model about agents or processes? Is the theory valid? Does the model make a valid use of the theory?

Aspects of model validation include both the requirements that the model is intended to meet as well as the technical details of the model and how the model relates to the relevant fields of knowledge upon which it is based.

Establishing Credibility

ABMS techniques are often used to model systems (e.g., large and complex social systems) that are often not amenable to being the subject of controlled experiments. In these cases, experiments on the real system cannot be designed or implemented to produce the data required for validating the model. Unlike physical systems, for which there are well-established procedures for model validation (see AIAA, 1998, for an example of V&V guidelines for assessing the credibility of computational fluid dynamics models), no such guidelines currently exist for ABMS.

In light of these facts, model validation tends to be a subjective process compared to model verification, which is an objective process in which a model is either verified or not. The challenge for validation is to develop a high degree of credibility for the model so that people will have collective confidence in the model and the results it produces. In the case of ABMS models that contain elements of human decision-making such as ABMS business applications, validation becomes a matter of establishing credibility in the model. In effect, the task is to establish an argument that the model produces sound insights and sound data based on a wide range of tests and criteria that "stand in" for comparing model results to data from the real system. The process is akin to developing a legal case in which a preponderance of evidence is compiled about why the model is a valid one for its purported use.

CYA: A Case Approach to Model Validation

Validation approaches are used to determine how well an ABMS model reproduces real business situations. The purpose is to ensure that however a model was built, the resulting system matches the appropriate parts of the real-world. One simple way to think about V&V is "covering cases" (i.e., "cover your analysis," CYA). Cases are reasonable combinations of inputs and expected outputs for a design, a model, or a subject. In practice, a model is fully validated when all of the model cases correctly match real-world cases and vice versa. For many substantial models, fully explicit coverage is difficult if not impossible. However, meaningful areas can be covered by systematic selection of the cases to consider, including:

- Real-world cases.
- Commonly believed scenarios should be included, with the caveat that the conventional wisdom as to results may be wrong.

- Known results from other modeling approaches such as analytical modeling.

There are three bases for comparison when it comes to validating a model:

1. Comparison of the model results for selected cases with the real system.
2. Comparison of the model results for selected cases with another model's results.
3. Comparison of the model results for selected cases to what would be expected by subject matter experts.

Whether or not the real system is available, other models for comparison are available, or subject matter experts are available as a basis for comparison of model results, the question then becomes, for what cases the model should be tested for the purposes of validation.

In principle, all possible cases for which a model could be exercised in practice could be enumerated and simulation results obtained. Comparable results for the real-world system will only be available for a limited number of cases or possibly for no cases at all. For example, in designing a new supply chain system that does not currently exist, no data on the real-world system are available for comparison to the model results. This is a common situation. Simulation models are often developed in advance of building a physical prototype to explore a wide range of possible design configurations with alternative model assumptions.

For an existing system in which data exist on current operations, the model could be validated against the limited number of test cases for which data are available, but it will not be possible to validate the model outside of the system's current operational range. At the other extreme in this continuum of validation challenges are real-world systems upon which it is possible to conduct controlled experiments. Such systems include many physical systems, wet-lab biological systems, and to a limited extent, systems that include a small number of human decision-makers.

Model Calibration

If real-world cases are available for the system under investigation, some of the cases can be used to estimate and set the values of model parameters. This is the process of model calibration, not to be confused with model validation. The calibration cases are then set aside, and the remainder of the test cases serve as validation targets for the model to replicate.

Parameter Sweeping

To ensure that important model cases have been identified for concentrating validation efforts, it is often useful to first explore the space of all assumptions and possible parameter inputs to the model. The goal is to explore the kinds of results and behaviors the model is capable of producing to identify the most interesting cases that warrant further exploration. The basic inputs are varied in systematic ways to achieve either sensitivity analysis (excursions in a single direction) or broad parameter sweeps (excursions in all directions). Sensitivity analysis involves testing small ranges of the input parameters surrounding key values. Broad parameter sweeps involve systematically covering a wide range of input parameter values, at either a coarse-grained or a fine-grained level. For example, in the supply chain model, the ordering parameter space of values between zero and one was divided into 10 equal units at 0.1 increments. A simulation run was made for each parameter value in this range. In the ideal case, samples covering the full range of all input parameter values may be tested. Normally, the computational demands of exploring broad parameter ranges require large step sizes and low-resolution coverage for the variables of interest. The basic inputs may themselves be varied to discover the full range of model results possible from a range of input values.

Another approach to exploring parameter spaces is intermediate between broad parameter sweeps and localized sensitivity analysis in terms of the number of model runs required. This approach consists of using stochastic search techniques to randomly select the next direction in the parameter space to search. The notion is that interesting cases have just as high a likelihood as uninteresting cases to be discovered through random search and at a fraction of the computational effort involved in broader parameter sweeps.

Parameter sweeps allow the results of agent-based simulations to be reproduced by covering the range of model variation at a cost of a substantial number of model runs. The coarseness of the parameter sweeps can be adjusted in incremental phases. If additional sweeps are conducted later at a finer-grain resolution for the parameters, the results of the fine-grain sweeps will be consistent with and complement the coarse-grain sweeps previously conducted.

Many ABMS models are stochastic in nature. That is, randomness is included in the model to characterize uncertainty in agent behaviors, parameter values, and so on. Randomness is characterized by assuming specific functional forms for the probability distributions for the uncertain parameters. A stochastic model is then run repeatedly with different random seeds each time, for the same basic set of inputs. The random seeds are varied in successive runs to discover the possible range of outcomes that the model is capable of producing. Stochastic variation adds another set of dimensions to explore as part of the parameter sweeping process and adds to the computational burden.

Multiple Models

Another validation approach that has been increasingly used concerns the use of two or more models to validate or invalidate each other. Although, in some other contexts, having two models address the same system or answer the same questions may be seen as duplicative or wasteful, recent evidence suggests that replicating simulation model results can be an important adjunct to model validation. When more than a single model is used, the models may differ in terms of the computational techniques employed, the level of detail included in the models, and their underlying assumptions.

In reality, using two models together does not validate the models even if the model results do agree. Agreement only increases the models' credibility. If the models do not agree, it opens up areas for further investigation into the underlying causes for the models' differences. Hales et al. (2003) have identified some interesting model comparison methods, some of which have clear implications for model validation:

- "Comparing different models that announce the same type of results and trying to see if they actually produce similar (or the same) results."
- "Comparing different models" to see if one is better than another at reproducing certain exogenously observed results.
- "Using one model as a post-hoc summary or abstraction of another model's results, thus constraining the scope of an existing model to enable more powerful techniques to be applied in a different computational framework."
- "Using models with different structures and assumptions to confirm each other's results."

These techniques turn out to be revealing, for it is not uncommon for alternative models of the same system to yield different results. For example, Hales et al. (2003) performed a double replication of a well-known published model based on available documentation. The replication revealed some weaknesses in the original model, which otherwise might not have come to light. This shows that unreplicated simulation models and their results cannot necessarily be trusted. A model represents a theory of the real-world system's structure and behaviors. As with other kinds of scientific theories and experiments, simulations may need to be independently replicated to confirm the theory's (and the model's) validity.

ABMS as a Special Case of Analytical Modeling

ABMS models are sometimes generalizations of analytical, that is, noncomputational, models. Looking at it from the other direction, if enough simplifying assumptions are made in the ABMS, the ABMS reduces to a computational version of the analytical model. That is, the ABMS produces the same results as the analytical model under a set of appropriate simplifying assumptions. If the analytical models are known to be correct through previous validation exercises, the analytical model can be used to partly validate the ABMS model.

An example is a complicated queuing system such as the checkout lines at a grocery store. Under appropriate simplifying assumptions about customer arrival rates, server rates, and the behaviors of consumers in the checkout line, an analytic queuing model may provide adequate information on average customer checkout times and server utilization. Assuming that the queuing model has been validated at least over a limited range of operational parameters, the ABMS can incorporate the same assumptions and should duplicate the same average customer checkout times, if the ABMS is a valid model. The ABMS can then be used to investigate additional situations in which these simplifying assumptions are relaxed.

Use of Subject Matter Experts

Subject matter experts (SMEs) can also play an essential role in model validation. The role of the SME is to provide in-depth technical expertise and educated judgment for the knowledge domain that the model covers. SMEs can provide a wealth of experience and insights into identifying important test cases that will validate or invalidate the model, and offer judgments critical to establishing face validity for the model.

Experience has shown that not every domain expert can provide useful guidance. It takes a special type of person who is able to understand the purpose of the model, what the model is trying to accomplish, and is willing to accept the tradeoffs required between a model that is too detailed and one that has too little detail. The latter aspect of model acceptance, referred to as the tension between model transparency and veridicality (Carley 2002), is the essential tension that exists between the extremes of the level of detail adopted in any modeling enterprise.

Validation of Agent Theories

ABMS has raised a new technical challenge regarding the validation of models. That challenge concerns the validation of (1) agent behaviors and interaction mechanisms and (2) emergent structures and properties that are produced by the ABMS. There is currently not a good theory of human behavior that is generally applicable to all situations and contexts upon which ABMS can be built. General programs for artificial intelligence (AI) have fallen short of expectations for yielding good, descriptive behavioral models.

However, in specific contexts of human behavior that are much better understood, well defined, and well structured, for example, supply chain management, capturing human behaviors or at least a range of plausible behaviors holds great promise. Aside from the individual agent behaviors, it is becoming increasingly recognized that social effects are an important determinant of system behavior. The mechanisms of agent interaction are very important in laying the groundwork for realistic agent models. An example is the supply chain model and how trust is established and maintained in relationships among supply chain agents (Macal 2004). Much progress has already been made in translating theories of social interaction into the realm of ABMS, and this is the subject of ongoing research in such fields as computational social science. In any event, it is likely there will be an ongoing need for validated theory regarding individual behavior and social interaction for incorporation into agent models embedded within ABMS.

Case Study: Validation of the Electric Power Market Model

This section describes a case study for validation of the deregulated electric power market model that has already been introduced. Since the deregulated electric power market being modeled does not currently exist, validation of the model presented special challenges. Comparing model results with the real-world deregulated system through formal statistical means was not an option, although the purely physical electric power grid models had been validated previously for the case of the regulated power market. First of all, the model was developed by a team of experienced domain experts consisting of electric power system engineers as well as economists. This proved critical to establishing a solid baseline model ready for validation. Validation consisted of building a case for and maximizing credibility on several counts: data, subject matter experts, physical system comparison, and comprehensive sweeping of the agent parameter and strategy spaces.

Extensive validation of the data on the existing system and planned developments and expansions in the future was conducted by checking the currency of the data with the original data sources and cross-checking data with interested third parties. For example, electric power generation companies have a vested interest in using accurate data on the current and future electric power system capacity in the model. In addition, extensive use of sophisticated visualization techniques was made to visualize the input data as well as the model outputs. Data gaps and inconsistencies were easily spotted through these visualizations.

Validation of the reduced form direct current (DC) model of the electric power grid was also necessary, since the DC model was only a good approximation to the more detailed alternating current (AC) model over a limited range of operational parameter settings. Validation of the DC model to the AC model was done by comparing results for an extensive number of cases from the DC model to the full AC model. In turn, the AC model had been validated against the actual physical power grid in numerous validation exercises that had been conducted previously.

Validating the interface between the physical system and the economic system was also essential for gaining model credibility. Independent subject matter experts (SMEs) from the electric utility industry were assembled (i.e., independent of the model developers) to review model assumptions and model outputs for a limited number of cases. SMEs included former utility operators, industry consultants, and former traders. The SMEs were selected on the basis that they had previously held professional positions that required them to most nearly duplicate on a day-to-day basis

the decisions made by the computational agents in the model. The SMEs provided critical industry experience and the ability to place themselves in the positions of agents in the deregulated markets. A workshop-style format was used in which the model developers stepped the SMEs through the model assumptions and case results.

Comprehensive testing of plausible agent strategies was essential to obtaining valid model results. It was not possible to draw general conclusions from only a handful of model runs because of the nonlinear, dynamic aspects of the agent behaviors and interactions. Extensive model runs served the dual purposes of verifying model behaviors that were expected, thereby increasing the confidence in the model, and discovering model behaviors that were unexpected. Discovering unexpected cases created focal points for further model runs and more in-depth analysis and explanation. This process resulted in identifying the need for hundreds of additional model runs. All model results and the answers to the obvious questions pertaining to the model results had to be explainable in plain English or they would not be useful to decision-makers. The model validation phase ended up taking as long as the model development phase. In the end, however, it was generally accepted that the model was a valid one for answering a wide range of important questions pertaining to electric power deregulation.

Related Aspects of V&V

Other aspects of V&V are potentially related to agent-based modeling. These include independent V&V, certification, and accreditation. Ideally, any agent-based model that is used in an operational environment would undergo a rigorous V&V process conducted by knowledgeable people other than the original model developers, would be certified for use in the organization's IT software environment, and would be accredited as solving the problems of main concern to the business. Time and money are required to satisfy these objectives, which are well beyond the initial investment in the model and software development.

Independent V&V

The V&V of a model is considered independent (IV&V) when it is conducted by knowledgeable people other than the original model developers. Since the original model developers have a vested interest in declaring the model verified and valid, biases may limit the ability of the original model developers to thoroughly perform V&V. On the downside, it can be a daunting, time-consuming, and expensive task for a third party to understand what a model is supposed to do well enough to develop a test plan and conduct comprehensive model testing. A key aspect of IV&V then concerns the necessity of having extensive and complete documentation on all aspects of the model in addition to the complete source code transferred to the independent V&V group. The full IV&V process requires information from the model developers in four areas:

- Requirements that the model is intended to meet.
- Technical details of the model and how it relates to the relevant fields, knowledgeable expertise, and underlying theories.
- Data and meta-data (such as source of the data, its currency, etc.).
- The underlying software implementation.

Requirements can be specified using the original proposal for the model development that indicated the problem that was to be solved or later requirements specification documents. In lieu of a formal requirements specification document, a statement of the requirements that the model is supposed to meet as originally intended is very useful.

The model design used to meet the requirements can be specified using briefings on the model as well as any written documentation. The goal is to describe what the model actually does relative to the specified requirements and explain how it does it. There are several types of documents that are helpful in this regard, including:

- Flowcharts and logic diagrams.
- Technical papers or articles published on the model, if available.
- Resource materials that were used in understanding the processes that were modeled, particularly if they distinguish between the present implementation of the model and what the developers intend to add in the future. These resources could include papers in the domain and other information sources.
- Notes on knowledge engineering sessions with domain experts.

Data helps clarify the model's design, confirm the tester's understanding of the model, and start the model-testing process itself. In addition to data itself, the important data-related documents include:

- Data dictionaries, describing data elements and data sources.
- Database design documents.
- Data dependency diagrams.

Of course, computational models are naturally embodied in software. The critical software and related documents include the following:

- Diagrams related to the source code, such as UML (Unified Modeling Language) diagrams that indicate the model components and the logical flow of the processes in the model, can speed up the testing process (Object Management Group 2001).
- The source code is useful in the initial stages of validation but essential in the later stages. As the evaluation matures, it is desirable to obtain the working source code for testing, replication and investigation.
- Descriptions of algorithms and heuristics that govern the processes and agent interaction mechanisms included in the model are helpful.

Certification

Certification is the formal process of ensuring that a model meets some standard or set of standards. For example, in distributed simulation there are sets of protocols or requirements that a model must meet to properly interface to other models complying with the overall simulation architecture. The High Level Architecture (HLA) is one such architecture that specifies the IEEE 1516 standard (IEEE 2001a, 2001b, 2001c). Under HLA, models and their components must be registered in a standard way that ensures their ability to communicate with other, unspecified models in a dynamic runtime environment. Certification is the process by which an independent group puts its stamp of approval on conformance of the model to the specified standard. Currently, agent-based modeling has no generally agreed-upon certification standards beyond those that exist for distributed simulation (HLA as described above) or object-oriented technology (CORBA). These are more general frameworks that embody much more than agent-based modeling implementations.

Accreditation

Accreditation is the formal process of determining whether a model is useful for a particular purpose and is applicable to answering a specific set of questions. Potential users of the model are an intrinsic part of the accreditation process to ensure that the model addresses the questions in an appropriate and credible way. Generally, models are developed for a specific, intended purpose as opposed to being generally applicable to a wide range of problems. However, it is not uncommon for a successful model that has been developed for one purpose to be applied to a similar problem in a different, though related, context. The reasons for that simply have to do with the fact that it might be less expensive to adapt or augment an existing model with additional details on the related application area than it is to build an entirely new model from scratch.

The formal process of accepting a model for use in a specific application area is called accreditation. Accreditation is a structured and formal process for ensuring that the necessary elements to address the related problem are included in the model, or to conclude that the model cannot be modified in some way to include the new requirements. For example, the Department of Defense (DoD) has a large number of logistics and deployment planning models, with a considerable investment, which are based on cold-war assumptions. These models need to be systematically analyzed and accredited for their applicability to new DoD missions.

Not all models are able to be accredited for similar uses. For example, a model may have the proper scope but not be detailed enough to adequately answer a question that it was not designed to answer. An example is a supply chain model that represents items moving through the supply chain as continuous flow variables, designed to answer the question of whether system capacity is adequate. If the new question for the model is where a single (discrete) item is in the supply chain at any point in time, the model cannot be accredited for this purpose.

Summary

This chapter has explored some of the main practical considerations and approaches to performing agent-based model V&V. The key goal of model V&V is to earn a high level of credibility for the model among its intended users.

Verification is conducted by comparing the model results for a carefully selected number of test cases to a set of documented model design specifications. Various approaches have been used to select the appropriate cases. Conceptually, as more cases are tested, uncertainty in the correctness of the model's implementation is reduced and the model comes closer and closer to achieving the verification ideal. Techniques from object-oriented modeling and computation are useful at isolating agents and behaviors, aiding in the verification process.

Validation is conducted by comparing model results for a specified number of cases to an authoritative referent, whether the referent is the real world, another presumably validated model, or a set of domain experts. Comprehensive sweeps over parameter spaces and alternative assumptions are becoming more practical as an aid to validation as computational capabilities continue to advance, yet remain time-consuming and resource-intensive. The selection of a limited number of important cases for validation, either through conscious design by subject matter experts or by computational means such as stochastic search, are alternatives to more comprehensive investigation. These approaches often yield acceptable results for business applications. The use of multiple models, using alternative approaches, assumptions, or data, should be considered as an adjunct to model validation. ABMS are often reducible to simpler (noncomputational) analytical models for special cases. If such analytical models are available, they can also be a valuable adjunct to the validation of ABMS. Other aspects of V&V will be useful for ABMS to be generally adopted in the future, including independent V&V, and model certification and accreditation.

Agent-based models have all of the V&V requirements of traditional models. Agent-based modeling brings the new requirement to traditional model V&V of verifying and validating agent behaviors and interactions and emergent processes. There are no perfectly general answers to V&V of computational models, agent-based models included. Fortunately, there are many practical ways to approach V&V.

References

AIAA (1998). *AIAA Guide for the Verification and Validation of Computational Fluid Dynamics Simulations*. Reston, Va.: American Institute of Aeronautics and Astronautics.

Beck, K. and E. Gamma (1998). Test Infected: Programmers Love Writing Tests. *Java Report* **3**(7): 37–50.

Carley, K. M. (2002). Simulating Society: The Tension between Transparency and Veridicality. *Proceedings of the Agent 2002 Conference on Social Agents: Ecology, Exchange and Evolution.* Chicago.

Dijkstra, E. (1976). *A Discipline of Programming.* Englewood Cliffs, N.J.: Prentice-Hall.

Edmonds, B. and D. Hales (2003). Replication, Replication and Replication: Some Hard Lessons from Model Alignment. *Journal of Artificial Societies and Social Simulation* **6**(4) (online).

Gries, D. (1981). *The Science of Programming.* New York: Springer-Verlag.

Hales, D., J. Rouchier, and B. Edmonds (2003). Model-to-Model Analysis. *Journal of Artificial Societies and Social Simulation* **6**(4) (online).

IEEE (2001a). IEEE Standard P1516: *HLA Framework and Rules.* Piscataway, N.J.: IEEE.

IEEE (2001b). IEEE Standard P1516.1: *HLA Federate Interface Specification.* Piscataway, N.J.: IEEE.

IEEE (2001c). IEEE Standard P1516.2: *Object Model Template (OMT) Specification.* Piscataway, N.J.: IEEE.

Jackson, D. (2006). Dependable Software by Design. *Scientific American* **294**(6): 68–75.

Knuth, D. (1999). Quoted in *Knuth: Frequently Asked Questions.* Stanford, Cal.: Stanford University Press.

Law, A. M. (2007). *Simulation Modeling and Analysis,* 4th ed. New York: McGraw-Hill.

Macal, C. (2004). Emergent Structures from Trust Relationships in Supply Chains, in C. M. Macal, D. L. Sallach, and M. J. North (Eds.), *Proceedings of the Agent 2004 Conference on Social Dynamics: Interaction, Reflexivity and Emergence,* ANL/DIS-05-6, co-sponsored by Argonne National Laboratory and the University of Chicago, Oct. 7–9, pp. 743–760, available at http://www.agent2004.anl.gov/.

Miller, J. H. (1998). Active Nonlinear Tests (ANTs) of Complex Simulation Models. *Management Science* **44**: 620–830.

Object Management Group (2001). *OMG Unified Modeling Language Specification Version 1.5.* Needham, Mass.: Object Management Group.

Woehr, V. (1996). An Interview with Donald Knuth: DDJ Chats with One of the World's Leading Computer Scientists. *Dr. Dobb's Journal,* pp. 16-22 (online).

12

A Visual Approach to Data Collection and Cleaning

Tasty Morsels

The classic phrase "garbage in, garbage out" or "GIGO" applies not just to agent simulations but to any type of model or software (Oxford 2004). Feeding appropriate facts into models is critical. Simply put, finding data is easy, finding good data is hard. In many ways, if data is like food, then raw data is like sugarcane in a field: you need to process it before it can be eaten. This chapter describes both what should be fed into agent models and how the appropriate inputs can be found. The discussion begins with a quick overview of the modeling "fact food pyramid" and then delves into the details of model care and feeding.

The Fact Food Pyramid

Modeling is about converting data and information into knowledge and ultimately wisdom. Note that the definitions of these words for the purposes of modeling are more specific than the common usage of the terms (Oxford 2004). A fact food pyramid that highlights the similarities and differences between these terms is shown in figure 12.1.

Following Sharma (2005), it should be noted that various versions of this pyramid have been published in several fields, including knowledge management (Ackoff 1989; Zeleny 1987), information science (Cleveland 1982), and poetry (Eliot 1934), under many different names including the "knowledge hierarchy," the "knowledge pyramid," the "information hierarchy,"

the "information pyramid," and the "data, information, knowledge, and wisdom hierarchy (DIKW)," among others. Following this noble naming tradition, the hierarchy is labeled in figure 12.1 as a "fact food pyramid." T. S. Eliot's (1934) version, quoted below, is arguably the earliest and most succinct:

> Where is the Life we have lost in living?
> Where is the wisdom we have lost in Knowledge?
> Where is the Knowledge we have lost in information?

The distinctions in the fact food pyramid are useful for this chapter and for practical modeling. The version of the pyramid presented here is specialized for applied modeling rather than, say, poetics. The authors provide their apologies to the departed T. S. Eliot.

For modelers, data consists of collected representations of facts or what are believed to be facts. This matches the common use of the term (Oxford 2004). Data shows what happened or provides the status of something at one moment and in one place. For example, the dollar amount and time of a sporting goods purchase is data.

Information is data that can be used for decision-making. This definition places more emphasis on decision-making than the typical use of the word (Oxford 2004). This is appropriate since practical modeling is all about improving decision-making. Information explains what happened or provides the status of something with enough contextual background to be

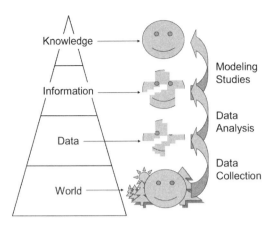

FIGURE 12.1 Fact food pyramid.

understandable. An example is the total dollar amount or volume of purchases in a sporting goods store. Whether something is data or information depends sensitively on the intended use.

Knowledge is information that has higher-level meaning to a decision-maker. Similarly to the modeling usage of the word "information," this definition of knowledge places more weight on decision-making

than the common definition (Oxford 2004). Knowledge indicates why something happened or why something is the way that it is in a situation. Continuing the sporting goods example, knowledge might be the fact that early spring tends to have high sales volumes due to shoppers' anticipation of improved weather. Further knowledge might be that early summer has high merchandise return rates due to shoppers' failure to actually use the equipment that they purchased. As with data and information, the dividing line between information and knowledge is set by the situation.

Wisdom in a given area is an understanding of what causes similarities and differences in outcomes in the area. This definition focuses more on strategic decision-making than the typical definition (Oxford 2004). Wisdom is the generalization of knowledge gleaned from many diverse situations. Wisdom explains why things happen or why things are the way that they are across a wide range of situations. Figure 12.2 indicates the way that wisdom builds on data, information, and knowledge that have been derived from several different but related situations. An example of wisdom in the sporting goods situation is being aware that good weather tends to increase sales of some

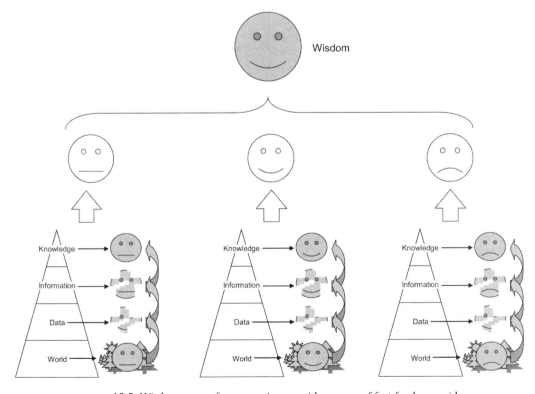

FIGURE 12.2 Wisdom comes from experiences with a range of fact food pyramids.

items and that adjusting pricing to match the weather increases long-term profits.

The use of accurate and appropriately detailed models can help decision-makers develop wisdom in particular areas by efficiently providing a range of diverse experiences. These experiences can include many situations that would be difficult to create or would take long periods to emerge in the actual environment. The experiences can also be delivered on accelerated time schedules to make the learning more time-efficient and improve the ability of decision-makers to learn by contrasting diverse experiences side by side. Thus, the use of models can deepen decision-makers' understanding of the situations they manage. Agent-based models can be especially useful in this regard since their bottom-up behavioral construction can allow a vast range of situations to be simulated and can provide realistic feedback to decision-makers.

Understanding the differences between data, information, knowledge, and wisdom helps to focus fact collection and processing efforts. Most models run on information rather than data. This is critical because it means that most data sources need processing before they are ready for modeling purposes. An overview of the required processing will be provided in the remainder of this section. The details will be discussed throughout the rest of this chapter. Following this lead, this chapter could easily be called "Information Preparation" rather than "Data Collection and Cleaning." Chapter 13, on "Understanding and Presenting ABMS Results," shows both how to convert model input information into knowledge and ultimately wisdom, as well as how to present the resulting knowledge and wisdom to decision-makers.

Data Collection

Data collection is used to accumulate measurements from real-world sources. There are a variety of approaches to data collection. Some of these approaches are mentioned later in this chapter. In the long term, collection of new data for agent models can be driven by intermediate findings derived from the model itself. While it is certainly possible to collect new data for modeling, most practical modeling efforts begin with existing data sources. This occurs because substantial data collection is usually expensive, many organizations have already collected substantial amounts of data on the issues of interest to them, and

because proxy or surrogate data can often be used to meet the remaining requirements. The use of proxy or surrogate data is discussed later in this chapter.

In the real world, modelers generally need to identify existing data sources, gain access to these sources, evaluate the contents, and then perform enhancements as needed. Effective approaches to identifying and obtaining existing data are described in the sections that follow. Standards for evaluating the data collection efforts are detailed in the section on data quality. Correcting errors in data is referred to as data cleaning, data scrubbing, or data cleansing (Rahm and Do 2000). Data cleaning is closely coupled with data collection (Rahm and Do 2000).

Data cleaning or error correction is hard to do and is time-consuming work. The work typically requires acute, sustained attention to detail. Successful data cleaning is very much dependent on finding the right kind of person to do the job. The best data cleaners are usually detail-oriented people who understand the need to check things out. Ideally, they will have a good knowledge of statistics and a solid understanding of the purposes for which the data is being cleaned. Not everyone has these traits, but those who do should be highly valued!

So, what should the data cleaners be doing? Data cleaning begins with an evaluation of the current quality of the data and should include careful logging of all data updates. If the quality level is too low for a given application, then it may be possible to correct or otherwise improve parts of the data. Many of the checks used to assess data quality can also be used to do this evaluation. Data quality measurement is usually passive in that data problems are only identified. Data cleaning is an active process in that data problems are both identified and corrected (Rahm and Do 2000). There are a variety of common errors to look for (Rahm and Do 2000):

1. There are several kinds of typographical errors, including incorrect data entry within fields and between fields.
2. As stated below, there are several types of measurement errors, including measurement logging errors, measurement bias errors, and improperly coded data.
3. Fabricated data can also be a problem.

To find these types of problems a variety of statistical checks and visual checks can be used as discussed later. Furthermore, additional data-cleaning methods are described later in this chapter along with the corresponding data quality evaluation standards. A variety of advanced techniques are also available (Ratnasingham 1999; Winkler 2003).

Data cleaning is ideally completed as a parallel activity to data collection. This allows feedback between the data collection and cleaning activities. For example, a data quality evaluation might indicate that many address entries in a sales database are improperly coded. If data collection is still ongoing, this finding can be fed back to the data collection managers. These mangers can in turn have their data collectors review the proper data-encoding standards before collecting more data. This feedback by itself will not correct data that has already been collected. However, it can result in improvements to the data yet to be collected. If data-cleaning efforts begin early enough, most of the data collection issues can be resolved before substantial amounts of problematic data are collected. In practice, data cleaning often follows data collection. This is particularly true for data applications that are different from the goals of the original data collection efforts. In this case, the data cleaning may have significantly different standards than the earlier efforts and thus require substantial updates to the data. Modeling is often in this category. Fortunately, these efforts in many cases can be incremental. This allows modeling efforts to proceed while data is slowly updated in the background.

Data Analysis

Data analysis converts collected data into information. Just as the categorization of facts as data or information depends on the intended use, data analysis is domain specific. However, there are some important general principles of data analysis. These principles include clear statements of the questions being answered, traceable descriptions of the data sources, and reproducible documentation of the data analysis techniques and suitable estimates of error.

Since the meaning of data analysis depends on the use, concretely defining the questions being answered is the key. This definition can be quite succinct. In fact, a paragraph or even a sentence can be enough in some cases. It must include the core question or concern being addressed by the analysis. This core goal can be the production of information for use in later analysis. Certainly, it can sometimes be correct to apply information for purposes other than the original

analytical intent. However, it is important to know the original intent to determine how far a field the new use is. If it is too far from the initial purpose for the data, then the effects of this difference on the results of the new use must be reviewed to avoid erroneous conclusions.

Traceable descriptions of the data sources contribute to long-term organizational learning, support study reproduction, and help with quality assurance. A description of a data source is traceable when the origin of the data is clearly identified and each data element can be tracked back to its fundamental source. Thus, the data sources can be traced. Traceability helps organizational learning by contributing to the accumulation of knowledge about the data sources within an organization and by maintaining an organization's ability to reconstruct data later when needed. In addition, traceability assists quality assurance by simplifying data audits.

Reproducible documentation of data analysis techniques means writing a description of how the analysis was performed. The documentation should be in the form of directions that are detailed enough to allow the analysis to be reproduced using the original data or similar data. The role of this documentation is to allow later auditing and reproduction of the work. The documentation should open with a short executive summary, but otherwise it need not be written at the management level. Rather, the directions should be written at a level of detail that is understandable by anyone with the same basic skills set and expertise as a typical data analyst in the given role. This means that the directions do not need to include substantial background information or references to tutorials, unless the techniques to be used are unusual in the specific analytical context. One of the best ways to ensure that documentation is written at an appropriate level is to have it briefly reviewed by an analyst with a relevant background who has not worked on the project. The reviewer should be asked if they feel that they could reproduce the study using only the documentation and the original data and without the ability to ask the questions of the documentation's author.

The data analysis should produce estimates of error bounds on all of the analytical results. These error bounds are critical since they allow later users of the data to understand the impact of the errors on any conclusions that are drawn. These estimates should describe the expected variability in the products of the analysis in either quantitative or qualitative terms.

Ideally, statistical estimates such as variances, standard deviations, quartiles, or higher moments can be used. In practice, these values can be difficult to determine for many data sets. However, error bounds of some type or other are still needed. If necessary, qualitative descriptions can be substituted if quantitative bounds cannot be found.

Modeling

Modeling is one approach to converting information into knowledge. Here the term "modeling" includes both agent-based modeling and other techniques as well. Modeling in this context is the production of a system representation that is somehow simpler than the system itself, yet still salient in some way. The system being modeled is called the referent. These modeling concepts are discussed in detail in chapters 4, 5, and 11.

The relationships embedded in a properly constructed model represent knowledge. In general, modeling allows these relationships to be expressed in a simpler form than the original system. This simpler form is the model. To be simpler, the model cannot include every detail from the original system. To be useful, the details that are eliminated must not substantially affect the model's results in the area of interest. The art of modeling is the ability to efficiently determine which details need to be included in the model and which do not. The iterative development approach that is discussed throughout this book is the most powerful technique for efficiently selecting details to model.

Modeling allows information to be in some sense intelligently summarized. These summaries take advantage of patterns in the underlying data. For modeling to be effective, these patterns must represent fundamental behaviors or facts. The summaries form knowledge.

Experience

Experience can convert knowledge of a range of situations into wisdom. As previously discussed, wisdom is the generalization of knowledge gleaned from many diverse situations. Clearly, there is no substitute for real experience. However, models can be used to accelerate learning. For example, the U.S. armed forces use battlefield simulations to train soldiers to deal with complex combat situations and to test new combat approaches (Wilson 1996; Infantry News 2002; McCaffrey 2003). Executives, managers, and operations personnel can also benefit from simulation exercises that allow them to rapidly broaden, deepen, and generalize their accumulated experience in both commonly and rarely encountered situations. Agent modeling is particularly helpful in this regard since it uses representations of real behaviors. This makes the model much more transparent to the users and allows users more flexibility in their responses. Model transparency is detailed in chapter 13.

A Model Diet

Every model has a set of input requirements for each possible use. Knowing the diet needed by a given model is the key to proper model use. The structure of the model itself defines the basic types of data that are needed. A simple agent-based market model may require only basic descriptive data on the general categories of market participants as well as the count of each kind of participant. An advanced agent-based model of competitive market behavior might require detailed business data on every market player. The specific questions that the model will be applied to assist with fleshing out and refining the basic needs. The scope of the questions and the required accuracy of the results each plays a role.

Several factors are critical when considering the input data requirements for a model application. The foremost among these issues is the required resolution of the input data. Examples include the fact that an hourly market model will probably need some type of hourly data source. While this at first seems trivial, a surprisingly large number of sophisticated organizations have failed to notice data resolution requirements until it was too late. Interpolating data or retrofitting models to run at new resolutions is costly and tends to produce lower-quality results than models run with properly matched inputs. Also, pay particular attention to the difference between data that should exist, data that does exist, and data that can actually be used.

Marshmallows and Campfire Stories

Most organizations have shared beliefs about the kinds of data that they collect and the form in which they collect it. As the authors have found in many cases, the beliefs about what is collected typically go well beyond that which is actually stored. The reasons for this are legion. Data collection systems managers have a stake in appearing thorough and proactive. Their subordinates have similar interests. The analytical members of the organization generally feel more capable and comfortable believing that huge amounts of detailed data are theoretically at their disposal. Managers at all levels like to impress customers, shareholders, and boards with their command of the business as demonstrated by hard data. One-of-a-kind or limited data collection efforts are often remembered far beyond their useful lifetime. Furthermore, these rare and expensive data collection events set expectations and mold mistaken beliefs. Ultimately, asking if an organization has specific types of data is not enough. Some member of the modeling team needs to see the data early in the project to ensure that the beliefs about what is available match the reality.

Directly seeing promised data does more than simply confirm that the data actually exists. It offers the opportunity to ensure that the data is in a usable form or can be converted into a usable form. The sad fact is that even substantial data collection efforts can easily amass huge amounts of essentially unusable data. This is particularly true when the data has not been statistically analyzed or used for other modeling purposes. In this case, no one really knows if the data is usable. Given the extra care that is needed to properly format, clean, and store modeling data, it is unlikely that anyone put in the effort.

Of course, even the existence of usable and properly formatted data is not enough for modeling. The data not only must be usable but available for use. The data that is most useful for modeling is often among the most jealously guarded resources in many organizations. Generally, data is useful for modeling when it describes or quantifies the behaviors of actors of interest. Within agent-based simulations, these actors are typically modeled as agents. The fact that a given set of data describes the behavior of such agents means that it details the behaviors of customers, suppliers, or competitors. Therefore, this data usually has substantial value to an organization. An organization's desire to protect this valuable resource may make it difficult to obtain the data. Fortunately, there are solutions to this problem. Several ways to work around this type of obstacle are described later in this chapter.

The value of data is not the only reason why it may be protected. In many cases, managers and staff members may wish to keep tight control of data sources for their own personal purposes. The approaches offered later in this chapter can provide technical routes around these problems. The best organizational approach is usually to form partnerships with the data holders by inviting them to participate at some level in the model development process. This is often far better than the usual attempt to force compliance from the top. Management support for a modeling project is generally extremely helpful. However, data transfer is complex. Even the most determined managers often find it extremely difficult to force data holders to hand over the right type of properly formatted data. Be sure to remain on good terms with data suppliers!

Cooking Times Vary

Collecting and properly formatting input data for model use is often the most time-consuming modeling activity. As will be discussed later, this is good news since it means that agent-based modeling money is being invested in better understanding the customer rather than on technology. Averaging over the many model applications the authors have participated in, about 80% of the cost of most model-based studies was consumed by input data collection, cleaning, and validation. On average, all of the other tasks inherent in large-scale modeling studies totaled about 20% of the final study cost. These other functions include requirements analysis, model selection if more than one model may be applicable, model development if a new model is needed, model execution, output analysis, and final report writing. As time-consuming as it may sound, even model development is a distant second to input data collection and formatting for properly completed studies. Actually, this seemingly disproportionate expense is quite appropriate if the significance of high-quality input data is carefully considered. Verfication and validation as well as data collection and cleaning are the most time-consuming parts of ABMS since they most directly touch the real world.

ABMS proceeds from the small to the large. Good data on the small is required to model the large. This small-scale data is sometimes referred to as "micro-data." High-quality micro-data is thus required. In many ways, this is good news. The major modeling investment is not in exotic technologies or advanced tools. It is in better understanding the customer, the client, or the market. With agent modeling, money is being spent where the most value is derived.

Defining a given model's required resolution or resolutions is the key. Naturally, agent models focus on individual behavior from a bottom-up perspective. The individuals are generally some type of decision-maker such as a person, family, or corporation. Selecting the size of the appropriate entity required for modeling helps to define the required data resolution. For example, if the fundamental agents in a consumer model of car purchases are people, then data on individual purchasing patterns is needed. However, if the fundamental agents in a consumer model of car purchases are a demographic group, then data on the demographic level is all that is needed. Clearly, data requirements vary with each model's requirements.

Data Quality

Data quality has several dimensions, each of which has important implications for modeling. These dimensions are shown in figure 12.3.

Accuracy

Accuracy is relative correspondence between the data and reality or how close the measured values are to the real values (Veregin 1998). It is the level of matching between the stored values and real values for a given data source. Highly accurate data has close correlation with the underlying values being measured. Considering an example of an automotive purchases database, the purchase price data would be highly accurate if almost all recorded prices were identical to the real transaction prices. This level of accuracy might be attained by using computerized connections to vehicle sales tax recording software.

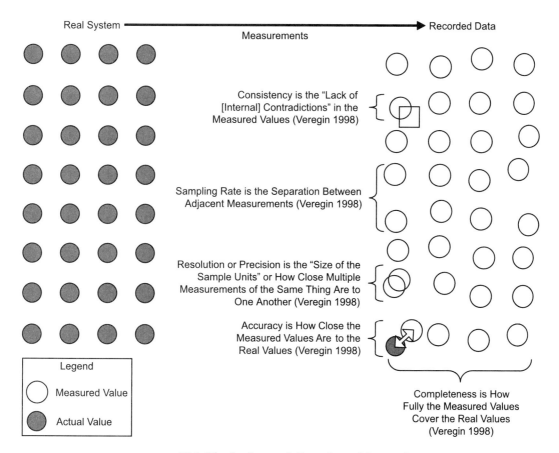

FIGURE 12.3 The fundamental dimensions of data quality.

The database would probably be relatively inaccurate if the recorded prices were manually entered some time after each of the transactions. Other issues discussed later such as completeness might also be questionable. Of course, even without these other issues, using the term "actual value" suggests that reality is always measurable (Veregin 1998)!

In some cases, reality cannot be fully observed. Sometimes reality cannot be observed due to economic or temporal limits (Veregin 1998). An example is polling all consumers in America about their sporting goods preferences. Clearly, statistical sampling techniques can be used to reduce this problem, but the underlying issue remains. It is often difficult to collect enough data to develop fully representative samples.

Sometimes reality is based on subjective perception rather than objective fact, such as when dealing with personal opinion (Veregin 1998). An example is a customer satisfaction survey. Clearly, the information that can be gained from such a survey may be interesting and useful. Even though many measurements are made of customer satisfaction, the actual idea of customer satisfaction can be difficult to concretely define. Such quantitative measurements of qualitative factors are commonly used for many types of decision-making outside of modeling. In practice, the same approximations that are made for other uses of such data can also be applied to agent modeling. In the end, accuracy should be assessed relative to data source specifications.

"Accuracy is the inverse of error" (Veregin 1998). While accuracy compares recorded data to the actual values being measured, error looks at the relative mismatches. Even though both terms focus on the same underlying issue, the terms have different connotations. Describing data as 95% accurate usually engenders greater confidence than describing the same data as being 5% in error. Positive and truthful data descriptions based on measures of accuracy tend to be the most persuasive in communicating data quality. However, when even small errors can have large consequences, it is more appropriate to discuss data sources in terms of error levels.

Precision or Resolution

Precision or resolution is the "size of the sample units" or how close multiple measurements of the same thing are to one another (Veregin 1998). Accuracy and precision are often used interchangeably, but they actually have different meanings. As previously discussed, accuracy is the correspondence between measured data and the real values (Veregin 1998). Precision or resolution are the differences between multiple measurements of the same thing. For example, the auto sales database might have poor accuracy due to faulty operator instructions to record the pretax sales price rather than the final sales price. The precision still might be high due to the systematic recording of numbers that are all wrong by exactly the same percentage!

The value of resolution or precision varies. In principle, higher resolution data is more useful. In practice it is best to have the resolution of the data match the resolution of the model. Higher resolutions can be better than lower resolutions for some applications and worse for others. Examples can be seen in modeling consumer purchases in a sporting goods store. If the goal of the modeling is to represent the purchasing patterns of individual consumers, then high-resolution data at the consumer level is best. Lower resolution data at the store or region level might be useful, but even a moderate number of consumer purchase histories would be quite helpful. However, if the goal of the modeling effort is to represent regional sales, then region-level information is needed. Data on the decisions of regional managers, and the context in which their decisions were made, is key. Consumer purchase information will still be helpful, but less detail may be sufficient. If the model only deals with consumer demand at the regional level, then having the purchase histories of individual consumers may actually be distracting. Note, though, that the resulting regional model can only be used to answer questions at the regional level or above. Questions that are more detailed would require a higher resolution model. The key is to make sure that the resolution level matches the modeling application. Resolution is related to accuracy since resolution is also an important part of a data source's description (Veregin 1998).

Sampling Rate

Sampling rate is the separation between adjacent measurements (Veregin 1998). According to Veregin (1998):

> Resolution is distinct from the spatial sampling rate, although the two are often confused with each other. Sampling rate refers to the distance between samples, while resolution refers to the

size of the sample units. Often resolution and sampling are closely matched, but they do not necessarily need to be. When the sampling rate is higher than the resolution, sample units overlap; when the sampling rate is lower than the resolution, there are gaps between sample units.

Consistency

Consistency is the "lack of [internal] contradictions" in data (Veregin 1998). Consistency is an internal property of data sources (Veregin 1998). These internal properties are typically contextual. Consider the previously mentioned data set on the decisions made by the regional managers of a retail sporting goods chain. The data sets might record the stock-keeping units or products to make available in their region. The data sets would lack internal consistency when different product codes are used for the same product at different times. This might happen due to coding

changes or simple data-recording errors. Consistency can be measured by cross-checking fully redundant or partly redundant fields. Visualization tools can be used to check data consistency.

There are several basic types of redundancy, including internal redundancy, one-to-one, one-to-many, and many-to-many redundancy. Each of these basic types of redundancy can be easily checked. Several tools can be used, including visualization systems and relational databases. In particular, visualization tools such as the VisAD or the Pajek package can highlight contradictions and other data consistency problems (Batagelj and Mrvar 1998, 2004; Hibbard 1998). Figure 12.4 shows a Pajek visualization of connections between a set of related web sites. In the figure, each vertex represents a web site and each edge represents a hyperlink between the connected sites. The vertices were positioned based on the relative connectivity of the sites. Web sites with more connections are

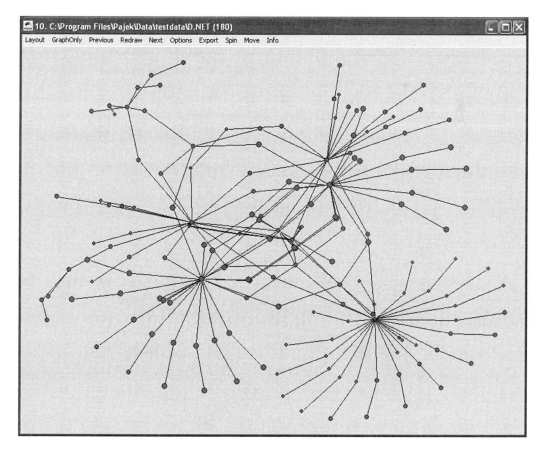

FIGURE 12.4 Pajek visualization showing example of web site connection data.
(From Batagelj and Mrvar 2004.)

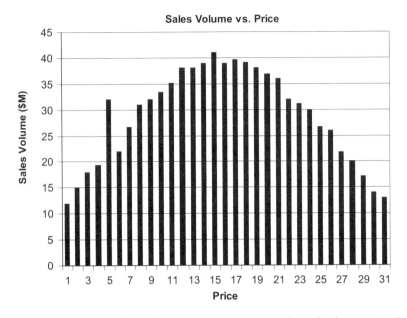

FIGURE 12.5 This example of a histogram raises questions about the data at price 5.

located closer to the center of the plot than proportionally less connected sites.

Other useful visual tools include histograms and scatterplots. Histograms can be used to see outliers in overall distributions as shown in figure 12.5. The items at price 5 are clearly different from the rest of the sample. Scatterplots can be used to find outliers in data sets with multiple variables. The example of a scatterplot in figure 12.6 indicates that the cluster in the lower right is unusual and suggests that this data should be investigated further.

Internal redundancy occurs when a data item can be checked against itself for correctness. An example is credit card numbers with built-in check sums (Gallian 1996). Credit card numbers assigned using this kind of process produce a predictable result when

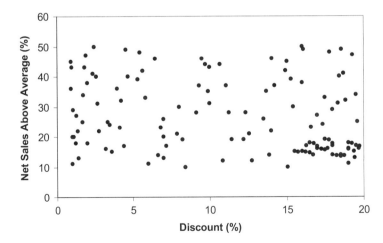

FIGURE 12.6 This example of a scatterplot suggests that the cluster in the lower right should be further investigated.

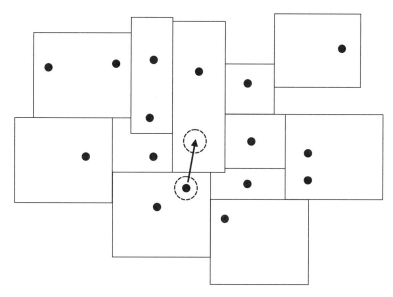

FIGURE 12.7 Example of facility locations and county boundaries with an incorrectly located facility highlighted.

they are run through a formula (Gallian 1996). This allows certain errors to be automatically recognized using the numbers themselves (Gallian 1996).

One-to-one redundancy occurs when two or more fields in each record contain information that is essentially the same or is easily translated. An example is driver's license numbers. Depending on the state, these numbers can encode several pieces of information about the holder, including their name (Gallian 1996). In a retail sporting goods customer loyalty program database, having both a driver's license number and a name field could technically be redundant. In practice, it is a good idea to keep both fields to simplify data access. Direct automated matching or visualization tools can be used to check one-to-one data consistency such as this.

One-to-many redundancy occurs when one or more database records contain fields with the same underlying information. This typically is the result of one field acting as a container for other fields as in a country that contains states. As an example, consider a facility location database with addresses that include both regular street addresses and county codes. The street addresses are used to locate the facilities and the counties are used to track county licensing. The facility street addresses can be used to find the county. Several facilities may be located in the same county. Some counties may not have a facility. However, each

facility is only in one county. The recorded county codes can be checked against facility street addresses. Data inconsistency would occur if some of the street addresses were not in the recorded county. As with one-to-one data consistency, automated matching or visualization tools can be used. An example of a visualization is shown in figure 12.7.

Many-to-many redundancy occurs when multiple fields in a data source encode overlapping values. For example, consider a service delivery database that contains customer street addresses, customer counties, and customer service delivery territories. The street addresses are used to locate the customers, the counties are used for tax purposes, and the territories are used for service delivery coordination. In this database several data consistency tests can be performed, including checking the county boundaries against the recorded service territories. As before, automated matching or visualization tools can be used to check many-to-many data consistency. An example of a visualization is shown in figure 12.8.

Completeness

Completeness is how fully the measured values cover the real values (Veregin 1998). There are two main types of completeness, namely data completeness and model completeness (Brassel et al. 1995). As with

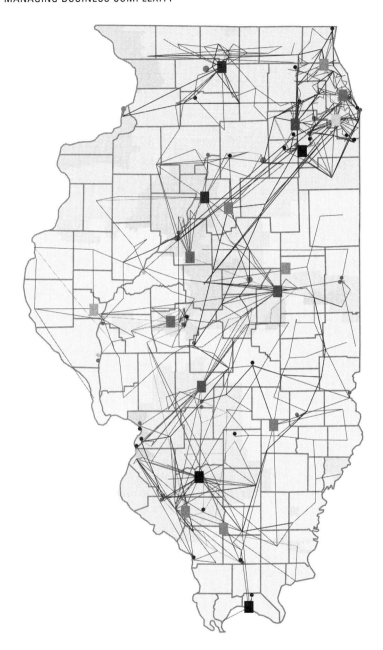

FIGURE 12.8 County boundaries and the service territories of major power companies in the state of Illinois, U.S.A.

consistency, visualization tools can be used to check completeness.

Data completeness means that everything that is said to be in a data source is actually in the data source. An example of a lack of data completeness is an automotive sales database that is supposed to contain all transactions from 1985 forward but that only

contains lists of new and used car sales at auto dealerships from 1985 onward. The sales of used cars by current private party owners might not be included due to difficulties with effectively collecting this data.

Model completeness is data source coverage relative to a particular "use" (Brassel et al. 1995). Model completeness means that everything that needs to be in a data source for a specific model is actually in the data source. Considering the automotive data source again, the data might be incomplete in terms of data but it still might have model completeness if the agent-based model to be constructed only needed data on car dealerships. However, if competition from private party sales were to be modeled, then this data source would be model incomplete. The missing data might be filled in using secondary sources from state vehicle licensing agencies.

Either way, completeness evaluations also assess the data that is actually in the data source versus the description of the data source (Veregin 1998). Two types of comparisons are normally made. The first is the data that is not present but is supposed to be included in the data source. The second is the data that is present but is not included in the data source description.

Completeness evaluations assess the data that is not present but should be. An example is a U.S. customer address data source missing parts of New York. In this example, there is clear data incompleteness. This may translate into model incompleteness if New York is a key state for agent model development, as might be the case for an organization with high sales volumes in this area. In this case, alternative sources of data probably can be used, including the use of proxy data from similar densely populated Eastern industrial states such as New Jersey. However, organizations with few sales in New York may consider this data source model complete for their purposes and may be able to use the data source without augmentation.

Completeness evaluations also assess the data that is present but should not be. An example is a U.S. customer address database that also happens to have some additional addresses for customers in parts of Canada. This extra data can be useful if it extends the coverage range or depth of a database. This additional data may be problematic if it biases results derived from analyzing the data or if it interferes with model runs using the data.

Completeness is related to data resolution. Low-resolution data is in some ways less complete than higher resolution but otherwise equivalent data. Resolution differs from completeness in that resolution is internal to the data set, resolution is systematic in its omissions, and resolution does not focus as strongly on comparing purported and actual data set contents. Resolution is internal to the data set because it involves the inclusion or exclusion of items throughout the source rather than from one specific area or region of the real data. Resolution is systematic in that it includes the selection or elimination of data in a regular or methodically patterned way. As was discussed earlier, resolution can vary throughout the data. However, even with internal variation, the inclusion or exclusion of items due to the resolution level of the data is still relatively systematic compared to selection or elimination caused by data incompleteness. Furthermore, completeness assessments explicitly evaluate the difference between the expected and actual data content while resolution checking does not focus on this type of comparison.

Interdependencies

These dimensions are partly, but not fully, independent. For example, increasing accuracy tends to simultaneously increase consistency. However, this effect is not necessarily linear. Many data sets can be divided or partitioned into subsets that have dramatically different quality levels. This is often caused by the distribution of the data collection work across different people, between various groups of people, or over periods of time. Increasing the accuracy of already highly consistent data sets may increase the overall accuracy of a data set without having much effect on the overall consistency.

Fabricated Data

Fabrication can be a pernicious data quality problem. Data is fabricated for a variety of reasons, including a lack of resources for proper data collection, sloppiness in data collection, and counterproductive incentives. Special approaches can be applied to find fabricated data in addition to the use of basic data quality checks. An example of a special technique is the use of Benford's Law (Berleant et al. 2003):

> Benford's Law . . . describes how in many data sets the probability that a datum begins with the numeral "1" is greater than the probability that it begins with "2," and so on with "9" having the lowest probability of being the most significant digit. It is likely that this tendency explains in part the fact that on Google.com, a leading Web search engine, the query term "18" has more hits than "28," which has more hits than "38," a trend that continues on with occasional exceptions and generally seems to apply to other sequences of

numbers [as well]. . . . One application of this is detecting faked data. Hill (1999) suggests that using Benford's Law for this purpose is only the beginning, and that the future holds great potential for advances in the detection of data fraud.

Hill (1999) notes that certain types of data are particularly difficult to fabricate:

Unexpected properties of truly random data sets make it difficult to fabricate numerical data successfully. . . . To demonstrate this to beginning students of probability, I often ask them to do the following homework assignment the first day. They are either to flip a coin 200 times and record the results, or merely pretend to flip a coin and fake the results. The next day I amaze them by glancing at each student's list and correctly separating nearly all the true from the faked data. The fact in this case is that in a truly random sequence of 200 tosses it is extremely likely that a run of six heads or six tails will occur (the exact probability is somewhat complicated to calculate), but the average person trying to fake such a sequence will rarely include runs of that length.

This is but one example of the well-documented observation that most people cannot generate truly random numerical data. A study published in 1953 by psychologist A. Chapanis describes his experiment in which subjects were asked to write out long sequences of numbers (digits 0 through 9) in random order (Chapanis 1953). His results showed that different individuals exhibit marked preferences for certain decimal digits, and that repetitive pairs or triplets such as 222, 333 are avoided, whereas preferred triplets usually are made up of digits all of which are different, e.g., 653 or 231. This tendency to avoid long runs and include too many alternations, as in my class demonstration, has been confirmed by many researchers.

Most recently it has played a role in the arguments of cognitive psychologists Gilovich, Vallone, and Tversky that the "hot hand" in basketball is nothing more than a popular misperception, since long streaks in truly random data are much more likely to occur than is commonly believed (Gilovich et al. 1985).

Questions have been raised about the statistical methodology used by Gilovich et al. However, the conclusion that people often misperceive randomness remains valid.

Evaluating Data Quality

A variety of approaches can be used in tandem to evaluate data quality. These basic data quality checks can be done by anyone with a solid quantitative background. However, it is highly recommended that detailed data quality evaluations be performed by either a trained statistician, an expert on the data in the area under consideration, or both.

A Recipe for Success

Data collection and cleaning are iterative. Data collection involves several iterated steps. First, the modeling data requirements should be identified based on the initial model design. Second, data sources that may meet these requirements should be identified. Third, the data should be obtained. Fourth, the quality of the data should be evaluated. Fifth, a decision should be made to accept the data as found, improve the data quality through data cleaning, or return to the first step and refine the model's data requirements. Each of these steps will be discussed in detail.

Identifying Modeling Data Requirements

Agent modeling is best performed using a process of stepwise refinement. This means that modeling data requirements, model design, and even model implementation normally proceed in iterative steps. The identification of modeling data requirements based on the initial model design is not intended to produce a result set in stone. Rather, it is intended to produce a useful starting point for later refinement.

The process of identifying data requirements from the initial design should include a review of three main types of data. These categories are input data, calibration data, and validation data.

Input data is the type of data that comes to mind most readily when considering data requirements. While certainly important, input data is only one of three main categories of data that need to be specified. The other categories will be discussed later. Input data is used to execute models for practical applications.

Input data generally populates the parts of the model that vary from situation to situation. The identities and context-specific properties of agents and the variable aspects of the environment are usually input data. Values that are constant across model runs may be stored within input data sources to simplify model tuning, but they are included in another category here. This category is usually the easiest to identify in the initial design. Simply look for the things that will change between different uses of the model. Talking through two or three examples of model applications can make these items clear. Diverse examples are the key here. If the examples are quite similar, then many things that actually may vary will seem to be constant. Ask what is different about the example situations. What facts and descriptions would need to be given to the model to set up the example? The answers generally define the input data. An example is a sporting goods retail model that is being used to answer questions such as the following:

1. How does the placement of the other stores' surrounding sporting goods sales locations affect retail results? How does a coffee shop on the same concrete pad as a sporting goods store affect sales? Does the relative pad location matter? How about just sharing the same parking lot?

2. How does the routing of vehicle flow around store parking lots and the resulting foot traffic outside stores affect sales? Are there interactions with the flows for neighboring stores? Can these flows be synergistically leveraged?

3. How can store promotional signage be configured to take advantage of the specific types and volumes of traffic passing on the way to other stores? Will periodic signage adjustments to match regular and predictable changes in flows help? How much could it help?

These questions all focus on the same underlying themes. With suitable input data, a single well-designed model can address all of these questions. At the same time, these questions are diverse enough to suggest the range of data variation needed for the model. Say that the initial model design calls for shoppers to be agents and for stores to be part of the environment the agents live in. Clearly, the varying shopping preferences that underlie the cited traffic patterns are agent input data. Store pad and parking lot layouts vary in the questions listed above. These are likely environmental input data. Information on the sporting goods stores, the neighboring stores such as coffee shops, and signage are also environmental input data. If the initial model design calls for stores to be adaptive in their signage or even long-term location, then the ranges are agent input data. In either case, all of these variable items are input data. So what, then, is calibration data?

Most models have embedded constants that are used for tuning or calibration. As previously mentioned, these values are often stored with the input data to simplify model tuning. Returning to the sporting goods example, calibration data might include information on vehicle driver responses to posted speed limits, driver reactions to parking lot markings, common parking patterns, pedestrian responses to parking lot markings, pedestrian usage of sidewalks, and pedestrian responses to signage.

How different is input data and calibration data? Naturally, the classification of data input into one category or another depends on the specific area being modeled. This means that one model's input data is another model's calibration data. The fundamental difference described here is that input data is expected to change regularly every time the model is used to answer a new question. Calibration data is not strictly expected to change at all. Technically speaking, the need to change calibration data suggests that the model was not properly calibrated in the first place. In practice, it is expected that calibration data will change very slowly over time as the world surrounding the model changes or better information becomes available. At the very least, calibration data should normally remain the same while answering several different questions with the model. Precisely classifying data into one category or the other is not necessarily a critical point for most practical applications. The critical point is that both types of data should be considered.

As discussed in detail in chapter 11, validation is the process of checking a model against the real system that it is supposed to represent. A variety of validation approaches are discussed in that chapter. The fundamental approach compares model results to actual situations. Validation data is special input data combined with the expected output results that are used in tandem to confirm the correct operation of the model. Validation data is special because both the input data for the model and the expected output data are available. Validation data is used to ensure that the model is properly reproducing real situations. Validation of both the model and the data should be completed while the model is being developed and whenever the model is updated. Validation performed during model construction demonstrates that the model is being properly built. Later updates are another story.

As discussed in chapter 14, models are usually updated during extended use. In fact, one sign of a dead model is a decline in update requests. This is particularly true for enhancement requests. It has been said that imitation is the highest form of flattery. For modeling, user requests for extensions to cover new applications are the highest compliment. A user that is actively thinking about new uses for a model is showing genuine respect for the modeling effort. However, honoring these requests raises an important question for the modelers. This question is, how can the modeling team ensure that the model is still working properly after the requested changes are completed? The answer is regression testing.

Regression testing is used to revalidate models after modifications are completed. Regression testing normally reuses validation data sets to rerun previously passed tests to ensure that the model still works as expected.

Continuing the sporting goods example, the validation data might include information on the shopping preferences, layouts, and signage details in specific malls as well as the resulting traffic flow and sales patterns. These values can be used to set up the input data for several test cases that can be checked against the recorded output results. The validation process is detailed in chapter 11. A validation data example is shown in figure 12.9.

Identifying Potential Data Sources

Identifying potential data sources means locating possible places to find the data called for by the model's requirements. When identifying potential sources, be sure to develop plans for obtaining the data from these sources. Locating data and gaining access to it are often two different things. In many cases, the division or group within an organization that develops models is often different from the ones that collect data. Data collection groups often equate modeling with statistics. These groups are most commonly embedded within product or service management teams, although they are sometimes independent. When they are part of customer-focused management teams, these groups usually collect data on the specific product or service lines they support. Thus, there is usually a need to work with several such teams when developing large agent models.

Regardless of their place in the organization, data collection groups typically develop statistical reports that the group is comfortable delivering to other parts of the organization. Requests for disaggregated or raw data are often considered a threat and are commonly viewed with suspicion by such groups. This distrust can be overcome, but this usually takes time and consistent efforts to develop trust. It is generally wise to budget at least two to four times the initial estimated calendar days for obtaining unprocessed data from other parts of an

Real Price	Model Price	Difference
$ 10.84	$ 10.35	-5%
$ 10.91	$ 10.41	-5%
$ 10.14	$ 9.81	-3%
$ 9.24	$ 9.33	1%
$ 9.04	$ 9.23	2%
$ 9.72	$ 9.57	-2%
$ 10.66	$ 10.19	-5%
$ 10.99	$ 10.49	-5%
$ 10.41	$ 9.99	-4%
$ 9.46	$ 9.44	0%

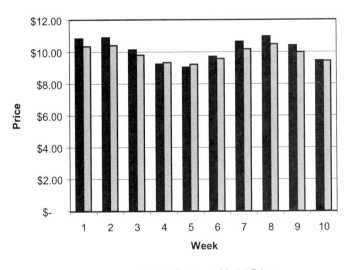

FIGURE 12.9 Matching modeled prices with real prices.

organization. Disaggregated data can and often is successfully obtained from other parts of an organization. It just takes some attention to the human factors involved and enough time to allow trust to be developed. If agent-modeling teams identify the kinds of data they need for the next iterative step early in the process, then the data will usually be available when it is needed.

Obtaining raw or lightly processed data from external organizations is usually more difficult than obtaining it from internal sources. The main hurdle is intellectual property concerns. Naturally, most outside organizations that make data available sell their data as a service. Similar to internal data collection groups, they usually provide this service in the form of statistical reports. Unlike internal groups, the source data is usually their core asset. If this data is shared in full detail, then the outside organization's ability to sell future services is reduced or eliminated. This makes these organizations generally quite reluctant to share this data without substantial fees. Fortunately, there are several solutions. These solutions include the use of data set samples and surrogate data sources. Data set samples are discussed next. The use of surrogate data sources is discussed later in this chapter.

In many cases, only a limited subset of the data held by external organizations is usually needed for agent modeling. For example, consider an outside organization that has surveyed a panel of 25,000 new and used car buyers about their car-buying habits over a ten-year period. This data certainly could be used as an important information source for an agent-based model of the new and used car market. However, not all of this data is actually needed for the modeling effort. Typically, the data from only a few thousand panelists will be needed to form a reasonable picture of the car buyer's habits. Furthermore, the average car buyer purchases a new vehicle every three or so years. Thus, only about six years of data will probably be needed to complete the model. Two or three years will most likely not be enough to capture the multiyear dynamics, but six or so years will cover most of this activity. Ultimately, only a few thousand purchaser or panelist traces are needed for each of six years from a ten-year 25,000 purchaser data set. This selected subset will be far more affordable then the full data set. When negotiating for such data, be sure to have the subsets drawn from the full panel data in a statistically representative way. While obvious at first glance, such considerations are often not made explicit in the heat of negotiations.

Another common challenge with obtaining data is making sure the data is in an appropriate format. This is not just a matter of simple file structure conversion. As will be discussed later, a variety of issues are involved, including ensuring that the data is internally traceable and can be tied back to external data sources.

Internal traceability refers to the ability to connect related records in a data set. Returning to the automotive purchases panel, the data would be internally traceable if all of the car purchases for each panelist could be uniquely identified so that individual purchase histories can be reconstructed. Ensuring that the data is internally traceable is a nontrivial challenge in large data sets collected over long periods. The biggest issue is ensuring coding consistency since it is common for coding standards to be periodically changed in long-term panels.

Ties back to external data sources are similar to internal traceability. In the car purchases panel, one example of an external tie is to connect both the panelists and their purchases to geographic locations. This could be used for a variety of purposes, including seeing whether panelists tend to purchase cars at dealerships near their homes or if the panelists tend to purchase at geographically clustered groups of dealerships. From an agent-modeling perspective, such data could be used to develop dealership site selection simulations. Having enough entries in the data set to connect records to external sources such as map databases or geographic information systems is critical when developing models to address questions broader than the data sets themselves. Geographic information systems are discussed in chapter 10.

Direct measurements of facts in a given business situation are sometimes difficult to obtain. In these situations, proxy or surrogate data can be a good alternative. Surrogate data consists of measurements of situations that are different from, but related to, the situation of interest. An example from the sporting goods arena is the measurement of customer satisfaction with the quality of purchased goods. Customer satisfaction and engagement can be challenging to measure, even excluding the occasional "customer from hell" (Knutson et al. 1999; Harris 2003). However, knowing something about customer satisfaction with purchases could be extremely useful. One hypothetical answer is to use a correlated variable such as return rates. This value may be a useful surrogate for the real value to be measured since increasing return rates probably indicate falling customer satisfaction.

The first key challenge with the use of surrogate variables is identifying or discovering them. The process of efficient discovery begins with knowledge of the domain or subject being modeled. Many variables to be modeled are already used for existing planning and operations. The starting point is to ask whether the needed values are currently being estimated using other values. If so, these estimates can usually be used. If not, then domain experts can be consulted to find values that they believe may be related. If the experts are stumped, a little creative thinking and a few foolish questions can go a long way.

Creative thinking about what might be related to the variables of interest means considering which inputs determine the results of interest and which outputs depend on these results. Simply put, if an organization cares about a variable, then that variable must have a quantitative effect somewhere at some time. Looking for the causes of a variable and for its effects can lead to a reasonable surrogate or surrogates. Returning to the customer satisfaction example from the retail store service side, maybe repeat business is a good surrogate. However, what if the chain is a high-volume discounter? Maybe combining two variables by considering repeat business while excluding price-cutting sales is a better indicator.

Foolish questions go hand in hand with creative thinking. The first few candidate surrogate variables suggested by a modeler will often seem a little strange to the experts. After all, the experts said they were stumped. Thus, the candidate variables actually have to sound at least somewhat strange at this point. If the potential surrogates are obvious, then the experts probably would have suggested these candidates themselves! Pressing the experts to consider possibilities outside of the usual range of thinking is required here! Following this approach, a clear understanding of the area being modeled combined with creative thinking can usually be leveraged to find proxy data sources.

The second key challenge with the use of surrogate variables is documenting or quantifying their utility. Once potential surrogate variables are identified, their correlation to the target variable must be documented. The fundamental issue is that, by definition, large samples of the target variable are not available. Generally, if target variable samples can be found, then statistical techniques such as calculating correlation coefficients can be used (Mendenhall et al. 1990;

McClave and Benson 1994). If samples of the target variable are not available, then expert opinion can be substituted. In any case, the potential level and range of correlation should be considered as well as any systematic biases. The level of correlation indicates how well a given variable or set of variables predicts the target. The range of correlation shows the bounds on the surrogate variables for which the correlations are valid. Systematic biases indicate the expected characteristic errors.

Obtaining the Data

The process of obtaining the data is discussed in detail in the "Identifying Potential Data Sources" section of this chapter. As previously stated, obtaining data usually requires the development of working relationships with either other groups within the organization or with outside groups. This process can and is regularly done. However, be sure to budget sufficient time to complete this process.

Evaluating the Quality of Data

Evaluating the quality of the data requires a significant amount of effort but is well worth the time. Properly vetted data is the foundation of effective modeling and reliable model use. The keys to understanding data quality were presented earlier in this chapter in the "Data Quality" section.

Selecting the Next Step

Once the data has been obtained and its quality has been evaluated, there are three options to deal with it. These options are to accept the data as it is, improve the data quality through data cleaning, or to return to step one and refine the model's data requirements.

Accepting the data in its current state is the simplest choice. Choosing this option requires that the evaluated quality of the data be high enough to support the questions to be answered with the model. As discussed in preceding sections, the real goal here is not to have data of arbitrarily high quality. The goal is to have data that is good enough to address the questions being asked. As discussed in chapter 2, if the questions are strategic, then 15% to 30% forecast accuracy is usually appropriate. Tactical questions generally need 10% to 15% forecast accuracy while operational questions are more commonly in the 3% to 10% range. Of course, all of these numbers depend on the area of interest. One word of caution, though: managers and executives typically overestimate the required accuracies. This is natural. Most people want other people's estimates to be as accurate as possible. Decision-makers who are responsible for making vital choices are even more motivated to have exact numbers. Personality selection factors that help people to become high-level decision-makers can amplify management interest in accuracy. However, accuracy is not free.

In general, the more accurate a model is, the more time is generally needed to design and develop the model. Obtaining increasingly accurate data is one of the major costs. The returns from modeling depend on the application but generally decrease with increasing accuracy. This is to say that initial improvements in model accuracy may yield substantial business returns. Further model accuracy improvements usually produce smaller business returns. Thus, determining the appropriate level of accuracy for a given model is a matter of efficient investment. The model should be accurate enough to yield meaningful results for decision-makers but not be more accurate, and thus more costly, than necessary. At first glance, finding this balance might seem quite difficult. Fortunately, there is a good approach to achieving this balance. The incremental model design and development process discussed throughout this book allows models to grow in stages over time with regular management feedback. Following this approach, the accuracy of the models can increase until the required levels are obtained while simultaneously limiting efforts to only those tasks that are necessary.

Dinner Is Served

Input data can be provided to models in several basic storage forms, including scalar form and vector form. The data itself can be either qualitative or quantitative (Svensson 1998). Each of these input types has different handling requirements.

Qualitative Data

Qualitative data describes nonnumeric situations in terms such as red or blue (Svensson 1998). Numeric encodings are commonly used for qualitative values, but these encodings are often arbitrary. Qualitative data can be unordered or ordered.

Unordered data is also called categorical data. Categorical data describes situations in groups or classes such as running shoes that are green, blue, or red. Arbitrarily assigned numbers are often used to encode the categories. An example is denoting green shoes with the value one, blue shoes with the value two, and red shoes with the value three. This encoding does not imply that red shoes are three times better than green shoes.

Ordered data is generally encoded using ordinal numbers (Svensson 1998). Ordinal numbers are numbers that imply an order but do not specify an amount (Oxford 2004). An example is a sporting goods store checkout system that first records the customer loyalty card, if any, then records the items to be purchased, and then finally processes the payment method, such as a credit card. Say that a value of one is assigned to the first checkout stage, two is assigned to the second stage, and three is assigned to the third stage. Clearly, recording the items to be purchased is not two-thirds as important as payment processing.

There are a variety of ways to use qualitative data in agent models. These methods are discussed in chapters 3 and 6.

Quantitative Data

Quantitative data describes situations with numbers that are in some sense measured. These quantitative values are generally encoded using cardinal numbers (Oxford 2004). Cardinal numbers are numbers such as prices that can be meaningfully compared to one another and can be used in ratios. Quantitative data is either discrete or continuous. Data is discrete when it is "individually separate and distinct," such as the numbers 1, 2, and 15 (Oxford 2004). Data is continuous when it is broken up, such as the numbers 0.9, 0.99, 0.999, 0.9999, and so on (Oxford 2004).

It is important to note that quantitative data only addresses the measured value. For example, a $75.00 running shoe is half the price of a $150.00 running shoe. However, the $75.00 running shoes may be better or worse than the $150.00 pair. The only thing the number indicates is that the $75.00 shoes cost only half as much as the $150.00 pair. Approaches to using quantitative data for agent modeling are described in chapters 3 and 6.

Data Storage Forms

Scalar data is the simplest type of quantitative data that can be used for modeling. Scalar data is individual point data. An example is the average historical price of crude oil worldwide. For practical purposes, there is one unique number. Storing scalars is usually easier than the other data types since they are simpler in structure. Scalar data is definitely used in business applications, but it is less common than more complex data types. Furthermore, because there is relatively little scalar data in most business applications, it is somewhat easier to manage.

Vector or indexed data can also be provided. Indexed data is data that can be meaningfully organized into a list of similar elements. An example is the annual average price of crude oil worldwide. There are many prices, in this case one for each year. Most business data is vector or indexed. Among indexed data, temporal data is the most common. However, other types of vector data are also used. This includes data that is spatially indexed such as sales regions or indexed by topic such as employee records. Indexed data is commonly stored in relational databases. It is important to note that the indexing referred to in this chapter is not relational database indexing. Relational database indexing is normally done to allow individual database records to be uniquely identified and to increase database execution speed. The indexing referred to in this chapter describes the overall structure of specific sets of data.

Temporal data is data that is indexed by time. The previously mentioned annual crude oil production data is an example that is indexed by year. Other examples of time-indexed data are customer sales records and monthly profit values. Time indexing is often combined with other indexing approaches. Customer sales records are normally indexed by the transaction time stamp and customer identifier. Profit values can be indexed by month and by business unit, among other indices.

Several formats of temporal data are commonly used, including time-indexed and event formats. These formats can store the same data. Both formats are commonly used since they provide different trade-offs between storage size and manipulation complexity.

Time-indexed input is the simplest form of time-series data storage. Time-indexed data stores a value for each time in a given range. Time-indexed data follows the classic spreadsheet style of storage with each column of data containing a different type of value and each row containing the values for each period. An example is weekly shoe retail prices. Ten weeks of data for one stock-keeping unit (SKU) for this example is shown in figure 12.10.

Storing temporal data in a time-indexed form has several advantages. First, it is a relatively simple format compared to event storage and thus is easy to understand. Second, time-indexed data is straightforward to work with. Most common business programs such as spreadsheets and databases can work directly in times-series format. Furthermore, most basic summary operations such as averages, minimums, maximums, and standard deviations can be immediately calculated from times-series data. Third, time series can be read into many models and simulations quite easily. The major disadvantage of time-series data is its size. Time-series data files often can be quite large since every value is included for every period. This is particularly true for situations where the data changes slowly. All of the values that are repeated from period to period can result in unnecessarily large files. This is one major reason for scripted or event-based data.

Scripted or event-based data only records data changes or new values instead of storing all values. Returning to the weekly running shoe price example, it can be seen that the shoe price is usually $91.00. These values could be recorded in time-indexed form. However, the result would be the repetition of the

Week	Shoe SKU 4186898 Sales Price
1	$ 91.00
2	$ 91.00
3	$ 91.00
4	$ 75.00
5	$ 91.00
6	$ 70.00
7	$ 91.00
8	$ 91.00
9	$ 72.00
10	$ 91.00
11	$ 91.00
12	$ 80.00

FIGURE 12.10 Example of time-indexed storage of weekly shoe prices for a selected shoe SKU.

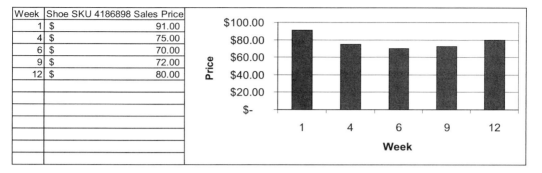

Week	Shoe SKU 4186898 Sales Price
1	$ 91.00
4	$ 75.00
6	$ 70.00
9	$ 72.00
12	$ 80.00

FIGURE 12.11 Example of event-based storage of sales prices for a shoe SKU.

same values over and over again. Instead, all that needs to be stored is the price values that deviate from the standard shelf price. Thus, only the initial price and the special sales prices need to be recorded. This is shown in figure 12.11. Here, by convention, the standard price is taken to be the first entry, in this case $91.00, and all of the remaining prices are taken to be sale prices for one week each. Continuing this example, the price for week 4 is $75.00 since this value is recorded in the data set. The price for week 5 is $91.00 since there is no entry for week 5 and $91.00 is the default price.

Event-based or scripted data has several advantages. First, event files can take up less space than times-series data since only the required data is stored. Second, event files can sometimes be processed faster than time-series data since only changes need to be read. Third, event files can sometimes fit more naturally into simulations since they can be used to update values only when there is a change rather than requiring continuous updates. Fourth, event data can sometimes be easier for people to interpret than time-series data since event data emphasizes changes. Unfortunately, there are also some disadvantages to the event data format.

The disadvantages of the event data format include complexity, difficulties in working with tools, and excessive size when the data repeatedly changes. As previously stated, the event format takes somewhat more effort to work with, particularly when tools such as spreadsheets are involved. In addition, event data files are only smaller than time-series files when the data rarely changes. If the data changes during most time intervals, then the savings from event data storage can be negligible. Furthermore, if the time intervals are predefined, then times-series data does not have to

contain the time stamps for the individual time steps. However, since event data does not imply a time step, the time stamp for each step must always be stored. This can make event data files for rapidly changing data larger than the corresponding fixed-step time-series files.

Of course, it is possible to create hybrid files that combine aspects of both the time-series and event data formats. These files can gain some of the performance advantages of each of the formats at the expense of greater complexity. Advanced approaches include the use of standard file formats such as the Hierarchical Data Format (HDF) (NCSA 2004). HDF files are discussed in more detail in chapter 10.

Other types of vector data can also be used. An example is the delta modulation technique inspired by analog signal processing (Steinmetz and Nahrstedt 2002). The delta modulation data format is a hybrid of the time-indexed and event data formats. With delta modulation, the changes from period to period are recorded for each period. The delta in the name refers to the subtraction of the last value from the current value. Modulation refers to the process of transmitting or storing changes over time. Delta modulation is sometimes used when the rate of change is the most important issue. It can also save space if the period-to-period differences or changes use much less space than the absolute values or few changes occur. An example showing delta modulation for the previous weekly running shoe prices is shown in figure 12.12. Since it is an optimization, delta modulation should only be used when simpler file storage formats such as time indexing or event storage are shown to take up too much space or when explicitly identifying differences is paramount. More advanced and complicated forms of compression can also be used. However, there is generally a sharp tradeoff with ease of access.

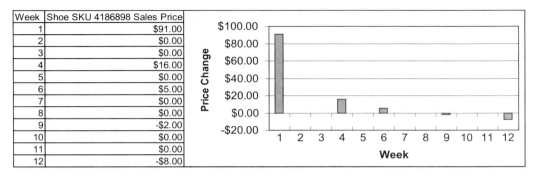

Week	Shoe SKU 4186898 Sales Price
1	$91.00
2	$0.00
3	$0.00
4	$16.00
5	$0.00
6	$5.00
7	$0.00
8	$0.00
9	-$2.00
10	$0.00
11	$0.00
12	-$8.00

FIGURE 12.12 Example of delta modulation storage of weekly shoe prices for a selected shoe SKU.

As discussed in chapter 6, objects are separable containers that encapsulate properties and behaviors. The properties define what an object is. The behaviors define what an object does. Objects are normally defined using a nested hierarchy of properties and behaviors. Each member of the hierarchy is called a class.

Each class defines a set of properties and behaviors. Classes normally are defined as incremental extensions to other classes. The extension classes are said to be children of the extended parent classes. An example of a Unified Modeling Language (UML) class hierarchy for sporting goods retail stores is shown in figure 12.13. UML is discussed in detail in chapter 6. The top-level class is the retail store itself. The subclasses show specialized types of stores such as freestanding stores, embedded mall locations, and online outlets.

The properties and behaviors in each class normally add to those of their parents. Individual objects are defined to be a representative of exactly one class. The behavior of individual objects is given by the class they represent. The content of individual objects is defined by the properties for each class. Thus, objects of a shared class all have the same behaviors but each object can potentially have different contents. It is differences in content that can allow two objects of the same class to respond differently to the same inputs.

Clearly, object data encodes the properties of individual objects. In some ways, object data can be seen as data that is indexed by topic. There are some

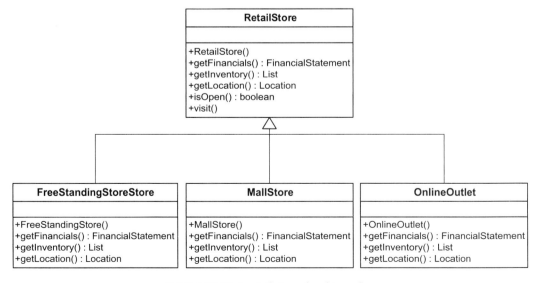

FIGURE 12.13 A retail store class hierarchy.

differences, though. Object data is concentrated by a single specific topic index, namely the objects themselves.

As further detailed in chapter 3, agents are self-contained objects. This means that agents are naturally thought of as objects with the special ability to sequence their own behavior. In this vein, agents can be considered objects with rules for behavior and "rules to change the rules" (Casti 1998). The basic rules sequence the agent's behaviors. The "rules to change the rules" allow adaptation so that the agent can modify its behavior over time (Casti 1998).

Storing objects is in many ways straightforward, with one catch. The properties of each object simply need to be stored. A basic row-oriented or spreadsheet-like style can be used as shown in figure 12.14. Figure 12.14 shows agent properties down each column and agents along each row. If dynamic changes in the object properties need to be recorded, then the basic row-oriented storage format can be elaborated to include a time-indexed value. Formats that are more sophisticated can of course be built on top of this basic idea. Unfortunately, there is a catch. The example only shows simple or primitive properties such as numbers and names. What about storing connections to other agents?

It is possible for an agent to have links to other agents. For example, a sporting goods chain district manager might have a list of store managers in their region. The result is an agent that maintains a list of agents. Another example is a retail manager agent that contains a reference to the retail store that it manages. Storing this more complex data leads to object serialization (Hericko et al. 2003).

"Object serialization is the process of writing the state of an object" in memory to a disk or other storage location (Hericko et al. 2003). Serialization requires storing the object itself and all of its connected objects. The term "serialization" is used since the objects are translated from a complex multidimensional web in computer memory to a linear or serial file on a disk. Serialization uses a type of link tracing that directly stores the primitive contents of objects in a simple form as well as storing references to other objects and their contents. Usually, the first time a new object is encountered it is assigned a unique identifier and then the contents of the object are stored. From then on, any additional reference to the object simply results in the storage of the unique identifier.

Object "deserialization is the process of rebuilding" stored data "back into an object" (Hericko et al. 2003). Deserialization requires restoration of the serialized object itself and all of its connected objects. Deserialization directly restores the primitive contents of objects as well as reconnecting references to other objects and their contents. Usually, the first time a new object is encountered it is created and then the contents of the object are restored. From then on, any additional reference to the object simply results in the reconnection of the object based on its unique identifier.

	Agent Name	Agent Type	Used Capacity (MWh)	Available Capacity (MWh)	Target Capacity (MWh)	Cost or Value ($/MWh)	Initial Price ($)	Current Price ($)	Current Profit ($)	Last Profit ($)
	(Offset 0)	(Offset 1)	(Offset 2)	(Offset 3)	(Offset 4)	(Offset 5)	(Offset 6)	(Offset 7)	(Offset 8)	(Offset 9)
3	Company 1	GENCO	141	141	58	$9.09	$10.00	$10.00	$815.14	$237.98
4	Company 2	GENCO	129	129	37	$9.04	$9.04	$14.04	$751.77	$223.73
5	Company 3	GENCO	113	113	15	$10.99	$10.99	$10.99	$438.30	$0.00
6	Company 4	GENCO	102	199	197	$9.87	$9.87	$14.87	$508.92	$180.03
7	Company 5	GENCO	0	195	186	$10.30	$10.30	$15.30	$0.00	$92.84
8	Company 6	GENCO	192	192	177	$10.39	$10.39	$10.39	$859.80	$73.89
9	Company 7	GENCO	163	163	103	$10.78	$10.78	$10.78	$667.21	$0.00
10	Company 8	GENCO	151	151	76	$10.86	$10.86	$10.86	$605.16	$0.00
11	Company 9	GENCO	0	200	200	$9.95	$9.95	$14.95	$0.00	$165.07
12	Company 10	GENCO	149	149	73	$10.87	$10.87	$10.87	$595.83	$0.00

FIGURE 12.14 Spreadsheet-style agent storage.

Object serialization is a natural storage format for agents. Fortunately, serialization tools are widely available in most object-oriented programming environments (Foxwell 1999; Archer 2001). In most object-oriented programming environments, serialization can be directly used to store whole agent simulations with a few lines of code. Furthermore, many enterprise databases such as the Oracle database system and Microsoft SQL Server directly support object serialization (Microsoft Corporation 2004; Oracle Corporation 2004).

A Market Example

The Electricity Market Complex Adaptive System (EMCAS) model simulates the operation of an electric power market. It includes a detailed model of the power grid, the companies that operate it, and the consumers that depend on it. The model requires several basic kinds of input data for each scenario:

1. The model requires data on electricity consumer types, locations, and demand levels. The types include residential consumers, commercial customers, and industrial customers. Consumer demands are normally related to several factors:
   (a) Consumer demands are usually related to the weather, with particularly warm or cold days yielding greater demands.
   (b) Consumer demands are usually related to the day of the week, with weekdays having more demands than weekends.
   (c) Consumer demands are usually related to special occurrences such as major sports events.
   (d) Consumer demands are usually related to the time of day on a diurnal cycle, with the time in late afternoon often having the highest demand.
   (e) Consumer demands are usually related to price, but only weakly and on a long-term basis.
   (f) Consumer demands are usually related to economic conditions, with better times yielding greater demand.
2. The model requires data on generation companies:
   (a) The company's current or expected future generator inventories need to be defined. The generator operating data such as capacity, type, and costs are required.

(b) The company's current or expected future financial figures are needed to the level of detail commonly found in a public balance sheet.
(c) The company's current operating strategies may need to be defined, if the modeling goal is to simulate the existing marketplace.
(d) The company's potential future range of strategies may need to be defined, if the modeling goal is to simulate possible future marketplaces. The range of strategies may be extremely broad if EMCAS's strategic adaptation features are used or may be much narrower if laws or corporate governance limits the company's options.
3. The model requires data on transmission companies:
   (a) The structure of the "long haul" transmission grid is required at least to the level of detail commonly found on regional transmission maps. Higher resolution data can be used to produce more detailed output results.
   (b) The financial and operating data for these companies is needed at the public balance sheet level of detail.
4. The model requires data on distribution companies:
   (a) As with the other companies, the financial data for distribution companies is needed at the public balance sheet level of detail.
   (b) The operating strategy for the "last mile" distribution grid is required at the consumer-type level of detail.

Of course, how this data is collected depends on the specific model use. For one study commissioned by a state regulatory agency, the goal was to study price stability and possible transmission line bottlenecks about three years into the future within their state. The agency was preparing to guide their state through the difficult transition from a highly regulated system to a deregulated market. This difficulty was compounded by the fact that the future market rules were not defined. Certainly, the rules were expected to promote competition, but not much else was known. In this vein, the authors spend enough time modeling markets that they are often asked if they believe in the "free market?" The answer is simple, "Yes, of course, but which free market?" There are many ways to structure market rules. Each of these approaches has different consequences that depend sensitively on the specific situation in which they are used. In fact, there are so many market rule options that market design is a meaningful specialty. For example, the EMCAS model can be used to support market design efforts.

Electric power market design is especially difficult due to the need to instantaneously balance supply and demand. In most markets, supply can temporarily mismatch demand by changing inventories. Demand can also exceed supply through curtailments. Unfortunately, with a few exceptions, electric power cannot be efficiently stored in bulk quantities. Demand curtailments do occur in power markets, but they often have serious consequences.

Planned changes in electric power systems tend to take place over long periods of time and with substantial publicity. For example, it usually takes several years to build a new power plant. Quite a few of these years are spent obtaining public permits. Power lines take even more time, if they can be built at all. Thus, the structure of the electric power grid expected for the period to be simulated was relatively well known. The question was how consumers and companies might fare in this future deregulated configuration under certain postulated market rules.

Generation company data was collected from a variety of public sources, including government databases and proprietary internal databases. The company's inventories were based on existing plants minus units scheduled to be shut down before the study period plus units scheduled for addition. The generator capacity and type data was available from public power pool data. This data was examined using a variety of tools and manually cleaned. Operating cost is highly confidential data for most companies since it sets practical lower bounds on bid pricing and is an important determinant of profits. Since this was a public study, the operating cost data was estimated strictly using the publicly available unit types. For example, large coal-fired units have well-known ranges of operating costs. Engineering judgments were used to select reasonable values in this range for each large coal-fired plant.

Since the simulation run was to start in a future year, data describing the likely future configuration of the companies was needed. Note, though, that the goal was not to predict the exact future situation, but rather it was to discover potential future weaknesses in the market. As such, repeated runs that tried alternative company strategies were needed. The results did not say which strategies each company would use or whether or not the companies would ever use such strategies. Instead, the results indicated which strategies, if any, the companies might be able to use to raise prices. Again, the goal was to find out if such strategies exist. Of course, the real companies might choose to avoid these strategies.

The transmission company data was collected and cleaned in much the same way as the generation company data. These data elements originally included only the operating and connection data but not the map locations. The locations were added using a specially written program that automatically looked up the power grid access point's address in a U.S. street database. The results of the program were then manually checked.

The distribution company data was collected and cleaned following the same approach used for the other companies. The "last mile" distribution grid data was obtained by combining tap point data from the long-haul transmission grid with information on consumer locations.

The consumer data was found by merging two public sources of data on power consumption and then scaling the results to account for future growth. The first data source gave detailed tap-by-tap demands but only for a few hours a year. The second data source provided hourly data for a full year but only at a highly aggregated level. To run the study the whole load needed to be recreated from the data slices that were available. This was accomplished by using a linear program to find a simple surface with the minimum simultaneous distance from all of the known points. This simple curve was used to fill in the remaining data. Linear programming is described in chapter 5.

Clearly, data for complex studies such as that discussed above requires combining many data sources over a period of time. Persistently following the recommendations of this chapter can and does pay off!

Summary

Data collection and cleaning is all about connecting data users to the appropriate data sources. Along the way, the data sources need to be evaluated and the data they contain may need to be cleaned. This chapter showed how to identify and evaluate appropriate data sources as well as how to clean them when required.

References

Ackoff, R. L. (1989). From Data to Wisdom. *Journal of Applied Systems Analysis* **16**: 3–9.

Archer, T. (2001). *Inside C#*. Redmond, Wash.: Microsoft Press.

Batagelj, V. and A. Mrvar (1998). Pajek—Program for Large Network Analysis. *Connections* **21**(2): 47–57.

Batagelj, V. and A. Mrvar (2004). *Pajek: A Program for Large Network Analysis*. Ljubljana, Slovenia: University of Ljubljana.

Berleant, D., M.-P. Cheong, C. Chu, Y. Guan, A. Kamal, S. Ferson, et al. (2003). Dependable Handling of Uncertainty. *Reliable Computing* **9**: 1–12.

Brassel, K., F. Bucher, E.-M. Stephan, and A. Vckovski (1995). Completeness. In S. C. Guptill and J. L. Morrison (Eds.), *Elements of Spatial Data Quality*. Oxford: Elsevier Science, pp. 81–108.

Casti, J. L. (1998). *Would-Be Worlds: How Simulation Is Changing the World of Science*. New York: Wiley.

Chapanis, A. (1953). Random-Number Guessing Behavior. *American Psychologist* **8**: 332.

Cleveland, H. (1982). Information as Resource. *The Futurist* (Dec.), 34–39.

Eliot, T. S. (1934). *The Rock*. London: Faber & Faber.

Foxwell, H. (1999). Java 2 Software Development Kit. *Linux Journal* (online).

Gallian, J. A. (1996). Error Detection Methods. *ACM Computing Surveys* **28**(3): 504–517.

Gilovich, T., R. Vallone, and A. Tversky (1985). The Hot Hand in Basketball: On the Misperception of Random Sequences. *Cognitive Psychology* **17**: 295–314.

Harris, R. (2003). Engagement: The Missing Link. *European Retail Digest* No. 38, 1–7.

Hericko, M., M. B. Juric, I. Rozman, S. Beloglavec, and A. Zivkovic (2003). Object Serialization Analysis and Comparison in Java and NET. *ACM SIGPLAN Notices* **38**(8): 44–54.

Hibbard, W. (1998). VisAD: Connecting People to Computations and People to People. *Computer Graphics* **32**(3): 10–12.

Hill, T. P. (1999). The Difficulty of Faking Data. *Chance* **12**(3): 27–31.

Infantry News (2002). The Integrated Unit Simulation System at the U.S. Army Soldier Systems Center Will Emerge, Beginning This Fall. *U.S. Army Infantry School Infantry News* (Summer).

Knutson, B. J., C. Borchgrevink, and B. Woods (1999). Validating a Typology of the Customer from Hell. *Journal of Hospitality and Leisure Marketing* **6**(3): 5–22.

McCaffrey, B. R. (2003). Lessons of Desert Storm. *Joint Force Quarterly* (Winter).

McClave, J. T. and P. G. Benson (1994). *Statistics for Business and Economics*. Englewood Cliffs, N.J.: Prentice-Hall.

Mendenhall, W., D. D. Wackerly, and R. L. Scheaffer (1990). *Mathematical Statistics with Applications*. Boston: PWS-Kent.

Microsoft Corporation (2004). *SQL Server*. Redmond, Wash.: Microsoft Corporation.

NCSA (2004). Hierarchical Data Format 5 Home Page. Champaign, Ill.: National Center for Super-computing Applications.

Oracle Corporation (2004). *Oracle Database System*. Redwood Shores, Cal.: Oracle Corporation.

Oxford (2004). *Compact Oxford English Dictionary Online*. Oxford: Oxford University Press.

Rahm, E. and H. H. Do (2000). Data Cleaning: Problems and Current Approaches. *IEEE Bulletin of the Technical Committee on Data Engineering* **23**(4): 3–113.

Ratnasingham, P. (1999). Risks in Low Trust Among Trading Partners in Electronic Commerce. *Computers and Security* **18**: 587–592.

Sharma, N. (2005). Available as http://www.personal.si.umich.edu/~nsharma/dikw_origin.htm

Steinmetz, R. and K. Nahrstedt (2002). *Multimedia Fundamentals*, Vol. 1: *Media Coding and Content Processing*. Indianapolis, Ind.: Prentice-Hall.

Svensson, E. (1998). Teaching the Measurement Process in Biostatistics. *Proceedings of the Fifth International Conference on Teaching of Statistics*. Singapore: International Association for Statistical Education.

Veregin, H. (1998). Data Quality Measurement and Assessment. *NCGIA Core Curriculum in GIScience*. Santa Barbara: University of California at Santa Barbara, National Center for Geographic Information and Analysis.

Wilson, J. R. (1996). Battle Labs: What Are They, Where Are They Going? *Acquisition Review Quarterly* (Winter), 63–74.

Winkler, W. E. (2003). Data Cleaning Methods. *Proceedings of the ACM Workshop on Data Cleaning, Record Linkage and Object Identification*. Washington, D.C.: Association for Computing Machinery.

Zeleny, M. (1987). Management Support Systems: Towards Integrated Knowledge Management. *Human Systems Management* **7**(1): 59–70.

13

Understanding and Presenting ABMS Results

Up to this point, this book has covered the fundamentals of agent modeling. Once the basics of agent modeling and how to build agent models are clear, there is a need to understand what comes out of agent-based models and how these results can be used to make an impact, to supply useful information, and to support decision-making. Agent-based model results are in many ways similar to results from traditional models and simulations, but the agent focus of ABMS adds some new dimensions and challenges. This chapter addresses some of the technical and practical issues involved in analyzing and interpreting results from agent-based models and simulations. It addresses questions such as the following:

- What kinds of results come out of agent-based simulation?
- What can be done with the results?
- What are the limitations of the results?

This chapter uses the agent-based supply chain simulation model introduced in chapter 5 to explore the types of results that are possible for agent models to produce. Along the way, the results of the model will be classified and analyzed. This chapter also considers the need for designing simulation runs and the need for designing sets of many simulation runs, many more than is the usual practice for standard simulation models, to fully understand system and agent behaviors. The key issue in analyzing agent simulation results is to understand how the micro-level behavioral rules of the agents, which are selectable or controllable in part, influence the macro-level behavior of the system as a whole. This chapter will also discuss how to take the results from an agent model, derive insights, and present them to decision-makers. This is the main objective—using an agent model to provide information and then to articulate that information to a decision-maker. The challenge is to take numbers and produce useful information.

Analyzing ABMS Results

We can do several things to extract the most important information from a model's results. In this chapter, the seven steps for understanding and presenting ABMS results are presented:

1. Record or log the model output. The model output log reflects the states of specific agents, the aggregate states of collections of agents, and the states of the system and the environment over time that are useful for explaining the model results.
2. Analyze the results through statistical analysis. Agent-based simulations produce substantial amounts of information on a wide range of possible outcomes. Statistical analysis can be applied to identify trends, likelihoods, and outliers. Unlike the assumptions often made in statistical analysis that all samples are independent and identically distributed, simulation models

produce time series of results in which there is a large degree of dependency among the values. Special statistical techniques are required.

3. Apply time-series analysis methods and pattern detection techniques to understand relationships among variables over time. Special methods developed for time-series analysis must be applied to understand the patterns embedded in the time-series data.

4. Conduct sensitivity analysis of key parameters. An important question concerning a model's results is how sensitive the results are to small changes, errors, or perturbations in the input data and agent parameters.

5. Sweep regions of the parameter space to understand agent and model behaviors over a broad range of parameter settings. Many times managers would like the system to operate primarily in regions where its behavior is predictable and even controllable. The key question is what agent operating parameter settings result in desirable system behavior.

6. Characterize model outputs over the parameter space. Sometimes understanding system behavior in regions of the parameter space is not enough, and managers need to characterize this behavior with reduced-form statistical models.

7. Present the results. How the results of a model are presented is often the key to their being understood and accepted by decision-makers. Advanced visualization techniques ease understanding and generate interest.

The Quest for Information from Models

Any model or simulation produces one or more of three types of results: (1) a single number, (2) a time series of numbers representing the behavior of important system variables over time, or (3) patterns of information that can be qualitatively described. For example, an optimization model produces a single number that represents the "optimal" solution or state of the system at some point in time. A simulation model by definition is a dynamic representation of a process and how it changes over time. Simulation models produce time series of numbers representing the important state variables of the system. These results are conditional upon the assumptions made about the system. Sometimes the interest in the output of a dynamic model is not so much with the actual numerical values as it is with a qualitative description of how the model, and presumably the

real system, behaves. For example, key information could be whether the industry will grow in the coming year rather than the precise amount by which it could grow.

From the analyst's perspective, the challenge is to classify the system's possible future behavior using understandable terminology that can be easily articulated to decision-makers. For example, important questions may be whether the process being modeled exhibits cyclic or periodic behavior and whether there are regular variations in the key state variables. If there are variations, how large are the troughs and the peaks, and when should the behavior be considered unstable versus stable? There is the issue of transient behavior. How can an analyst tell whether a system is going through a turbulent transition period that will in the end give way to stability without additional action? How does an analyst tell how long the transients will be? These are all important questions for which insights can be developed through an in-depth analysis of model outputs.

Example Results from the Supply Chain Model

The simple supply chain model was introduced in chapter 5. The remainder of this chapter will focus on analyzing the results from this model, which, although simple, is a remarkably rich source of system and agent behaviors. Model results presented in this chapter were originally produced by the systems dynamics version of the Beer Game simulation (Mosekilde et al. 1991). These results, including figures 13.1–13.17, and 13.19–13.20, are reproduced here using the agent-based version of the supply chain model introduced in chapter 5.

Figure 13.1 shows the inventory levels resulting from running the supply chain simulation for 60 periods. In this case, the inventory ordering parameter is set to 0.30 and the ratio of pipeline to inventory parameters is 0.15. This is a very simplified model of a supply chain, but it is capable of producing the full range of complex system behaviors observed in large-scale supply chain models and in real supply chains. And this complexity occurs solely by varying the settings for the two control parameters in the agent rules! For this case of order parameter settings, the supply chain appears to exhibit chaotic behavior (this can be shown to be true chaotic behavior in the mathematical sense). Initially, orders build as stocks are depleted in response to the ramp-up in customer demand from

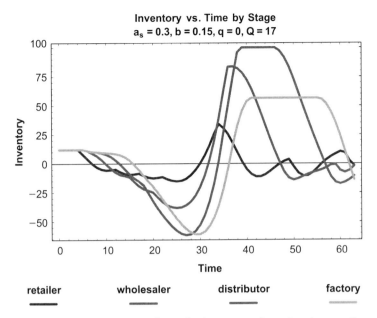

FIGURE 13.1 Inventory levels over time for all supply chain stages for a chaotic case. (Reproduced from Mosekilde et al. 1991, fig. 5a.)

four to eight items per period that occurs at time period 5.

The result of the agents' application of the ordering rules is to amplify the orders at each stage as they are received by upstream agents. Eventually shipments begin to arrive to fill the orders and, because of the delays in ordering and shipping, continue to build the inventories at each stage far beyond desirable levels. And then agents stop ordering altogether. This causes inventory levels to eventually crash, as no items are left in the pipeline to replenish stocks. The system continues through this process of building up and crashing almost in a cyclical fashion. In real supply chains, this amplification effect as one moves up the supply chain is called the "bull-whip effect" (Lee et al. 1997).

Figure 13.2 shows the customer orders and receipts for this case. Although the customer ordering rate is very regular, at four items for each of the first four time periods and eight items thereafter, customer deliveries fluctuate drastically as a result of the fluctuations in inventory. The situation is even worse than simply having the inventories fluctuate wildly—customers are not being satisfied.

One might expect that if the supply chain simulation were run long enough, it might settle down and

eventually stabilize. Figure 13.3 shows that this is not the case. Even if the simulation were run for thousands of periods, the system never settles down. There is not even a predictable pattern to the supply chain behavior that results. The system simply cannot adjust to the one-time change in customer demand that occurs at time 5!

Considering the inventory costs in the simple supply chain model, the results are even more ominous. Applying a stock-holding charge ($0.50/item/period) and a backorder charge ($2.00/item/period) to inventory levels gives a time series of the costs incurred. Figure 13.4 shows the inventory costs for the supply chain. The fluctuations in cost directly correspond to the fluctuations in inventory levels. Clearly, this rapidly changing and unpredictable behavior for the supply chain would be highly undesirable and unpleasant for all involved in its operation.

But is this chaotic behavior always the result of operating this particular supply chain, or are other behaviors possible? A slight variation in the ordering parameters for the agent decision rules can produce drastically different outcomes. Figure 13.5 shows a case where the system eventually settles down and adjusts to a stable state.[1] In this case, the initial shock

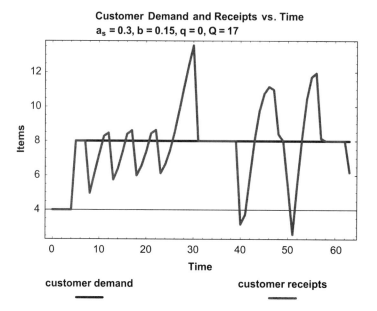

FIGURE 13.2 Customer orders and receipts for a chaotic case. (Reproduced from Mosekilde et al. 1991, fig. 5b.)

to the system when customer demand ramps up can be absorbed by the system as the individual agents adjust their ordering policies. The agent behaviors tend to counteract and dampen the effect rather than amplify it as in the previous chaotic case. Here, the net effect of the agent behaviors is to stabilize the system. Every agent's inventory and pipeline levels stabilize close to their desired levels. Managers generally would much prefer to operate the supply chain under stable rather than chaotic conditions

Besides these two types of behaviors, chaos and stability, other types of behaviors are possible. Periodic

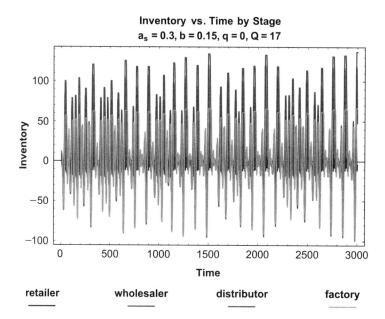

FIGURE 13.3 Long-run inventory levels for supply chain stages for a chaotic case. (Reproduced from Mosekilde et al. 1991, fig. 6a.)

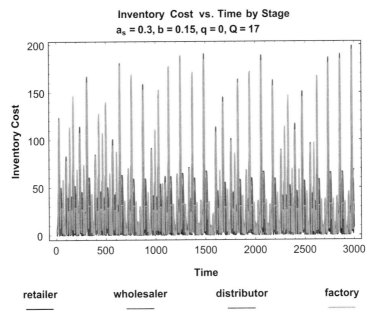

FIGURE 13.4 Long-run inventory costs for supply chain stages for a chaotic case.

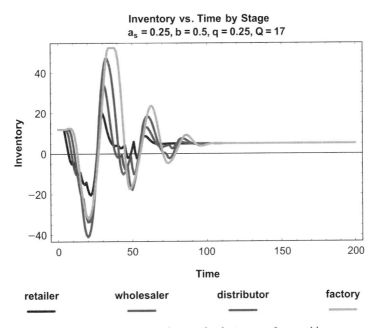

FIGURE 13.5 Inventory costs by supply chain stage for a stable case.

behavior is where the system exhibits recurring cycles or oscillations that are very predictable and easily described. Figure 13.6 shows the supply chain exhibiting periodic behavior for another set of agent ordering parameters.[2] Other behaviors are even more chaotic than that shown in figure 13.1. Changing the agent parameter settings slightly again results in the supply chain exhibiting what is known as hyperchaos, shown in figure 13.7.[3]

Some settings for the agent ordering parameters cause the system to exhibit unstable behavior in the short run, but without any further changes or shocks to the system, eventually give way to stable behavior in the long run. Figure 13.8 shows one such example.[4] The results of this simulation include large fluctuations in inventory in the short run, but these settle down in the long run to much smaller fluctuations that continue indefinitely. Here is a case where it might be worth considering whether it is desirable to ride out the pain incurred in the short run to get to a more acceptable longer-run situation.

An interesting aspect of this particular simulation is that customer demand and receipts completely stabilize in the long run even though inventories continue to fluctuate throughout all the stages of the supply chain— but at least the customers are satisfied. In fact, as shown in figure 13.9, in this case different stages of the supply chain exhibit different types of long-run behavior.[5] For example, the retailer is fairly stable, consistent with the observed stable provision of orders to customers. Going up the supply chain to the factory level, the stages find themselves in progressively more unstable situations. The factory experiences the most unstable behavior compared to the other stages. In this supply chain, the factory would have good reason to complain as it takes the brunt of the instabilities in the system.

This section has discussed some of the types of results that are produced by the simple but representative agent-based supply chain model. A wide range of system behaviors were observed, covering the spectrum from pure chaos to stability. All of these behaviors were the result of varying the ordering parameters in the agent decision rules. The supply chain model, although simple, produces all of the behaviors observed in most agent models. This makes it a useful tool for illustrating how to analyze the results of agent models in general. The following sections will discuss techniques and technical approaches to analyzing and boiling down these results into useful information.

Techniques for Analyzing ABMS Results

Agent-based simulations produce large amounts of information over a range of possible outcomes and assumptions. How can this vast amount of data be

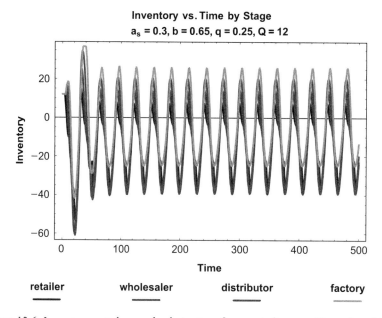

FIGURE 13.6 Inventory costs by supply chain stage for a periodic case. (Reproduced from Mosekilde et al. 1991, fig. 8.)

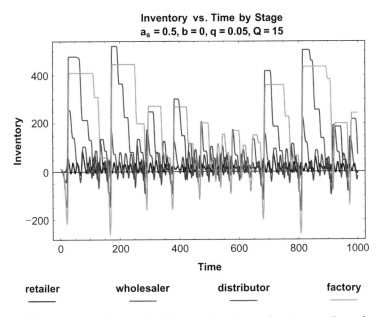

FIGURE 13.7 Inventory costs by supply chain stage for a hyperchaotic case. (Reproduced from Mosekilde et al. 1991, fig. 7a.)

reduced into a manageable amount of information? Traditional methods for analyzing the outputs of dynamic simulation models are used in conjunction with methods that specifically address ABMS results.

Statistical Analysis

Statistical analysis is the first line of analysis of model output. Model results can be analyzed for likely trends, outliers, and patterns. It is often the goal of statistical analysis to identify the underlying probability

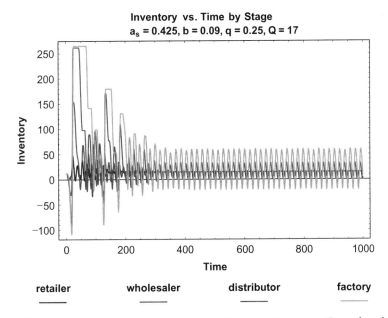

FIGURE 13.8 Inventory costs by supply chain stage for a transition case. (Reproduced from Mosekilde et al. 1991, fig. 9.)

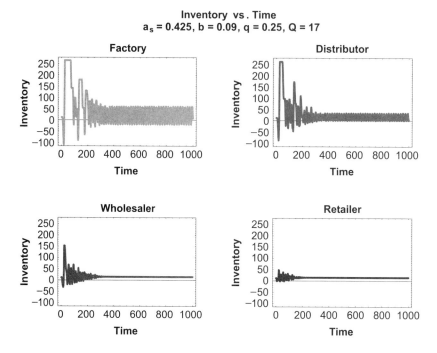

FIGURE 13.9 Inventory costs for all supply chain stages for a transient case.

distribution that characterizes the process that generated a given time series. This is possible if the underlying process is not changing or is stationary in statistical terminology. For example, in the supply chain model, after customer demand has ramped up to its new level of eight at time 5, the supply chain process is stationary. After the system adjusts to the ramp-up in customer demand, meaningful statistics on the process can be estimated.

Consider a typical discrete-event simulation model in which some of the variables have random values, that is, a stochastic simulation. In some cases, if an analyst were to look only at the time-series data coming out of a simulation model, not knowing the nature of the underlying processes in the simulation, it may be difficult to discern whether the model was stochastic or deterministic in nature. As has been discussed, the example supply chain model is completely deterministic, but the model results exhibit a great deal of variability for the chaotic cases.

Various statistics can be derived from the outputs of a simulation time series. Perhaps the most important statistic concerns the estimate of the mean or average value of a process. To take an example, suppose the

flow of customers through a grocery checkout line is simulated, and an analyst wishes to estimate the average customer waiting time. The waiting times vary from customer to customer depending on the time it takes for each customer to be checked out, which in turn depends on the particular items the customer purchases. Good modeling practice for a stochastic simulation dictates that the analyst performs many replications of the simulation runs. Each simulation run begins with a different starting value for the random number generator used in the simulation. By varying the random number seed, as it is called, from run to run, the model will produce a different outcome, a different realization of customer waiting times. When the outputs of all the simulation runs are taken together, the result is a distribution of waiting times for all the customers that is statistically significant. Then key questions can be meaningfully addressed using statistics, such as:

• What is the mean customer waiting time?
• What is the confidence interval for the mean?

Having a handle on the underlying probability distributions that allows us to estimate such things as the probability that a variable will exceed a threshold value or the probability that people will balk at waiting in long lines is important information for practical decision-making. Estimating the true mean of an observed quantity, say the mean number of people waiting in line, from a time series generated by a stochastic simulation model is not a simple task. Since the sample mean, which is computed as the average of a limited number of values observed in the simulation time series, is only an estimate and is itself a random variable, it is desirable to develop confidence estimates on how close the sample mean approximates the true mean. Establishing these confidence intervals requires estimating the variance of the sample mean. Unlike the assumptions made in elementary statistical analysis that all samples are independent and identically distributed, simulation models produce time series of results in which there is a large degree of dependency or autocorrelation among the time-series values. Because of this dependency, estimating the variance of the sample mean requires estimating various correlations among the time-series variables, an involved process. Sophisticated techniques for estimating the variance, such as batch means, must be employed. Variance reduction techniques include control variates, stratified sampling, antithetic variates, and importance sampling. Standard texts on tools for discrete-event simulation output analysis contain detailed descriptions of these procedures (Fishman 1973; Law 2007).

For purposes of statistical estimation, one might be able to make simplifying assumptions on the form of the underlying probability distributions for the processes being modeled. The typical assumption is that the underlying distribution is normal or Gaussian. Parametric statistics requires analysts to make strong assumptions about the form of the data being analyzed. For example, conventional hypothesis testing often requires that data be in the form of a bell-shaped curve (i.e., the data is in the form of a normal or Gaussian distribution). The parameters being referred to in the name "parametric statistics" are those of the assumed distributions. By using parametric statistical techniques and assuming normality, it is possible to simplify the estimate of the variance for the mean. On the other hand, nonparametric statistics assume comparatively little about the underlying process behind the data. Nonparametric statistics is an approach to characterizing numeric data that

does not require strong assumptions, such as normality, about the structure of the underlying data sources. For example, nonparametric monotone function statistics only assume that the underlying data is increasing in value over time (Hellerstein 1995). Other types of nonparametric statistics make different assumptions. There is a tradeoff when deciding between parametric and nonparametric statistical methods. For example, conventional hypothesis testing usually produces results with a greater probability of being true, or substantially tighter confidence intervals, than those from monotone functions. Parametric statistical methods usually produce more precise results than nonparametric statistics. However, nonparametric statistics can be properly applied in many situations where parametric statistics cannot be correctly used (Downey and Feitelson 1999).

Much has been written about the use and misuse of statistical methods. The use of statistics in analyzing ABMS results is not immune to misuse. Unfortunately, parametric statistics are often applied to situations that do not meet the requirements for their use (Downey and Feitelson 1999). An example of such misuse is the application of bell curve hypothesis testing with data that are not distributed in the shape of a bell curve. This problem most often occurs when the form of the underlying data is not known but parametric statistics that require specific forms are applied anyway. This inappropriate use can result in misplaced confidence in statistical results. Two of the leading causes of this type of statistical error are lack of knowledge and lack of tools. Lack of knowledge can combine with organizational habits to produce high confidence in low-quality forecasts. Lack of tools is another problem. Even if analysts know about the weakness of certain techniques and know how to do better, they may not have the computational tools to make nonparametric statistics practical.

Most of the common business computational environments such as spreadsheets and mathematical scripting environments can perform nonparametric statistics. However, special extensions, plug-ins, or add-ins are often required for this capability. This additional software at best usually needs to be custom loaded onto analysts' computers and often needs to be specially ordered as well.

Statistics for a supply chain simulation factory inventory are shown in figure 13.10. Key statistics summarizing the time series include the mean,

Statistics for Data Set:
  Factory Inventory Time Series

Time series length:	1600
Min value:	-74.25
Max value:	42.55
Range:	116.80
Sample mean:	3.89
Sample variance:	1032.9
Sample skewness:	-0.48
Sample kurtosis:	2.27
Quartiles:	{-17.21, 5.38, 36.63}
Mode:	42.12

FIGURE 13.10 Statistics for supply chain factory inventory.

median, mode, variance, skewness (provides information on the symmetry of the underlying probability distribution, 0 for a symmetric distribution), kurtosis (provides information on the tails of the underlying probability distribution, 3 for normal distribution), and quantiles. Figure 13.11 shows the frequency of attaining various inventory levels for the long-run portion of the simulation after the initial transients have dissipated. Although the mean inventory level is close to zero, large fluctuations occur over the range of −74 (the maximum backorders) to 42 (the maximum stock). Clearly, the inventory levels are not normally distributed. The most likely situation is for the inventory stock to be at its maximum level of about 42, indicated by

the mode. This is the point, as determined in the simulation, at which the factory stops placing orders because inventory levels have vastly exceeded desirable levels and orders from manufacturing are beginning to be filled.

The histogram in figure 13.11 shows that the distribution of factory inventory is far from normally distributed. Goodness-of-fit testing using various statistical tests, such as chi-squared and Kolmogorov–Smirnov, could be applied to this data to select the underlying probability distribution that best fits or characterizes the data.

Characterizing System Behavior

Classifying system behaviors and discovering the conditions under which the system exhibits these behaviors is important for managing any system. This chapter has discussed the results from a number of cases of the supply chain model in which only the agent parameters varied from simulation to simulation. At the highest level, systems exhibit either stable or unstable behaviors. Stable behavior is steady and predictable as the name implies. Unstable behavior comes in two forms: increasing without bound or varying continuously in ways that may or may not be predictable. The latter type of instability is of particular interest as it often arises in agent-based models.

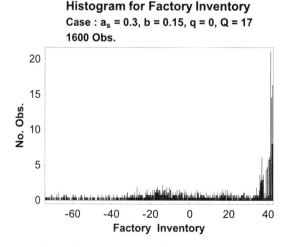

Histogram for Factory Inventory
Case : a_s = 0.3, b = 0.15, q = 0, Q = 17
1600 Obs.

FIGURE 13.11 Histogram for supply chain factory inventory.

We can begin to summarize the results for an entire time series by what is called a phase plot. In figure 13.12, the factory inventory is plotted along the horizontal axis and the distributor inventory is plotted along the vertical axis. At each step of the simulation, the factory and distributor inventories are plotted as a point in the two-dimensional plane of the phase plot. For the chaotic case shown in figure 13.12, groups of points that never repeat themselves but are contained within a bounded area can be observed. For a system that exhibits periodic behavior, the phase plot consists of a tight loop as shown in figure 13.13, in which inventory levels repeat themselves indefinitely. For a system that exhibits long-run stable behavior, every point in the time series eventually is the same, and the phase plot consists of a single point, the combination of stable values for the distributor and factory inventories. Phase plots summarize a time series in a way that reveals distinctive patterns of system behavior.

Time-Series Analysis and Pattern Detection

Periodic behavior is observed for many real-world business processes such as supply chains (Chen and Dreznen 2002) and business cycles (Helbing 2003). The supply chain example offers an opportunity to perform more sophisticated time-series analysis to see if there are any natural patterns or cycles embedded in the data. This would be useful information to manage the inventory. The factory inventory time-series is shown in figure 13.14. A sophisticated time-series pattern detection technique known as fast Fourier transform (FFT) analysis was applied to the factory inventory time-series to produce figure 13.15. The analysis of the factory inventory time-series reveals distinct periodic behavior embedded in the inventory fluctuations, as shown in figure 13.15. The peak frequency at which the inventory levels repeat themselves is 0.03 cycles per day, which corresponds to a cycle length or period of approximately 30 days. Every 30 days inventory levels nearly repeat themselves for both positive (stock) and negative (backorder) levels. There is a natural periodicity to the system in terms of factory inventory levels, yet there is nothing cyclical in the input data that is causing this periodic system behavior! The single increase in demand that occurred at time 5 created a wave in the supply chain operation that persists indefinitely,

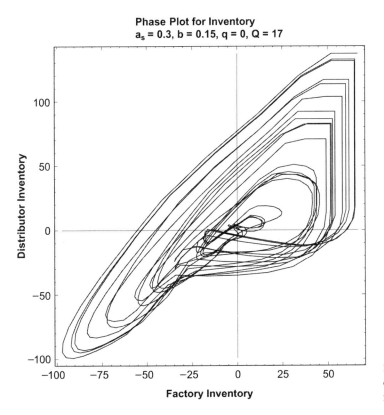

FIGURE 13.12 Phase plot for distributor and factory inventory for a chaotic case.

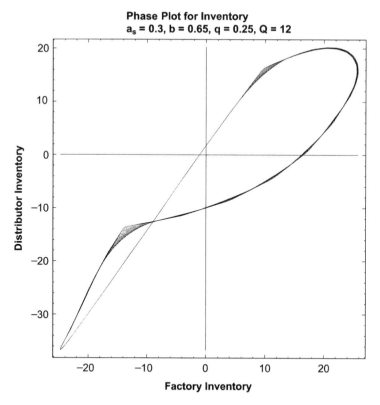

FIGURE 13.13 Phase plot for distributor and factory inventory for a periodic case.

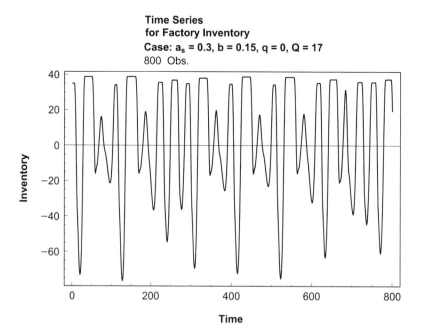

FIGURE 13.14 Factory inventory time series for a chaotic case.

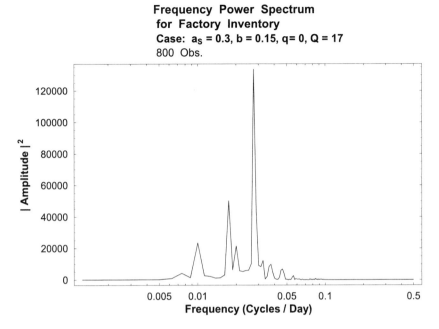

FIGURE 13.15 Time-series analysis of factory inventory.

even after the original cause has long passed. This example demonstrates that even in data that appears to be highly chaotic, there may be strong patterns that provide useful information for managing operations.

Sensitivity Analysis

The objective of sensitivity analysis is to understand how a given variable affects the overall model results. Sensitivity analysis is a useful technique for identifying key data and information that the modeling effort should concentrate on.

Sensitivity analysis consists of varying model parameters, often one parameter at a time, in a limited range and observing how the simulation results vary. The goal is to see the effects of varying the values either because there is uncertainty in the chosen input values, or because there is a need to better understand the effects of the variable on the overall system behavior. In the grocery checkout line example, suppose it is known that, on average, 10 customers per hour arrive at the checkout line, but there could be as many as 20 and as few as none. Should more checkers be hired or should the number of checkout lines be increased? Hiring more checkers increases costs but reduces customer waiting times and

improves the customer experience. Does hiring more checkers mean higher profits or lower profits? This question could be addressed through sensitivity analysis in which the number of checkout lines in the simulation is varied, to see the effects on customer waiting times and profits.

A practical and important application of sensitivity analysis to ABMS is to explore the effect of various agent decision rules and parameters for the rules on the system as a whole. Often there is uncertainty about what rules should be used for the agents in the model. Perhaps there are several plausible candidates for agent rules. In business, people often learn a standard set of rules to conduct their business either through schooling or from experience. Successful rules for managing operations diffuse throughout an industry and eventually become standard practice. Agents learn and employ similar rules, and this narrows down the range of possible rules that need to be considered as candidates in modeling agent behaviors. Sensitivity analysis has applications for understanding the agent behaviors and the rules that have been adopted for the agents in the model.

The ability to conveniently modify or deactivate the behavior of a given agent allows the influence of that agent to be easily tested. This is another type of agent sensitivity testing. What is less obvious is the business value of this type of sensitivity testing. In practical applications, the authors have found that determining the influence of critical agent behaviors on model results allows a range of important questions to be answered and can greatly improve the effectiveness of using the model. Sensitivity analysis is also particularly useful in addressing the uncertainty inherent in the agent rules. Rules can be categorized on the basis of how much intelligence or creativity the agents are assumed to have. For example, it is possible to start with zero intelligence such that the agent rules are fixed and the agents do not adapt at all. Beyond the zero intelligence rules, it is possible to add some adaptive capabilities for the agent rules and explore the effects of adaptive behaviors.

Another use of sensitivity analysis is to balance the simplicity versus complexity of agent rules. The challenge is to identify the simplest rules that credibly reproduce the behaviors of the agents. If an agent model is too simple, it lacks credibility and is not sensitive to the effects of key variables. If an agent model is too complicated, it is difficult to understand and gain any insights into agent behavior. If a model with the simplest rules for describing agent behaviors exhibits the same types of system behaviors that are observed in the real world, then it is likely that an agent model with more complex rules would also exhibit the same behavior. Sensitivity analysis can be an important tool when applied to understanding the degree of complexity needed for adequately capturing the agent rules of behavior.

Determining the influence of an agent's behavior on model results immediately reveals the importance of the behavior, the possible returns from further investigating the behavior, and the potential value of enhancing the fidelity of the behavior's representation in the simulation. Gauging the relative importance of a behavior can be directly beneficial for organizations when the behavior can in some sense be controlled. What can be done if a specific behavior is identified as important but cannot be controlled? Quantifying the possible returns from learning more about the behavior is a solid step. Once the value of understanding the behavior is quantified, the knowledge that may be gained from enhancing the agent's behavior model can be considered. The authors have found that the importance of individual agent behaviors to system outcomes is often surprising to business experts. The authors have seen several situations

where it was widely assumed that certain behaviors were central to familiar outcomes. ABMS sensitivity analysis showed that these behaviors had little to do with the actual results.

Focused sensitivity analysis of results identifies the types of outcomes most critical to decision-making, such as best- or worst-case scenarios. There can be a focus on the precursors to the results, such as the types of choices by competitors that influence the final outcomes. There can be a concentration on critical points or inflection points of greatest sensitivity and uncertainty. Exploration of the possible outcomes through sensitivity analysis can be the basis for detailed investigations into the issues of critical importance using ABMS.

Sensitivity analysis is useful for identifying which variables or parameters may be most important in producing system behavior. But sensitivity analysis provides little information on what behaviors might be encountered over the entire range of cases that could be modeled. In sensitivity analysis, one parameter at a time is varied while the values of all the other variables are held constant. This amounts to exploring the local space surrounding an initial solution. Beginning with another solution in another part of the model solution space would, in general, give a different result in terms of how the system behaves in response to varying the same parameter. The exception to this would be if the system could be described as a "linear" system. In the linear case, the sensitivity of the system to its parameters would be the same through the entire model solution space. However, the systems of greatest interest to agent modelers often turn out to be highly nonlinear. This is due to the nonlinear nature of the agent interactions that typically comprise such models.

Advances in computational capabilities now allow more comprehensive exploration of the model solution space by providing the capability to perform a larger number of simulations in an ever-shortening amount of time. Vast numbers of simulations can be performed systematically so as to explore large regions of the parameter space and allow the results to be put into a comprehensive view of the system and agent behaviors. This systematic process is what is referred to as parameter sweeping.

Parameter Sweeps

The objective of parameter sweeping is to identify all the possible behaviors that a model is capable of generating and to understand the conditions and assumptions under which the behaviors will result.

In the real world many variables change simultaneously, and there is a need to explore the effects of changing combinations of these variables over the entire model solution space. Traditionally these techniques are called response surface methodologies. The goal of response surface methods is to derive a statistical model that "connects all of the dots" of the simulation outputs and represents how the model outputs are related to the inputs by a single, statistically valid equation. The response surface is usually smooth, owing to the statistical methods used to derive it, and gives a visual picture of how the system responds to various inputs over a wide range of parameter settings. The nonlinearities inherent in agent models, however, do not lend themselves to this smooth correspondence between model inputs and outputs, as will be seen for the case of the supply chain model.

Consider the two agent ordering rule parameters for the supply chain model, the inventory and pipeline parameters. There is a need to understand how the supply chain behaves for all possible combinations of these agent parameter settings. To perform this parameter sweep, an analyst can take the following steps:

1. Segment the range of values for the inventory and pipeline parameters (from 0 to 1) into 25 segments, and take combinations of these two values to specify an individual simulation run. This creates a total of 25×25 runs or 625 cells.
2. For each cell, do one simulation run corresponding to the parameter settings for the cell. Run each simulation for 1,000 time periods.
3. Classify the long-run behavior of the time series from the simulation in terms of a key state variable, in this case the factory inventory (we could do the same for any number of important system variables).
4. Finally, plot the results for each of the simulation cells and color each cell so that it indicates the long-run system behavior: lightly shaded for stable to strongly shaded for chaotic (a chaotic solution showing strong periodicities), for example.

Figure 13.16(a) shows the resulting inventory levels for the 625 simulations. For simulations in the northwest portion (left, top) of the parameter space, corresponding to low values of the inventory control parameter and high values of the pipeline parameter,

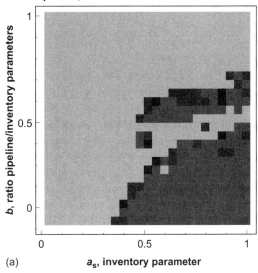

Distribution of Modes for Factory Inventory
q = 0.25, Q = 17

b, ratio pipeline/inventory parameters

a$_s$, inventory parameter

(a)

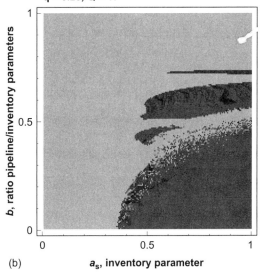

Distribution of Modes for Factory Inventory
q = 0.25, Q = 17

b, ratio pipeline/inventory parameters

a$_s$, inventory parameter

(b)

FIGURE 13.16 System behavior classification over an agent parameter space: (a) results of parameter sweeps for coarse-grained simulations; (b) results of parameter sweeps for fine-grained simulations. (Reproduced from Mosekilde et al. 1991, fig. 10.)

the system attains stable behavior in the long-run. But in the southeast portion (right, bottom) chaotic solutions arise, corresponding to high values of the inventory control parameter and low values of the pipeline parameter. Between the solutions exhibiting chaotic and stable behaviors there is a transition area in which the behavior is periodic or quasi-periodic, a mix of chaotic and periodic behaviors. This situation is typical—an area of periodic behavior separating areas of stability and chaos.

The results of the simulation experiments are sensitive to how finely grained the parameter space is partitioned, especially in the areas close to the boundaries where the behavior transitions from stable to chaotic. A proper analysis should consider this fact. It is advisable to investigate the effect of a more finely grained level of detail for the inventory and pipeline control parameters. As before, divide up each parameter space into segments along each axis, but this time use 200 segments rather than 25. This results in a total of 40,000 (200 × 200) cells, each cell specifying a combination of agent rule parameters for a simulation. Figure 13.16(b) shows the results of running the simulation for these 40,000 simulation runs. The behaviors observed are similar to the previous case, but now the tight intermixing of stable and chaotic solutions in some regions close to the boundary is much more obvious.[6]

What do the various system behaviors mean for the bottom line, the cost of operating the supply chain? Figure 13.17 shows the costs for each of 40,000 simulation runs.[7] The cells are shaded according to the long-run average cost of operating the supply chain. White indicates the lowest cost solutions, black indicates the highest costs, and shades of gray represent intermediate values. There are several solutions that produce the same minimum cost, indicated by the row of lighter cells (cells having a value for b of about 0.7). For the simulations that exhibit chaotic behavior, inventory levels fluctuate continuously, and there are many stockout situations that result in backorders, which are very costly. In contrast, for stable behavior, inventories level out at low stock levels, resulting in low costs. The stable region of the parameter space is shown by the light-gray sections in the figure. The stable region is large and continuous, a nice calm place to operate the supply chain.

Emergent Behavior

Agent models are built upon the dynamic processes of agent interaction. Often, the process of agent interaction, as it unfolds over time, is of as much interest as the long-run, end state that the system may eventually achieve. One of the objectives of agent simulation

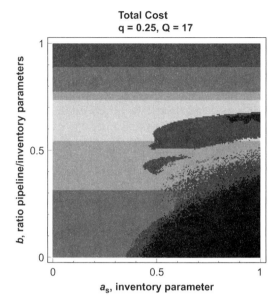

FIGURE 13.17 Supply chain costs over an agent parameter space. (Reproduced from Mosekilde et al. 1991, fig. 12.)

output analysis is to understand how the behavioral rules of the agents influence the system as a whole. Agent models show the transitory processes of how the system evolves to its long-run state. Some of the outcomes of the agent interactions may result in what is termed "emergent" behavior. Emergent behavior is the result of the agent behaviors and interactions within the model that are not directly specified as part of the behaviors of the agents in the model. In simple terms, emergent behaviors are system outcomes that are more complicated than the simple sum of the constituent parts.

For example, can consumer buying frenzies emerge in an agent model if detailed buying behavior is not directly specified for the individual agents? Yes, if the agent behaviors include a capacity for imitation. Suppose a given person makes contact with three people who have just purchased a new item. The given person might imitate the other people's behavior, which effectively results in the given person buying the same product, even though they had no intention of buying this product originally. The mechanisms that operate at the individual level, such as how consumers decide to buy particular products and why people join groups, often result in counterintuitive behavior at the system level. People see how their friends, neighbors, relatives, and other influential people react to events, and this in turn influences their behavior. This imitation effect can cascade from one agent to another through a social network of agent interactions. The cascading effect that results leads to a self-reinforcing feedback loop that builds upon itself, and ultimately leads to the formation of a durable, emergent structure.

Emergent behavior is often in the form of discernable patterns or a recognizable structure that is internally generated by the agent behaviors and agent interactions embedded within the agent model. The Schelling model of housing segregation introduced in chapter 4 is a good example. Figure 13.18 shows the results of the Schelling modeling in which there are two types of agents, differentiated by their degree of shading.[8] Initially, they are randomly distributed throughout the space. Each agent has a rule to the

effect that it requires 25% of neighbors to be of the same color. If the rule is not satisfied at any time in the simulation, the agent moves to a new location in which the required condition is satisfied. After 25 generations, patterns in the agent locations are clearly discernible. The agents segregate into clusters of similar agent types, based entirely on the agent rules that are applied using only locally available information. Analysis of ABMS results includes the need for identifying and characterizing these types of internally generated, or endogenous, patterns and clusters.

The final big question is how to effectively explain ABMS results to decision-makers. If agent modeling is to realize its full potential and create new information to solve real-world problems that have not been possible to solve before, agent models must provide new information to decision-makers in novel ways.

(a)   **Schelling-Type Model: Generation 0**

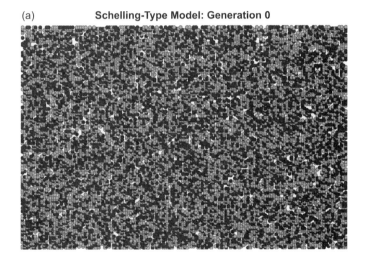

(b)   **Schelling-Type Model: Generation 24**

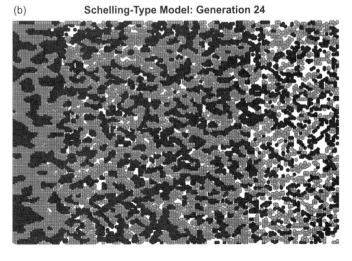

FIGURE 13.18 Results from the Schelling segregation model: (a) initial random distribution; (b) clustering after 25 generations.

Presenting ABMS Results

ABMS models can deal with more realistic conditions and generate newer insights into difficult problems than models based on conventional approaches. Agent-based modeling is particularly good at addressing aspects of systems that have not been addressed by traditional models, such as:

- transient, nonequilibrium conditions;
- phase transition points;
- stable and unstable regions;
- individual agent behavior; and
- dependence on initial conditions.

However, decision-makers are generally not familiar with how to interpret and use the results from agent-based models. For example, explaining an extreme dependence on initial conditions to decision-makers can be difficult. The following quote sums up the situation (author unknown):

> A hundred years ago, every scientist would have said: "Of course, if you know the initial condition and you know the law, you can predict what will happen." Now we know that's absolutely untrue . . . tiny, tiny changes in initial conditions can distort the outcome by huge amounts. [The translation to business is that it's frequently impossible to find a "best" strategy. Instead] what is most important is to have a family of strategies, such that one can vary the response to one's changing circumstances according to success.

ABMS Results for Decision-Making

ABMS models are seldom used with the intent of predicting the future unconditionally, without regard to specific assumptions. As with virtually all major scientific advances, something less important must be sacrificed to make progress in a direction that is more important. For example, moving from classical to quantum mechanics required scientists to abandon their hopes for absolute measurement precision to gain much greater statistical predictive power. Similarly, ABMS requires modelers to abandon their hope for exact, numeric predictions in exchange for the ability to represent and investigate the complex behaviors of real-world systems. For deeply complex systems, this tradeoff is more than just an option. It is required, since none of the point prediction methods

can be adequately relied on when it comes to agents and their behaviors. Rather than predicting the future, ABMS models are used to:

- Generate insights into complex processes.
- Relate micro-level process knowledge to global-level system results.
- Envisage ranges of possible outcomes and contingencies.

ABMS can provide many types of useful information to decision-makers based on agent interactions that are embedded in the models. Decision-makers can use ABMS results to answer several types of questions, such as the following:

- Will a small number of firms tend to dominate the market?
- Will change come quickly or be slow in the offing?
- Will the market always be in a state of turbulence or will it settle down after an initial transition?
- How will a market respond to different marketing strategies targeted at different segments of the consumer market?
- What is the significance of observed market patterns and early indicators?
- Which evolutionary paths and directions is it likely that the market will take?

Agent-based modeling allows decision-makers to understand and predict which agent behaviors cause specific market outcomes. An ABMS also allows decision-makers to recognize disequilibrium situations early in their development and to link these situations to others like it and to their likely causes. The model allows decision-makers to identify the sources of greatest uncertainty.

As has been shown in this chapter with the supply chain model, deterministic chaos can result in inventory levels throughout the supply chain as a result of myopic ordering policies. Other ordering policies result in stable inventory levels at all stages of the supply chain and tend to balance agent behaviors. The implications of the rules are not obvious from the rules themselves. Understanding the connections between micro-level and macro-level behaviors is critical to interpreting the results from an ABMS and is the challenge of presenting ABMS results to decision-makers.

Communicating ABMS Results

The insights gained from ABMS must be clearly understood and effectively communicated to decision-makers to be useful. These are several things to keep in mind when presenting results from ABMS models. Presenting ABMS results starts with education. Decision-makers need to know that they are seeing something different than they have seen in the past. Decision-makers need to know the strengths and weakness of ABMS. Decision-makers need to be shown the appropriate ranges of output rather than simply being told that "this is the answer." The reasons for the results need to be explained to decision-makers in a complete, straightforward, logical, problem-domain-specific way.

Ideally the model results should be explained completely independently of references to the ABMS or any other modeling technique employed. To do this requires preparation on the part of the model user to be in a position of being able to answer all the questions that might be asked concerning the "why" of the model results. Any time a decision-maker asks a question about the model results that cannot be answered by the analyst, the model's credibility and value are reduced in the eyes of the decision-maker. An explanation ability for model results in general, and of agent behaviors in particular, should be developed to support decision-makers' questions concerning model results. Usually the model user or analyst accomplishes this by thorough inspection and detailed analysis of the model results, and thinking through the observed effects to identify their causal factors in the model.

Cognitive styles of decision-makers, that is, how they respond to and pick up new information, are important to discern and consider when presenting results. People have different cognitive styles when it comes to how they see and understand results. Some people are visual thinkers, and they respond best to being shown figures and graphs based on ABMS results. Some people are numeric thinkers, and they respond to statistical analysis of ABMS results. Some people are strictly qualitative, and they respond to being "told an accurate story" or given a narrative in plain language based on the ABMS results. When it comes to presenting results to many people at one time, it is important to discern and consider the cognitive styles of the people who will be in the audience, if that is possible to know in advance. If the cognitive styles of the people in the audience are unknown, it is

wise to prepare for all possible styles—have something for everyone.

Many times decision-makers tend to seize on a particular model result, to the exclusion of all other results, for better or for worse. Anticipating which result decision-makers will seize upon, whether it be in the form of a chart, a graph, or a set of numbers, can have sizable benefits in terms of getting the main modeling message across. How can this be anticipated in advance of giving a major presentation to upper management? If the same model results are presented repeatedly to different audiences, it is often possible to identify which results are most memorable based on the reactions and comments of the audience members.

Organizational issues are also critical to having models accepted, used, and change the ways of doing business. Individual champions are not enough; the fit to the organization is just as important. Each organization has its own culture, which influences the way in which new information is received and disseminated and how new ideas are accepted. Having a successful modeling activity is at least as much an organizational challenge as it is a technical challenge. The fit should consider several dimensions:

- The organization's specific needs should be considered. The model has to fit the organization in terms of both how it is developed and how it is intended to be used. Two critical questions should be answered: (1) Who are the users? and (2) Who are the decision-makers who will use the results?
- The modeling project's scale compared to the organization's scale, in terms of the resources available to be applied in response to the presentation's recommendations and the time frame for implementation of the results, should be considered.
- Expectations on the part of the organization for how beneficial the results will be and the extent of their implications for the organization, as well as how soon the results can be provided, and how much it will cost should be considered.

Sometimes an organization's needs for information are immediate. Even in the context of immediacy, ABMS can be used in a form of modeling similar to extreme programming in software development. Conversational modeling, also called conversation speed modeling, is a way to use fast simulations to run live interactive tests of proposed options in real time during strategic planning meetings.

Visualizing Results

Visualization is one of the most effective ways to present key model information to decision-makers. Advanced visualization and animation software is readily available for desktop computing and ABMS applications, whereas just a few years ago visualization tools were the sole province of powerful scientific workstations. This section shows how advanced visualization techniques can be used to illustrate key information from the supply chain simulation.

Illustrating Robustness

Figure 13.19 shows the same supply chain costs as in figure 13.17, but this time costs are plotted in three dimensions. The height of the plotted data corresponds to the average long-run cost for the simulation. The peaks are the higher-cost areas, and the troughs and valleys represent lower-cost solutions. The figure illustrates that the minimum-cost solutions, in the row with dark-colored cells, are situated in a long valley at about $b = 0.7$. At the end of the valley there are several peaks indicating that the minimum-cost solutions are situated right next to much more costly solutions,

This visualization drives home the point that if someone accepts the minimum-cost bid without further reflection, they could easily end up in a dangerous area of the solution parameter space where a tiny variation in the data, a tiny perturbation of customer demand, or a tiny mistake made in ordering causes the space to shift to a solution that incurs much higher costs. The darkly shaded cells are minimum-cost solutions that are truly situated on the edge of chaos. If a manager chooses one of these solutions, then they are going to subject themselves to the possibility of a catastrophic failure. Most people operating

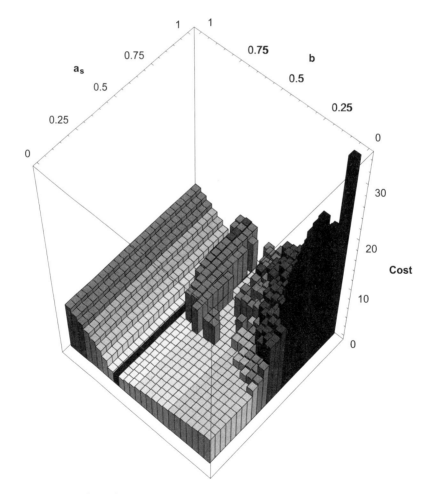

FIGURE 13.19 Total supply chain costs over an agent parameter space. (Data reproduced from Mosekilde et al. 1991, fig. 10, in 3D.)

Supply Chain Beer Game Simulation
Case: aS = 0.3, b = aSL/aS = 0.15, r = 0, Q = 17
Desired Inventory = 14.8, Desired Pipeline = 14.8

Supply Chain Beer Game Simulation
Case: aS = 0.3, b = aSL/aS = 0.15, r = 0, Q = 17
Desired Inventory = 14.8, Desired Pipeline = 14.8

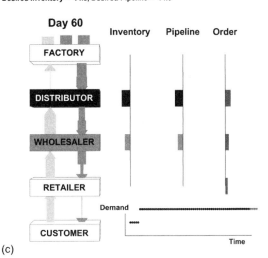

(a)

(c)

Supply Chain Beer Game Simulation
Case: aS = 0.3, b = aSL/aS = 0.15, r = 0, Q = 17
Desired Inventory = 14.8, Desired Pipeline = 14.8

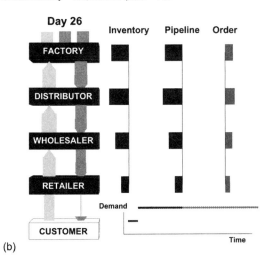

(b)

FIGURE 13.20 Visualization of supply chain flows and the status of orders and shipments: (a) day 1; (b) day 26; (c) day 60.

a system, running a business, or trying to make a profit or reduce costs, would prefer to operate in an area of stability, where small changes produce small and predictable results. Most managers would much prefer to operate at a robust solution point. Policies should be robust as well as efficient. This example demonstrates that the world is not Newtonian—a small change here or there may result in a very big change elsewhere in the system. Business systems may be highly optimized as every inefficiency is squeezed out, but at the expense of robustness. The example also illustrates that although the rules constructed for the agent behaviors may be continuous and smooth and thoroughly predictable, the behavior of the system that the agents comprise may be far from smooth or predictable.

Animating a Dynamic Process

Animation is an advanced visualization technique used to illustrate the dynamic behavior of a process.

Animation uses recognizable objects of the system as opposed to abstract data and statistics. Animations are very computationally intensive, but as computer power continues to increase, more is becoming possible in the animation world.

Figure 13.20(a) is a visualization of the state of supply chain simulation for a particular time slice. The visualization encapsulates all of the main information from the simulation on the state of the supply chain at that time. It illustrates the flows of orders and goods in shipment, and the status of inventory, pipeline, and customer orders. An animation can be created by combining the sequence of such scenes for each of the time periods in the simulation. The animation shows and emphasizes the dynamic elements of behavior as the system changes over time.

Seven Steps

This chapter has presented a seven-step process for dealing with ABMS results:

1. Recording or logging the model output.
2. Analyzing the results using traditional statistical analysis techniques.
3. Applying sophisticated time-series analysis methods.
4. Conducting sensitivity analysis and identifying key parameters and agent rules.
5. Sweeping regions of the parameter space.
6. Characterizing model outputs over the parameter space.
7. Presenting the results to decision-makers, and using advanced visualization techniques and other means to get the main points across.

Several output analysis techniques were demonstrated and it was shown how model results can be boiled down into useful information. Finally, this chapter discussed various strategies for presenting results to decision-makers for maximum impact.

Notes

1. The system stabilizes for inventory and pipeline ordering parameters, 0.25 and 0.50, respectively.
2. The system reaches true periodic behavior for inventory and pipeline ordering parameters, 0.30 and 0.65, respectively.
3. The system exhibits highly chaotic behavior for inventory and pipeline ordering parameters, 0.50 and 0.0, respectively.

4. The system exhibits highly chaotic behavior in the short run and periodic or stable behavior in the long run for inventory and pipeline ordering parameters, 0.425 and 0.09, respectively.
5. The system exhibits chaotic behavior in the short run, but transitions to periodic (factory and distributor) and stable (wholesaler and retailer) behavior in the long run.
6. The plot in figure 13.16(a) represents 625 (25×25 grid) individual simulations and the classification of long-run behavior of the time series: dark shading indicates chaotic behavior, light shading indicates stable behavior, and medium shading indicates periodic or quasi-periodic behavior. The plot in figure 13.16(b) is the same as in figure 13.16(a), but at a much more finely grained segmentation of the parameter space. The plot represents 40,000 (200×200 grid) individual simulations.
7. The plot represents 40,000 (200×200) individual simulations. a_s is the inventory gap parameter, b is the ratio of the pipeline and inventory gap parameters.
8. The clustering is based on agent rules that require 25% of neighbors to be the same shade.

References

Chen, F. and Z. Dreznen (2002). Quantifying the Bull-Whip Effect in a Simple Supply Chain. *Management Science* **46**(3): 436–443.

Downey, A. and D. Feitelson (1999). The Elusive Goal of Workload Characterization." *ACM SIGMETRICS Performance Evaluation Review* **26**(4): 14–29.

Fishman, G. S. (1973). *Concepts and Methods in Discrete Event Simulation*. New York: Wiley.

Helbing, D. (2003). Modeling Supply Networks and Business Cycles as Unstable Transport Phenomena. *New Journal of Physics* **5**: 90.1–90.28.

Hellerstein, J. L. (1995). Constructing Quantitative Models Using Monotone Relationships. *IEEE Transactions* **7**(2): 294–304.

Law, A. M. (2007). *Simulation Modeling and Analysis*, 4th ed. Boston: McGraw-Hill.

Lee, H. L., V. Padmanabhan, and S. Whang (1997). The Bullwhip Effect in Supply Chains. *Sloan Management Review* (Spring), 93–102.

Mosekilde, E., E. R. Larsen, and J. D. Sterman (1991). Coping with Complexity: Deterministic Chaos in Human Decision Making Behavior. In J. L. Casti and A. Karlqvist (Eds.), *Beyond Belief: Randomness, Prediction, and Explanation in Science*. Boston, CRC Press, pp. 199–299.

14

ABMS Project Management

The ABMS Business Function

As discussed throughout this book, agent-based modeling and simulation (ABMS) projects have the potential to substantially improve an organization's ability to manage complex situations. Gaining this transformative ability requires organizations to develop and apply a set of new business processes. The transformative nature of agent modeling combined with the potential number of new business processes suggests that ABMS in many ways represents a new "business function."

The new ABMS business function allows organizations to understand and control external and internal processes that were previously considered unfathomable and unmanageable. This function allows organizations to investigate both radical and minor behavioral changes before such behaviors are tested in the real world. It empowers organizations to consider challenges before they are faced in the real world, and integrates or fuses detailed, low-level data into coherent global pictures. This integration occurs during both model development and model usage. During development, the various available agent behavioral designs and data sets are compared, contrasted, and merged as needed. During model usage, data is integrated while creating the needed model inputs and while running the model. However, doing these things requires that a model be created and that the input data be rendered in definite forms.

As previously mentioned, the ABMS business function involves more than the simple production of models. It includes the online testing of models and it defines how users integrate, run, and view models. Detailed techniques for testing models are presented in chapter 11. Methods for preparing model input data are presented in chapter 12. Approaches to using models and communicating the results are discussed in chapter 13. This chapter considers how these techniques are managed within organizations and the roles that various participants play in the process.

The Fundamentals

Management of agent-based modeling projects begins with fundamental project management. The same core skills required to complete any type of substantial project are also needed for agent-modeling projects. In addition, such projects have special requirements that go beyond the core management skills. These special requirements include the need to understand the central concepts of agent modeling, the ability to articulate these concepts, the need to apply an iterative development process, and the need to focus development efforts throughout the process. The central concepts of agent modeling are explained in the earlier chapters of this book. The iterative ABMS development process is also discussed in the earlier chapters of this book. This process will be detailed here in the context of project management. Focusing of development efforts is also discussed later in this chapter. Naturally, the depths of each of these requirements depend on the scale of the project being managed.

It is widely held that project managers have three overall control levers: the project's requirements; the project's delivery schedule; and the project's budget or resources. Any of the levers can be moved, within reason, as long as the others move a proportional amount in the opposite direction. Carefully trading off these factors is often said to be the key to success.

Project Goals

The real key to ABMS project management is a clear grasp of the problem to be solved. This may seem too obvious to mention, but it is commonly absent from many projects. Lacking a good understanding of the problem to be addressed at each stage of the project life cycle is not just an issue for agent models. In fact, any type of project can fall victim to this issue, and many do. The real test is to be able to state the goal of the project in one or two sentences. For example, consider a retail consumer model such as the agent spreadsheet detailed in the chapter 8. Here is an example of a clear project goal:

> The goal of the project is to represent the flow of retail customers on a department store sales floor at about a 4-foot resolution rectangular grid to test the effects of different floor plans on the percentage of trips with successful purchases, the volatility of trips with successful purchases, the average customer frustration level, and the customer frustration volatility level.

Here are some less clear alternatives:

- The goal of the project is to model where retail consumers go in department stores to buy items of interest.
- The goal is to find the best way to lay out department store floor plans using agents.
- The goal of the project is to model department store consumers on a rectangular grid.
- The goal of the project is to model the flow of retail consumers in department stores with different rectangular grid floor plans to see which one is best.

None of these goals is inherently bad. They are simply so general as to be difficult to implement. How can good goals be recognized? Good goals can be achieved and the achievement of good goals can be clearly recognized. When evaluating a goal, ask "How will the developers know when the model is done?" Certainly, the verification and validation details may require substantial work. However, if the overall answer is relatively obvious, then the goal is probably specific enough. If the goal seems appropriately specific, then ask if the potential questions to be addressed by the model seem to justify the development effort.

One question that is regularly raised about the need for clear goals is about the role of iterative development. After all, if agent modeling should be done iteratively to take advantage of learning during development, then what is the point of starting with clear goals? Will such goals just get in the way by stifling creative exploration? The answer is no!

Defining clear goals is not that same thing as mandating permanent targets. Project goals are intended to evolve over time as the model and the modeling team members' understanding of the problem evolve. The goals should be regularly reviewed and updated based on the modeling progress and the project team members' experiences. The difference between projects with evolving and permanent targets is like the difference between a remote-controlled airplane and a bottle rocket. Remote-controlled airplanes may be started in the right direction, but they get where they are going due to regular guidance and feedback from their controller. A bottle rocket is pointed at its target, its fuse is lit, it heads off on its preordained ballistic course, and it usually explodes along the way. The agent model development process detailed in this book works like an airplane. Regular feedback is critical. For ABMS, the joystick on the remote-control unit is like the project goals. ABMS projects with inflexible targets often end up exploding like bottle rockets. It is best to use an airplane!

Stopping Mission Creep

The usual personnel and administrative concerns found in nearly all projects also occur with agent model development. Beyond the usual personnel issues, the most common is mission creep. Mission creep is the incremental addition of a series of new requirements each of which is a reasonable step by itself but that together produce an unreasonable aggregate result (Siegel 2000). On agent-modeling projects, mission creep occurs either when a simulation is incrementally expected to model more that it was originally designed to handle or when more and more requirements are added to a project without sufficient budget and schedule adjustments. ABMS mission creep has two common causes.

The leading cause of mission creep is poorly managed excitement about project successes. Mismanaged excitement occurs when managers build up expectations about what a model can do before they work out the costs of these capabilities. For a variety of reasons, many users assume that the capabilities being discussed will be available free after the first phase of the modeling effort is completed. This runaway excitement can be nipped in the bud by reminding users what will actually be delivered for each phase of the project and letting them know that more can eventually be done, for a price.

The second leading cause of mission creep is ineffectual budgetary bartering. Ineffectual budgetary bartering occurs when new requirements are traded for more, but not enough, money. The usual project management advice is to take each estimated task completion cost and double it. This advice works well here too.

Champions

Virtually all successful agent-modeling projects have a champion who supports the simulation effort. Champions are leaders who work to protect and grow the project within an organization. Champions usually invest some of their own organizational identity into a project. In return, champions receive the lion's share of the credit for project accomplishments.

Who are the champions? Champions are usually innovators who are continually seeking ways to improve their organization. Champions are usually not experts on agent modeling but they are typically quick to learn at least the basic concepts. Champions tend to have a high level of curiosity and an interest in intellectual growth. Champions are usually willing to take risks to achieve meaningful rewards. Champions have long-term vision and a willingness to work hard to realize their vision. Many champions are also influential at some level in their organization. They either manage significant resources themselves or have the ability to talk to people who do. Champions with a smaller amount of formal influence can still be invaluable—the willingness to stand up and be counted brings its own special form of influence.

Finding and maintaining champions is one of the most important long-term project management activities. So, how are champions found? The good news is that champions often identify themselves. They are the kinds of people who ask questions and seek out new opportunities for their organizations. To find a champion, look for people who are looking for change!

Keeping a champion involved in a project requires a careful attention to giving the champion what they need to be successful. Ask them what they need to show to their management for the project to be considered valuable. Be sure to find out not only the type but also the form of the needed feedback and then provide this to them! Arm them with information on the value of agent modeling and the status of the project. Remind them of the results of the project, since it is easy to lose sight of incremental progress amid daily distractions. Modelers are only successful when their champions are successful. Treating champions well is the secret of modeling success!

The Domain Skills Pyramid

Chapter 12 discussed data, information, knowledge, and wisdom as part of a fact food pyramid (Cleveland 1982; Eliot 1934). Following up on this, it is often useful to divide project team members into one of four rough categories of domain-specific skills. The categories of domain skills are ignorance, awareness, literacy, and expertise. These skill categories form an inverted pyramid with the bottom level, ignorance, representing no domain skills at all and the various depths of expertise at the top collectively representing increasingly high levels of skills.

Ignorance is simply a lack of data, information, knowledge, or wisdom about the selected domain. For practical purposes, people in a state of ignorance about a domain have never even heard of the area. In colloquial terms, such people have not even "heard the talk" and certainly cannot "talk the talk" or "walk the walk."

Awareness is the possession of at least some data about the selected domain. Generally this data pertains simply to the existence of the domain and a few, often misunderstood, features of its structure. People who only have an awareness of a domain have heard of the area but know essentially nothing about it. In colloquial terms, such people have "heard the talk," but cannot "talk the talk" or "walk the walk."

Literacy is the possession of at least some data and information, and possibly knowledge, about the selected domain. People with literacy in a domain know about the existence of the domain, have an essentially correct, but simple, view of the domain's fundamental structure, and are able to hold workable discussions about the domain with others. However, such people have a difficult time resolving ambiguous situations involving the domain and have limited or no ability to make effective judgments about the domain. In colloquial terms, they can "talk the talk" but not "walk the walk."

Expertise is the possession of data, information, knowledge, and possibly wisdom about the selected domain. Experts have a detailed view of the structure of a domain; can resolve complicated and ambiguous situations involving the domain; and can make effective judgments about the domain. The most sophisticated experts have deep wisdom about the domain and clearly understand how the domain intersects with neighboring domains. In colloquial terms, experts can "walk the walk." The best can run too.

Naturally, assignment to one of the four categories is a function of the domain of interest. An expert in a given domain may be, and often is, completely ignorant of unrelated areas. Furthermore, there is normally a gradation of skills within each category and an indistinct boundary between them. For example, there are many depths of expertise from basic competence to profound wisdom. As another example, the boundary between high literacy and basic expertise is somewhat nebulous. In general, despite the gradations and indistinctness, these categories can be useful for approximately gauging project communications requirements and roughly assessing the need for individual domain-specific training.

ABMS Project Structures

There are several fundamental ABMS project structures. These structures are one-stop modeling, generalist modeling, and specialist modeling. One-stop modeling is completed by a single individual. Generalist modeling employs a small team that shares the work. Specialist modeling employs team members who are each focused on an individual specialty or specialties. Every actual agent-modeling project structure is an elaboration of one of these structures. In practice, the dividing lines between these structures are somewhat indistinct. For example, groups may be organized following the specialist modeling approach, but have one person who does both data collection and model validation in the generalist style. The goal of these project classifications is not to rigidly pigeonhole projects into one of the categories. Rather, the intent is to describe the range of commonly used structures and detail the requirements of each structure.

The structural pattern existing in a given organization is usually driven by the scale of the project being developed. In addition to the inherent fuzziness of the lines between the structures, it is quite common for projects to move between these structures in evolutionary steps over time. The most common sequence is to start with one-stop modeling, move to generalist modeling, and then to specialist modeling as the project requirements and resources grow.

One-Stop Modeling

One-stop modeling is the simplest approach to ABMS development. In this approach, a single highly motivated individual does all the work. Since only one person is involved, a limited amount of effort can be expended on the model and a finite range of skills are employed. As a result, the models that are produced using one-stop modeling tend to be simpler than with the other structures. In this regard, one-stop modeling is often used to start the agent-modeling process. This is particularly true in organizations that have not previously used ABMS.

Many models produced by a single individual are primarily used to extract insights that make sense and that are explainable to that individual. The model results or even the model itself may not be obvious or even seen by others. This most commonly occurs with models developed while learning agent modeling. The later models that are developed based on deeper experience are usually much clearer.

As with all of the project structures, one-stop modeling can be effective if the individual model developer is clear about their goals. The major issue is to focus the modeling effort on an issue small enough to be reasonably addressed by one individual in the available time. In particular, if the purpose is to learn about agent modeling, then the individual should expect their initial models to be quite limited in scope. If the purpose is to demonstrate the value of agent modeling for a specific organization or a specific problem, then the individual should target a small to moderate-sized component of the problem that has high value. Well-designed agent models are inherently structured to be extensible over time. If the purpose is to develop the foundation for a larger modeling effort, then the individual should target a limited set of the core or fundamental components found in the full problem. Of course, these goals can overlap. In this case, the focus should be on the minimal intersection of the requirements for each goal.

With ABMS, large projects come from medium-sized projects. Where do medium-sized projects come from? They come from small projects, of course! Iterative development means incremental growth. Elvis Presley once said, "Ambition is a dream with a V8 engine." If there is one message to be derived from this discussion, it is that big goals can be achieved by starting small. For one-stop modelers, the real goal should be to get some useful subcomponents working and then grow these components over time. This applies equally well to larger projects!

One-stop modeling requires a wide range of skills in varying amounts. These skills are needed on all agent-modeling project teams, but one-stop modeling means that these capabilities need to be concentrated into one person. The required ingredients are a clear grasp of the problem being modeled, an awareness of the area being modeled, an understanding of agent modeling, knowledge of at least one model development tool, a handle on data collection, and capabilities with model output analysis and presentation.

As previously stated, a clear grasp of the problem to be solved is obvious but necessary. A lack of clear goals is a fast route to project failure. Clear goals are the path to success!

Awareness of the area being modeled requires more than just clear goals. Knowing the area being modeled means that the developer can recognize agent behaviors that are good candidates for inclusion in the model and can eliminate less interesting behaviors. One of the purposes of agent-based modeling is to determine which behaviors influence system outcomes and which behaviors do not. Theoretically, all behaviors are potential candidates for modeling. In many areas, there is debate over which individual behaviors cause which system-level outcomes. However, on a practical basis, some behaviors are much more likely to be influential than others. Everything else being equal, these behaviors should be modeled first. Of course, everything else is rarely equal. Other influences on this decision include how well understood a behavior is, how complicated it is, and if there are any existing models available for a given behavior. Better understood, simpler, and previously modeled behaviors are good starting points for

agent modeling. Even in the numerous areas where there is debate over the influence of various behaviors, it is important to know enough to be able to itemize and ultimately model the contending opinions.

An understanding of agent modeling is definitely needed by one-stop modelers. Fortunately, this book provides the core knowledge. Enough experience for at least basic one-stop modeling can be gained by developing several models following the instructions in this book.

Knowledge of at least one model development tool is necessary for one-stop modelers to implement working simulations. The tool to use depends on the modeler's current skill levels. Modelers that know how to use modern spreadsheets such as Microsoft Excel can start with these tools following the instructions in chapter 8. Those who know mathematical scripting languages such as Wolfram Research Mathematica or MathWorks MATLAB can follow the example in the same chapter. People without these skills or those with an interest in using a tool with direct support for agent-based modeling should consider the other options discussed in that chapter, including Repast Py, NetLogo, and StarLogo. Finally, people with a reasonable background in either structured or object-oriented programming can consider using one of the large-scale ABMS tools discussed in chapter 10. However, even experienced programmers are advised to start small and use one of the other tools for initial model prototyping.

Having a handle on data collection is another obvious, but often ignored, issue for one-stop modelers. Here the question is simple: once there is a hungry mouth in the form of a model, how will it be fed? This does not have to be a hard question. If the model is primarily intended for learning, then it probably needs very little data. If the model is a demonstration of capability, then only enough data is needed to show the potential of the system. For larger efforts, it often makes sense to recruit a data expert in the organization to provide the needed inputs, at least on a part-time basis. This can also help with model credibility since it signals to managers that the data is trustworthy.

Last but not least, capabilities with output analysis are needed. As with data collection skills, the level of output analysis capabilities required on a project depends on the project's goals. Learning projects require only enough analysis capabilities to allow the modeler to evaluate the quality of their model. Demonstration projects require enough skills to show the value of the model to senior management. Larger projects require a complete output analysis skill set. This argues for specialization in larger projects. Output analysis is discussed in detail in chapter 13.

Generalist Modeling

One-stop modeling assigns all of the project tasks to one person and thus requires them to have a full range of skills. Generalist modeling spreads tasks over several people but still requires each of them to have at least some involvement in each task. In this way, one-stop modeling projects are in some sense performed by generalist teams of one. In practice, one-stop modeling is common enough and working alone is different enough to warrant a separate category. Because of the sharing of functions and the concomitant broadening of skills, generalist teams are cross-functional teams.

With generalist modeling, one integrated team does all of the work, with modelers and users functionally indistinguishable within the team. In fact, the modelers are often the current or future users of the system. This project structure is a natural extension of one-stop modeling from one team member to several team members. Generalist modeling teams are sometimes supplemented with occasional advice and assistance from agent-modeling experts. This can be particularly helpful with new teams, organizations that are just starting to work with agent simulation, or for complex modeling tasks. The required agent-modeling expertise can sometimes be found within an organization but is often provided by outside consultants. The use of agent-based modeling consultants is discussed later in this chapter.

Generalist teams require the same capabilities as one-stop modeling teams, namely a clear grasp of the problem being modeled, an awareness of the area being modeled, an understanding of agent modeling, knowledge of at least one model development tool, a handle on data collection, and capabilities with output analysis. The difference is that the number of tasks that can be accomplished grows somewhat as the number of team members rises. Notice the use of the term "somewhat" in the last sentence. In the immortal words of Fred Brooks, "adding manpower to a late software project makes it later" (Brooks 1975). Projects do not have to be late to fall victim to this problem. Adding people to a project does not necessarily increase productivity and it certainly does not increase

productivity in linear proportions. The key issue to watch is clear assignment of separable responsibilities.

In principle, generalist teams share responsibility for each of the required tasks. In practice, this can work if the team consists of two or three people. As the number of participants grows, the need to identify task leaders becomes more acute. Since the point of generalist teams is to maintain broad skills and exchange ideas, the task leaders are not required to specialize in the tasks that they manage. Rather, the tasks may be completed by any of the team members. Hopefully, several people will contribute to each task both directly and in a review capacity. Each task leader's assignment is to see their tasks through to completion. As projects grow, the assignments become increasingly difficult and the efficiency that can come from specialization is often needed. When this happens, generalist teams often tend to evolve into specialist teams.

Specialist Modeling

Specialist modeling extends the generalist approach by assigning specific types of work to individual team members, usually based on the team member's current or expected future skills. The same competencies needed for both one-stop modeling and generalist modeling are also required for specialist modeling. These capabilities are a clear grasp of the problem being modeled, an awareness of the area being modeled, an understanding of agent modeling, knowledge of at least one model development tool, a handle on data collection, and capabilities with output analysis. On specialist modeling project teams, these competencies are the domain of specific existing or emerging experts. The major roles are high-level leaders, managers, analysts, developers, and consultants.

Many organizations have one group or individual build the model and another group or individual use the resulting model. In this case, high-level executives and senior managers have a particularly important leadership role. High-level leaders want to be confident that the system is providing useful information. In particular, they want to see what is going on and are concerned with the project status. Agent-based modeling's focus on regular intermediate results fits well with high-level leaders' needs to be kept in the loop. Providing these leaders with regular status reports and model demonstrations, as well as heeding the resulting feedback from them, will go a long way toward gaining and maintaining their support.

Managers

Managers have a critical coordination role. Managers usually have a direct stake in the model's success. They typically have no hands-on use of the model, but they direct specific model questions through to the appropriate analysts. Managers may or may not understand the workings of the model, but with support from analysts, they must be able to articulate to high-level leaders both how the model works and how it benefits the organization. A manager's ability to articulate the model's usage and value to high-level leaders has several basic requirements. No one will ask all of the questions associated with these requirements. In fact, some of the questions will never be asked, but some will. Being able to address all of these questions will increase managers' confidence in the model, increase their ability to present it to others regardless of whether it ever becomes an actual issue in a real meeting, and will provide a good backup in case someone wants to know.

First, managers need to know enough to be able to provide a cogent summary of the inner workings of the model and to answer questions about how the model works. Few high-level leaders will actually ask about such details, but some will. The small number of leaders who ask are often the strongest supporters of modeling efforts. Be warned that many high-level leaders have enough industry-specific background experience to ask how the model handles the lower-level business functions that the executives once worked in. Some of them will ask about these areas. This often occurs, in part, to use the answers as a litmus test for the quality of the rest of the model. Finally, note that one management technique that is occasionally used to evaluate something that is too complicated for full-fledged examination is to ask a relatively random question about the details of the system. The answers to these probing questions are not judged using technical content but on the presentation style of the response. If the response, is confident, relatively quick, and seems to be appropriately detailed, then the answer is accepted. Making sure that managers know enough to provide immediate and accurate answers to such questions is critical.

Managers need to be able to describe the basic inputs and model setup costs. This is particularly important when they describe the model to potential new users. Having an example of the types of required input data is useful. Letting users look at an example of an input spreadsheet can often answer in a few seconds questions that might otherwise take minutes or hours.

Managers need to be able to describe execution and model runtime costs. This can be as simple as saying that a model run takes between five and ten minutes depending on the data. Be sure to consider the kinds of computers the users have when providing such estimates, as opposed to the runtimes recorded on development machines. Users often have less powerful computers than developers, so the differences can be meaningful.

Managers need to be able to describe model deployment and training costs, if the model can be distributed. Even if the model is to be used in-house by a limited number of users, the training process needs to be defined. Training for the model may be quite simple, but there still needs to be a plan in place for how to bring new users up to speed. Managers need to be able to articulate the plan once it is formulated.

Managers need to be able to describe model maintenance costs. Buildings eventually require maintenance. Cars eventually require maintenance. Models need maintenance too. Having a plan in place for keeping the model up to date and letting managers know how to explain this plan to others makes a big difference. An important part of the plan is model maintenance skills. Selecting modeling tools with a large and growing number of developers such as spreadsheets or toolkits based on widely used languages helps greatly in this regard.

Managers need to be able to describe model outputs and the value of the model. Being able to relate the outputs to useful questions of value to the business is particularly important. Methods for doing this are provided in chapter 13. One particularly common type of question that comes up has to do with the pet theories of high-level leaders and users. It is natural for people who think deeply about challenging business questions to develop personal theories about how things work or how things might be improved. Often, it is difficult to test such theories directly in the real world, so questions remain. Agent models often provide a natural framework to answer these questions. Thus, people who see an agent-modeling project will tend to ask if the resulting model could be used to test their pet theories. Of course, the answer depends on the fit between the model and the question. Considering the audience's potential pet theories in the context of the model is worth the time. The model does not necessarily have to address these theories, but if it does not, then a reason should be provided.

Managers need to be able to compare the model to those of competitors and those in related industries. Most organizations already have a wide variety of traditional models. Many organizations have or are currently developing agent models. Being able to compare and contrast the current modeling effort with those of the competition and those in related industries helps high-level leaders put the current effort into perspective.

Finally, managers need to be able to provide a detailed description of the status of the project. It is critical that this status reporting be phrased in terms understandable to the audience. This often means putting things in terms of model capabilities rather than tasks. For example, saying that the model will be able to answer basic questions about competitor price changes in two weeks is usually better than saying that the competitive price response behaviors will be designed, implemented, verified, and validated in two weeks.

Analysts

Analysts are model users. Analysts are usually experts on the business being modeled and often have had extensive previous experience in these business units. If not, then they generally have highly analytical backgrounds or equivalent experience. Analysts have an ongoing and continuous need to derive information from the simulation. As such, analysts need to know the model's strengths and weaknesses in detail.

Good analysts are not passive recipients of modeling software. Over time, analysts can and do provide information on new potential and actual model uses. This feedback comes from understanding models and then using them to answer real questions.

It is common for skilled analysts to make models do things that the simulations were not built to do. It is also common for them to use models to answer questions that the simulations were not specifically designed to answer. These activities can be a great thing if the usage fits the model's range of validity. In fact, some of the best uses of models that the authors have ever seen were invented by creative analysts who took the time to understand their models. However, this tendency can also be a problem when analysts use a model outside its range of validity. Mirroring the previous observation, some of the worst uses of models that the authors have ever seen were invented by creative analysts who failed to take the time to understand their models. The difference between these two results is a solid knowledge of the each model's

strengths and weaknesses. Setting these ranges is discussed in chapter 11.

If a model cannot do something that matters, skilled analysts quickly find this out. They also recognize when changes in the world create new or different requirements for models. Regular feedback from analysts is one of the best sources of recommendations on long-term model maintenance.

Input data collectors and cleaners are closely related to analysts. In many cases, analysts take on this role. For large models and in large modeling teams, input data preparation is a specialized task assigned to one or more people. Data preparation specialists need to be highly detail-oriented as discussed in chapter 12.

Developers

Model developers build the model. They need to be skilled with one or more of the agent-modeling tools discussed in chapters 8 and 10. Developers commonly have a substantial background in software engineering or a closely related discipline such as computer science, but this is not strictly required. Those who lack such a background normally have substantial work experience in software development.

Model developers understand how the model works from a development perspective. Model developers may or may not also be analysts. If they are not analysts, then they will often lack the special modeling awareness that comes from using a model for long periods. Developers who build but do not use models often say that they know how models work, but not how to use them. This is not necessarily a problem as long as these developers receive regular feedback from actual users about what works and what does not. Even for developers who do use their own models, this type of user feedback is essential since analysts' impressions of models are often quite different from those of developers.

Modelers

Modelers are experts in agent-based discovery, design, and development. They understand how agent modeling works, what it works for, and usually know two or three development tools. The best agent modelers have extremely diverse backgrounds, including degrees or substantial experience in several divergent fields. This background helps them to think about systems holistically from a bottom-up perspective rather than to employ the usual stovepipe approach used within individual specialized fields. The best agent modelers have substantial quantitative training and experience as well as a strong background in computer science or information technology.

Every project that uses the specialist team structure should include at least one agent modeler on the team to provide detailed guidance on ABMS techniques. Large projects often have more than one agent modeler guided by a lead agent-modeling architect. Many agent modelers on large-scale projects are consultants.

Consultants

Agent-based modeling consultants are often retained to assist with agent modeling. These consultants can help in-house developers or managers or can directly build complete models. ABMS is an area where a theoretical background and practical experience both make a real difference. Hiring agent-modeling consultants is particularly beneficial to organizations that are just starting out in agent modeling, that do not plan on developing in-house agent-modeling expertise, or that would like to be able to draw on the expertise of full-time agent-modeling specialists. Agent-based modeling consultants with specific experience in the area of interest can help to jumpstart projects and keep them moving smoothly. Agent-modeling consultants with experience in modeling several genuinely different systems can be especially useful since this broad background can provide a wide range of knowledge and substantially reduce surprises.

In all cases, managing consultants requires attention to detail and clear feedback from in-house participants. Attention to detail ensures that both the organization and the consultants have a well-documented understanding of what needs to be done and that this documentation is followed. Clear feedback from in-house participants ensures that the work being done matches the business's needs.

Clear written statements of work are generally recommended. Managers should also be aware of the differences between short-term and long-term contract management. Short-term contract management attempts to wring as much as possible as soon as possible from the other party. Long-term contract management looks to find profitable results for both parties to encourage them to continue the collaboration. Agent-based modeling touches on the core areas of most businesses. This commonly brings agent-modeling consultants into the heart of many businesses. As such,

it is recommended that long-term contract management be used. After all, who wants heart surgery performed by the lowest bidder?

From the consultant's perspective, all agent-based modeling projects should be approached with a long-term view. It is possible to work with an organization as a consultant for significant amounts of time. Even if the engagement is shorter, the good recommendations and positive word of mouth that can be generated by high-quality results are well worth the effort. Most new projects come from successful projects, either directly through follow-on work or indirectly through recommendations. Not every business has prefect customers, as Knutson has shown by studying the "customer from hell" in the retail setting (Knutson et al. 1999). However, most people want to be reasonable. As a consultant, treating people fairly encourages fairness in return.

Other types of consultants may also be employed, including software development professionals and data analysts. The more they know about agent modeling, the better the overall results will tend to be.

One key contact individual from the client organization and one key contact individual from the consulting organization should be identified at the beginning of the project. These two people should be mutually responsible for management communications. Other people can certainly communicate between the organizations, but the key contacts should ultimately be responsible for the management of the project.

Consultants can be paid with flat fees or with time and materials payments. Flat fees set a single price for the completion of a statement of work, regardless of the number of hours worked by the consultant. Time and materials payments set a charge rate for consultant time and materials used. The payments for a project vary with the number of hours worked. Time and materials payments are by far the most common for ABMS consulting due to the highly flexible nature of agent modeling.

Regular feedback from in-house participants helps agent-based modeling consultants focus their work and measure their progress. Keeping a regular dialog going between ABMS consultants, users, and in-house developers is good for everyone on the project.

Project Evolution

Of course, the one-stop modeler and the specialist team approaches are extremes. Most successful modeling enterprises are somewhere in between. ABMS project management is as iterative as the agent-modeling process itself. It is common for projects to evolve through the various project management structures.

The ABMS Business Process

A high-level roadmap of ABMS development and use is shown in figure 14.1. The steps in the figure describe the core requirements for model development and use. These steps are not intended to suggest a rigid process, but rather they are intended to provide a solid conceptual framework for ABMS project management. The figure shows structured steps, but in practice the steps are highly fluid and have fuzzy boundaries. Large amounts of feedback and iteration often occur between the steps. The feedback loops often reach backward across many steps. Work often can, and sometimes must, proceed simultaneously on several steps with appropriate feedback between steps. Furthermore, agent-modeling project mangers should customize the steps to match their specific requirements.

In this section, each step on the roadmap in figure 14.1 will be described using three stages and will be illustrated with an energy sector example:

- "Before" items are required preconditions for a given step to be successful.
- "During" items are expected actions to be completed within a given step.
- "After" items are expected outcomes from a given step.

ABMS Development

The development of agent-based models requires prototyping; architectural design; agent and agent rule design; agent environment design; implementation; and verification and validation. When properly performed, these steps yield a model that is ready for use.

Prototyping

Prototyping allows alternative ABMS formulations to be considered. The considerations are shown in table 14.1.

Architectural Design

Architectural design defines the foundation to be used for later implementation. The considerations are shown in table 14.2.

Agent and Agent Rule Design

Agent and agent rule design specifies behaviors. The considerations are shown in table 14.3.

Agent Environment Design

Agent environment design focuses on the specification of the agent's world. The considerations are shown in table 14.4.

Implementation

Implementation converts designs into working software. The considerations are shown in table 14.5.

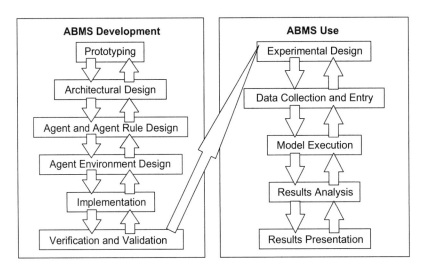

FIGURE 14.1 The ABMS business process.

TABLE 14.1 Prototyping considerations

Project status	Considerations	Example
Before	• Potential questions or areas of concern to be addressed have been identified	• A question is asked: "Are there generation companies with possible market power in a given electricity system?"
During	• Overall ABMS approaches to the issue are tested in outline form • Several decisions are made, namely (1) whether or not to use ABMS, and (2) if ABMS is to be used, an approach should be selected	• Live actors ("agents") are used to understand the modeling requirements • Viewing each generation company as an agent seems to have the potential to lead to useful insights and conclusions
After	• If ABMS is to be used, an ABMS approach has been specified and tested in outline form	• An ABMS approach with generation companies as agents is selected and tested in outline form

TABLE 14.2 Architectural design considerations

Project status	Considerations	Example
Before	• An ABMS approach has been specified and tested in outline form	• An ABMS approach with generation companies as agents is selected and tested in outline
During	• ABMS tools, general software tools, and hardware that may be used are considered and selected • The structure of the application is considered and defined	• Java and Repast (discussed in chapter 10) are selected for the simulation engine • Java Servlets with a Java-based web server are selected for the interface • The application is divided into multiple layers, each representing a different time horizon
After	• Implementation tools are specified • The overall structure of the application is specified	• The development tools and platform are specified • The application structure is defined

TABLE 14.3 Agent and agent rule design considerations

Project status	Considerations	Example
Before	• Implementation tools and platforms are specified • The overall structure of the application is specified	• Java/web-based tools and platforms are specified • The application structure is defined

During	• Possible agents are considered and selected
	• Possible rules for agent behavior are considered and selected
		• A variety of agents in addition to generation companies, such as consumers, are defined
		• Behavior rules for each agent are developed, for example:
		  ○ Companies seek profits and selectively avoid risks
		  ○ Consumers seek to reduce bills and control risk

After	• The agents for the model are specified • Behavior rules for each agent are specified	• The agents and behavior rules for the model are specified

TABLE 14.4 Agent environment design considerations

Project status	Considerations	Example
Before	• The agents for the ABMS are specified • Behavior rules for each agent are specified	• The agents and behavior rules for the model are specified
During	• An appropriate agent world is considered and selected • Appropriate data structures and algorithms to support the specified agent world are considered and selected	• The agent world is defined to include a market and complex power systems engineering constraints • Data structures and algorithms to support the market and the complex physical constraints are developed
After	• An agent world is specified • Data structures and algorithms to support the specified agent world are specified	• A market structure and constraints are specified • Data structures and algorithms to support the market and the constraints are specified

Verification and Validation

Verification and validation check agent-modeling software against both its design and reality. The considerations are shown in table 14.6.

ABMS Use

The use of agent-based models begins with a properly verified and validated model. An experimental design is then completed for the questions at issue. Data is collected and formatted for the model. The model is executed as many times as are needed. The results are analyzed and then the results are presented. As previously mentioned, these steps are often conducted iteratively and in parallel. They are presented here sequentially for clarity.

Experimental Design

Experimental design poses an answerable question and defines a rigorous way to answer the question. The considerations are shown in table 14.7.

Data Collection and Entry

Data collection and entry provides the inputs required for meaningful model execution. The considerations are shown in table 14.8.

Model Execution

Model execution converts raw inputs into raw outputs. The considerations are shown in table 14.9.

TABLE 14.5 Implementation considerations

Project status	Considerations	Example
Before	• An architectural design is specified • Agents and their rules are specified • An agent environment is specified	• A Java/web-based architectural design is specified • Companies, consumers, regulators, and other agents and their rules are specified • An agent environment with a market and with complex physical constraints is specified
During	• Software is written to match the architectural design, agent and agent rule design, and the agent environment design	• Java software is written to match the specified designs
After	• ABMS software is available for verification and validation	• The software is available for verification and validation

TABLE 14.6 Verification and validation considerations

Project status	Considerations	Example
Before	• ABMS software is available for verification and validation	• The energy sector ABMS software is available for verification and validation
During	• The ABMS software is tested to make sure that it matches its design (verification) • The ABMS software is tested to make sure that it matches the real-world issues of interest (validation)	• Structured code walk-throughs are used to test the software against its design • Analytically solvable special cases are used to test the software against known theories • Historical event recreation is used to test the software against the real world
After	• The ABMS software has been verified to match its design and validated to match the real-world issues of interest • The ABMS software is ready for use	• The ABMS software has been verified and validated • The software is ready for use

TABLE 14.7 Experimental design considerations

Project status	Considerations	Example
Before	• A potential question to be addressed has been identified • Verified and validated ABMS software that may address the question is available	• Again, a question is asked: "Are there generation companies with possible market power in a given electricity system?" • The verified and validated ABMS software is available
During	• The question is refined until it can be effectively answered with the available tools • A plan for applying the ABMS software to address the refined question is created	• The question is refined to: "Are there generation companies that can increase prices by at least 25% over the cost of production using a specific class of adaptive strategies?" • A list of stochastic scenarios to be run is created
After	• An answerable question is defined • A plan for applying the ABMS software to address the selected question is specified	• An answerable question is defined • A plan to answer the question is specified

TABLE 14.8 Data collection and entry considerations

Project status	Considerations	Example
Before	• An answerable question is defined • A plan for applying the ABMS software to address the selected question is specified	• An answerable question is defined: "Are there generation companies that can increase prices by at least 25% over the cost of production using a specific class of adaptive strategies?" • A list of stochastic scenarios to be run has been created
During	• The data specified by the plan is collected • The collected data is "cleaned" to ensure that it is at least up to the level of accuracy required by the experimental design • The collected data is reformatted to match the ABMS input requirements	• The required electric power system data such as branches (lines), buses (connections), costs, and loads are identified • Intellectual property and nondisclosure concerns surrounding the data are addressed • The data is collected, cleaned, and reformatted
After	• Data of the required quality is ready for use in the model	• Data is ready for use in the model

TABLE 14.9 Execution considerations

Project status	Considerations	Example
Before	• An answerable question is defined • Verified and validated ABMS software is available • A plan to answer the question is specified • Raw input data of the required quality is ready for use	• An answerable question is defined • Verified and validated ABMS software that addresses the question is available • A plan for applying the ABMS software to address the selected question is specified • Data is ready for use in the model
During	• The model is executed, usually many times, to match the experimental design	• The model is executed several hundred times for each scenario specified
After	• Raw ABMS outputs are available for analysis	• A large amount of raw ABMS output is available for analysis

Results Analysis

Results analysis converts raw outputs into meaningful information. The considerations are shown in table 14.10.

Results Presentation

Effectively presenting ABMS results makes model outputs useful to decision-makers. The considerations are shown in table 14.11.

Growing Up

In many ways, agent-based modeling and simulation represents a new business function. Dispersed organic or "grassroots" approaches to this business function that open up communications with business operations are still best. These approaches leverage innate interest, existing data sets, and current resources to develop ABMS models. Over time, the momentum generated by accumulating success can be directed

TABLE 14.10 Results analysis considerations

Project status	Considerations	Example
Before	• An answerable question is defined • A plan for using raw ABMS outputs to address the selected question is specified • Raw ABMS output is available for analysis	• An answerable question is defined and a plan to answer the question is specified • A large amount of raw ABMS output is available for analysis
During	• The raw outputs are processed based on the experimental design and the professional judgment of analysts • The use of professional judgment is documented	• The raw outputs are statistically processed to identify typical results, outlying results, and the probabilities of each result type • The results and their probabilities are used to identify generation companies that can unilaterally increase prices by at least 25% over the cost of production using a specific class of adaptive strategies
After	• Insights and conclusions based on the ABMS runs are available • Known limits to the insights and conclusions are specified • The use of professional judgment is documented	• Producers with possible market power under the given definition are identified, the use of professional judgment is noted, and the study limitations are noted

TABLE 14.11 Results presentation considerations

Project status	Considerations	Example
Before	• Insights and conclusions based on ABMS runs are available • Known limits to the insights and conclusions are specified	• Producers with possible market power under the given definition are identified, the use of professional judgment is noted, and the study limitations are noted
During	• Reports and presentations that effectively convey the insights and conclusions derived from the ABMS work, along with the known limits, are developed	• Reports and presentations listing the companies with possible market power and the conditions under which they may have market power are written • Study assumptions, such as the definition of market power and the range of strategies considered, are clearly noted
After	• Appropriate decision-makers understand the insights and conclusions derived from the ABMS work, along with the known limits	• Appropriate decision-makers understand which companies may have market power under specific assumptions of the study

toward obtaining new resources. The iterative nature of ABMS development encourages organic project management that incrementally grows projects over time.

References

Brooks, F. P. (1975). *The Mythical Man-Month: Essays on Software Engineering*. Boston: Addison-Wesley.

Cleveland, H. (1982). Information as Resource. *The Futurist* (Dec.), 34–39.

Eilot, T. S. (1934). *The Rock*. London: Faber & Faber.

Knutson, B. J., C. Borchgrevink, and B. Woods (1999). Validating a Typology of the Customer from Hell. *Journal of Hospitality and Leisure Marketing* 6(3): 5–22.

Siegel, A. (2000). Mission Creep or Mission Misunderstood? *Joint Forces Quarterly* (Institute for National Strategic Studies, National Defense University, Washington, D.C.) 25: 112–115.

15

Rising to the Challenge

The Who, What, Where, When, Why, and How of Agents

This book has addressed the who, what, where, when, why, and how of agents. The book presents answers to these and other questions and has provided a wealth of illustrative examples.

Who needs agents? Understanding the audience for agent-based modeling as a technique and as an information-creating enterprise is the key to its successful use. Anyone in a decision-making capacity who deals with systems having complex elements that include people should know about agent modeling and what benefits it could provide to their organization. Agent modeling can be done by many people, from teams of people engaged in traditional information technology, to research and development groups looking for new methods to bring into the corporation or government agency, to individual analysts who can only rely on desktop computing resources. People who use the information generated by agent-based models for decision-making need to have an in-depth understand of agent-based modeling capabilities and limitations.

What agents? The agent-based modeling approach represents a natural view of how people think about and understand systems that before now has been barely tapped. Agents are discrete units that have behaviors and some degree of autonomy. Agent-based modeling provides the tools to build models that include the full diversity of agent behaviors that has been lacking in traditional modeling approaches.

Where agents? The growing preponderance of candidate areas for agent-based simulations means that there is no need to look far for promising applications. Agent modeling has been used to model everything from diverse business processes and organizations, to the demands on the healthcare system from aging populations composed of individuals with varied healthcare needs. Agent modeling provides information that it has not been previously possible to provide.

When agents? Situations for which agent-based modeling can offer distinct advantages over more traditional modeling approaches, reveal new insights, and answer long-standing questions are becoming better understood every day. Briefly, agent modeling should be used:

- When there is a natural representation as agents.
- When there are decisions and behaviors that can be defined discretely (with boundaries).
- When it is important that agents adapt and change their behavior.
- When it is important that agents learn and engage in dynamic strategic behavior.
- When it is important that agents have a dynamic relationships with other agents, and agent relationships form and dissolve.
- When it is important that agents form organizations, and adaptation and learning are important at the organizational level.
- When it is important that agents have a spatial component to their behaviors and interactions.
- When the past is no predictor of the future.
- When scaling-up to arbitrary levels is important.

- When process structural change needs to be a result of the model, rather than an input to the model.

Why agents? Agent-based modeling offers the agent focus and perspective as its central concepts and natural starting point. There is a natural evolution in the understanding of agent behaviors and the behaviors of the system as a whole. Fewer assumptions have to be made in terms of aggregating agent behaviors or working with only "representative" agents. Finally, agent-based modeling allows us to work with models of real, or supposed, agent behavior rather than idealized versions and to see what the logical implications are of agent interactions on a large scale.

How agents? This book has provided a very explicit and detailed approach to (1) how to think about agents and agent-based systems in general, and (2) how to build agent-based models. The approach is widely applicable to a broad range of application areas. The approach extends from the verbal description of the modeled system, to the development of the conceptual model, to the model's implementation and analysis of the results produced by the model, to the explanation of the findings from the model to decision-makers. This approach covers the full range of application complexity, from the simple model, easily computable on the desktop using spreadsheets, to the extremely complicated model that requires the use of distributed computing resources.

With the answers to these critically important questions, anyone who has heard about agent-based modeling or is considering undertaking an agent-based modeling enterprise has a roadmap to success.

Useful, Usable, and Used

Agent-based modeling and simulation is a sustainable new advance for business and government decision-making. ABMS can provide leaders in industrial and government organizations the information they need on the complex systems that they manage.

ABMS is founded on the notion that the whole of many systems or organizations is greater than the simple sum of their constituent parts. To manage such systems, the systems or organizations must be understood as a collection of interacting components. Each of these components has its own rules and responsibilities. Some components may be more influential than other components, but none of them completely controls the behavior of the system. All of the components contribute to the system-level behaviors in large or small ways. ABMS provides the qualitative and quantitative tools to understand and ultimately manage such systems.

ABMS is not just a fad or a theoretical research activity. Of course, there is ongoing research that is extending and refining the underlying techniques. However, ABMS is now being successfully applied to many long-standing unsolved practical problems. ABMS builds on proven, highly successful techniques such as discrete-event simulation and object-oriented programming. ABMS leverages these and other techniques as much as possible to produce returns more directly and quickly. Discrete-event simulation provides an established mechanism for coordinating the interactions of individual components or "agents" within a simulation. Object-oriented programming provides well-tested frameworks for organizing agents based on their behaviors. ABMS combines these techniques with a rigorous focus on bottom-up model construction. This unique focus makes agent-based models verifiable, validatable, scalable, extensible, and robust.

ABMS as a field is growing rapidly on several fronts. Experience with ABMS applications is growing, as successes accumulate in a variety of industries. Practical approaches to going about managing and engineering both the models and the model development process are being extended. The theoretical underpinnings of the technique that ensure its validity and sustained usefulness are deepening. User-focused simulation environments that reduce the time and effort of model development are becoming available. In fact, the authors believe that in the future virtually all computer simulations will be agent-based because of the naturalness of the agent representation and the close similarity of agent models to the predominant computational paradigm of object-oriented programming.

The goal of ABMS is to create multifunction tools for evolutionary discovery. First, ABMS can catalyze user insights into complex processes. Second, ABMS can help users relate micro-level process knowledge to global-level system behaviors and results. Third, ABMS can help users to envisage ranges of possible outcomes.

Returning to the beginning, ABMS works much like a wave in a crowded stadium. To start a wave, a row of fans in a stadium stands up quickly and then sits back down a moment later. The next row of fans starts to stand in turn and then also sits down. The wave moves forward as rows progressively stand up and sit down. The individual people are each simply standing up and sitting down occasionally. The group as a whole forms a human wave that can sweep the entire stadium. ABMS works by applying the same concept. Each person or agent makes small, simple movements, but the group as a whole produces huge, complex results.

Applying this analogy, what senior managers know about consumers, employees, and business processes is much like what sports fans know about the behavior of people forming a wave in the crowd. The wave represents the large-scale system outcomes that every leader needs to know about ahead of time. Knowing about these outcomes and being able to relate them to their underlying causes can lead directly to the discovery of innovative answers to long-standing questions. ABMS allows managers' knowledge of the components, such as people, to be converted into knowledge about system-level results, much like the wave. Thus, with ABMS, senior managers can use their knowledge of consumers, employees, and business processes to discover strategic solutions for their enterprises.

In practice, ABMS focuses on incremental discovery, design, and development to ensure stakeholder buy-in and progressively document return-on-investment. These stages are identifiable for the purposes of exposition, but they are highly integrated during real projects. On the best-managed ABMS projects, the stages of discovery, design, and development all occur simultaneously at varying levels appropriate to the stage of the project itself.

The discovery phase of ABMS allows partial models to be built and then tested to yield insights. These insights can lead to both real-world innovations and improved model designs. These innovations and designs in turn can fuel further model development. This cycle can be repeated incrementally as desired.

The design phase of ABMS is fully integrated with the discovery phase. During design, models are specified. Then these specifications are tested using progressively more detailed prototypes. These prototypes are used to provide regular intermediate feedback to the future model users. The purpose of the design prototypes is to incrementally build toward the fully developed model.

The development phase of ABMS flows naturally from the discovery and design stages. This means that agent-based models are best built over time in simple stages or steps that accumulate into the final product. Each development stage adds new capabilities to the model and expands the range of business and government questions that it can answer. Individual ABMS development steps are purposely small, so that each stage requires only a limited investment and can be completed quickly.

ABMS is a useful, usable, and used technique that can do many things for organizations. ABMS is useful to tie experience with detailed processes to understanding of systems as well as to reveal unexpected possibilities in complex situations. ABMS is usable in stages on a progressive basis. ABMS is used to solve real-world business and government problems.

The usefulness of ABMS arises from its ability to show the emergent connections between system components, tie experience with detailed processes to system-level knowledge, and to identify possible outcomes that are outside the range of typical thinking. Showing the connections between system components allows users to investigate possible interactions and test potential interventions. Discovering the ties between micro-level behavior and macro-level results increases the value of detailed expert experience by allowing this business experience to be leveraged in new ways. Expanding strategic managerial vision by revealing otherwise unanticipated potential outcomes allows business and government leaders to make better-informed decisions.

ABMS is usable due to the iterative model construction process. This process starts with an initial description of the behavior of individual components or agent behaviors as well as supporting data. This description is then converted to a functioning model that can be executed with the given data. The resulting model is run and the initial results are examined. The agent behavior definitions in the model are then updated based on the initial results and the model is rerun. This progressive refinement process is continued until the model reproduces both the behaviors and results of the target system. Once this is complete, the resulting model can be used to answer business and government questions.

ABMS is used for a variety of practical business and government proposes. ABMS is used to increase the capabilities of experts to grasp micro-level behavior and to relate this behavior to macro-level outcomes. Agent-based models are used to expand the scope of future possibilities considered in decision-making.

This is particularly critical when business and government leaders face new and rapidly changing circumstances. As previously mentioned, what leader has not been surprised by unexpected events? ABMS can reduce surprise and increase awareness.

Ultimately, this is an increasingly complex world, and the systems that need to be analyzed are becoming more complex. Planning and management tools must capture this emerging complexity. ABMS is a useful, usable, and used solution!

Index